CREDO SERIES

Living and Loving as Disciples of Christ

*Based on the Curriculum Framework
Course VI: Life in Jesus Christ*

TEACHER'S RESOURCE

VERITAS
USA Office: Frisco, Texas

www.veritasreligion.com

CREDO SERIES CONSULTANT: Maura Hyland
PUBLISHER, USA AND THEOLOGICAL EDITOR:
Ed DeStefano
WRITERS: Eleanor Gormally (chs. 1–10);
Brendan O'Regan (chs. 11–12)
CONTRIBUTIONS: Joseph F. McCann,
Thomas H. Groome, Hosffman Ospino
COPY EDITOR: Elaine Campion
DESIGN: Lir Mac Cárthaigh
TYPESETTING: Heather Costello

INTERNET RESOURCES
There are internet resources available to support this
text. Log on to *www.credoseries.com*

Nihil Obstat and *Imprimatur* pending

Copyright © 2013 by Veritas Publications

All rights reserved. No part of the material may be
reproduced or transmitted in any form or by any means,
electronic or mechanical, including photocopying or
by any information or retrieval system, adapted, rented
or lent without written permission from the copyright
owner. Applications for permissions should be addressed
to the publisher: **Veritas, 313 Larchbrook Drive, Garland,
Texas 75043; info@veritasreligion.com**

SEND ALL INQUIRIES TO:
Veritas, Customer Service
P.O. Box 789
Westerville, OH 43086
Tel. 866-844-0582
info@veritasreligion.com
www.veritasreligion.com

ISBN 978 1 84730 284 7 (Student Edition)
ISBN 978 1 84730 418 6 (Teacher Resource Edition)
ISBN 978 1 84730 420 9 (E-book: Student Edition)

Printed in the United States of America

CONTENTS

INTRODUCTION **5**

CATECHESIS FOR YOUNG PEOPLE: JOSEPH F. MCCANN CM **8**

A SHARED CHRISTIAN PRAXIS APPROACH: THOMAS H. GROOME **10**

CULTURAL AWARENESS IN RELIGIOUS EDUCATION: HOSFFMAN OSPINO **14**

Chapter 1	**God Desires What Is Best for Us**	**17**
	Introduction	17
	Notes and Guidelines for Student Activities	22
	Worksheets	26
	Review of Chapter 1	42
Chapter 2	**Jesus' Response; Our Response**	**46**
	Introduction	46
	Notes and Guidelines for Student Activities	50
	Worksheets	55
	Review of Chapter 2	71
Chapter 3	**God's Law for a Good Life**	**75**
	Introduction	75
	Notes and Guidelines for Student Activities	80
	Worksheets	85
	Review of Chapter 3	96
Chapter 4	**The Reality of Sin**	**100**
	Introduction	100
	Notes and Guidelines for Student Activities	105
	Worksheets	110
	Review of Chapter 4	134
Chapter 5	**The Liberating Power of the Ten Commandments**	**138**
	Introduction	138
	Notes and Guidelines for Student Activities	142
	Worksheets	146
	Review of Chapter 5	161
Chapter 6	**Love the Lord Your God: The Second and Third Commandments**	**165**
	Introduction	165
	Notes and Guidelines for Student Activities	169
	Worksheets	174
	Review of Chapter 6	196

Chapter 7   **Honor Your Father and Your Mother: The Fourth Commandment** **200**
Introduction 200
Notes and Guidelines for Student Activities 204
Worksheets 209
Review of Chapter 7 222

Chapter 8   **Living the 'Way' of Life and Truth: The Fifth and Eighth Commandments** . **226**
Introduction 226
Notes and Guidelines for Student Activities 230
Worksheets 235
Review of Chapter 8 260

Chapter 9   **The Gift of Human Sexuality: The Sixth and Ninth Commandments** **264**
Introduction 264
Notes and Guidelines for Student Activities 269
Worksheets 274
Review of Chapter 9 294

Chapter 10 **Building a Just and Compassionate Society: The Seventh and Tenth
Commandments** **298**
Introduction 298
Notes and Guidelines for Student Activities 303
Worksheets 309
Review of Chapter 10 338

Chapter 11 **Living New Life in Christ Jesus** **342**
Introduction 342
Notes and Guidelines for Student Activities 346
Worksheets 349
Review of Chapter 11 364

Chapter 12 **Sustaining the Moral Life as Disciples of Jesus** **368**
Introduction 368
Notes and Guidelines for Student Activities 372
Worksheets 375
Review of Chapter 12 387

STUDENT ACTIVITY TOOL KIT **391**

ANSWER KEY TO CHAPTER REVIEWS **401**

ACKNOWLEDGMENTS **407**

Introduction

The aim of any Catholic high school theology program must surely be to help participants to become better disciples of Jesus Christ, more open to the Holy Spirit, and to grow stronger in their faith in God, a faith that is lived out every day. This can only be achieved by enabling the young people to explore and discover the Truth contained within the Word of God as spoken through Scripture, Tradition and the teaching of the Church. Knowledge of the Truth, then, should lead the young people to action; that is, to Christian living in the world.

With this aim as our central focus, the *Credo* series presents the whole story and vision of Catholic faith in a manner appropriate to young people of high school age. It is a Christ-centered curriculum, in that all the books, in one way or another, are Christological, constantly referring to the Christ of Faith and the Jesus of History. The curriculum adheres precisely to the detailed prescriptions of the United States Conference of Catholic Bishops' *Doctrinal Elements of a Curriculum Framework for the Development of Catechetical Materials for Young People of High School Age* (2007), which champions Christology as an organizing theme for all texts and topics. The Introduction to the Framework states:

> The Christological centrality of this framework is designed to form the content of instruction as well as to be a vehicle for growth in one's relationship with the Lord so that each may come to know him and live according to the truth he has given to us. In this way, disciples not only participate more deeply in the life of the Church but are also better able to reach eternal life with God in Heaven.

Though the texts do not often use the language of spirituality, there is an intentional emphasis throughout the curriculum on spirituality. All of the books in the series emphasize and encourage the students' personal appropriation and deep individual engagement with the Catholic faith. The teaching dynamic seeks to engage the 'souls' of the young people, to delve into what they really think and feel, and how they will decide to live their faith in the light of what they have learned. The pedagogy or dynamic of the series may be summarized as 'bringing Life to Faith and Faith to Life'. And so the generative theme of each chapter is brought to the resources of Catholic faith for its spiritual wisdom—in order to bring it back to life again as owned Christian wisdom, as lived Christian faith in the world.

The program is 'apologetic' in approach, in line with the recommendation in the Framework that it should attempt 'to help those same young people develop the necessary skills to answer or address the real questions that they face in life and in their Catholic faith', offering them a reason 'for the hope that is within [them]' (1 Peter 3:15). Hence the *Credo* series presents the 'content' of the faith as a great and wise way to live one's life in the world; appeals to young people's best desires and hopes; offers coherent and persuasive rationale for faith convictions, and often points to the lived witness of people from both past and contemporary times who are faithful witnesses to Jesus Christ and the faith taught and lived by his Church.

Credo possesses a real commitment to active parental involvement in the catechetical instruction of young people, and so offers suggestions to encourage a 'Faith Connect' with the young people's family and parish.

Credo is strongly committed to justice and, therefore, the social and personal responsibilities of Christian faith are integrated into all the books and topics. While we present the Catholic faith as offering Good News and great hope for young people today, we also remind young people that living as a Christian presents a real challenge, that being a disciple of Jesus brings great personal and social responsibilities. This sense of both consolation and challenge, of hope and demand, can have particular appeal to adolescents. There is much 'therapeutic' religion—a consoling experience—around today, but little challenge, whereas young people need both.

The *Credo* series is also deeply and consistently committed to what the Church now calls a 'New Evangelization'. Moving beyond the 'old' evangelization which emphasized 'bringing them in' (converting into the Church anyone not yet Catholic), the 'New Evangelization' advocates 'bringing Christians out' into the world with a faith alive. Thus, evangelization means to live one's faith

INTRODUCTION | 5

with enthusiasm in every arena of life, to be joyful and living witnesses to the Truth. The pedagogy that underpins the *Credo* series—from Life to Faith to Life—is essentially a mode of evangelization.

The material in the *Credo* series may easily be adapted to a parish youth catechesis program that meets once or twice a week or at intervals over a more extended period.

TITLES IN THE SERIES

The *Credo* series covers the six core courses as outlined in the Curriculum Framework mandated by the United States Conference of Catholic Bishops.

The six core courses are:

I.   God's Word Revealed in Sacred Scripture
II. Son of God and Son of Mary
III. The Promised One: Servant and Savior
IV. The Body of Christ: The Church
V.   Encountering Christ in the Sacraments
VI. Living and Loving as Disciples of Christ

The framework also lists five electives, and the *Credo* series will offer texts on a number of these. In all, the *Credo* series will constitute a four-year, eight-semester catechesis of the students. It is strongly recommended that the six core courses be taught in the order given in the Framework. Schools are asked to choose *two* from the five elective subject themes.

STRUCTURE AND PEDAGOGY

The teaching method used in the *Credo* series reflects the commitments and five 'movements' of the Shared Christian Praxis Approach as proposed by Thomas Groome. (For a comprehensive explanation of this approach, see Tom Groome, *Christian Religious Education: Sharing our story and vision;* San Francisco: Harper and Row (1980), now published by Jossey-Bass, San Francisco.)

The pedagogy or dynamic of the program may be summarized as 'bringing Life to Faith and Faith to Life'. The content of each chapter is presented under five major headings, used consistently within each chapter and reflected in the design. (See notes on design and layout below.) The primary intent is that the young people not simply *learn about* the content (though this is important) but that they *learn from* it and integrate it into their lives.

The first major heading, **Attend and Reflect**, establishes the generative theme of the chapter and engages the young people's interest. It encompasses **Movement One** of Groome's praxis approach (inviting the students to express their present praxis—thoughts, feelings, experiences and so on—around the theme), and **Movement Two** (inviting their deeper level of

reflection on this praxis, personally or socially, using their reason, memory and/or imagination). The two movements are worked through under a variety of subheadings—such as *'Talk it over'*, *'Let's probe deeper'* and *'Over to you'*—all fulfilling a function in the underlying dynamic of Life to Faith and Faith to Life.

Movement Three, encompassing three major headings—**Hear the Story**, **Embrace the Vision** and **Think It Through**, presents the Story and Vision of Christian faith through an exploration of Scripture and Tradition and theological reflection around the lesson theme. It highlights the spiritual wisdom of Catholic faith for young people today, what it offers and asks of their lives, and how it can be life-giving for both themselves and the world. Movement Three demands a certain amount of 'figuring out', as the philosophy and theology underpinning the Scripture and Tradition is 'unpacked' in a manner and at a level appropriate to young people and their world.

Each of the three sections involved in Movement Three also incorporates elements of Movements One and Two—mini attend-and-reflect moments—so that these mid-chapter sessions are not all teaching and instruction and presentation. Every session should see young people bringing Life to Faith! Also, every session will conclude with an opportunity for the young people to begin to bring Faith to Life. These middle weekdays offer features such as: *'Faith Word'* (defining a term or phrase in religious language or theological discourse), *'Talk it over'* (inviting reflective discussion) and *'What about you personally?'* (challenging the young people to question themselves).

Movement Four and **Movement Five**, which are interlocked and explored mainly under the heading **Judge and Act**, move the dynamic back to life again.

We invite the young people first to *judge*; that is, to appropriate the content, make its spiritual wisdom their own, take it to heart, familiarize themselves with its implications for living, and affirm it as part of their worldview. This involves reflecting back on the material studied in the chapter and responding to it, both orally and in writing. Here we also offer the young people a *'Learn by example'* (recounting the life of a saint or contemporary model of good living). The exercises offered at this point include *Journal Work* (personal reflection and writing in response to the chapter theme), *Research Projects* and more.

Then comes the final and perhaps the most important invitation, to *act*; to take what they have learned into everyday practical living, apply it, implement its suggestions, and enlist the support of others, especially family and close friends, in carrying it through. Here we find headings such as *'Share faith with family and friends'*, *'Reflect and Discern'* and *'Learn by heart'* (usually a short quotation from Scripture summarizing the theme of the chapter), as well as various exercises and questions that encourage the young people to make decisions in relation to the challenge of living as disciples of Jesus. Throughout the *Credo* series there is a vast array of activities, ranging from research projects and journal work to debates and role-plays. In seeking to connect with young people where they are 'at', we also take seriously the intense encounter of adolescents with modern media and pop culture. And so we include activities that encourage media literacy and support religious and Catholic values.

Through all of these means, we seek to enable the young people to deepen their relationship with God the Father and with the Risen Jesus and with the Holy Spirit, the Advocate and Teacher. In each chapter, through different personal and group activities, we encourage the young people to ponder on the signs of God's loving presence in their lives.

There is a strong liturgical note running throughout the *Credo* series. In addition to a specific study of the Mass, the Sacraments and prayer in the appropriate texts, there are many opportunities for ritual prayer and meditation. We invite the young people to reflect on Scripture passages and to engage in quiet moments of personal prayer so that they may become more alert to God's presence and more open to his call. Each chapter ends with a closing prayer or ritual that 'captures' the central teaching of the chapter. The rituals, which are written specifically for young people, contain traditional prayers that are rooted in the Tradition of the Catholic Church and they also focus on the everyday issues and experiences young people encounter in living their faith. We encourage the young people to respond in prayer. Throughout the program we also encourage them to make prayer a part of their daily lives, not just in school.

In summary, in each book of the *Credo* series we invite young people to: **attend and reflect** on their lives; **hear** the story of God's love for them; **see** the vision of what God wants for them; **think** about what this means; and finally, having encountered the Word of God in Scripture, in the teaching of the Church and in the experience of Christians through the ages, **judge** how it might apply to their lives and make a decision to **act** according to God's will and as disciples of Jesus.

The confidence and support of the teacher is paramount where catechesis is concerned, for it is the faith and enthusiasm and spirit of the teacher that is communicated to the disciple now and always. The *Credo* series provides all the necessary tools to bring Jesus and the proclamation of the Kingdom into the classroom.

DESIGN AND LAYOUT OF STUDENTS' TEXT

In order to give the *Credo* series a distinct personality that is accessible and relevant to young readers, we have employed a hand-drawn motif in the margins of the students' text. Since the Middle Ages, embellishment by hand has formed a vibrant part of Christian visual tradition. Even now, over five hundred years after the invention of printing, calligraphic decoration is still to be found on blessings, cards, candles and so on.

The style of hand embellishment adopted for the margins of our text is inspired by the doodle—a ubiquitous feature of teenage life. Many teachers of high school theology and other areas of religious education have begun to employ the act of doodling as a technique to assist prayer. In much the same way that monastic scribes could focus their minds on God while copying and illuminating their codices, the act of doodling can provide a focus for the young person that acts as an aid to contemplation. The *Credo* series makes use of this by offering suggestions for the use of 'doodling' as a means of helping the young people to focus during their reflections on Scripture.

Each of the five chapter sections has its own color. Text and illustrations follow this color pattern throughout the series, making it very easy for both students and teachers to navigate the text.

The *Credo* series is illustrated with artwork that spans a variety of media and traditions. For centuries the Church has been one of the major patrons of artistic endeavor, and this relationship is reflected in the diversity of sacred imagery included in the *Credo* series.

TEACHER'S RESOURCE

The teacher's resource provides background theological notes and general advice for teachers. It also contains supplementary support and extend activities for each chapter. We offer these to help the young people (and you) to deepen their understanding of the concepts presented in the students' text, thus enabling them to connect and integrate the content with their own life experiences. Most of the activities are offered as photocopiable worksheets and they are also available on the *Credo* website.

INTRODUCTION | 7

JOSEPH F. MCCANN CM

Catechesis for Young People

A CATECHETICAL EDUCATION

Catholic religious formation (catechesis) and religious education in high schools in the United States is based on three documents: the *General Directory for Catechesis* (1998), the *National Directory for Catechesis* (2005) and the *Doctrinal Elements of a Curriculum Framework for the Development of Catechetical Materials for Young People of High School Age* (2007). These documents are the foundations for the high school texts that form the *Credo* series.

Catholic catechesis or Catholic religious education and formation must always focus on the Person of Jesus Christ. Its purpose is 'to put people . . . in communion and intimacy with Jesus Christ' (*General Directory for Catechesis* [GDC], no. 80). The *Directory* uses the word 'apprentice', suggesting that young people should learn to know Jesus, love Jesus and follow Jesus as a matter of personal decision and habitual action. Catechesis, it says, should promote 'full and sincere adherence to his person and the decision to walk in his footsteps' (GDC, no. 53). Like an apprentice, too, the student should learn the appropriate responses and practice the behaviors and skills that follow from this decision: 'an apprenticeship in the entire Christian life' (GDC, no. 30).

So, whether we use the word 'catechize' or the phrase 'religious education' or 'religious formation', what we do in a Catholic high school Theology class should present Jesus Christ to young people in a warm and appealing way, as well as make sure that they are knowledgeable and well informed about the Catholic faith. Perhaps the best description for that process would be 'catechetical education'.

All the books in the *Credo* series are, in one way or another, centered on Jesus Christ. Instead of a book on Jesus and a book on Sacred Scripture and one on the Sacraments and another on the Church and so on, the texts in this series focus on Jesus in relation to the individual topics.

The books offer a comprehensive study of the major themes of Catholic Christian faith in a manner and language appropriate to young people of high school age.

RELIGION AND LIFE

Often people confine their religion to their time in church on Sunday, and do not see it as relevant to the rest of their lives. When this happens, religion becomes more of a private matter than a communal one. It becomes more about personal relationships and individual devotions, with little to say about public life, social issues or world problems. Today, more and more people profess to be 'spiritual', meaning a kind of mental culture, but fail to recognize that a religious stance implies, or should imply, the deepest convictions about life, the most cherished commitments and the most crucial life decisions.

The Second Vatican Council recognized this 'dichotomy between the faith which many profess and their day-to-day conduct' as 'one of the gravest errors of our time' (*Constitution on the Church in the Modern World* [*Gaudium et Spes*], no. 43). Hence the *Directory* wants to see Christian faith and daily life integrated in religious teaching and learning and returns to this theme on a number of occasions. It refers to 'experience' as 'a necessary medium for exploring and assimilating the truths which constitute the objective content of Revelation' (GDC, no. 152). It describes 'catechetical pedagogy' (method of teaching) as 'interpreting and illuminating experience with the data of faith' (GDC, no. 153). It employs a striking verb to describe the task of the religious educator: 'Correlating life and faith' (GDC, no. 207). This involves bridging 'the gap between belief and life, between the Christian message and the cultural context' (GDC, no. 205). This is a striking idea because it points to a 'disconnect' between the teaching of Christian theology and the life of the contemporary world.

FROM LIFE TO FAITH TO LIFE

The *General Directory for Catechesis* wants the theology teacher to bring the human experiences of the students to the timeless truths of the Christian faith. This can be simply described as helping young people to 'bring their lives to the Christian faith' and, then, 'bring Christian faith to their lives'. The intended result—the teaching objective—is 'lived Christian faith'. In a nutshell, the movement is 'life to faith to life'. This is also the essential dynamic of the 'shared Christian praxis approach' to catechesis and religious education, as taught by Thomas Groome, the general editor of the *Credo* series. This approach is explained in detail in Groome's own article on page 10 of this resource.

The great twentieth-century Catholic thinker Bernard Lonergan SJ outlined how a person learns in four steps: first, turning one's attention to something; second, arriving at an understanding of something; third, coming to judgment about something; and finally, making a decision about something. The stages are often summarized in two simple commands: Be attentive; Be responsible.

Accordingly, a method of teaching that enables young people to 'know their faith' will:

⊙ engage and promote their interests, in order that they pay attention to their own lives;
⊙ help them to reflect critically on and learn from their lives in the world;
⊙ encourage them to pay attention to and come to understand thoroughly the content of Christian faith;
⊙ help them to make judgments correlating and integrating their 'lives' and 'faith';
⊙ help them to reach decisions—about knowing, feeling and acting—regarding both life and faith.

These aims inform the structure for Groome's shared Christian praxis and the pedagogy in the *Credo* series.

WHAT CONTENT SHOULD WE TEACH?
The *General Directory for Catechesis* makes clear that the 'content' of catechesis is 'the Gospel message'. In this endeavor, the teaching of the Bible, Sacred Scripture, 'should have a pre-eminent position' (GDC, no. 127). The teacher should ensure, moreover, that interpretation of the Bible follows authentic Catholic teaching. The whole tradition of Catholic teaching should be faithfully taught; it does not do to 'cherry-pick'; that is, choose only the bits that suit our temperament and disposition or situation. The *Catechism of the Catholic Church* should be the guiding light for matters of doctrine, or, as the *Directory* says, 'the doctrinal point of reference for all catechesis' (GDC, nos. 93 and 121).

But teaching should not be purely factual and knowledge-based. The Christian faith has 'cognitive, experiential, and behavioral' aspects (GDC, no. 35). These three aspects are reflected in a very ancient phrase: *'lex credendi, lex orandi, lex vivendi'* or 'The law for believing is the law for praying and the law for living' (GDC, no. 122). Religious education is nothing if not 'holistic'. The theology teacher should engage people's heads, hearts and hands.

In response to the question of which topics to teach, the US bishops issued the document entitled *Doctrinal Elements of a Curriculum Framework for the Development of Catechetical Materials for Young People of High School Age* (2007). Its purpose is to provide a framework to help publishers and writers produce instructional material for catechesis. It takes up from the *Directory*, affirming its aim of centrality on Christ and involving Christian knowledge, personal relationship and responsible living. The *Credo* series adheres precisely to the detailed prescriptions outlined in this document.

Thorough knowledge and familiarity with Christian faith invites youth into the deep currents that have constituted the great river of Catholic thought and life for two thousand years. This includes Catholicism's *anthropology* (its positive understanding of the person and the covenant of nature and grace); its *cosmology* (a sacramental outlook on life and the universe); its *sociology* (that we 'are made for each other' and are our brothers' and sisters' keepers); its *epistemology* (merging our knowledge into spiritual wisdom), and so on. In this manner, catechetical education powerfully reinforces and, indeed, fulfills and completes education in secular subjects.

RELIGIOUS EDUCATION IS NOT CONFINED TO SCHOOL
The Christian community is needed to collaborate in the crucial task of Christian catechesis and Catholic religious education (GDC, no. 245).

Education cannot be successfully carried out if it is confined to the school alone. Young people must be aware of personal support and good example from friends, family, Church, from community groups and, indeed, from the wider society where appropriate. In the same way, religious formation takes place in the Christian faith community, including 'the family, parish, Catholic schools, Christian associations and movements, basic ecclesial communities' (GDC, no. 220).

What this means is that each Catholic is, at the same time, both catechized and catechist, learner and teacher in faith. One assists, as one can, in the formation of our youth, and, on occasion, is assisted in one's own growth in faith by the challenges and achievements of young Christians. The teacher who is not constantly learning in the classroom is hardly teaching at all. Galileo said in old age: *'Ancora imparo.'* (I am always learning.) There can be no better motto for a catechist.

JOSEPH F. MCCANN: INTRODUCTION | 9

THOMAS H. GROOME

A Shared Christian Praxis Approach

For many years I've been working to promote a 'shared Christian praxis approach' to catechesis and Religious Education. Originally much influenced by the conscientizing, emancipatory and praxis-based pedagogy of Paulo Freire, over the years, and from its employ across a great variety of contexts and cultures, age levels and time frames, this approach has developed and matured in its own right.

At core, a shared Christian praxis approach honors God's revealing presence and saving grace in the ordinary and everyday of people's lives and likewise the revelation and spiritual wisdom mediated by the Bible and Christian tradition. Its intent is to enable people to integrate their 'life' and 'Christian faith' into 'lived Christian faith', using a pedagogy that brings life to the Faith and brings the Faith to life.

That catechesis must teach Christian faith is patently obvious, but why attend to and actively engage people's lives as well? Clearly there is a whole underlying theology here of both Revelation and sacramentality, of how God continues to manifest his will and mediate his grace through the ordinary and everyday of life, as well as through Scripture/ Tradition and the seven great Sacraments. However, the pedagogical rationale for engaging people's lives in order to teach for Christian discipleship is stated forcefully by the *General Directory for Catechesis*— placing a shared Christian praxis approach squarely within the present mind of the Church regarding catechetical methodology.

By way of pedagogy, the *General Directory* calls for 'a correct . . . correlation and interaction between profound human experiences and the revealed message' (no. 153). For it is by 'correlating faith and life' (no. 207) that 'catechesis . . . bridges the gap between belief and life, between the Christian message and the cultural context' (no. 205). Christian religious educators must not only teach the faith tradition but also engage people's lives in the world because 'experience is a necessary medium for exploring and assimilating the truths which constitute the objective content of Revelation' (no.

152). Thus, effective catechesis should present every aspect of the faith tradition 'to refer clearly to the fundamental experiences of people's lives' (no. 133). Catechists should engage participants' own lives in the world as integral to the catechetical curriculum because 'one must start with praxis to be able to arrive at praxis' (no. 245).[1]

Let me now review briefly what I have explained at length elsewhere[2]: the core components and the pedagogical movements of a shared Christian praxis approach.

An Approach: I deliberately refer to shared praxis as an approach to catechetical education rather than a method; in fact, many different methods can be used within its overarching commitments. 'Bringing life to faith and faith to life' suggests a heuristic framework for how a religious educator might craft an intentional teaching/learning event. As people embrace and practice its commitments and dynamics, however, it becomes their general style and can be effected in varied ways and circumstances.

Praxis: Since Paulo Freire resurrected 'praxis' in educational discourse, there has been debate about what precisely the term means. Indeed, much educational literature still favors the term 'experience' instead and I often refer simply to 'life'—as in 'learning from life'. However, praxis has a more agential meaning than experience. Praxis is reflective activity in which one is an initiator or agent, whereas experience connotes something that one undergoes. John Dewey struggled to transcend this passive connotation of 'experience' throughout his writings, never with complete success.

I understand and use praxis to mean purposeful human activity, what we do reflectively and imaginatively or how we reflect upon and intend what we are doing. As such, it attempts to hold theory and practice in a dialectical unity while imagining the outcome and consequences. So, praxis embraces reflective, active and creative activity. A praxis way

10 | CREDO | LIVING AND LOVING AS DISCIPLES OF CHRIST

of knowing is intentional reflection upon what one is doing or what is going on in order to imagine consequences and create new possibilities.

The active dimension of a praxis way of knowing engages any and all bodily, mental and volitional activities, and likewise pays attention to whatever is being done in people's 'life-world'. It can engage what people know, how they feel, what they do, or what is going on in the historical reality of their social/cultural context. The reflective aspect of praxis entails the whole human capacity for knowing, engaging reason, memory and imagination, to intentionally learn from and for life in the world. It entails critical reflection not as a negative exercise but as a positive act of discernment (from the Greek *krinein*) that looks inward through self-reflection and outward at the public world through social analysis. The creative aspect recognizes the likely consequences of present praxis, imagines what might be or should be, and acts to bring about the desired end.

Christian: Christian religious educators are under mandate to teach with integrity the fullness of Christian Revelation that is mediated through Scripture and Tradition. Not only must we teach the constitutive truths, values and practices of Christian faith but also make explicit its meaning and demands for the lives of disciples today. Favoring a narrative language pattern for good catechetical reasons,[3] I find it helpful to highlight both the 'Story' and 'Vision' of Christian faith. I use these terms as metaphors to symbolize the whole historical reality of Christian Revelation and the demands/promises that it makes upon the lives of its adherents and communities. Together this Story and Vision constitute the spiritual wisdom of Christian faith for lives today and how we are to live for God's Reign as disciples of Jesus—doing of God's will 'on earth as in heaven'.

Shared: A shared praxis approach entails creating a community of conversation among participants, encouraging them to engage actively in the teaching–learning dynamic. It calls them into partnership with each other, to learn together. The exchanges among participants should entail all the give and take, listening and sharing, agreement and disagreement, cherishing one's own truth while being open to the truth of others that is the mark of good conversation. 'Shared' in the title also reflects the intent to help people bring 'life' and 'faith' together, to integrate Christian faith into daily life as 'lived faith'. This amounts to people appropriating its spiritual wisdom as their own, coming to see for themselves and embrace its truth and meaning for their lives.

In summary, a shared Christian praxis approach to Religious Education/catechesis involves creating a community of conversation and active participation in which people reflect together critically on their own historical agency in time and place, and on their socio-cultural realities; have access together to the spiritual wisdom of the Christian Story and Vision; and are encouraged to appropriate this wisdom with the intent of renewed praxis of Christian faith toward the coming of God's Reign.

PEDAGOGICAL MOVEMENTS OF A SHARED CHRISTIAN PRAXIS APPROACH

The movements of a shared praxis approach should be much more symphonic than sequential; it should not be practiced as a lock-step process. This being said, the dynamic of 'bringing life to faith, and faith to life' suggests a pattern of pedagogical moves that fulfill the foundational commitments of this approach. I outline its dynamics as a focusing activity and five subsequent movements.

The Focusing Activity: Here the educator's intent is twofold:

⊙ to engage people as active participants in the teaching–learning event;
⊙ to focus a curriculum topic as something of real interest to the lives and/or faith of participants.

Thus, it should dispose people to participate actively by turning them to look at their own lives in the world, and begin to engage them with a generative theme, symbol or text—something of real import to their present praxis of life or faith or both.

Movement One (M1): Expressing the Theme as in Present Praxis: The educator's intent here is to encourage participants to express themselves around the generative theme, symbol or text from the perspective of their present praxis. They can express what they do themselves or what they see others doing, their own feelings or thoughts or life-centered interpretations, or their perception of what is going on around them in their socio-cultural context. The key is that people 'pay attention' to the focus and name what emerges as their own encounter with the theme, symbol or text—how they see it, engage it, interpret it, or whatever. Their expressions can be spoken, written, drawn, constructed or mediated by any means of human communication.

Movement Two (M2): Reflecting on the Theme of Life/ Faith: The intent here is to encourage people to reflect critically on what they expressed in Movement One. As noted, critical reflection can engage reason, memory,

THOMAS H. GROOME: A SHARED CHRISTIAN PRAXIS APPROACH | 11

imagination or a combination of them; such reflection can be both personal and social. Reason questions or questioning activities can ask why things are the way they are; what causes them to be this way; what their meaning might be; why participants' own perceptions or interpretations are as they are, and so on. Memory questions or questioning activities might ask participants about the origins of their present praxis, their own recall or past experiences regarding it, to uncover how the social history is shaping their expressions and to recognize how their own biography or social location influence how they respond to the theme, symbol or text, and so on. Imagination-type questions or activities invite people to imagine beyond present praxis for its likely consequences, its possibilities and its desired outcomes.

Movement Three (M3): Christian Story and Vision: Here the pedagogical task is to teach clearly the Christian Story and Vision around the particular theme, symbol or text, and to do so with integrity and persuasion. Though this will often entail a doctrinal review, it is more important that people have persuasive access to the spiritual wisdom of Christian faith around the particular life/faith focus. Likewise, it is important to intentionally raise up the Vision out of the Story, what Christian faith teaches and means for lives now around the topic and how best to respond.

Movement Four (M4): Appropriating the Wisdom of Christian Faith to Life: M4 begins the dynamic of moving back to life again with renewed Christian commitment (M5). The pedagogy here encourages people to come to see for themselves what the wisdom of Christian faith might mean for their everyday lives, to personally appropriate this wisdom and to 'take it to heart' in who they are and how they live. So the educator might inquire how participants are feeling, or what they are coming to recognize for themselves, what they agree with or disagree with or might add to what has been presented in M3, and so on.

Movement Five (M5): Making Decisions for Christian Faith: Here the intent is to give participants an opportunity to choose how to respond to the spiritual wisdom of Christian faith. Decisions can be cognitive, affective or behavioral—what people believe, how they might worship or relate with God in prayer, or the ethics and values by which to live their lives. The imperative is that all decisions be 'real', influencing how participants live their Christian faith and grow in identity as disciples of Jesus Christ.

Though I lay out these movements sequentially, let me reiterate that they have great flexibility and many possible combinations. I have often combined the focusing activity with M1, and M1 with M2; I've borrowed from M3—briefly—as a focusing activity to engage people's interests; I've often shared from M3 as the conversation of M1 and M2 unfold; I've done M3 and then some M4 to return to M3 again before going back to M4 and eventually on to M5; I've combined M4 and M5 only to return again to M3 for more access to the wisdom of the faith tradition. And many times the decisions made in M5 have constituted the focusing activity for the next gathering of an ongoing community of conversation.

More important than the movements are their underpinning commitments. The focusing act reflects commitment to engage participants in the teaching/learning dynamic and with something generative for their lives. M1 reflects commitment to have people pay attention to their own lives in the world and to express their present praxis. M2 reflects commitment to critical reflection, encouraging people to think for themselves, personally and socially, to question and probe, to reason, remember and imagine around the life/faith theme, symbol or text from the perspective of their present praxis. M3 reflects commitment to give people access to the Story and Vision of Christian faith, enabling participants to encounter its spiritual wisdom for their lives. M4 reflects commitment to appropriation, encouraging participants to integrate their lives and Christian faith, to make its spiritual wisdom their own. M5 reflects commitment to invite people to decision, choosing a lived faith response to the spiritual wisdom they have encountered.

These commitments to participation and conversation, to engaging and attending, to expressing and reflecting, to accessing and appropriating, and to decision-making should run throughout the process. In other words, engagement does not end with the focusing activity but must be maintained throughout; likewise expression is not limited to M1, nor reflection to M2, nor decision-making to M5, and so on. Rather, the religious educator should promote these activities throughout the whole event.

By way of 'educating faithful Christians in a dissenting world', I make explicit the following points. Overall, a shared Christian praxis approach is set within a community of conversation and shared faith, reflecting the broader community of the Church. The dialectics of conversation—the shared faith of the group—provides a buffer against unduly individualized discernment and whimsical decision-making; all is tested within a community of discourse. Then, its dynamics invite people to active participation, encouraging them to be agents of their faith rather than dependents; in this regard it

12 | CREDO | LIVING AND LOVING AS DISCIPLES OF CHRIST

seems more likely, by God's grace, to encourage faith development toward Christian maturity.

Then, its focusing act and opening movements honor people's own wisdom from life and God's presence in their lives. However, the pedagogy here also encourages critical reflection, personal and social, inviting people to 'think twice' about their actions and reflections rather than settling for personal bias or blithely accepting the influences of their social and cultural contexts.

Movement Three gives access to the 'whole Story' of Christian faith and its Vision for people's lives now, doing so with integrity; it should never compromise anything that is constitutive of Christian faith. However, the fact that Christian Story/Vision is mediated into the context of people's lives (their own stories and visions), highlighting its spiritual wisdom for life, enables the religious educator to present Christian faith in a persuasive way and yet without indoctrination—in a mode respectful of but also appealing to participants.

Movements Four and Five encourage people's own discernment and decision-making but assure that both are well informed by the constitutive truths of Christian faith. If people are intent on dissenting they will do so anyhow, regardless of the pedagogy. Shared praxis certainly does not encourage dissent but that people's honest thoughts and feelings be brought to explicit discourse in the teaching/learning community. There they can be addressed and tested in ways more likely to lead to lived faith as disciples of Jesus. No approach can promise more.

NOTES

1. Congregation for the Clergy, *General Directory for Catechesis*, USCCB: Washington, DC, 1998. It is fascinating that the Directory refers to this pedagogy which integrates 'life' and 'faith' as 'the pedagogy of God' (no. 139) and likewise of Christ (no. 140).

2. My most complete statement of a shared praxis approach is in *Sharing Faith: A Comprehensive Approach to Religious Education and Pastoral Ministry*, San Francisco, CA: HarperSanFrancisco, 1991; now published by Wipf and Stock Publishers, Eugene, Oregon, USA, 97401. See especially Chapters 4–10.

3. See ibid., pp. 138–142, for my rationale to favor a narrative paradigm for Christian Religious Education.

This article is an extract from *Exploring Religious Education: Catholic Religious Education in an Intercultural Europe*, Chapter 22, 'Educating Faithful Christians in a Dissenting World' by Thomas H. Groome (Dublin: Veritas, 2008).

HOSFFMAN OSPINO

Cultural Awareness in Religious Education

The education of Christians in their faith does not happen in a vacuum. It is a process that builds on and integrates with the cultural values and convictions that educators and students learn from family, friends, society and Church. We are cultural beings. The Second Vatican Council reminded Catholics that sharing the Good News happens in the context of the 'living exchange between the Church and the diverse cultures of people' (*Constitution on the Church in the Modern Word* [*Gaudium et Spes*], no. 44). Subsequent ecclesial documents introduced the term 'inculturation' to name such living exchange. For instance, the *General Directory for Catechesis* published in 1997 dedicates several sections to exploring the relationship between catechesis and culture through the lens of inculturation. According to the *Directory*, awareness about culture in catechesis is more than mere adaptation (no. 109) or translation (no. 112) of religious categories into any particular language. Cultural awareness is rather a process of discernment on the part of the faith community that affirms the elements of culture that give meaning to people in their everyday lives and have the potential to mediate the experience of God while preserving the integrity of the Gospel message (cf. nos. 109–113). Likewise, they must challenge the aspects of culture that are contrary to their faith. These affirmations and negations are a good starting point for our reflection as religious educators.

One of the most significant outcomes of contemporary globalization is the increased appreciation of the many cultures that shape the lives of women and men in our families, communities and schools. Not only are we able to know more about other cultures through the media, the internet and the myriads of literary resources that fill our libraries, but we can also engage in dialogue with people around us who see and interpret the world according to cultural criteria different from our own. Cultural diversity is inescapably present in our cities, our parishes, our schools and our classrooms. Some diversity has always been with us, but our awareness

of it has been heightened by modern transportation and communication, by migration and globalization. Religious educators must develop a deepened sensibility about diversity and be more attentive to the impact of this reality on the way we educate in faith. This is a gift.

But every gift brings its own challenges. Some of us may feel more at ease with the idea of sharing different cultural perspectives on a particular issue or practice than others; some may prefer to focus on the common aspects of our human experience rather than on the differences. The truth is that it does not have to be either/or but should be both/and. Educating Christians in culturally diverse contexts like many of our schools and faith communities demands that we affirm our own cultural experiences *and* those of the people who walk with us on our life journeys; we must find that which we share in common *and* learn to appreciate that which makes us different. In some sense this is what makes our experience fully *catholic*.

Another challenge that the gift of cultural awareness poses for religious educators is how sincerely to embrace cultural diversity when we educate in faith and to affirm the cultural experiences of all the people we encounter (that is, teachers, students, administrators, parents). A quick look at the history of Christianity shows at least four attitudes: (1) Indifference before cultural diversity while focusing on the 'objectivity' and 'universality' of content; (2) Open rejection of cultural perspectives that are not similar or equal to those of a dominant group; (3) Adoption of some form of tolerance that expects progressive assimilation into a given culture, usually the culture of those who have the power to set the directions for the educational enterprise; (4) Openness to discovering elements of wisdom and truth in the various cultural contexts where Christian believers live, thereby enriching the experience of all participants in religious education. This last attitude is deeply ingrained in the nature and purpose of Catholic education, making it possible for Christianity

14 | CREDO | LIVING AND LOVING AS DISCIPLES OF CHRIST

to take root and become indigenous in every corner of the world. However, at various points in history the former attitudes, or some variations of these, have prevailed, contradicting the 'catholic' (that is, universal, inviting, inclusive, open) character of Christian religious education. Thus, it is imperative that we develop approaches to religious education that continue to affirm the wisdom of the Christian tradition in all possible forms *and* engage culture as a valid mediation of our encounter with God in history. In the culturally diverse contexts in which we educate Christians today, we must be attentive to and welcome the many cultural perspectives that people bring to the conversation.

Awareness of cultural diversity in religious education places before us a twofold invitation: (1) to understand better how God enters into relationship with us in history and (2) to acknowledge the experiences that we bring as human beings to that relationship. From this invitation then emerge two powerful insights that can significantly enrich the way we educate people in Catholic faith today:

1. *God becomes present to us through history and culture*

God comes to the encounter of women and men in the midst of our history and culture(s). God meets us in the here and now of our lives. One of the central convictions of our Judeo-Christian tradition is that God has a plan for us, that God has something to share with us, and we know about this because God has revealed it to us, especially through Jesus Christ.

Christians listen to, embrace and live God's message in different ways according to the historical and cultural conditions that shape our existences. From the first moments of historical Revelation, God has become present to women and men living in particular cultural contexts through words, actions, symbols and people; that is, ways that are unique to people's experiences and thus they can understand. Biblical language, for instance, is filled with rich Semitic imagery that affirms the relational character of human experience. Some Christians have used classical philosophical language to speak of God's divine presence and message, yet with the help of more abstract concepts and categories. Artists use their imagination to capture their experience of God and the Gospel message through a rich variety of expressions (for example, music, painting, architecture). Some cultures favor oral traditions to share their faith convictions with the younger generations. Others affirm the value of ritual and symbol to interpret their relationship with God.

Regardless of how we articulate our faith in the everyday of our lives, we do it with the resources that our culture provides. The greatness of the divine Revelation is manifested in that God freely and gratuitously chooses to enter into relationship with us according to the cultural experiences that shape our lives. Since we are much more aware of the diversity of cultural symbols, rituals and stories that mediate the experience of God in our diverse communities and schools, it is imperative that religious educators become aware of such cultural mediations and affirm their value for Christian education.

2. *We see the world through the lenses of our particular culture*

Culture is our human way of life; it is who we are, what we do and what we hope. In this sense, every human person simultaneously belongs to a culture and contributes as an architect of her or his own cultural reality. Culture is the matrix in which we are born and become human. At times the word 'culture' is understood as something merely external or artificial or something that some people have but we are not sure if we do too. This limited understanding is sometimes the consequence of our inability to name our own culture because we are seldom asked to do so. Is culture mainly defined by language or ethnicity or race or education or social location or religion or politics or history? The best answer that we can give to this question is: all of the above. Whenever we can identify the criteria and modes through which we interpret our immediate reality, then we are talking about culture.

This observation is very important when educating Christians in their faith. Most of the language, symbols, rituals and values that we use to talk about our faith are borrowed from the immediacy of our cultural experiences. It is easy to assume that when our young people hear the word 'church', each one of them has the same understanding, but we would be surprised. Let us think of a culturally diverse group of young people in a Catholic high school in the United States. For a young person raised in a Euro-American family, hearing the word 'church' may suggest a group of people to which one chooses to belong—or not. For a Hispanic student, 'church' may evoke images of family life. For an African-American student, to hear the word 'church' may lead her or him to think of Protestant Christianity, since these are the most common churches in neighborhoods that are predominantly Black.

The cultural circumstances that shape the lives of the women and men whom we encounter in religious education are the same circumstances that shape the language and categories that they use to express their faith. We must be attentive to such categories, intentionally integrating them into how we communicate Christian faith and how we encourage people to live it.

Furthermore, those whom we educate in faith are not the only ones who are shaped by particular cultural circumstances. Educators are as well. As religious educators we need to identify our own cultural assumptions and evaluate them on a continuous basis. How we teach, what we teach and why we teach (all curriculum questions) very much reflect our cultural values and convictions. The more aware we are about these values and convictions, the better we are able to foster authentic relationships with our young people and make responsible pedagogical decisions.

We enter the religious educational experience as human beings shaped by the richness of our own particular culture(s). Nonetheless, we are not exempt from biases and errors. For decades White Christian educators in the United States denied fellow Black Christians access to their schools on account of the color of their skin. In mission territories some Christian educators forced native populations to accept a faith that the latter did not understand. Sometimes religious educators may embrace inadequate or incomplete understandings of the Christian tradition and fail to present it with faithfulness. These educators do not necessarily mean harm or evil toward the people affected by their decisions, yet they operate according to unchecked cultural standards. It is crucial that we remain attentive about our cultural assumptions, affirm those that make us more human and authentic Christians, and question those that do not.

CONCLUSION

Cultural awareness is a pedagogical virtue. As such, we must learn it, cultivate it and perfect it on a continuous basis. We cannot lose sight that our contemporary societies, faith communities and schools are culturally diverse. We have the responsibility to learn what elements of culture mediate the experience of God for the people whom we encounter in our educational settings, and to challenge the aspects that counter God's presence. As Christian educators, then, we have the obligation to be culturally responsive and responsible when educating in faith. Our lives and the lives of those whom we encounter are deeply shaped by unique cultural experiences. Through these cultural values and convictions, we enter into relationship with one another and with God. May this be an invitation to grow in awareness about our own cultural being and that of the people we educate in faith.

16 | CREDO | LIVING AND LOVING AS DISCIPLES OF CHRIST

CHAPTER 1

God Desires What Is Best for Us

INTRODUCTION

Let the hearts of those who seek the LORD rejoice.
—Psalm 105:3

Chapter 1 focuses on the human search for happiness. We help the young people to recognize that true and lasting happiness rests in God alone and in following God's plan for our lives.

Chapter 1 is developed under five major headings:

◉ **ATTEND AND REFLECT:** How do you seek happiness?

◉ **HEAR THE STORY:** The divine path for the human pursuit of happiness

◉ **EMBRACE THE VISION:** We are images of God

◉ **THINK IT THROUGH:** Overcoming obstacles to happiness

◉ **JUDGE AND ACT:** (*Activities and exercises that encourage the young people to integrate what they have learned in the chapter into their daily lives*)

Theological Background for the Teacher

JOURNEYING TOWARD PERFECTION

[God] is not far from each one of us. For 'In him we live and move and have our being'; . . . 'For we too are his offspring.'
—Acts 17:27–28

God is the Creator of all things, the 'master of the world and of its history' (*Catechism of the Catholic Church* [CCC], no. 314). The Book of Genesis affirms that the world and everything in it have their origin, ground and final goal in God. Created out of love, God's creation is 'in a state of journeying' toward the full realization of God's dream for the world and for all that is within it.

The universe was created 'in a state of journeying' (*in statu viae*) toward an ultimate perfection yet to be attained, to which God has destined it.
—CCC, no. 302

True and lasting happiness rests in knowing God and following God's plan for us. We are created to share eternal love and happiness with God. Thus we are called to be participants in God's divine plan—to seek to live, to know, to create and to love like God. To this end God has entrusted the world to us. In accordance with God's will and command, we strive to continue God's work by transforming the world and making it a suitable dwelling-place for all God's children. Working in and through us, God gives us the responsibility of being stewards of the earth, of respecting all life and taking care of all the earth's creatures.

THE DIGNITY OF THE HUMAN PERSON

The dignity of the human person is rooted in his creation in the image and likeness of God.
—CCC, no. 1700

The principle of human dignity is based on the belief that God is the source and Creator of all life. In the Book of Genesis we learn that humankind is God's masterpiece; man and woman are the climax of God's creative activity. The Catholic Church teaches that we are created in God's image and likeness with the capacity to know and love God like no other creature. 'The divine image is present in every man' (CCC, no. 1702). Our relationship with God, therefore, is at the core of our human dignity.

Being in the image of God the human individual possesses the dignity of *a person*, who is not just something, but someone. He is capable of self-knowledge, of self-possession and of freely giving himself and entering into communion with other persons.
—CCC, no. 357

Human dignity must be understood in the context of human freedom, because human dignity is grounded in human freedom. God invites us to cooperate with him in bringing about his divine plan, and he has granted us the dignity of acting with intelligence and free will. Thus, we are free to accept or to reject the invitation to enter into the ongoing work of creation that God has entrusted to us.

CHAPTER 1: GOD DESIRES WHAT IS BEST FOR US | INTRODUCTION | 17

It is essential to a human being freely to direct himself. . . . By his deliberate actions, the human person does, or does not, conform to the good promised by God and attested by moral conscience.

—CCC, no. 1700

We are free to shape our lives and to influence the world in which we live. We direct our own lives by freely making our own contribution to our growth and development. When we choose to continue the work of creation, we act in accordance with the will and command of God. In so doing we act as children of God, made in God's image and likeness.

FALL AND REDEMPTION

As intelligent and free creatures, both angels and human beings must make their way to their ultimate destinies by using their intellect and will to make free choices. They can and must choose between loving God—who has shown his love for them in creation and Revelation—and loving something else.

—*United States Catholic Catechism for Adults* (USCCA), 57

In spite of our aspirations for a better life and a better world, and in spite of God's command to us to love one another, much unhappiness, evil, pain and suffering exist in our world. Why does evil exist? Could God not have created a world so perfect that it was devoid of evil and suffering? In order to understand the existence of evil we have to remember that the world that God created in wisdom and goodness is a world moving toward its ultimate perfection, in which we are all called to play our part. While we await the achievement of this state of ultimate perfection, evil will exist alongside good.

Central to our journey of faith is the awareness of forces within us that oppose each other and cause us conflict.

—USCCA, 72

We have the capacity to hear the voice of God urging us toward what is good. However, we sometimes refuse to cooperate with God's plan for creation and we allow obstacles to inhibit God's desire for us from becoming a reality. God has given us the free will to seek out what is true and good and beautiful; however, we sometimes choose what is evil rather than what is good (see USCCA, 319). This is moral evil—the evil of sin. We are all aware of the struggle between good and evil that resides within our human hearts.

The story of humankind's relationship with God is revealed in the Genesis narrative. Using symbolic language, Genesis 3 reveals how the harmony and perfection of creation was shattered by Adam and Eve's desire to seek happiness through their own resources and by their refusal to obey God. As a consequence of that first sin (Original Sin), Adam and Eve became estranged from God. Genesis reveals that as a result of the actions of our first parents, our human nature has been weakened and we are subject to suffering and death. The impact of Original Sin has darkened our minds, weakened our wills and inclined us toward sin (see USCCA, 319).

By his sin Adam, as the first man, lost the original holiness and justice he had received from God, not only for himself but for all human beings.

—CCC, no. 416

Such is the unconditional nature of God's love and mercy that, despite all of this, he refuses to abandon us. Through the power of the Holy Spirit and the life, Death, Resurrection and Ascension of his only Son, Jesus Christ, God offers us redemption and 'humanity is restored to a right relationship with God' (USCCA, 70).

JESUS CHRIST IS THE FULFILLMENT OF GOD'S PROMISE

It is in Jesus Christ that God's promise of redemption has been fulfilled. Jesus Christ has revealed to us the divinity within our humanity and the potential each of us has to grow in intimacy and communion with God. A 'model of holiness' (CCC, no. 459), he draws us toward perfect union with God the Father. Through Jesus' life, Death, Resurrection and Ascension, God's plan has been restored.

The only-begotten Son of God, wanting to make us sharers in his divinity, assumed our nature, so that he, made man, might make men gods.

—CCC, no. 460, quoting St. Thomas Aquinas

Jesus is the Word of God, 'the image of the invisible God, the firstborn of all creation' (Colossians 1:15). He is the Incarnate Son of God, the Second Person of the Holy Trinity, who became man in order that we might come to know God.

The son, accordingly, came, sent by the Father, who before the foundation of the world chose us and predestined us in him to be his adopted sons and daughters. For it is in him that it pleased the Father to restore all things (cf. Ephesians 1:4–5 and 10). To carry out the will of the Father, Christ

18 | CREDO | LIVING AND LOVING AS DISCIPLES OF CHRIST

inaugurated the kingdom of heaven on earth and revealed his mystery to us.

—*Lumen Gentium (Constitution on the Church)*, no. 3

The *Catechism of the Catholic Church* teaches: 'The Word became flesh for us

⊙ in order to save us by reconciling us with God;
⊙ so that thus we might know God's love;
⊙ to be our model of holiness;
⊙ to make us "partakers of the divine nature".'

—CCC, nos. 457–460

In Jesus Christ, the Word of God became man, ever drawing us toward God the Father. It is Jesus Christ who shows us how to respond to God's love in our lives. He alone enables us to live the moral life to which we are called as children of God. He alone leads us, by the power of the Holy Spirit, 'to maturity, to the measure of the full stature of Christ' (Ephesians 4:13).

GRACE: THE UNDESERVED GIFT FROM GOD

Grace is the free and undeserved assistance God offers us so that we might respond to his call to share in his divine life and attain eternal life. God's grace, as divinely offered gift, does not take away or restrict our freedom; rather, it perfects our freedom by helping us overcome the restricting power of sin, the true obstacle to our freedom.

—USCCA, 329

The word 'grace' comes from the Latin word *gratia*, meaning 'free'. Grace is a freely given, unearned, spontaneous gift from God that enables each one of us to 'respond to his call to become children of God, adoptive sons, partakers of the divine nature and of eternal life' (CCC, no. 1996). As Christians, God's grace is constantly at work in our lives, enabling us to journey in faith, love and justice. The grace of God guides us to live in accordance with God's divine plan and to be true disciples of Jesus Christ.

We do not always take the time to reflect on the depth of God's love for us. Often, we do not recognize God's grace at work in our day-to-day lives. Indeed, it is not always easy for us to allow ourselves to truly accept the unearned and gracious love of God. Pope Francis addressed this difficulty in his homily in the chapel of the Domus Sanctae Marthae at the Vatican in June 2013 when he said:

'It is more difficult to let God love us than to love Him! The best way to love Him in return is to open our hearts and let Him love us. . . . Let Him draw close to us and feel Him close to us. This is really very difficult: letting ourselves be loved by Him.'

And yet, being loved by God is at the core of Christian morality. Pope Francis went on to urge us to pray for the ability to accept God's love which resides in all our hearts.

'Lord, I want to love You, but teach me the difficult science, the difficult habit of letting myself be loved by You, to feel You close and feel Your tenderness!'

This chapter offers us an opportunity to affirm for our young people in real and explicit ways that they are much loved by God, and so lead them to uncover for themselves the myriad ways in which the love of God is present to them, guiding, supporting and sustaining them to live their lives with justice, truth and love.

ADDITIONAL BACKGROUND READING

Catechism of the Catholic Church, nos. 302–314, 410, 456–460, 1700–1706; *United States Catholic Catechism for Adults*, chapters 1 and 2; **James F. Keenan, S.J.,** *Moral Wisdom* (Rowan and Littlefield, 2009).

CHAPTER OUTCOMES

In all learning situations it is important to assess what the young people have learned and are striving to integrate into their lives. Learning builds on prior knowledge and experiences. A 'Prior Knowledge Assessment' tool is available on line at *www. credoseries.com*. Assessing the young people's prior knowledge of the key faith concepts presented in each chapter will both help you to present your lessons more effectively and also help the young people to grow in their Catholic identity.

In each chapter of this text there are two overarching desired outcomes. They are: (1) that the young people will come to a deeper understanding of the teaching of the Catholic Church and so be able to give an account of the faith; (2) that they will choose to co-operate with the grace of the Holy Spirit and strive to grow in their own personal faith and in their relationship with God.

The purpose of this text and the other texts of the *Credo* series is to help the young people to both grow in their understanding of the faith and become articulate, faith-filled people, whose faith gives direction to their lives and influences how they live. While it is reasonably easy to assess how well the young people remember and have understood the knowledge of the faith (the information presented in a lesson), it is not quite so easy to assess their progress in terms of their faith formation. To facilitate the latter, we have incorporated the use of multiple strategies as identified by Bloom's taxonomy and its revision by Anderson and Krathwohl. We have also set out two sets of outcomes for each chapter: *Learning Outcomes*, which focus on the information presented in the chapter, and *Faith-formation Outcomes*, which focus on the opportunities provided for young people to integrate the knowledge of the faith of the Church into their lives—both of which help the young people to grow as people of faith.

All of the outcomes reflect the six tasks of catechesis as identified in the *General Directory for Catechesis* (1997) and the *National Directory of Catechesis* (2005). The tasks, which are integrated into all the texts in the *Credo* series, as stated in the National Directory, are:

1. Promote knowledge of the faith.
2. Promote knowledge of the meaning of the Liturgy and the Sacraments.
3. Promote moral formation in Jesus Christ.
4. Teach the Christian how to pray with Christ.
5. Prepare the Christian to live in community and to participate actively in the life and mission of the Church.
6. Promote a missionary spirit that prepares the faithful to be present as Christians within society.

CHAPTER OUTCOMES

Learning Outcomes

As a result of studying this chapter and exploring the issues raised, the young people should be able to:

⊙ recognize that the pursuit of happiness is universal among human beings;
⊙ identify some of the commonly perceived routes to happiness in society;
⊙ understand the Catholic Church's teaching on the path to 'true' happiness;
⊙ recognize how the two accounts of Creation in the Book of Genesis help us to understand why God created the world;
⊙ know that we are invited to play our part in the unfolding of God's plan of goodness by following the example of Jesus Christ and the guidance of the Holy Spirit;
⊙ understand that the dignity of the human person is rooted in our being made in the image and likeness of God;
⊙ know that God has gifted human beings with intellect and free will, thus giving us the ability to choose between good and evil;
⊙ recognize that our ultimate goal is to respond to God's grace and live in the presence of God for all eternity;
⊙ understand the Catholic Church's teaching that human nature is weakened as a result of Original Sin;
⊙ recognize that everyone experiences temptation;
⊙ know that Jesus' redeeming mission was and continues to be the restoration of humanity to the state of original holiness and original justice;
⊙ know the story of St. Augustine of Hippo.

Faith-formation Outcomes

As a result of studying this chapter and exploring the issues raised, the young people should also:

⊙ come to appreciate that it is only in God that will they find truth and lasting happiness;
⊙ recognize that faith in God can help people to become fully alive;
⊙ identify ways in which they can play a part in God's plan for creation;
⊙ identify in their own lives where the gift of God's grace helps them to live their faith;
⊙ recognize moments of temptation in their lives;
⊙ ask for God's grace to know, resist and reject temptation;
⊙ be inspired by the story of St. Augustine of Hippo to seek happiness in places and ways that lead to God.

20 | CREDO | LIVING AND LOVING AS DISCIPLES OF CHRIST

Teacher Reflection

As you prepare to engage your group in a study of the human search for happiness, take a moment to read this reflection from the fourteenth-century hermit and spiritual writer Julian of Norwich.

> We cannot be blessedly saved until we are truly in peace and in love, for that is our salvation.
>
> . . . We are sure and safe by God's merciful protection, so that we do not perish. But we are not blessedly safe, possessing our endless joy, until we are all in peace and in love, that is today wholly contented with God and with all his works and with all his judgments, and loving and content with ourselves and with our fellow Christians and with everything which God loves, as is pleasing to love. And God's goodness does this in us.
>
> So I saw that God is our true peace; and he is our safe protector when we ourselves are in disquiet, and he constantly works to bring us into endless peace.

REFLECT

Identify and reflect on those times when you have felt 'wholly contented with God'; when you have experienced the presence of God drawing you into his peace and happiness.

CHAPTER 1: GOD DESIRES WHAT IS BEST FOR US | INTRODUCTION | 21

Notes and Guidelines for Student Activities

ATTEND AND REFLECT

How do you seek happiness?

Learning Outcomes

That the young people would:

- ⊙ recognize that the pursuit of happiness is universal among human beings;
- ⊙ identify some of the commonly perceived routes to happiness in society;
- ⊙ understand the Catholic Church's teaching on the path to 'true' happiness.

Faith-formation Outcome

That the young people would also:

- ⊙ come to appreciate that it is only in God that will they find truth and lasting happiness.

Overview

Chapter 1 begins by inviting the young people first to reflect on their own pursuit of happiness and then to become aware of the growing influence of consumerism and secularism on the general pursuit of happiness in society. We introduce the young people to the Catholic Church's teaching that true and lasting happiness has its source in our relationship with God the Father, Son and Holy Spirit. We seek to awaken in them the realization that our innate longing for happiness can only be satisfied by communion with God, who cares deeply for each one of us and who continually seeks us out. Finally, we invite the young people to reevaluate where they seek happiness and to reflect on how focusing their pursuit of happiness on their relationship with God might impact their own lives and the lives of those around them.

Supplementary Activities for 'Attend and Reflect'

Worksheet 1: 'Can Money Buy Happiness?' (*page 26 of this resource*) seeks to heighten the young people's awareness of the false attractions of our consumerist society, which tells us that *all* things, including happiness, can be bought. We invite them to explore and reflect on the fact that true and lasting happiness cannot be found in possessions and material goods.

Worksheet 2: 'What Is Happiness?' (*page 28 of this resource*) invites the young people to define and share their understanding of happiness. This worksheet also presents some biblical verses on happiness that the young people may decide to 'take to heart' in their lives.

HEAR THE STORY

The divine path for the human pursuit of happiness

Learning Outcomes

That the young people would:

- ⊙ recognize how the two accounts of Creation in the Book of Genesis help us to understand why God created the world;
- ⊙ know that we are invited to play our part in the unfolding of God's plan of goodness by following the example of Jesus Christ and the guidance of the Holy Spirit.

Faith-formation Outcomes

That the young people would also:

- ⊙ recognize that faith in God can help people to become fully alive;
- ⊙ identify ways in which they can play a part in God's plan for creation.

Overview

In section two, 'Hear the Story', we explore with the young people why God created the world. We discuss the Church's teaching that the world was created for the glory of God and that God the Creator invites each of us to be part of the unfolding of his divine plan of goodness for all creation. We emphasize that God invites us to bring life, love, goodness, truth and beauty to the world. We encourage the young people to identify how they can be instruments for change and good in the world and we remind them that Jesus, the Incarnate Son of God, came to live among us to show us the 'way' to fulfill this responsibility. Finally, we recall Jesus' promise that he would be with us always and that he would send the Holy Spirit to be our teacher and helper.

22 | CREDO | LIVING AND LOVING AS DISCIPLES OF CHRIST

Supplementary Activities for 'Hear the Story'

Collage Activity
Encourage the young people to search through newspapers and magazines for stories about people who are working to make the world a better place. They could work individually or in groups and cut out headlines, images and short paragraphs for a large class collage on this topic. The young people might also write out some relevant Scripture quotations to accompany the collage. Finally, invite them to agree on a title for the collage and to display it in a prominent location in the school.

Worksheet 3: 'Eulogy' (*page 30 of this resource*) is a creative exercise that requires the young people to write an imaginary eulogy about themselves in order to help them focus on the kind of person they would like to become. You might like to play instrumental music in the background while the young people reflect upon and compose their material.

Worksheet 4: 'When Hope and History Rhyme' (*page 31 of this resource*) uses words from Nobel prize-winning poet Seamus Heaney (1939–2013) to help the young people begin to contemplate what our world would be like if 'hope and history' were to 'rhyme'.

Worksheet 5: 'I Have a Dream' (*page 32 of this resource*) presents a selection of quotations from some famous people talking about their dreams as a starting point for encouraging the young people first to articulate their own dreams for their lives and then to situate those dreams within the context of God's dream for each one of them.

EMBRACE THE VISION

We are images of God

Learning Outcomes
That the young people would:
- understand that the dignity of the human person is rooted in our being made in the image and likeness of God;
- know that God has gifted human beings with intellect and free will, thus giving us the ability to choose between good and evil;

- recognize that our ultimate goal is to respond to God's grace and live in the presence of God for all eternity.

Faith-formation Outcome
That the young people would also:
- identify in their own lives where the gift of God's grace helps them to live their faith.

Overview
In section three, 'Embrace the Vision', we lead the young people to an understanding of the implications of our being made in God's image and likeness. God has gifted us with imagination, free will, reason and intellect. God does not control us; rather, we have the freedom to shape our own lives and our world. With this comes immense responsibility, which lies at the very heart of the Christian challenge to live a moral life. God has implanted in us a desire for happiness that we can freely choose to pursue. We seek also to deepen the young people's understanding of grace as the free gift by which God enables us to share in his life. We guide the young people to appreciate that our ultimate purpose and goal is to respond to God's grace and live in the loving presence of the one God, who is Father, Son and Holy Spirit, for all eternity.

Supplementary Activities for 'Embrace the Vision'

Worksheet 6: 'Acrostic Verse or Prayer' (*page 34 of this resource*) uses words from St. Paul's greeting to the early Christian community, 'Grace to you and peace from God our Father and the Lord Jesus Christ', as a framework for the young people to write an acrostic poem or prayer that affirms the gift of God's grace in their lives.

Worksheet 7: 'Choosing Our Way' (*page 36 of this resource*) invites the young people to read an excerpt from Victor E. Frankl's *Man's Search for Meaning* as the basis for a discussion on the human capacity to exercise one's free will in spite of obstacles and challenges. From this we encourage the young people to reflect on their own capacity to make decisions and to choose their own 'way' or 'attitude' in life.

Worksheet 8: 'Moments of Grace' (*page 37 of this resource*) guides the young people to discover how the Samaritan woman's encounter with Jesus at the well of Jacob was a 'graced' moment. From this we

CHAPTER 1: GOD DESIRES WHAT IS BEST FOR US | NOTES AND GUIDELINES | 23 encourage them to identify 'graced' moments in their own lives—moments when God has touched and moved their hearts.

Worksheet 9: 'My Relationship with the Triune God' (*page 38 of this resource*) invites the young people to create a visual representation of their own relationship with the Triune God.

THINK IT THROUGH

Overcoming obstacles to happiness

Learning Outcomes

That the young people would:

⊙ understand the Catholic Church's teaching that human nature is weakened as a result of Original Sin;

⊙ recognize that everyone experiences temptation;

⊙ know that Jesus' redeeming mission was and continues to be the restoration of humanity to the state of original holiness and original justice.

Faith-formation Outcomes

That the young people would also:

⊙ recognize moments of temptation in their lives;

⊙ ask for God's grace to know, resist and reject temptation.

Overview

We begin section four, 'Think It Through', by heightening the young people's awareness of obstacles to happiness and helping them to recognize times in their lives when they fail to live up to the inherent goodness that God has placed in the heart of all human beings. Through recalling the account of the Fall in the Book of Genesis, we lead them to appreciate that the causes of sin are rooted in human selfishness and in the human person's capacity to choose evil over good. The section also explores how we share in the saving work of making God's Kingdom a reality here on earth. We help the young people to understand that through the Paschal Mystery of Jesus' life, Death, Resurrection and Ascension, God has fulfilled the divine promise of redemption and freed us from the power of evil and sin.

Supplementary Activities for 'Think It Through'

Worksheet 10: 'Joseph's Story' (*page 39 of this resource*) invites the young people to study the story of Joseph, son of Jacob, in the Book of Genesis and to explore and discuss how Joseph's faith in God's plan for him sustained him through difficult times and how good outcomes can sometimes result from bad or evil choices.

Research Activity

Invite the young people to work in pairs to find stories or articles from newspapers or the internet that reflect how people can use their intellect and free will to sabotage God's dream for humanity. They could prepare a visual presentation for the class by writing a short summary of each example, or cutting out or printing headlines or paragraphs that capture the essence of the stories, along with photographs or other images.

Worksheet 11: 'Living God's Dream' (*page 40 of this resource*) offers the young people an opportunity to review and reassess their own efforts at living as disciples of Jesus and making God's dream for them a reality.

JUDGE AND ACT

Learning Outcome

That the young people would:

⊙ know the story of St. Augustine of Hippo.

Faith-formation Outcome

That the young people would also:

⊙ be inspired by the story of St. Augustine of Hippo to seek happiness in places and ways that lead to God.

Overview

In section five, 'Judge and Act', the young people review and discuss the teachings of the Church that they have learned about in this chapter. They learn about St. Augustine of Hippo and how his long and painful search for meaning led him to find happiness in Christ. The young people also learn about St. Monica, Augustine's mother and a devout Christian, whose prayer and perseverance played such a positive role in her son's faith journey.

24 | CREDO | LIVING AND LOVING AS DISCIPLES OF CHRIST

Supplementary Activities for 'Judge and Act'

Research Activity

Invite the young people to research or recall the lives of other saints who encountered challenges and obstacles in their journey to faith in Christ. They could share their findings with the class.

_____

Media Project 1

Encourage the young people to identify popular movies and television programs that reflect the human quest for happiness, and then to discuss to what extent the characters in the movies/programs found the answer to true and lasting happiness.

_____

Media Project 2

Invite the young people to work in groups to find recent newspaper articles or stories or photographs that depict people working toward the creation of a better and more just world. Ask each group to compose a song or rap based on the example that they found most inspiring. Each group may then perform their song or rap for the class.

Additional Prayer Suggestions

Guided Meditation: 'Each step is a prayer'

(*See 'Student Activity Tool Kit', pages 394–6 of this resource, for further helpful suggestions in relation to conducting guided meditations.*)

Ask the young people to take up a position suitable for meditation. Encourage them to still their bodies and to become aware of their breathing.

Invite the young people to listen as you read the following Scripture verse slowly:
'God saw everything that he had made, and indeed, it was very good' (Genesis 1:31).

Continue to lead the young people in quiet prayer:
Imagine God looking at creation today.
What would God see?
Quietly give thanks to God for all the good things in creation.

Repeat the Scripture verse:
'God saw everything that he had made, and indeed, it was very good.'

Then continue to lead the young people in prayer:
Now imagine God looking at you.
God sees not only your physical self, but right into your heart and your mind.
Think of all the good things God sees in you . . . some things that no one else will ever see!
Quietly give thanks to God for all the good that is in you.

Help the students to situate themselves back in the classroom and end the prayer by praying the Sign of the Cross.

_____

Scripture Reflection

(*See instructions for the use of doodling in prayer in the 'Student Activity Tool Kit', page 394 of this resource.*)

Use this Scripture verse to engage the young people in prayer:

For we are what he has made us, created in Christ Jesus. . . .

EPHESIANS 2:10

CHAPTER 1 | WORKSHEET 1

NAME:

Can Money Buy Happiness?

This worksheet offers you the opportunity to explore and reflect on whether or not happiness can be bought. In other words, can happiness be found through the acquisition of possessions and material goods?

GROUP ACTIVITY 1
◉ Work in groups of three or four.
◉ Imagine you are going on a shopping spree. You have a credit card that has no financial limit but it can only ever be used five times.
◉ Discuss the scenario together and try to agree on five things you would buy with the card.
◉ List your choices on the lines provided below.

1. _____

2. _____

3. _____

4. _____

5 _____

◉ Now look again at the choices you made. Before completing the grid below, discuss why you chose each item and how you think each item could contribute to your happiness.

26 | CREDO | LIVING AND LOVING AS DISCIPLES OF CHRIST

CHAPTER 1 | WORKSHEET 1 (CONTD.)

Why we chose to buy this item
1.
2.
3.
4.
5.

GROUP ACTIVITY 2

- Once again, work in groups of three or four.
- Do a brainstorm on the things that money cannot buy.
- Agree together on the top five things that money cannot buy that you think would help you live a happy and fulfilled life.
- List your 'top five' choices on the chart below.

Five Things that Money Cannot Buy
1.
2.
3.
4.
5.

REFLECT AND RESPOND

- If you were told that you could have everything on this list or the top five from your imaginary shopping spree, which would you choose, and why?
- Share your thoughts on this with the group.

DECIDE FOR YOURSELF

- What insights have you gained from the exercises on this worksheet?
- How might these insights impact your pursuit of happiness from here on?

CHAPTER 1: GOD DESIRES WHAT IS BEST FOR US | WORKSHEET 1 (CONTD.) | 27

CHAPTER 1 | WORKSHEET 2

NAME:

What Is Happiness?

All human beings desire happiness. This worksheet invites you to reflect further on your understanding of what constitutes happiness.

REFLECT AND RESPOND

⊙ Begin by closing your eyes and thinking about the word 'happiness'. What comes to mind?

⊙ Allow any words, phrases, lines from songs, images or scenes from films or books or personal experiences to emerge.

⊙ Now list what came up for you.

_____

_____

_____

_____

_____

_____

COMPARE AND SHARE

With a partner, share and compare lists. Discuss:

⊙ What do your lists have in common? What insights or understanding about the meaning of happiness do they reflect?

⊙ Has your understanding of what happiness means changed over the course of your life? In what way?

⊙ Work together to see if you can come up with your own definition of happiness.

READ AND REFLECT

Read and reflect on these biblical verses about happiness.

> Happy is everyone who fears the LORD,
>   who walks in his ways.
> You shall eat the fruit of the labor of your hands;
>   you shall be happy, and it shall go well with you.
>   —Psalm 128:1

28 | CREDO | LIVING AND LOVING AS DISCIPLES OF CHRIST

CHAPTER 1 | WORKSHEET 2 (CONTD.)

[H]appy are the people whose God is the LORD.
—Psalm 144:15

Happy are those . . .
whose hope is in the LORD their God.
—Psalm 146:5

Happy are those who find wisdom,
and those who get understanding.
—Proverbs 3:13

Those who despise their neighbors are sinners,
but happy are those who are kind to the poor.
—Proverbs 14:21

[H]appy are those who keep the law.
—Proverbs 29:18

CHOOSE AND DESCRIBE

⊙ Choose one of the above Scripture verses that you would like to 'take to heart' in your life.
⊙ Reflect on and then write about the difference taking this piece of wisdom to heart might make to your life.

_____

_____

_____

_____

_____

_____

_____

_____

_____

CHAPTER 1: GOD DESIRES WHAT IS BEST FOR US | WORKSHEET 2 (CONTD.) | 29

CHAPTER 1 | WORKSHEET 3

NAME:

Eulogy

This worksheet offers you the opportunity, through a creative activity, to imagine the kind of person you would like to become.

CREATIVE EXERCISE

Imagine that you have died and that your family, friends and neighbors have gathered for the funeral Mass to say their goodbyes to you. At the end of the ceremony the priest invites someone to talk about you and your life as a Christian. On the lines provided write the kind of eulogy you would like to hear people give in remembrance and celebration of your life.

A TRIBUTE TO THE LIFE OF

_____ (*your name*)

_____

_____

_____

_____

_____

_____

_____

_____

_____

REFLECT AND SHARE

⊙ Reflect upon and share the insights you have gained about yourself from doing this exercise. For example, think about and then discuss:
  – What have you identified to be the things that really matter in life?
  – What contribution would you like to make to the world you live in?
⊙ What would you need to change in the way you live your life in order to truly become the person you described in your 'eulogy'?

30 | CREDO | LIVING AND LOVING AS DISCIPLES OF CHRIST

CHAPTER 1 | WORKSHEET 4

NAME:

When Hope and History Rhyme

This worksheet invites you to reflect on what the world would be like if, in the words of the Irish poet Seamus Heaney, 'hope and history' were to 'rhyme'.

READ, REFLECT AND RESPOND

⊙ Read and reflect on these words of wisdom from the Irish Nobel prize-winning poet Seamus Heaney (1939–2013).

> History says, Don't hope
> On this side of the grave.
> But then, once in a lifetime
> The longed-for tidal wave
> Of justice can rise up,
> And hope and history rhyme.

⊙ What do you think Heaney meant when he spoke of hope and history rhyming?
⊙ If hope and history were to 'rhyme' in terms of the world we live in, what would change? What would such a world look like?
⊙ On the lines provided, write what you imagine such a world would be like.

_____

_____

_____

_____

_____

_____

_____

_____

CHAPTER 1: GOD DESIRES WHAT IS BEST FOR US | WORKSHEET 4 | 31

CHAPTER 1 | WORKSHEET 5

NAME:

I Have a Dream

All of us have dreams. We dream about how we would like life to be for ourselves, for those whom we love and for the future of the world. Being aware of the dreams we hold dear in our hearts can help us bring them to fruition. This worksheet invites you to identify your own dreams for your life and then to situate those dreams within the context of God's dream for you.

READ, REFLECT AND RESPOND

People have always believed that their dreams help their future take shape and become a reality. Here is how some famous people articulated their dreams for the future:

Clergyman and civil rights activist **Reverend Martin Luther King Jr.** said:
'I have a dream that my four children will one day live in a nation where they will not be judged by the color of their skin but by the content of their character. . . . I have a dream that one day every valley shall be exalted, every hill and mountain shall be made low, the rough places will be made straight and the glory of the Lord shall be revealed and all flesh shall see it together.'

Olympic athlete **Jesse Owens** said:
'We all have dreams. But in order to make dreams come into reality, it takes an awful lot of determination, dedication, self-discipline, and effort.'

Film producer and director **Walt Disney** said:
'All our dreams can come true, if we have the courage to pursue them. . . . If you dream it, you can do it.'

Politician **Robert Kennedy** said,
'There are those who look at things as they are and ask "why?" I dream of things that never were and ask "why not?"'

Reflect now on your own dreams for the future—for yourself and for the world. Describe your top dream for yourself.

_____

_____

_____

_____

32 | CREDO | LIVING AND LOVING AS DISCIPLES OF CHRIST

CHAPTER 1 | WORKSHEET 5 (CONTD.)

Describe your top dream for the world.

_____

_____

_____

God, too, has a dream for all of humanity and God invites us to participate in making that dream become a reality.

Describe what you think God's dream for you is right now.

_____

_____

Describe what you think God's dream for the world is right now.

_____

_____

_____

MAKING GOD'S DREAM A REALITY

List three ways in which you can help make God's dream for you a reality.

1. _____

2. _____

3. _____

List three ways in which you can help make God's dream for the world a reality.

1. _____

2. _____

3. _____

CHAPTER 1: GOD DESIRES WHAT IS BEST FOR US | WORKSHEET 5 (CONTD.) | 33

CHAPTER 1 | WORKSHEET 6

NAME:

Acrostic Poem or Prayer

St. Paul frequently opened his Letters to the early Christian community with the greeting: 'Grace to you and peace from God our Father and the Lord Jesus Christ.' (See, for example, Romans 1:7; 1 Corinthians 1:3; 2 Corinthians 1:2.) In so doing, St. Paul reaffirmed for the early Christian community that God was ever present to them. This worksheet invites you to use St. Paul's words of greeting to write an acrostic poem or prayer that affirms the gift of God's grace in your own life.

GET CREATIVE!
Using some of the words from St. Paul's greeting as a framework, write a poem or prayer about the presence of God's grace in your life.

G _____

R _____

A _____

C _____

E _____

A _____

N _____

D _____

P _____

E _____

A _____

C _____

E _____

34 | CREDO | LIVING AND LOVING AS DISCIPLES OF CHRIST

CHAPTER 1 | WORKSHEET 6 (CONTD.)

F _____

R _____

O _____

M _____

G _____

O _____

D _____

CHAPTER 1 | WORKSHEET 7

NAME:

Choosing Our Way

Viktor E. Frankl (1905–97) spent three years in Auschwitz, Dachau and other concentration camps during the Second World War. As a result of these experiences he wrote *Man's Search for Meaning*. This worksheet presents an excerpt from this inspirational book and invites your response.

READ, REFLECT AND RESPOND

Read and reflect upon this passage from *Man's Search for Meaning* and then share responses to the questions that follow.

> We who lived in concentration camps can remember the men who walked through the huts comforting others, giving away their last piece of bread. They may have been few in number, but they offer sufficient proof that everything can be taken from a man but one thing: the last of the human freedoms—to choose one's attitude in any given set of circumstances, to choose one's own way.

- What do you think might help a person to exercise their free will courageously and for good in spite of obstacles?
- Does this excerpt give you renewed hope? If so, why?

OVER TO YOU

Name three ways in which you are choosing your 'own way' or your 'own attitude' in life right now.

1. _____

   _____

2. _____

   _____

3. _____

   _____

JOURNAL EXERCISE

Choose one of the 'ways' that you named in the previous exercise and describe how your choosing this 'way' or 'attitude' is helping to shape you as a person right now.

36 | CREDO | LIVING AND LOVING AS DISCIPLES OF CHRIST

CHAPTER 1 | WORKSHEET 8

NAME:

Moments of Grace

This worksheet invites you to read and reflect upon the story of Jesus' conversation with the Samaritan woman at Jacob's Well in order to help you recognize the role of God's grace in that encounter but also in your own life.

JESUS REVEALED GOD'S GRACE

The *Catechism of the Catholic Church* teaches: 'Grace is a *participation in the life of God*' (CCC, no. 1997). During his time on earth Jesus sought to draw people to God. Through his words and his actions he sought to open people's minds and hearts to the reality of God in their lives, to help them be aware of how they were 'graced' by God's love and called to participate in the realization of God's dream for all humanity.

- ◉ In John 4:5–26 we read about Jesus entering into conversation with a Samaritan woman at the well of Jacob. Take a few moments now to read and recall that story.
- ◉ As you read it, try to enter into the mind and heart of the Samaritan woman and begin to discern how she came to understand the depth of what Jesus was saying to her about life and about God.
- ◉ What had to happen within the Samaritan woman to allow her to discover the capacity and courage to respond in such a way to Jesus' gift of love? Think about the role that God's grace played in her response.

GOD'S GRACE IN *MY* LIFE

- ◉ We can call the Samaritan woman's encounter with Jesus a 'graced' moment. It was God's grace that enabled her to respond as she did to Jesus' gift of love.
- ◉ Recall and write about a time when you experienced a 'graced' moment— a time when God touched and moved your heart.

_____

_____

_____

_____

_____

_____

_____

CHAPTER 1: GOD DESIRES WHAT IS BEST FOR US | WORKSHEET 8 | 37

CHAPTER 1 | WORKSHEET 9

NAME:

My Relationship with the Triune God

We are made in the image of the Triune God, who is Father, Son and Holy Spirit, one God in a communion of love. Each one of us is embraced in this communion of love. This is God's grace, God's free and undeserved gift to us. This worksheet invites you to create a visual representation of your own relationship with the Triune God.

PAUSE AND REFLECT
Spend a little time reflecting quietly on your relationship with the Triune God. These questions may help you focus your thoughts.

⊙ What is the nature of that relationship? In what ways do you engage with the Triune God?

⊙ Perhaps there are certain prayers or songs or hymns or poems that help you relate to the Triune God. Try to name some of those.

⊙ Perhaps there are special places that help you tap into the presence of the Triune God in your life. Again, try to identify some of those places.

⊙ Perhaps there are images or icons that help unwrap and reveal the beauty of the Triune God to you. Recall some of those.

⊙ Think about how you feel when you are communicating with the Triune God. How is it a positive experience?

⊙ How does this relationship offer you comfort, support or hope during challenging times?

MY RELATIONSHIP WITH THE TRIUNE GOD
Each one of us relates to the Triune God in our own unique way. See if you can create an image that depicts your personal relationship with the Triune God, an image that helps describe and name the significance of the Triune God in your life. Draw this image in the box below.

38 | CREDO | LIVING AND LOVING AS DISCIPLES OF CHRIST

CHAPTER 1 | WORKSHEET 10

NAME:

Joseph's Story

This worksheet invites you to study the story of Joseph, son of Jacob, in the Book of Genesis and to explore how Joseph's faith in God's plan for him sustained him through difficult times and how good outcomes can sometimes result from bad or evil choices.

READ AND REFLECT

This is a brief summary of the story of Joseph, son of Jacob.

Joseph's brothers were jealous of him and they sold him as a slave. Joseph was taken to Egypt, where he had a hard life and was even falsely imprisoned before Pharaoh heard about his ability to interpret dreams. Joseph interpreted Pharaoh's dreams and predicted that a famine would take place in Egypt. Pharaoh was so impressed with Joseph that he made him governor of Egypt. When the famine eventually came, adequate preparations had been made and there was enough food in Egypt to feed everyone.

When Joseph's brothers arrived in Egypt to buy food, they were shocked to discover that Joseph was the governor. They became afraid of what Joseph might do to them because of how they had treated him. However, Joseph looked at the situation in a different way. Throughout his suffering he had been aware of God's plan for him. Joseph said to his brothers, 'And now do not be distressed, or angry with yourselves, because you sold me here; for God sent me before you to preserve life. . . So it was not you who sent me here, but God' (Genesis 45:5, 8).

Read the full account of this story in Genesis 37 and 40–45.

RESPOND

⊙ How does the story of Joseph show that while evil can never create good in itself, good can result from bad choices?

⊙ The above summary states: 'Throughout his suffering he had been aware of God's plan for him.' What is the plan that is being referred to here, and how did it sustain Joseph through his difficult times?

⊙ Share any aspects of Joseph's story that resonate with your own life.

⊙ What character do you most identify with? Why is this?

⊙ What character do you least identify with? Why is this?

CHAPTER 1: GOD DESIRES WHAT IS BEST FOR US | WORKSHEET 10 | 39

CHAPTER 1 | WORKSHEET 11

NAME:

Living God's Dream

God calls each one of us to participate in his divine plan of goodness for all of creation. As disciples of Jesus Christ, we are challenged each day of our lives to make God's dream a reality within ourselves, within our relationships and within the wider world. This worksheet invites you to review and reassess your efforts at living up to this responsibility.

REFLECT AND RESPOND

Take some time to think about how you are responding to God's dream for you at this moment in time. Then see if you can articulate briefly how you would rate your progress in each of the areas mentioned in the following questions.

Where do you seek happiness? Does your search for happiness coincide with the path that Jesus showed us, or are you searching in other places?

_____

_____

_____

_____

How do you think you are succeeding in living as an image of God, as someone who is alive with the very breath of God? How, for example, do you show respect for the dignity of all people, and try to bring love, goodness and truth into your relationships with others?

_____

_____

_____

_____

_____

40 | CREDO | LIVING AND LOVING AS DISCIPLES OF CHRIST

CHAPTER 1 | WORKSHEET 11 (CONTD.)

How do you show respect and care for the natural world, which God has entrusted to our stewardship?

_____

_____

_____

_____

Has anything that you have learned so far in this chapter caused you to reassess how you are living out God's dream for you? What might you try to change from here on? What new approaches might you take?

_____

_____

_____

_____

A DAILY REMINDER
Find a Scripture verse that will remind you of God's dream for you and sustain you in your efforts to live as a disciple of Jesus Christ. Write the verse out on a large piece of card and hang it in your bedroom as a reminder each morning of how each new day is a new opportunity to make God's dream for you a reality.

CHAPTER 1: GOD DESIRES WHAT IS BEST FOR US | WORKSHEET 11 (CONTD.) | 41

CHAPTER 1 | CHAPTER REVIEW

NAME:

Review of Chapter 1

I. **True/False. Mark the true statements 'T' and the false statements 'F'. In the case of each false statement, cross out and rewrite the incorrect words to make the statement true.**

_____1. Aristotle taught that happiness is the chief desire of the human heart.

_____2. The Catholic Church teaches that human beings can only find true happiness by pursuing a life lived in relationship with God.

_____3. The Catholic Church teaches that God created the world out of fear.

_____4. God wills to share his divine life only with those who never sin.

_____5. God invites only specific people, such as priests, to join with him in bringing about the changes for good that he desires in the world.

_____6. The human person is the summit of God's plan.

_____7. God creates the human person with an intellect but without free will.

_____8. Only evil people face temptation.

42 | CREDO | LIVING AND LOVING AS DISCIPLES OF CHRIST

CHAPTER 1 | CHAPTER REVIEW (CONTD.)

_____9. Because of Adam and Eve's sinfulness, God eventually turned his back on humanity.

_____10. Jesus abolished the Law of Sinai.

II. Matching. Write the letter of the term from column 2 next to its best match in column 1. There are two more items in column 2 than you need.

COLUMN 1	COLUMN 2
_____ 1. An attraction to act contrary to right reason and the commandments of God	A. Secularism
_____ 2. 'You have made us for yourself alone and our hearts are restless until they rest in you'	B. Two C. Morality D. freedom
_____ 3. Number of Creation accounts in the Book of Genesis	E. One F. Sin G. St. Augustine of Hippo
_____ 4. An abuse of the freedom that God gives to created persons	H. St. Monica I. Temptation
_____ 5. Jesus' Death, Resurrection and Ascension	J. Paschal Mystery K. St. Catherine of Sienna
_____ 6. A vision and philosophy of life that separates religion and life	L. Society
_____ 7. St. Augustine's mother	
_____ 8. The power God gives us to say 'yes' or 'no' to him	
_____ 9. A group of persons bound together organically by a principle of unity that goes beyond each one of them	
_____ 10. The goodness or evil of human acts	

CHAPTER 1: GOD DESIRES WHAT IS BEST FOR US | CHAPTER REVIEW (CONTD.) | 43

CHAPTER 1 | CHAPTER REVIEW (CONTD.)

III. Write a brief answer. Explain the teaching of the Catholic Church on 1 or 2.
  1. Original Sin
  2. Human beings are endowed with intellect and free will.

_____

_____

_____

_____

_____

_____

_____

_____

IV. How would you respond? A friend tells you that she does not need God in order to be fully happy.

_____

_____

_____

_____

_____

_____

_____

_____

_____

_____

_____

_____

CHAPTER 1 | CHAPTER REVIEW (CONTD.)

V. Make a 'disciple decision'.

1. What is the most important wisdom for life that you discovered in this chapter?

_____

_____

_____

_____

_____

_____

2. Name several ways you can put this wisdom into practice. Choose one of the ways you identify and describe how you will make that wisdom part of your life right now.

_____

_____

_____

_____

_____

_____

_____

_____

CHAPTER 1: GOD DESIRES WHAT IS BEST FOR US | CHAPTER REVIEW (CONTD.) | 45

CHAPTER 2

Jesus' Response; Our Response

INTRODUCTION

The world will never be the dwelling place of peace, till peace has found a home in the heart of each and every man, till every man preserves in himself the order ordained by God to be preserved.

—Pope John XXIII, *Pacem in Terris (Peace on Earth)*, no. 1

The call to Christian morality is situated in the context of our relationship with God and our response to God's unconditional love for us. God alone can satisfy the human desire for true and eternal happiness. God draws all things to himself by continuing 'to watch over creation, sustaining its existence and presiding over its development and destiny' (*United States Catholic Catechism for Adults* [USCCA], 510). The love that God offers is unearned, given freely without condition or coercion. God reaches out and beckons to us, inspiring in us a response of love.

Chapter 2 is developed under five major headings:

- ⊙ **ATTEND AND REFLECT:** How should we respond to God, who is Love?
- ⊙ **HEAR THE STORY:** We are called to be 'blessed'
- ⊙ **EMBRACE THE VISION:** The Beatitudes and God's free gift of joy
- ⊙ **THINK IT THROUGH:** What it means to live the Beatitudes
- ⊙ **JUDGE AND ACT:** (*Activities and exercises that encourage the young people to integrate what they have learned in the chapter into their daily lives*)

Theological Background for the Teacher

RESPONDING TO GOD'S LOVE: THE WAY OF SELF-GIVING

The call to Christian morality is a call to love in response to God's love for us. As baptized Christians, we are invited to answer that call by entering into a real and personal relationship with God—a relationship that promises to satisfy the deepest longings of our human heart. Our response to

God's love shapes who we are and who we aspire to become. It determines our 'way of being' in the world, defines our fundamental life orientation, and shapes how we engage with others and with the world around us.

The practice of the moral life animated by charity gives to the Christian the spiritual freedom of the children of God. He no longer stands before God as a slave, in servile fear, or as a mercenary looking for wages, but as a son responding to the love of him who 'first loved us'.

—*Catechism of the Catholic Church* [CCC], no. 1828

Because we were loved first, human beings have deep within themselves the capacity to love in return. We grow and develop as human beings in relation to the 'other'. We are challenged to push the boundaries of our own self-containment and connect with the humanity of others. As human beings, we grow through mutuality and discover our true selves through self-giving.

Self-giving is how human beings find themselves; it is the meaning of human relationships. This is because of a more fundamental truth. Human self-giving reflects the mutual self-giving of the divine life itself. We human beings are at our best when we sincerely give ourselves to others, because we are created in the image and likeness of a self-giving God. In our relationship with each other the love of God is made visible.

—Bishop Donal Murray, *Keeping Open the Door of Faith*

The love of God and our capacity to love in return lies at the heart of the Christian moral call.

JESUS: THE WAY OF LOVE

For God so loved the world that he gave his only Son, so that everyone who believes in him may not perish but may have eternal life.

—John 3:16

46 | CREDO | LIVING AND LOVING AS DISCIPLES OF CHRIST

Founded on love, the Incarnation makes us 'aware of the depth of God's love for us' (USCCA, 86). In Jesus we have the fulfillment of God's Revelation, the model of how we should respond to God. Jesus' whole life was a response of love and obedience to the Father.

> The Word became flesh *so that thus we might know God's love*: 'In this the love of God was made manifest among us, that God sent his only Son into the world, so that we might live through him [1 John 4:9].'
>
> —CCC, no. 458

Jesus reveals the will of the Father. He is 'our model of holiness' (CCC, no. 459), pointing the way to the Father, inviting us to share in God's divine nature and to become sons and daughters of the Father (see CCC, no. 460). Jesus came to proclaim the Good News that the Kingdom of God is at hand. He is the love of God made visible in the world.

> God's approach to us is made out of sheer love. The friendship he offers in his Son is 'the goal of human history, the focal point of the longings of history and of civilization, the center of the human race, the joy of every heart and the answer to all its yearnings' [*Gaudium et Spes*, (*Constitution on the Church in the Modern World*), no. 45].
>
> —Bishop Donal Murray, *Keeping Open the Door of Faith*

The Christian moral life is a response to the love of God the Father, through Jesus Christ, by the power of the Holy Spirit.

> The Word of God . . . reveals to us that 'God is love' (1 John 4:8) and at the same time teaches that the fundamental law of human perfection, and consequently of the transformation of the world, is the new commandment of love.
>
> —*Gaudium et Spes*, no. 38

THE BEATITUDES: PATHWAYS TO THE KINGDOM OF GOD

The Sermon on the Mount presented in Matthew's Gospel account summarizes a collection of significant statements that Jesus made during his earthly ministry. The statements, called the Beatitudes, form the heart of Jesus' teaching on the Kingdom. The New Testament affirms this '*vision of God*' (Matthew 5:8), speaking of it as an '*entering the joy of God*' (Matthew 25:23); an '*entering into God's rest*' (Hebrews 4:7–11); an invitation to become '*participants of the divine*

nature' (2 Peter 1:4). The Kingdom is not a place but an invitation to be embraced in the love and activity of God who is already present in our midst.

> The Beatitudes reveal the goal of human existence, the ultimate end of human acts: God calls us to his own beatitude.
>
> —CCC, no. 1719

The call to live the Beatitudes is a call to enter into the unconditional love that God gifted to us. Jesus teaches these Beatitudes

> . . . as the foundations for a life of authentic Christian discipleship and the attainment of ultimate happiness. They give spirit to the Law of the Ten Commandments and bring perfection to moral life. That spirit is ultimately the spirit of love.
>
> —USCCA, 308–9

Using rich and evocative language, Jesus outlines how God calls us to live out that 'spirit of love'. In the Sermon on the Mount Jesus makes it quite clear that the people who understand and experience the reality of the Kingdom are a particular kind of people: they are ego-free and other-focused, at ease with their own vulnerability and ready and willing to reach out in compassion and love; they do not resist grief and sadness and they recognize pain to be part of the human condition; they fight for justice and equality and are tuned into and sensitive to the activity of God in the world. We know when we have encountered these people for they radiate a deep sense of authenticity, inner happiness and joy.

> The Beatitudes confront us with decisive choices concerning earthly goods; they purify our hearts in order to teach us to love God above all things.
>
> —CCC, no. 1728

By the power of the Holy Spirit we are challenged to avoid storing up material goods for ourselves; to share the earth's resources; to confront our prejudices; to break down barriers; to place our trust in God in times of sorrow; to work toward a just world where people live in peace; to foster an attitude of forgiveness; to be honest and truthful in our dealings with others. This is the Beatitude vision.

> The Decalogue, the Sermon on the Mount, and the apostolic catechesis describe for us the paths that lead to the Kingdom of heaven. Sustained by the grace of the Holy Spirit, we tread them, step by step, by everyday acts. By the working of the

CHAPTER 2: JESUS' RESPONSE; OUR RESPONSE | INTRODUCTION | 47

Word of Christ, we slowly bear fruit in the Church to the glory of God.

—CCC, no. 1724

THE CALL TO DISCIPLESHIP IN CHRIST

And [Jesus] said to them, 'Follow me....'

—Matthew 4:19

In calling people to follow him, Jesus drew them into a new and exciting way of being in the world. Many people took Jesus' words to heart and their lives were changed forever. Many came away feeling nourished and satisfied. Others, however, were not able to take up Jesus' challenge and they went away downhearted and saddened.

What he [Jesus] is searching for is people who will really accept that God is the God of creation who lovingly created the world so that he might coax from his creatures the free response of love to his creative love.

—Eamonn Bredin, *Disturbing the Peace: the Way of Disciples*

Jesus called his disciples to reflect in their own lives the love with which he loved them, the very love of God. To be a disciple of Jesus is to enter into the love of God and to become 'participants of the divine nature'. It is a vocation, a choice to see things with different eyes.

This vocation is addressed to each individual personally, but also to the Church as a whole, the new people made up of those who have accepted the promise and live from it in faith.

—CCC, no. 1719

The call to live the Beatitudes is a call to work toward transforming our world so that God's presence reigns in our lives and God's dream for reality is fulfilled.

Do you not know that all of us who have been baptized into Christ Jesus were baptized into his death? Therefore we have been buried with him by baptism into death, so that, just as Christ was raised from the dead by the glory of God the Father, so we too might walk in newness of life.

—Romans 6:3–4

This is the challenge of every baptized Christian: 'birth into the new life in Christ' (CCC, no. 1277). We are called to live a life focused on Christ, to be truly Christ-ian.

It is by looking to him in faith that Christ's faithful can hope that he himself fulfills his promises in them, and that, by loving him with the same love with which he has loved them, they may perform works in keeping with their dignity: 'I ask you to consider that our Lord Jesus Christ is your true head, and that you are one of his members. He belongs to you as the head belongs to its members; all that is his is yours: his spirit, his heart, his body and soul and all his faculties. You must make use of all these as of your own, to serve, praise, love and glorify God. You belong to him, as members belong to their head. And so he longs for you to use all that is in you, as if it were his own, for the service and glory of the Father' [St. John Eudes]. 'For to me, to live is Christ' [Philippians 1:21].

—CCC, no. 1698

This chapter offers you and the young people an opportunity to affirm your baptismal promises and to explore the 'be-attitude' ways of Jesus, which, when incorporated into our everyday lives, will lead to true discipleship and authentic moral living.

ADDITIONAL BACKGROUND READING

Catechism of the Catholic Church, nos. 1716–1729, 1812–1832; *United States Catholic Catechism for Adults*, 308–321; **Pope John Paul II**, *Veritatis Splendor*.

48 | CREDO | LIVING AND LOVING AS DISCIPLES OF CHRIST

CHAPTER OUTCOMES

See general note on page 19 of this resource.

Learning Outcomes

As a result of studying this chapter and exploring the issues raised, the young people should be able to:

- recognize that they are called to love as Jesus loved and as God loves;
- become familiar with the Beatitudes in Matthew's account of the Gospel;
- understand the Beatitudes to be the attitudes and actions characteristic of the Christian life;
- examine the Beatitudes within the context of the Sermon on the Mount;
- understand that the Beatitudes invite us to see life as a blessing;
- know the Golden Rule, 'In everything do to others as you would have them do to you';
- understand the actions and attitudes revealed in each of the Beatitudes;
- understand how the Theological Virtue of hope deepens our faith and sustains us in our efforts to truly become 'Beatitude' people;
- recognize that Jesus, in his life, Death, Resurrection and Ascension, embodied the Beatitudes;
- know the story of St. Maria Faustina, an 'apostle of mercy' who witnessed to the spirit of the Beatitudes.

Faith-formation Outcomes

As a result of studying this chapter and exploring the issues raised, the young people should also:

- become more aware of God's love in their lives;
- strive to live the values of the Beatitudes;
- come to a deeper understanding of the challenges inherent in being a disciple of Jesus;
- apply the insights they have gained from studying the Beatitudes to their own lives;
- begin to make real decisions about changing their attitudes and actions to reflect the values of the Beatitudes;
- identify ways in which they too could be 'apostles of mercy'.

Teacher Reflection

As you prepare to engage your group in a study of how we should respond to God's unconditional love for us, take a moment to read and reflect on these words from Jean Vanier, from his book *Tears of Silence*.

But
> who will bring life to
> > the despairing,
> > to crushed and dying hearts
> > to those whose future is barred
> > to the mentally sick
> > to the aged and alone
> > to the despised and anguished
> > to the burnt out

statesmen are called upon to enact laws
but who is called to give hope to the despairing
how to approach him
> he, repulsive and fearful
> i, with my fear and my security

and yet. . . . .
> i feel. . . . .in some mysterious way
> that there is a calling
> the silent crying out of misery

tears of silence
> and in my deepest being i hear this call
> a sort of whispering
> > that life has meaning, but
> > in the degree that i find love

no reasons. . . . .no reasons why. . . . .only a sort of. . . . .
> an act. . . . .
an act of faith that i can enter into some vast and
> powerful movement
of life and life giving

REFLECT

When and where could you offer hope to those without hope, love to those who do not feel loved, and compassion to those marginalized by society?

CHAPTER 2: JESUS' RESPONSE; OUR RESPONSE | INTRODUCTION | 49

Notes and Guidelines for Student Activities

ATTEND AND REFLECT

How should we respond to God, who is Love?

Learning Outcomes

That the young people would:
⊙ recognize that they are called to love as Jesus loved and as God loves;
⊙ become familiar with the Beatitudes in Matthew's account of the Gospel;
⊙ understand the Beatitudes to be the attitudes and actions characteristic of the Christian life.

Faith-formation Outcomes

That the young people would also:
⊙ become more aware of God's love in their lives;
⊙ strive to live the values of the Beatitudes.

Overview

Section one, 'Attend and Reflect', begins by inviting the young people to reflect on their own experiences of loving and being loved. From this we lead them to a deeper appreciation of the nature and breadth of God's divine love for each one of them—a love that is beyond our human comprehension. We then turn to the Beatitudes, which proclaim Jesus' attitude to life in the world. We help the young people to understand that these eight fundamental attitudes and actions are a blueprint for how God has created us to act in the world. Jesus' invitation to us to live the Beatitudes each day of our lives is an invitation to share in the Kingdom and be partakers of God's divine nature.

Supplementary Activities for 'Attend and Reflect'

Class Debate

Invite the young people to prepare for a class sharing of ideas on the motion: 'The Beatitudes are a series of utopian value statements that have no place in the twenty-first century.' Each student will then speak to the class for two or three minutes either for or against the motion. Afterward, have a whole-class discussion on the insights gained from this activity about the attitudes of today's young people in relation to the values Jesus preached.

Worksheet 1: 'Our Human Values' (*page 55 of this resource*) invites the young people to identify the values that they hold to be most important for human relationships and for the good of the whole human family.

Worksheet 2: 'Living the Beatitudes' (*page 57 of this resource*) offers the young people an opportunity to tease out what living the values of the Beatitudes means in the world today. They do this through group research and sharing of their own experiences.

HEAR THE STORY

We are called to be 'blessed'

Learning Outcomes

That the young people would:
⊙ examine the Beatitudes within the context of the Sermon on the Mount;
⊙ understand that the Beatitudes invite us to see life as a blessing;
⊙ know the Golden Rule, 'In everything do to others as you would have them do to you'.

Faith-formation Outcome

That the young people would also:
⊙ come to a deeper understanding of the challenges inherent in being a disciple of Jesus.

Overview

In section two, 'Hear the Story', we take a closer look at the Sermon on the Mount and explore how it is a summary of Christian discipleship and of the New Law that Jesus lived and taught. We explain that the New Law is the Law of Love, the Law of Grace and the Law of Freedom. We examine the historical context of the Sermon on the Mount and we then invite the young people to reflect on the radical nature of the world view at the heart of Jesus' teaching and to relate it to their own lives.

Supplementary Activities for 'Hear the Story'

Research Activity

Invite the young people to recall the saints and other holy people whom they have met already in the 'Learn

50 | CREDO | LIVING AND LOVING AS DISCIPLES OF CHRIST

by Example' profiles in the *Credo* series. Ask them to choose one person from this group and to create a profile of this person based on their living out the values of the Beatitudes. The young people may work alone or in groups at this task. On completion of their research, they might like to present their findings to the class.

Beatitude Rap

Invite the young people to work in groups to create a 'Beatitude Rap' that would make it easy for people to remember the eight Beatitudes. When they have completed the project, encourage them to perform their 'Beatitude Rap' for the class.

Life's Blessings Diary

Invite the young people to take time out to review the blessings that life has bestowed on them. Suggest that they create a *Life's Blessings Diary* and begin a weekly practice of writing down blessings they have received over the course of their week.

Worksheet 3: 'Reflection on the Golden Rule' (*page 58 of this resource*) invites the young people to recall a time when they found themselves in conflict with another person and to examine how the situation and outcome might have been different if they had applied the Golden Rule of Jesus to dealing with it.

Worksheet 4: 'Being Authentic' (*page 60 of this resource*) seeks to heighten the young people's awareness of the times in their lives when they do not act with authenticity; in other words, when they do not live up to being the person God calls them to be. We invite them to acknowledge those times when there is disharmony between their aspirations to live up to the goodness to which God calls them and their actual everyday 'way of being' with others.

Worksheet 5: 'The Spirit of the Beatitudes' (*page 62 of this resource*) invites the young people to identify stories or parables or statements of Jesus from the four Gospel accounts that echo the values of the Beatitudes.

EMBRACE THE VISION

The Beatitudes and God's free gift of joy

Learning Outcome

That the young people would:

⊙ understand the actions and attitudes revealed in each of the Beatitudes.

Faith-formation Outcome

That the young people would also:

⊙ apply the insights they have gained from studying the Beatitudes to their own lives.

Overview

In section three, 'Embrace the Vision', we explore the attitudes and actions behind each of the Beatitudes and we guide the young people to reflect on how and where they might put these attitudes and actions into practice in their everyday lives.

Supplementary Activities for 'Embrace the Vision'

Charity Research Activity

Invite the young people to work in groups to research charities in their locality or city. Each group will choose one charity and prepare a short presentation under the headings:

 – Mission statement
 – Goals and objectives
 – Examples of work projects
 – Outcomes/impact

Invite the young people to conclude their presentation with a statement on the ways in which they believe the charity inspires, challenges, supports and transforms their locality or city and how it embodies the vision of the Beatitudes.

Beatitude Prayer/Ritual

Invite each of the young people to write an acrostic prayer using the letters of one of the core virtues of the Beatitudes (for example, Humility; Compassion; Mercy; Justice). Afterward, you might use these prayers as the focus of a class prayer-reading ritual on the theme of the Beatitudes.

CHAPTER 2: JESUS' RESPONSE; OUR RESPONSE | NOTES AND GUIDELINES | 51

Worksheet 6: 'Wisdom in Story' (*page 63 of this resource*) presents an ancient story from the Jewish Hasidic tradition and invites the young people to reflect on the wisdom it holds for their own lives, especially in light of the vision of the Beatitudes.

Worksheet 7: 'Worldly Beatitudes versus Jesus' Beatitudes' (*page 65 of this resource*) invites the young people to identify the dominant values in the world today and to create a set of 'Worldly Beatitudes' to compare with the values of the Beatitudes that Jesus preached and lived.

THINK IT THROUGH

What it means to live the Beatitudes

Learning Outcomes
That the young people would:
⊙ understand how the Theological Virtue of hope deepens our faith and sustains us in our efforts to truly become 'Beatitude' people;
⊙ recognize that Jesus, in his life, Death, Resurrection and Ascension, embodied the Beatitudes.

Faith-formation Outcome
That the young people would also:
⊙ begin to make real decisions about changing their attitudes and actions to reflect the values of the Beatitudes.

Overview
Section four, 'Think It Through', delves more deeply into what it means to respond to Jesus' call to live the Beatitudes. The section opens with an extract from a homily that Blessed Pope John Paul II addressed to young people, which leads into a discussion about the challenges Christians are likely to face in trying to live the Beatitudes in a world that often upholds a very different set of values. This is where the Theological Virtue of hope comes into play. Hope deepens our faith and commitment to 'love' as Jesus loved and commanded us to love—even when that may not be the popular thing to do. We reassure the young people that we have the ability to meet the challenge of living a life of holiness and justice because we have received the gift of God's grace to help us. In Christ God assures us of the grace that will enable us to realize the happiness that God has willed for us from the beginning.

Supplementary Activities for 'Think It Through'

Creative Exercise
Invite the young people to imagine that Jesus has been asked to give the keynote address at a Global World Conference. Their challenge is to write the address as they think he might write it, under the title 'A Declaration of Hope for Today's World'.

Share Your Story
You might consider inviting the young people, if they feel comfortable in doing so, to share with the class any decisions they have made or actions they have taken recently based on the challenges set out in the Beatitudes. They might talk about the consequences of such decisions or actions, for themselves or others, and share any insights or wisdom they have gained from those experiences.

Worksheet 8: 'Living as the Body of Christ' (*page 67 of this resource*) offers the young people the opportunity to study the words of St. Paul in Romans 12:9–18, in which he advises on how disciples of Jesus should live as members of the Body of Christ.

JUDGE AND ACT

Learning Outcome
That the young people would:
⊙ know the story of St. Maria Faustina, an 'apostle of mercy' who witnessed to the spirit of the Beatitudes.

Faith-formation Outcome
That the young people would also:
⊙ identify ways in which they too could be 'apostles of mercy'.

Overview
In section five, 'Judge and Act', the young people review and discuss the teachings of the Church that they have learned about in this chapter. We introduce them to the life story of Helen Kowalska, who would become St. Maria Faustina. Maria experienced a series of private revelations and visions of Jesus, in which Jesus asked her to model in her life the mercy of God. Maria took this message to heart and lived as 'an apostle of mercy'. Her diary has become the handbook for devotion to Divine Mercy and her message is now being spread throughout the world. We encourage the young people to find inspiration in

52 | CREDO | LIVING AND LOVING AS DISCIPLES OF CHRIST

Maria's life and attitude for their own lives as disciples of Jesus.

Supplementary Activities for 'Judge and Act'

Media Search
Encourage the young people to search various media for evidence of Christians throughout the world whose lives are an inspiration to us all. They could look for stories, documentaries, reports, articles, films and images to use as examples. Invite them to share their findings with the class.

Worksheet 9: 'Apostles of Mercy' (*page 69 of this resource*) invites the young people to reflect upon and identify what being an 'apostle of mercy' might mean in today's world. We offer them the opportunity to work together in groups to come up with some practical suggestions for how they as young people might become 'apostles of mercy' at this point in their lives.

Additional Prayer Suggestions

Beatitude Circle Blessing: Giving and Receiving a Blessing

Before the Ritual
- Divide the class into two groups: A and B.
- Invite each young person to choose a Beatitude blessing from the list provided below. Explain to them that they will bestow this blessing upon everyone in the opposite group during the ritual.
- For the first part of the ritual, As will be invited to give the blessings while Bs receive the blessings. The roles will then be reversed.
- You might like to suggest that the person giving the blessing would bless the recipient with holy water on the forehead or hands as they are saying the words. Alternatively, they could place their hands on the shoulder of the person receiving the blessing.
- You might like to play quiet music in the background as the blessing ritual is taking place.

Each student chooses one blessing from this list:

Beatitude Blessings
Blessed are you (*name*) when you are poor in spirit, for the kingdom of heaven is yours.
Blessed are you (*name*) when you mourn, for you will be comforted.
Blessed are you (*name*) when you are meek, for you will inherit the earth.
Blessed are you (*name*) when you hunger and thirst for righteousness, for you will be filled.
Blessed are you (*name*) when you are merciful, for you will receive mercy.
Blessed are you (*name*) when you are pure in heart, for you will see God.
Blessed are you (*name*) when you make peace, for you will be called a child of God.
Blessed are you (*name*) when you are persecuted for righteousness' sake, for yours is the kingdom of heaven.

Gather the class in a circle (standing or sitting, depending on what works best for your situation).

Leader
We gather here today to remember that Jesus calls us to be Beatitude people, that is, people whose attitude toward others reflects the values that Jesus preached and lived. We gather as a Christian community supporting one another on our journey toward the fulfillment of God's desire for each one of us.

Take a moment to read and reflect upon the Beatitude blessing you have chosen for today's ritual. Perhaps this Beatitude resonates with you in a special way. Perhaps you know people who live this Beatitude in their everyday lives. Perhaps this Beatitude challenges you in your own life. (*Pause*)

I now invite everyone in group A to come forward, one by one, and bless each person in group B with their chosen Beatitude.

When the group A students have completed their blessings:

Leader
Let us pray.
God our Father, bless all those who are working for your Kingdom. (*Pause*)

I now invite those who have received a blessing to return the blessing.

CHAPTER 2: JESUS' RESPONSE; OUR RESPONSE | NOTES AND GUIDELINES | 53

Students in group B move around the group, blessing each person with their Beatitude.

When the group B students have completed their blessings:

Leader
Let us pray:
May the love of God fill
our hearts,
our minds,
our souls,
our beings.

All
Amen.

Let us say the Lord's Prayer together, remembering that we are called to be Beatitude people.

All
Our Father . . . .

Scripture Reflection
(See instructions for the use of doodling in prayer in the 'Student Activity Tool Kit', page 394 of this resource.)

Use this Scripture verse to engage the young people in prayer:

> **Your word is a lamp to my feet and a light to my path.**
> **PSALM 119:105**

54 | CREDO | LIVING AND LOVING AS DISCIPLES OF CHRIST

CHAPTER 2 | WORKSHEET 1

NAME:

Our Human Values

This worksheet invites you to reflect on and identify the values that you hold to be most important—in yourself and in others.

REFLECT AND RESPOND

⊙ In the box provided, name all the 'values' that you would consider to be of importance to you; for example, values such as honesty, compassion, empathy, concern for the less fortunate and so on.

⊙ Now, on the chart, identify the five values that you would consider to be the most important for human relationships and for society in general. Place these values in order of their importance, with number 1 being the most important.

⊙ Beside each value, write a brief explanation as to why you think it is of such importance.

Important human values	Why this value is important
1.	
2.	
3.	
4.	
5.	

CHAPTER 2: JESUS' RESPONSE; OUR RESPONSE | WORKSHEET 1 | 55

CHAPTER 2 | WORKSHEET 1 (CONTD.)

COMPARE AND SHARE

- Share your list of the five most important values with a partner and note the similarities and differences in your choices.
- Recall together incidents from the life of Jesus in which he lived out each of the values that you listed.
- Then share ideas on 'new' ways in which you might live these values in your everyday lives as young people—in your home, in your school and in the wider community.
- Record your best ideas here and then share them with the class.

56 | CREDO | LIVING AND LOVING AS DISCIPLES OF CHRIST

CHAPTER 2 | WORKSHEET 2

NAME:

Living the Beatitudes

The Beatitudes outline for us how God wants us to live. They challenge us to our very core. They challenge our assumptions about ourselves and about others. They challenge the way we configure our lives and contribute to shaping the communities and the world in which we live. They challenge our understanding of justice and compassion—and demand a response from the heart. This worksheet seeks to help you to identify what living the values of the Beatitudes means in the world today.

GROUP ACTIVITY

⊙ Form eight groups. Each group takes a different Beatitude.
⊙ Each group undertakes the following tasks:
  – Spend a few minutes brainstorming the meaning of your chosen Beatitude.
  – Then take turns to share examples of times when you have lived this Beatitude or have seen others live this Beatitude.
  – Recall examples from the media or from films or literature that portray this Beatitude being lived out in the world today.
⊙ Work together to prepare a short presentation on the outcome of your explorations, which one person from your group may present to the class. The presentation might include:
  – The insights you gained from the activity;
  – The challenges it presented for how you might change your way of living;
  – Any questions your discussions may have raised.

FOLLOW-UP DISCUSSION

You might like to use these questions as a guide for a class discussion following the presentations:
⊙ What examples of people living the Beatitudes impressed you the most?
⊙ What personal challenges did this activity throw up for you?
⊙ Did you make any resolutions as a result of this activity? If so, you might like to share them with the group.
⊙ What are the greatest challenges to living the Beatitudes today?
⊙ If Jesus were to join in this discussion, what do you think he might say about the activity you have just completed?

JOURNAL EXERCISE

Choose one Beatitude that you would like to live by and describe how you would go about making it a part of your daily life.

CHAPTER 2 | WORKSHEET 3

NAME:

Reflection on the Golden Rule

Jesus summarized his teachings in the Sermon on the Mount with what has become known as 'The Golden Rule': '*In everything do to others as you would have them do to you*' (Matthew 7:12). Respect for others lies at the heart of the moral life. By attending to the needs of others as we would wish them to attend to our needs, we can unlock a key to true and lasting happiness. In relating with respect, justice, compassion and love to others, we connect with the goodness of our own humanity and we reflect the goodness and love of God. This worksheet invites you to reflect on how your way of 'being' with others might change if you were truly to live by the Golden Rule.

REFLECT AND RESPOND

⊙ Recall a time in your personal life when you experienced conflict with another person that continued for some time or that was never completely and favorably resolved; for example, with a family member or friend, or with someone in authority, perhaps in your school or local community.

⊙ Think about what it was that caused the situation first to develop and then to continue and get worse.

⊙ Without naming the situation or the other person who was involved, try to articulate in general terms what you found most challenging or annoying about the other person's behavior. For example, perhaps it was their refusal to engage with you and discuss the problem; perhaps it was their stubbornness or self-righteous attitude; perhaps it was their selfishness or cruelty in acting the way they did.

_____

_____

_____

_____

_____

58 | CREDO | LIVING AND LOVING AS DISCIPLES OF CHRIST

CHAPTER 2 | WORKSHEET 3 (CONTD.)

◉ Now describe in general terms how you responded, once again without naming the person involved or giving specific details. For example, you may have told them exactly what you thought of them and perhaps made it clear that you wanted no more to do with them; you may have accused them of being cruel or cowardly or selfish or whatever.

_____

_____

_____

_____

_____

◉ Now take some time to read back over and really reflect upon what you have written. Consider how the outcome might have been different if you had applied the Golden Rule of Jesus to the situation. Try to describe first of all how you might have acted or responded in a different way, and then try to imagine the likely outcome of that different approach.

_____

_____

_____

_____

_____

_____

_____

JOURNAL EXERCISE
Write a brief summary of what you have learned from this activity.

CHAPTER 2: JESUS' RESPONSE; OUR RESPONSE | WORKSHEET 3 (CONTD.) | 59

CHAPTER 2 | WORKSHEET 4

NAME:

Being Authentic

Jesus was truly authentic. He said, 'love your neighbor as yourself' (Matthew 22:39), and he reached out to tax collectors, thieves and prostitutes. He said, 'love the Lord your God with all your heart, and with all your soul, and with all your mind' (Matthew 22:37), and his life was a continuous response of love to God the Father. It was this integrity and authenticity that attracted people to him. This worksheet invites you to recognize those times in your life when you have not been authentic, when there has been a contradiction between your words and your actions.

REFLECT AND RESPOND

All of us have encountered someone who is authentic, someone whose way of being with themselves and others is in harmony with what they say. We also have a sense of what it is like to be true to our real selves, and at such times we connect with those around us in a way that is life-giving and rich. As disciples of Jesus, we are called to be people of integrity and truth.

◉ Think of some things you typically say you will do for others; for example, you might offer to get together with a classmate to tackle some difficult homework; you might promise to visit an elderly neighbor; you might say you will meet up with a school friend for coffee.

◉ Now reflect back on the past week. List five things you promised to do for or, perhaps, with others. They don't have to be 'big' things—just things that you said you would do.

_____

_____

_____

_____

_____

_____

60 | CREDO | LIVING AND LOVING AS DISCIPLES OF CHRIST

CHAPTER 2 | WORKSHEET 4 (CONTD.)

⊙ Now, taking each of the items you listed, review for yourself whether or not you actually followed through on what you had said or promised you would do. (That is, assuming that no other external event or happening prevented you from fulfilling your promise.)

For those times when you kept your promise, can you:
– remember how you felt?
– remember how the other party reacted or felt or responded?
– identify what helped you to follow through on your promise with this person?

Where you did not do as you had said you would, can you:
– remember how the other person reacted or responded?
– identify what it was that prevented you from fulfilling your promise?

JOURNAL EXERCISE

⊙ Write about any insights you gained about yourself and the values you hold to be important as a result of doing the above exercise.

⊙ See if you can identify and describe the source of any contradictions between what you typically say you will do and what you actually do.

⊙ Finally, reflect upon and write about how specific teachings of Jesus might help you to be more authentic and reliable.

CHAPTER 2: JESUS' RESPONSE; OUR RESPONSE | WORKSHEET 4 (CONTD.) | 61

CHAPTER 2 | WORKSHEET 5

NAME:

The Spirit of the Beatitudes

Jesus' whole life was lived in response to the love of God the Father. Jesus mirrored the spirit of the Beatitudes in everything he said and did: in how he related to those around him, in the words he used, the stories and parables he told, the miracles and acts of mercy, healing and forgiveness he performed. This worksheet offers you the opportunity to search the four accounts of the Gospel for stories or parables or statements of Jesus that echo the values of the Beatitudes.

GROUP WORK
- Work in groups of three or four.
- In any of the four accounts of the Gospel locate examples of stories, parables, sayings, miracles or other actions of Jesus that reflect the values of each of the Beatitudes.
- Then complete the chart below by naming one example from Scripture for each Beatitude, along with its biblical reference. (The first one has been done for you.)

Beatitude statement	Example from the Gospel
Blessed are the poor in spirit, for theirs is the kingdom of heaven.	The tax collector's prayer in the parable of the Pharisee and the Tax Collector (Luke 18:9–14)
Blessed are those who mourn, for they will be comforted.	
Blessed are the meek, for they will inherit the earth.	
Blessed are those who hunger and thirst for righteousness, for they will be filled.	
Blessed are the merciful, for they will receive mercy.	
Blessed are the pure in heart, for they will see God.	
Blessed are the peacemakers, for they will be called children of God.	
Blessed are those who are persecuted for righteousness' sake, for theirs is the kingdom of heaven.	

62 | CREDO | LIVING AND LOVING AS DISCIPLES OF CHRIST

CHAPTER 2 | WORKSHEET 6

NAME:

Wisdom in Story

This worksheet offers you the opportunity to hear a story from the Jewish Hasidic tradition of the late seventeenth and eighteenth centuries in Eastern Europe and to reflect on the wisdom it holds for you today as you strive to live as a disciple of Jesus in the spirit of the Beatitudes.

READ AND REFLECT

Read and reflect on this story before answering the questions below.

Once upon a time, there was a very holy rabbi. He loved the Torah and God and his people, who were very poor and persecuted in their country. He loved his country too, and he loved the others who were not Jews, but they did not make it easy to love them. He spent most of his days preparing his weekly Torah portion, studying and praying, and listening to the many needs of his people, financial, medical and spiritual. It was a hard life and he often doubted whether anything he did was useful. He knew the people looked up to him, so he tried hard to be faithful, to bring them hope and to encourage them with the Torah and the daily prayers and rituals.

One Sabbath afternoon he was in his study when suddenly the prophet Elijah appeared before him. He was terrified! He cried out in distress, but Elijah was quick to calm his fears, saying, 'The Holy One, blest be His name, is pleased with you! And He has sent me to bring you a gift for your faithfulness and for all that you do for his suffering and struggling people!' The rabbi was stunned—a gift from the Holy One! 'What would you like?' Elijah asked. The rabbi stood there in shock, but he had wondered about Paradise-Gan-Eden so often, and he'd heard that they studied Torah in heaven on Sabbath afternoons—all the great leaders, patriarchs and matriarchs; if only he could have a visit to heaven, that would make all the difference to his difficult world. He didn't even have to speak the thought aloud, yet Elijah said, 'Fine, Paradise it is.' And he snapped his fingers and he and the rabbi stood at the gates of Paradise. They opened, and the rabbi and Elijah walked into a world that was lovely beyond description, lush, like the Garden of Eden was in the beginning perhaps. It smelled unbelievably fresh and it was filled with light. The rabbi wandered around in a daze, filled with an enormous sense of peace and well-being.

Elijah said nothing and let the rabbi just soak it all in. It took the rabbi a while but he began to realize that there were very few people in heaven! There were a few clusters of people here and there studying Torah, walking as friends, laughing, singing, making music, eating . . .

CHAPTER 2: JESUS' RESPONSE; OUR RESPONSE | WORKSHEET 6 | 63

CHAPTER 2 | WORKSHEET 6 (CONTD.)

but there really weren't many people in Paradise. The rabbi grew distressed as he walked around, and he finally turned to Elijah and asked, 'Where is everyone? After all these years only these few people made it to Paradise?' Elijah laughed and said, 'You, too, Rabbi. I would have thought that you would have known!' 'Known what?' the rabbi asked. Elijah looked solemnly and said, 'The saints are not in Paradise! Paradise is in the saints! Most people realize that as soon as they get here, and then they go back to earth to live and bring hope and light to all the world. They bring Paradise back to earth with them.' Then Elijah snapped his fingers and the rabbi was back in his study, alone. It was late afternoon on the Sabbath and he stood there stunned.

He began to pray, rocking back and forth, his heart and his mind filled with so many feelings. Then he stopped and wondered to himself: had he ever really looked at anyone here on earth? Had he ever caught a glimpse of Paradise in people's eyes, in their faces? And then, more soberly, he asked himself: does anyone see Paradise in my face, in my eyes? In that moment, his life was changed forever. He walked the streets of his village, looking intently into the faces of everyone, not just the Jews he knew who came to his services, but everyone: the beggars, the strangers, the visitors. He knew what to look for now and where to find Paradise: Heaven is in the saints and Paradise is here on earth.

When he died, crowds came to his funeral, and everyone spoke of how he had brought light and hope and such joy with him, and that he always looked you right in the eyes and smiled, his face lighting up when he saw you—as though he saw something there that no one else did.

How do you think this story ties in with the vision of life described in the Beatitudes?

_____

_____

_____

_____

What wisdom or insights might you take from this story for your life today?

_____

_____

_____

_____

_____

64 | CREDO | LIVING AND LOVING AS DISCIPLES OF CHRIST

CHAPTER 2 | WORKSHEET 7

NAME:

Worldly Beatitudes versus Jesus' Beatitudes

Jesus' Beatitudes are paradoxical and juxtapose values that the world often does not naturally hold to be true. He challenges his hearers to re-examine all that they had previously taken for granted. He alerts them to a new and radical way of living. He presents a world in which the love of God reigns, a world where the poor, the marginalized, the sick and infirm, the bereaved and children are 'blessed'. This worksheet invites you to identify the dominant values in today's world and to create a set of 'Worldly Beatitudes' to compare with the values of the Beatitudes that Jesus preached and lived.

BRAINSTORM

⊙ Work as a single class group and use a board or flipchart to write down all the words or phrases you can think of that reflect the attitudes and actions that are commonly believed to bring happiness and contentment in the world today.

⊙ Leave these words on view, as you may need to refer back to them during the following activity.

GROUP ACTIVITY

⊙ Form small groups.

⊙ Work together to create a set of eight 'Worldly Beatitudes' based on attitudes and values prevalent in the world today that are regarded as recipes for happiness and contentment. For example, 'Blessed are those who hunger for promotion, for they will be satisfied.'

⊙ It would be a good idea to write your suggestions for these 'Worldly Beatitudes' on a different sheet of paper initially, as you are likely to change your choices several times before deciding on the final eight.

⊙ When you have agreed on your eight choices, complete the chart below.

Jesus' Beatitudes	Worldly Beatitudes
Blessed are the poor in spirit, for theirs is the kingdom of heaven.	
Blessed are those who mourn, for they will be comforted.	

CHAPTER 2: JESUS' RESPONSE; OUR RESPONSE | WORKSHEET 7 | 65

CHAPTER 2 | WORKSHEET 7 (CONTD.)

Jesus' Beatitudes	Worldly Beatitudes
Blessed are the meek, for they will inherit the earth.	
Blessed are those who hunger and thirst for righteousness, for they will be filled.	
Blessed are the merciful, for they will receive mercy.	
Blessed are the pure in heart, for they will see God.	
Blessed are the peacemakers, for they will be called children of God.	
Blessed are those who are persecuted for righteousness' sake, for theirs is the kingdom of heaven.	

REFLECT AND DISCUSS

⊙ Look back over the 'Worldly Beatitudes' that you have just created. What might happen to the way we relate to others if we were to adopt the attitudes and actions of these 'Worldly Beatitudes'?

⊙ What might happen to the way we judge ourselves and others, and thereby to how we shape our lives?

⊙ How would all of this impact the world we leave behind for future generations?

JOURNAL EXERCISE

Look back at the second part of each of Jesus' Beatitudes; for example, 'for theirs is the kingdom of heaven' and so on. Then look at the second part of the 'Worldly Beatitudes' that you composed yourself. Do you notice a big difference in the goals in both sets of Beatitudes? Reflect on the difference and then describe what you think these contrasting goals reveal about the motivations, actions and attitudes of people in the world today.

66 | CREDO | LIVING AND LOVING AS DISCIPLES OF CHRIST

CHAPTER 2 | WORKSHEET 8

NAME:

Living as the Body of Christ

This worksheet offers you the opportunity to study some words of advice from St. Paul on living as members of the Body of Christ.

READE AND RESPOND
- ⦿ Work in pairs.
- ⦿ Read Romans 12:9–18.
- ⦿ Then pick out and list on the lines provided twenty pointers that St. Paul gives for living as true Christians.

1. _____

2. _____

3. _____

4. _____

5. _____

6. _____

7. _____

8. _____

9. _____

10. _____

11. _____

CHAPTER 2: JESUS' RESPONSE; OUR RESPONSE | WORKSHEET 8 | 67

CHAPTER 2 | WORKSHEET 8 (CONTD.)

12. _____

13. _____

14. _____

15. _____

16. _____

17. _____

18. _____

19. _____

20. _____

JOURNAL EXERCISE

From the list above, choose the six pieces of advice for Christian living that you think have most relevance for young people today. Write a brief description of why you think living according to each of these principles is important for young people.

68 | CREDO | LIVING AND LOVING AS DISCIPLES OF CHRIST

CHAPTER 2 | WORKSHEET 9

NAME:

Apostles of Mercy

You have learned about St. Maria Faustina, who took to heart the Gospel command to 'be merciful even as your heavenly Father is merciful' and so lived as an 'apostle of mercy'. This worksheet invites you to reflect upon and identify what being an 'apostle of mercy' might mean in today's world.

BRAINSTORM
- Work as a single class group and use a board or flipchart to write down all the words or phrases that come to mind when you think of the concept of mercy.
- Include feelings that are associated with mercy; for example, compassion and empathy.
- Include outcomes that are associated with mercy; for example, comfort and relief.
- Include people whom you think might need mercy; for example, a prisoner or a homeless person.
- Leave these words on view, as you may want to refer back to them during the following activity.

GROUP ACTIVITY
- Form small groups.
- Work together to create a list of ten suggestions for how you as young people might be 'apostles of mercy' in the world today.
- When you have agreed on your ten choices, write them on the lines below.
- Afterward, compare your list with those of the other groups.

ACTIONS OF MERCY

1. _____

_____

2. _____

_____

3. _____

_____

CHAPTER 2: JESUS' RESPONSE; OUR RESPONSE | WORKSHEET 9 | 69

CHAPTER 2 | WORKSHEET 9 (CONTD.)

4. _____

_____

5. _____

_____

6. _____

_____

7. _____

8. _____

_____

9. _____

_____

10. _____

_____

70 | CREDO | LIVING AND LOVING AS DISCIPLES OF CHRIST

CHAPTER 2 | CHAPTER REVIEW

NAME:

Review of Chapter 2

I. **True/False. Mark the true statements 'T' and the false statements 'F'. In the case of each false statement, cross out and rewrite the incorrect words to make the statement true.**

_____1.   In the First Letter of John we read: 'God is love.'

_____2.   The Beatitudes may be found in all four accounts of the Gospel.

_____3.   Matthew situates the Sermon on the Mount on the seashore.

_____4.   Jesus' 'golden rule' for finding happiness is, 'In everything do to others as you would have them do to you.'

_____5.   A beatitude is a form of Hebrew song found only in the Book of Psalms.

_____6.   Biblical scholars agree that it is unlikely Jesus delivered the Sermon on the Mount word for word at one time and in one place.

_____7.   Authentic disciples of Jesus hunger for justice, fairness and equality in the world, as Jesus did.

_____8.   Concern for oneself is a characteristic of a disciple of Christ.

CHAPTER 2: JESUS' RESPONSE; OUR RESPONSE | CHAPTER REVIEW | 71

CHAPTER 2 | CHAPTER REVIEW (CONTD.)

_____9. The first words the risen Christ said when he appeared to his disciples were, 'Come follow me.'

_____10. Sr. Maria Faustina experienced visions of Jesus during her time on a small farm in Poland.

II. Matching. Write the letter of the term or phrase from column 2 next to its best match in column 1. There are two more items in column 2 than you need.

COLUMN 1	COLUMN 2
_____1. Blessed are the merciful, for they will. . . .	A. Humility
_____2. Blessed are those who mourn, for they will. . . .	B. be comforted
	C. inherit the earth
_____3. Blessed are those who hunger and thirst for righteousness, for they will . . .	D. be called children of God
	E. be filled with pity
_____4. Blessed are the peacemakers, for they will. . . .	F. receive mercy
	G. Peace
_____5. Blessed are the meek, for they will. . . .	H. be filled
	I. _Kenosis_
_____6. Blessed are the pure in heart, for they will. . . .	J. the kingdom of heaven
	K. Apostle of Mercy
_____7. Blessed are the poor in spirit, for theirs is. . . .	L. see God
_____8. A title given to St. Maria Faustina	
_____9. Selfless, self-emptying love	
_____10. The virtue by which a Christian acknowledges that God is the author of all good	

72 | CREDO | LIVING AND LOVING AS DISCIPLES OF CHRIST

CHAPTER 2 | CHAPTER REVIEW (CONTD.)

III. Write a brief answer. Explain the teaching of the Catholic Church on 1 or 2.
   1. The Beatitudes are pathways on the journey toward happiness both here and hereafter in the eternal presence of God.
   2. The literary form and historical context of the Sermon on the Mount.

_____

_____

_____

_____

_____

_____

_____

_____

_____

_____

IV. How would you respond? A non-Christian friend who does volunteer work with the homeless says to you, 'I don't believe in God but I want a just and fair world too. How is that different from the vision Jesus set out in the Beatitudes?'

_____

_____

_____

_____

_____

_____

_____

_____

_____

_____

_____

CHAPTER 2 | CHAPTER REVIEW (CONTD.)

V. Make a 'disciple decision'.

1. What is the most important wisdom for life that you discovered in this chapter?

_____

_____

_____

_____

_____

_____

_____

_____

_____

2. Name several ways you can put this wisdom into practice. Choose one of the ways you identify and describe how you will make that wisdom part of your life right now.

_____

_____

_____

_____

_____

_____

_____

_____

_____

_____

74 | CREDO | LIVING AND LOVING AS DISCIPLES OF CHRIST

CHAPTER 3

God's Law for a Good Life

INTRODUCTION

Through his life, Death, Resurrection and Ascension, Jesus revealed the depth of God the Father's love for each one of us. Jesus draws us, by the grace of the Holy Spirit, into God's love and enables us to live out of the goodness that is at the core of our humanity; he calls each one of us to be a 'beatitude' person.

> The beatitude we are promised . . . teaches us that true happiness is not found in riches or well-being, in human fame or power, or in any human achievement . . . but in God alone, the source of every good and of all love.
> —*Catechism of the Catholic Church* (CCC), no. 1723

The *Catechism* also teaches that 'the beatitude we are promised confronts us with decisive moral choices' (CCC, no. 1723). God has gifted us with the capacity to think freely and to make choices that shape our lives.

In chapter 3 we look at the natural law, a law that God has written in the hearts of all human beings. We examine how this innate sense of right and wrong guides us toward what is good and helps us to fulfill God's desire for us to grow to our full potential as human beings.

Chapter 3 is developed under five major headings:

◉ **ATTEND AND REFLECT:** What is the source of moral law?

◉ **HEAR THE STORY:** An understanding mind

◉ **EMBRACE THE VISION:** Developing an 'understanding heart'

◉ **THINK IT THROUGH:** The freedom to choose to follow Jesus

◉ **JUDGE AND ACT:** (*Activities and exercises that encourage the young people to integrate what they have learned in the chapter into their daily lives*)

Theological Background for the Teacher

THE ETERNAL LAW OF GOD

> God saw everything that he had made, and indeed, it was very good.
> —Genesis 1:31

All creation is a reflection of the goodness of God, who rules the universe with love and wisdom. Made in God's image and likeness, the human person is called to flourish in God's love, to work in partnership with God's eternal law and to help bring God's dream for all creation to completion.

The eternal law, which embraces all of creation, is the wisdom of God that moves all things to their final end. It is because of our capacity to reason and reflect that we can come to know the eternal law of God.

> The natural law is nothing other than the light of understanding placed in us by God; through it we know what we must do and what we must avoid.
> —CCC, no. 1955

The divine or eternal law can be either natural or revealed. Through the natural law we get a glimpse of the goodness of God and uncover what it is that God desires for us. The natural law applies to all humans everywhere. St. Paul addressed the universal nature of the natural law when speaking of the Gentiles:

> When Gentiles, who do not possess the law, do instinctively what the law requires, these, though not having the law, are a law to themselves. They show that what the law requires is written on their hearts, to which their own conscience also bears witness.
> —Romans 2:14–15

The *Catechism of the Catholic Church* teaches that the natural law enables us to discern that which is true and good and is the means by which we come to know the moral law.

CHAPTER 3: GOD'S LAW FOR A GOOD LIFE | INTRODUCTION | 75

The natural law states the first and essential precepts which govern the moral life. It hinges upon the desire for God and submission to him, who is the source and judge of all that is good.

—CCC, no. 1955

Desire for God is what urges us to seek out that which is good and to avoid that which diminishes our potential as human beings. Natural law gives expression to our innate sense of right and wrong. It is that inclination of our human nature that urges us to discern the moral values and precepts that protect and enshrine the good. We all possess natural inclinations and desires. All of us at some stage in our lives have experienced things that we are naturally drawn toward—like beauty and integrity; justice and truth; the preservation of life; loving relationships; loyal friendships. Such inclinations and desires are a part of being human. Natural law, then, is our innate wisdom that guides our inclinations and desires 'with a view to the true and the good' (CCC, no. 1954). When we pay attention to this wisdom, when we honor the fundamental thrust of our human nature toward what is good, we have the capacity to discover the core values that enable humanity to grow and to flourish. In this chapter we lead the young people to tap into this innate wisdom which resides in the heart of each of them, in the hope that they may come to a deeper understanding of the integrity of the Christian moral call and reflect its truth in their everyday lives.

NATURAL LAW AND REASON
The natural law concept goes back to the ancient Greeks. Philosophers like Aristotle and the Stoics believed in the existence of natural moral principles in our human nature. However, it was St. Thomas Aquinas who expanded this understanding in the thirteenth century. He understood the natural law to be a moral code, created by God and present in every person. For Aquinas, the natural law offers a framework for human freedom, a reasoned reference point for the rules of conduct that contribute to the well-being and potential of all.

Law is an ordinance of reason for the common good.

—St. Thomas Aquinas, *Summa Theologiae*
1–11, 90, 4

The human person is the pinnacle and climax of God's creation. Unlike all other creatures we alone are endowed with the gifts of reason, intellect, intuition and imagination; we alone have the capacity to make choices about ourselves, about the way we relate to and engage with others, and about how we shape

the kind of world we live in. However, the natural law is not something that we can create or invent ourselves. Neither is it something that we passively receive. Rather, it is to be discerned in and through deep imaginative reflection on what it means to be human. Grounded in our own experience, we have the capacity to discover what is right and what is wrong —and in so doing we discover the will of God.

NATURAL LAW AND FREEDOM
St. Thomas Aquinas helps us make the distinction between the natural law and the laws of nature. Unlike the instinctive laws of nature or of the animal world or the fixed laws of science that operate to an inevitable pattern, the natural law is a moral law. What distinguishes it from the laws of nature is that it applies to human action and to the human person's capacity to choose. As human persons we possess the freedom to incline our lives toward the inherent goodness within us or to decide to move away from that goodness and to seek happiness in other ways.

For God willed that men and women should 'be left free to make their own decisions' [see Ecclesiasticus 15:14] so that they might of their own accord seek their creator. . . . Their dignity therefore requires them to act out of conscious and free choice, as moved and drawn in a personal way from within, and not by their own blind impulses or by external constraint.

—*Gaudium et Spes (Constitution on the Church in the Modern World)*, no. 17

Without freedom, we cannot speak meaningfully about morality or moral responsibility. Human freedom is more than a capacity to choose between this and that. It is the God-given power to become who he created us to be and so to share eternal union with him.

—*United States Catholic Catechism for Adults (USCCA)*, 310

NATURAL LAW AND DIVINE LAW
This fundamental thrust toward the good expressed in the natural law is evidenced throughout Sacred Scripture. Echoing the moral norms and precepts discerned from natural law, time and again the Scriptures point us in the direction that enhances the human person. Situated within the historical contexts of the Old and New Testaments, Sacred Scripture offers concrete examples of how best to live as the chosen People of God.

We see the application of the natural law made manifest in the lives of the Old Testament prophets in their demand to live justly; to uphold the dignity of

76 | CREDO | LIVING AND LOVING AS DISCIPLES OF CHRIST

the widow; to give voice to the poor; to safeguard the socially marginalized.

> He has told you, O mortal, what is good; and what does the Lord require of you but to do justice, and to love kindness, and to walk humbly with your God?
>
> —Micah 6:8

The Decalogue belongs to God's Revelation; it urges us to be honest, to be faithful; to be true to ourselves; to be loyal to our neighbor. All are laws that are discerned by reflecting on our human nature.

> At the same time they [the Ten Commandments] teach us the true humanity of man. They bring to light the essential duties, and therefore, indirectly, the fundamental rights inherent in the nature of the human person. The Decalogue contains a privileged expression of the natural law.
>
> —CCC, no. 2070

Many of the parables of Jesus reveal what happens when the goodness inherent in the heart of all human persons is reflected in what we do and say. Indeed, we see the fulfillment of the moral law in the life, Death, Resurrection and Ascension of Jesus Christ himself.

CONSCIENCE

> A genuine personal conscience is not presented to us by life as a gift and is not by any means an automatic attainment. It has to be forged in the smithy of the individual's soul.
>
> —Vincent MacNamara, *The Truth in Love*

Because of the general manner in which the word 'conscience' is used in everyday conversation, it can be difficult to confine its meaning to a simple definition. Often, conscience is talked about as if it was a faculty of the mind that we call on when making a moral judgment. This understanding is sometimes reflected in statements like 'my conscience told me' or 'my conscience would not allow me' or 'I couldn't go against my conscience'.

But conscience is not a 'thing' that we possess. It is not a specific faculty that we can take out and 'use' when faced with a moral issue or situation. Neither is it an extra 'sense' or 'intuition' or an extra function of our brains that deals specifically with moral matters. At its simplest meaning, conscience is the person making a moral judgment and coming to a sense of what is right and wrong. This can often be a complex process of thinking, reflecting and reasoning involving consideration of all the facts,

seeking advice, drawing on the wisdom of past experience and on the shared experiences of others. For Christians, it can involve referring to the Sacred Scripture, to Tradition and to the authority of the Church to help discern what is the will of God.

In *Gaudium et Spes* the official teaching of the Catholic Church on conscience is clearly presented:

> Deep within their consciences men and women discover a law which they have not laid upon themselves and which they must obey. Its voice, ever calling them to love and to do what is good and to avoid evil, tells them inwardly at the right moment: do this, shun that. For they have in their hearts a law inscribed by God. Their dignity rests in observing this law, and by it they will be judged.
>
> Conscience is the most secret core and the sanctuary of the human person. There they are alone with God whose voice echoes in their depths. By conscience, in a wonderful way, that law is made known which is fulfilled in the love of God and of one's neighbor. Through loyalty to conscience, Christians are joined to others in the search for truth and for the right solution to so many moral problems which arise both in the life of individuals and from social relationships.
>
> —*Gaudium et Spes*, no. 16

Conscience, then, is an inner awareness that life has a moral dimension and that there are truths to be learned in living. It helps us to discern the kind of person we are, to articulate the kind of person we are becoming through our choices and decisions, and it reminds us of the kind of person we are called to become as children of God. Conscience calls us back to that basic thrust inherent in the heart of all humans that encourages us to grow as full human beings. Through the activity of our conscience we tap into that innate goodness, that natural inclination of our human nature to love and to flourish and to uphold the dignity of our humanity. Conscience cannot be imposed externally; rather, it comes from deep within the sacred core of each one of us. It is in this sense that we can speak of conscience as the voice of God 'speaking' and 'echoing' in our hearts. As *Gaudium et Spes* (no. 16) teaches: conscience is our 'secret core', our inner 'sanctuary'.

DEVELOPMENT OF CONSCIENCE

Conscience both invites and demands. It invites us to reflect God's image and likeness in the sort of person we are. But it also demands that we take responsibility for becoming the sort of person God invites us to

CHAPTER 3: GOD'S LAW FOR A GOOD LIFE | INTRODUCTION | 77

become. We grow in and through our interpersonal relationships and personal choices. Who we are is fashioned by how we forge our lives, by our way of being in the world, and is given expression in our daily moral acts and reasoned choices. This is a lifetime process. Thus, conscience is formed and developed over time.

We grow in maturity of conscience through education, experience and prayer. We are not born with a 'fully formed' conscience. Rather, we grow toward maturity of conscience as we develop our core moral values. We are educated in the process of developing our conscience through the influence of our parents and teachers; through reflection on our everyday experiences; through our traditions and our faith; and through the guidance of Sacred Scripture and the teachings of the Church. The *United States Catholic Catechism for Adults* puts this very clearly when it teaches:

> A good conscience requires lifelong formation. Each baptized follower of Christ is obliged to form his or her conscience according to objective moral standards. The Word of God is a principal tool in the formation of conscience when it is assimilated by study, prayer, and practice. The prudent advice and good example of others support and enlighten our conscience. The authoritative teaching of the Church is an essential element in our conscience formation. Finally, the gifts of the Holy Spirit, combined with regular examination of our conscience, will help us develop a morally sensitive conscience.
>
> —USCCA, 314

Through Baptism we become partakers of God's divine wisdom and sharers in new life with Christ. We receive God's grace to help us to lead moral lives and to live in accordance with the goodness that God has written in our hearts. In the Sacrament of Confirmation the grace received at Baptism is perfected (see CCC, no. 1316) when the bishop invokes the outpouring of the Holy Spirit (see CCC, no. 1299).

ADDITIONAL BACKGROUND READING
Catechism of the Catholic Church, nos. 1719, 1777–1785, 1790–1794, 1950–1974; *United States Catholic Catechism for Adults*, 314–315, 320, 327–328, 335, 336, 379–380, 383, 390, 437, 442; *Gaudium et Spes*, 16, 17, 26.

CHAPTER OUTCOMES

See general note on page 19 of this resource.

Learning Outcomes
As a result of studying this chapter and exploring the issues raised, the young people should be able to:

⊙ know that natural law is the source of all moral law and the foundation on which moral rules and civil law are built;

⊙ appreciate that all people possess this natural law within themselves;

⊙ know that the concept of the natural law has been accepted throughout history by pagan as well as Christian philosophers;

⊙ be aware of attitudes to the natural law in Greek and Roman philosophical traditions;

⊙ be familiar with the teachings of St. Thomas Aquinas on the natural law;

⊙ recognize the relationship between natural law and divine law as revealed in the Scriptures;

⊙ understand the connection between natural law and civil law;

⊙ understand the connection between natural law and conscience;

⊙ know the Church's guidelines for forming and informing one's conscience;

⊙ be aware of the challenges to following one's conscience;

⊙ recognize the sources of erroneous judgments of conscience;

⊙ know what is involved in an examination of conscience;

⊙ be familiar with the practice of the Examen;

⊙ know about the life of St. Thomas More.

Faith-formation Outcomes
As a result of studying this chapter and exploring the issues raised, the young people should also:

⊙ recognize the natural divine law in their own hearts and appreciate how it enhances their dignity;

⊙ reflect on how they are called to follow the natural and the divine law in their daily lives;

⊙ implement the Church's guidelines for informing their conscience;

⊙ develop the habit of examining their conscience regularly;

⊙ understand that conscience grows and develops in accordance with one's intellectual, emotional and spiritual maturity;

⊙ be inspired by St. Thomas More's loyalty to his conscience and his faith;

⊙ integrate the 'justice' principles they identified into their daily lives.

78 | CREDO | LIVING AND LOVING AS DISCIPLES OF CHRIST

Teacher Reflection

As you prepare to engage your group in a study of the eternal natural law
of God, take a moment to read and reflect on these words of wisdom from
Bishop Ken Untener of Saginaw.

Prophets of a Future Not Our Own

It helps, now and then, to step back and take a long view.

The kingdom is not only beyond our efforts,
it is even beyond our vision.

We accomplish in our lifetime only a tiny fraction
of the magnificent enterprise that is God's work.
Nothing we do is complete, which is a way of saying
that the kingdom always lies beyond us.
No statement says all that could be said.
No prayer fully expresses our faith.
No confession brings perfection.
No pastoral visit brings wholeness.
No program accomplishes the church's mission.
No set of goals and objectives includes everything.

This is what we are about.
We plant the seeds that one day will grow.
We water seeds already planted,
knowing that they hold future promise.

We lay foundations that will need further development.
We provide yeast that produces far beyond our capabilities.

We cannot do everything, and there is a sense of liberation
in realizing that. This enables us to do something,
and to do it very well. It may be incomplete,
but it is a beginning, a step along the way,
an opportunity for the Lord's grace to enter and do the rest.

We may never see the end results, but that is the difference
between the master builder and the worker.

We are workers, not master builders; ministers, not messiahs.
We are prophets of a future not our own.

CHAPTER 3: GOD'S LAW FOR A GOOD LIFE | INTRODUCTION | 79

Notes and Guidelines for Student Activities

ATTEND AND REFLECT

What is the source of moral law?

Learning Outcomes
That the young people would:
◉ know that natural law is the source of all moral law and the foundation on which moral rules and civil law are built;
◉ appreciate that all people possess this natural law within themselves.

Faith-formation Outcome
That the young people would also:
◉ recognize the natural divine law in their own hearts and appreciate how it enhances their dignity.

Overview
In section one, 'Attend and Reflect', we explore the natural law, which is the source of all moral law and the foundation on which moral rules and civil law are built. We present the Church's teaching that all moral law is part of the divine plan of original justice and original holiness that God willed for his creation. We explain to the young people that this divine or eternal law can be either natural or revealed. It is 'natural' in that all people possess this law within; through reason, we can come to know what is right and just. We guide the young people to understand that natural moral law, unlike other laws, is fulfilled only in so far as we make good moral choices. And God created us with an intellect and free will to enable us to do that. We have the God-given ability to think about our life, to weigh evidence and consequences and to decide how we can best live according to the will of God. We explain that the natural moral law is also 'revealed' in the ancient law of the Old Testament, notably the Ten Commandments, and in the teaching of Christ, notably the Sermon on the Mount, which perfects the ancient law.

Supplementary Activities for 'Attend and Reflect'

Worksheet 1: 'Wisdom from Life and Scripture' (*page 85 of this resource*) invites the young people first to identify wisdom they have gained from their own life

experiences and relationships, and then to explore some of the wisdom that is offered in the Book of Sirach. The young people then select a particular piece of wisdom that resonates with them in a special way.

Worksheet 2: 'Natural Law and the Parable of the Prodigal Son' (*page 88 of this resource*) invites the young people to examine the parable and try to identify how the judgments and actions of each character—the father and the two sons—reflected or did not reflect the wisdom of the natural law. From this the young people move into a discussion on the factors that shape and influence one's moral choices.

Note: Worksheet 2 requires the young people to illustrate their conclusions on a flow chart or mind map. You might like to read out to the young people the notes on creating mind maps on page 392 of the 'Student Activity Tool Kit'. There are also some examples of flow charts at the end of the tool kit.

HEAR THE STORY

An understanding mind

Learning Outcomes
That the young people would:
◉ know that the concept of the natural law has been accepted throughout history by pagan as well as Christian philosophers;
◉ be aware of attitudes to the natural law in Greek and Roman philosophical traditions;
◉ be familiar with the teachings of St. Thomas Aquinas on the natural law;
◉ recognize the relationship between natural law and divine law as revealed in the Scriptures.

Faith-formation Outcome
That the young people would also:
◉ reflect on how they are called to follow the natural and the divine law in their daily lives.

Overview
Section two, 'Hear the Story', opens with Pope Benedict XVI's 2011 address to the German parliament in which he referred to the prayer of King Solomon that God would grant him 'an understanding mind' so that he would be able to discern well between good and evil and so govern with justice. In this reference

80 | CREDO | LIVING AND LOVING AS DISCIPLES OF CHRIST

Pope Benedict was emphasizing the natural law whereby through reasoned reflection human beings can discern what is right and just and derive the moral norms that make for good living. The section moves on to explore how respect for the natural law was reflected in the Greek and Roman philosophical traditions. We then examine the teachings of St. Thomas Aquinas on the natural law. Aquinas taught that through honoring the natural law the human person participates in the eternal law of God. The young people learn about the relationship between natural law and the more explicit divine law as revealed in the Scriptures. The section ends with the message that we cannot simply depend on our own disciplined efforts to overcome the challenge of living by the natural law or the revealed law. We need and are empowered by the grace of God through Jesus Christ, which we receive in Baptism. We also rely on the teachings of Jesus, which are taught with authority by the Church.

Supplementary Activities for 'Hear the Story'

Research Activity
Invite the young people to work in small groups to research what understanding of the dignity of the human person is most prevalent in today's society. Encourage them to search through local and national newspapers for stories that highlight where the dignity of the person has been: (1) upheld, (2) denied, (3) challenged. They could look through current affairs articles, sports articles, fashion articles, education articles, advertisements, headlines, letters to the editor and so on. Ask them to select one story and to present this story and their analysis of it to the class group. Their presentation may be visual (poster/collage/PowerPoint) or verbal (drama/song/poem/lecture).

Afterward, you might conduct a whole-class discussion on the insights gained from the activity. Here are some suggestions for questions to guide the discussion:
- What do we mean by upholding the dignity of the person?
- How is human dignity affirmed most visibly in society today?
- Where is there evidence of a lack of respect for the dignity of the human person?
- Where is there room for improvement?
- How can young people help?

Worksheet 3: 'Human Rights' (*page 89 of this resource*) encourages the young people to come up with a written statement on what human rights means to them. We then invite them to examine the famous painting *The War of Human Rights* by Fitz Maurice and ask them to review their statement in light of any insights they gain from the painting. Finally, we encourage them to find a biblical phrase or passage that offers them hope in relation to the fulfillment of human rights and the honoring of the human person.

EMBRACE THE VISION

Developing an 'understanding heart'

Learning Outcomes
That the young people would:
- understand the connection between natural law and civil law;
- understand the connection between natural law and conscience;
- know the Church's guidelines for forming and informing one's conscience.

Faith-formation Outcome
That the young people would:
- implement the Church's guidelines for informing their conscience.

Overview
In section three, 'Embrace the Vision', we explore the relationship between natural and civil law. We begin by reminding the young people that all societies need moral rules so that people may live with dignity. We help them to recognize that many rules of social order—for example, not to steal, lie, harm or cheat—are based on the natural inclination of people to live justly and peacefully with one another. In other words, the natural law provides the foundation for the rules that guide our human communities. We also help them to recognize that in a pluralistic society such as ours, people do not always agree on how the dictates of the natural law are to be interpreted. This can lead to civil laws that the Church judges to be contrary to both the natural law and the revealed law. This is where conscience and our God-given gift of freedom comes into play. We remind the young people that we are free to choose not to live by the natural moral law that God has implanted in our heart. We explore the Church's teaching on the need to develop and form our conscience so that we may make practical judgments according to reason that are in conformity with the will of God as revealed in

CHAPTER 3: GOD'S LAW FOR A GOOD LIFE | NOTES AND GUIDELINES | 81

Scripture and Tradition. Finally, we present some key disciplines that the Church has proposed to help us form and inform our conscience correctly so that we may build up the moral capacity to make good choices.

Supplementary Activities for 'Embrace the Vision'

Research Activity: Violations of the Natural Law
Invite the young people to work in pairs and select an example from history or the present day of civil law violating the natural law; for example, legalized racial segregation; Nazi Germany; slavery; child labor; denial of women's rights; the death penalty. Ask the young people to research the violation and (1) situate it in its historical context; (2) name the civil laws in question; (3) name the violation(s) of the natural law; (4) identify what may have happened to change the law(s), or attempts currently taking place to do so.

_____

Worksheet 4: 'Lead Kindly Light' (*page 90 of this resource*) presents the text of the well-known hymn 'Lead Kindly Light' by Cardinal John Henry Newman (1801–90), along with a quotation in which Newman explores the meaning of conscience. We invite the young people to examine Cardinal Newman's images and explanations for conscience and then to come up with their own definition of conscience.

_____

Worksheet 5: 'The Prophets and Social Justice' (*page 92 of this resource*) focuses on the prophets of the Old Testament and their call for a just and fair society. We invite the young people to read a selection of passages from the writings of the prophets and to explore the relevance of their message for today's world. The young people will then compose their own statements on justice and use them to create a 'Justice Speaks Out' booklet.

THINK IT THROUGH

The freedom to choose to follow Jesus

Learning Outcomes
That the young people would:
⊙ be aware of the challenges to following one's conscience;

⊙ recognize the sources of erroneous judgments of conscience;
⊙ know what is involved in an examination of conscience;
⊙ be familiar with the practice of the Examen.

Faith-formation Outcomes
That the young people would also:
⊙ develop the habit of examining their conscience regularly;
⊙ understand that conscience grows and develops in accordance with one's intellectual, emotional and spiritual maturity.

Overview
Section four, 'Think It Through', deals with our God-given freedom to make moral decisions and act according to our conscience. We begin our exploration by reminding the young people that following one's conscience is not always easy and we discuss some of the ways in which they may be tempted to abuse this freedom. We help them to recognize that a judgment of a person's conscience can, at times, be erroneous, and we inform them of the Church's teaching in relation to possible sources of such erroneous judgments. We advise the young people on the importance of examining their conscience regularly and we advocate the use of the Examen as a method of discernment to guide them in living according to God's will by responding to the promptings of the Holy Spirit.

Supplementary Activities for 'Think It Through'

TV News Survey
⊙ Invite the young people to select and watch a TV news program—alone or in small groups. Ask them to make a note of: the topics covered; the images that accompany the topics; the assumptions underpinning the analysis of the topics; the order in which the topics are presented; particular words used to describe the topics.
⊙ This activity could be extended by asking the young people to follow a particular TV news program for a week and to feed back to the group their insights and findings.
⊙ When the young people have completed the activity, have a class discussion in which they share the insights they gained from doing this exercise. You might like to use some or all of these questions to guide the discussion:

82 | CREDO | LIVING AND LOVING AS DISCIPLES OF CHRIST

- Whose voice was the strongest in the news stories?
- Were there voices that could have been heard but weren't? Explain.
- Who decides whose voice gets the greatest hearing in such news bulletins?
- What images of society were portrayed through the news items?
- What understandings of social justice were portrayed?

⊙ Finally, the young people could prepare short presentations based on the insights they gained from the activity. Topics might include, for example, how their own assumptions, judgments and attitudes impact their responses to news coverage; the power of the media in relation to the message that is sent out; the view of society portrayed through the news; how Jesus might react to TV news coverage.

Worksheet 6: 'The Seven Principles of Catholic Social Teaching' (*page 94 of this resource*) introduces the young people to the seven key principles that provide the foundation for the Social Teaching, or Social Doctrine, of the Catholic Church. We invite them to work together in small groups to represent one principle in image form and to find a suitable Scripture story or phrase to accompany the image. The young people will then make a presentation of their work for the class.

Worksheet 7: 'My Conscience-Formation Timeline' (*page 95 of this resource*) offers the young people an opportunity to explore the process involved in the growth and development of their conscience and to identify on a timeline the people, events, circumstances and teachings that have influenced the shaping of their conscience.

JUDGE AND ACT

Learning Outcome
That the young people would:
⊙ know about the life of St. Thomas More.

Faith-formation Outcomes
That the young people would also:
⊙ be inspired by St. Thomas More's loyalty to his conscience and his faith;
⊙ integrate the 'justice' principles they identified into their daily lives.

Overview
In section five, 'Judge and Act', the young people review and discuss the teachings of the Church that they have learned about in this chapter. They also learn about the life of St. Thomas More.

Supplementary Activity for 'Judge and Act'

Media Activity: A Man for all Seasons
You might like to show your students the 1966 movie *A Man for All Seasons*, starring Paul Scofield as Sir Thomas More and Robert Shaw as King Henry VIII, which is widely regarded as the quintessential film on issues of conscience. The film depicts the moral integrity of Sir Thomas More when faced with Henry's desire to divorce his wife Catherine in order to marry Anne Boleyn. More refused to give his approval on the basis of his religious beliefs. His response to his peers who urged him to change his mind was: 'When we die and you are sent to heaven for doing your conscience, and I am sent to hell for not doing mine, will you come with me for fellowship?' His decision not to go against his conscience cost More his life. After viewing the film, the young people could discuss the ways in which More remained true to himself and his conscience even when dealing with Cardinal Wolsey, Richard the Duke of Norfolk and his own family members.

Additional Prayer Suggestions

This Prayer Reflection seeks to help the young people to grow in the knowledge that God is the center of our being and that he desires what is best for each one of us. God enfolds us in love and compassion. When we call upon God, it is not God who comes to us, for God is always with us; rather, it is we who are opening our hearts to God.

Leader
Open up your hearts to God. (*Pause*)

All
O Lord, my heart is ready,
My heart is ready to feel your presence.

Leader
Creator of all, come to me.
Let your presence renewing be.

CHAPTER 3: GOD'S LAW FOR A GOOD LIFE | NOTES AND GUIDELINES | 83

All
O Lord, my heart is ready,
My heart is ready to feel your presence.

Leader
Savior of all, come to me.
Let your peace enfolding be.

All
O Lord, my heart is ready,
My heart is ready to feel your presence.

Leader
Spirit of all, come to me.
Let your power refreshing be.

All
O Lord, my heart is ready,
My heart is ready to feel your presence.

Leader
Close your eyes.
Know that God accepts you whoever you are. (*Pause*)
God loves you. (*Pause*)
God is in the very core of your being. (*Pause*)
You are in the presence of God. (*Pause*)
You are in the arms of God. (*Pause*)
You are in the love of God. (*Pause*)
You are in the kingdom of God. (*Pause*)
You are in the heart of God. (*Pause*)

In the name of the Father,
and of the Son,
and of the Holy Spirit.

All
Amen.

Scripture Reflection

(*See instructions for the use of doodling in prayer in the 'Student Activity Tool Kit', page 394 of this resource.*)

Use this Psalm verse to engage the young people in prayer:

To you, O Lord, I lift up my soul.
O my God, in you I trust.

PSALM 25:1–2

CHAPTER 3 | WORKSHEET 1

NAME:

Wisdom from Life and Scripture

The Catholic Church teaches that God continues to rule the universe with wisdom and directs it toward divine fulfillment. Much of the wisdom we learn in life comes from our own experiences. We also gain wisdom from listening and attending to the experiences of others. This worksheet offers you the opportunity first to identify the wisdom you have gained from your life experiences and relationships, and then to explore some of the wisdom that is offered in the Book of Sirach. Finally, we will invite you to select a particular piece of wisdom that resonates with you in a special way.

WISDOM FROM LIFE
Brainstorm the wisdom you have gleaned so far in your life from:
⊙ your own experiences
⊙ the people you live with
⊙ grandparents and older people
⊙ teachers or leaders
⊙ books, films, poetry

MY 'TOP TEN' NUGGETS OF WISDOM
Select the top ten pieces of wisdom that are most significant to your life today.

1. _____
   _____
2. _____
   _____
3. _____
   _____
4. _____
   _____
5. _____
   _____
6. _____
   _____
7. _____
   _____

CHAPTER 3: GOD'S LAW FOR A GOOD LIFE | WORKSHEET 1 | 85

CHAPTER 3 | WORKSHEET 1 (CONTD.)

8. _____

_____

9. _____

_____

10. _____

_____

WISDOM FROM THE BOOK OF SIRACH

The Book of Sirach, which is also known as the Book of Ecclesiasticus, is one of the great collections of wise sayings in the Old Testament. Read the following references from this book and take note of those that you particularly like.

In praise of wisdom 1:1; 1:4; 1:13; 1:14; 1:22; 1:23; 1:24; 1:26; 1:27; 1:29; 1:30	**Friendship** 6:14–17; 7:11–12
Duties to God 2:6; 2:12; 2:13; 2:14	**Relations with others** 7:18–19; 7:32–36
Duties to parents 3:3–7; 3:12–14	**Choice of friends** 9:10–11; 9:14–16
Humility 3:17–18; 3:23–26	**The sin of pride** 10:6–7
Duties to the poor and oppressed 4:1; 4:2; 4:3; 4:5–6; 4:8; 4:9; 4:10	**Concerning humility** 10:26–27; 10:28–30
Precepts for everyday living 5: 1–2; 5:9–12; 5:14–15	**Responsible use of wealth** 14: 9–10

Select your ten favorite 'wisdom quotes' from the Book of Sirach and write them on these lines.

1. _____

_____

2. _____

_____

3. _____

_____

86 | CREDO | LIVING AND LOVING AS DISCIPLES OF CHRIST

CHAPTER 3 | WORKSHEET 1 (CONTD.)

4. _____

_____

5. _____

_____

6. _____

_____

7. _____

_____

8. _____

_____

9. _____

_____

10. _____

_____

REVIEW AND SHARE

⊙ Compare and contrast the words of wisdom that you selected from the Book of Sirach with your own 'Top Ten' pieces of wisdom.

⊙ Pair up with a partner and compare your lists.

⊙ Discuss which pieces of wisdom would have the greatest relevance to young people's lives.

⊙ Work together to design a web page on the topic 'Words of Wisdom for Young People Today' and share the nuggets of wisdom that you have gathered with other students and friends.

A DAILY REMINDER

Select one piece of wisdom from the Book of Sirach that resonates with you in a special way. Write this on a piece of card and hang it in your bedroom.

CHAPTER 3: GOD'S LAW FOR A GOOD LIFE | WORKSHEET 1 (CONTD.) | 87

CHAPTER 3 | WORKSHEET 2

NAME:

Natural Law and the Parable of the Prodigal Son

Jesus directed his parables at the hearts of his listeners. Using ordinary situations that people could identify with and rich imagery that had the power to challenge and transform, Jesus encouraged people to look within themselves and rediscover the inner wisdom and goodness that God had planted in their hearts. He challenged them to become aware of the values that were underpinning and informing their thoughts and judgments, their beliefs and deeds.

It is not surprising that many of the parables Jesus told appeal to the natural law, that natural capacity within each of us to discover what needs to happen if we are to flourish with dignity and justice and fulfill the potential that God desires for us. This worksheet offers you the opportunity to reread the parable of the Prodigal Son and identify how the actions of each of the characters in the parable reflected or did not reflect the wisdom of the natural law.

READ AND RESPOND
⊙ For this activity you will need three sheets of paper to create three flow charts or mind maps—one for each of the characters in the parable of the Prodigal Son. (Your teacher will be able to guide you in creating these charts.)
⊙ Read the parable in Luke 15:11–32.
⊙ As you read it, begin to identify the values, attitudes, beliefs or judgments of each character. Write these on the charts.
⊙ Then pay attention to how those values, attitudes, beliefs or judgments are reflected in the characters' actions, thoughts or words, and identify those actions, thoughts or words on the charts.
⊙ Which of the values, attitudes, beliefs or judgments of the characters in the story can you find in your own life?

PAIR AND SHARE
⊙ Share your charts with a partner.
⊙ Discuss what emerged for each of you from this activity.

CLASS DISCUSSION
⊙ What or who might have helped shape the values you live by?
⊙ What might impede you from living out of the values reflected in the natural law?

88 | CREDO | LIVING AND LOVING AS DISCIPLES OF CHRIST

CHAPTER 3 | WORKSHEET 3

NAME:

Human Rights

In protecting human rights, society seeks to uphold the dignity of all human persons in a way that leads to wholeness and fullness of life for all. This worksheet offers you the opportunity to reflect upon and discuss the concept of human rights and to come up with a statement on what human rights means to you. You will then examine the famous painting *The War of Human Rights* by Fitz Maurice and share your insights with the group.

GROUP ACTIVITY

⊙ Work in small groups.
⊙ Share your views on what the term 'human rights' refers to.
⊙ Then work together to come up with a statement on what 'human rights' means to you.

Human rights means. . . .

_____

_____

_____

_____

OBSERVE AND SHARE

The War of Human Rights is a famous painting by the American artist Fitz Maurice. The painting was first exhibited at the 1993 United Nations World Conference in Vienna, which was attended by world leaders such as the Dalai Lama and President Clinton, and it became an international symbol of human rights.

⊙ Do an internet search for the painting *The War of Human Rights* by Fitz Maurice.
⊙ Take some time to examine the painting.
⊙ Compare the statement the group produced above with the image that Fitz Maurice has created.
⊙ What strikes you about the way the artist has depicted the dignity of the human person and human rights?
⊙ What strikes you about the color, images, lines and curves the artist has used?
⊙ What do you think the artist is trying to say through this painting?
⊙ If you were an artist, how might you depict human rights? How might you depict the dignity of the human person? What sort of images might you use? Share your ideas.

JOURNAL EXERCISE

See if you can find a biblical phrase or passage that supports the importance of human rights.

CHAPTER 3: GOD'S LAW FOR A GOOD LIFE | WORKSHEET 3 | 89

CHAPTER 3 | WORKSHEET 4

NAME:

'Lead Kindly Light'

This worksheet presents the well-known hymn 'Lead Kindly Light' by Cardinal John Henry Newman (1801–90), along with a quotation in which Newman explores the meaning of conscience. We invite you to examine Newman's images and explanations for conscience and then to come up with your own explanation of what conscience means.

JOHN HENRY NEWMAN

John Henry Newman was born in London in February 1801. He was a member of the Church of England but he converted to Catholicism in 1845. During his life he had a profound spiritual and theological influence on the Catholic Church. He was made Cardinal by Pope Leo XIII in 1879 and was beatified by Pope Benedict XVI on September 19, 2010. Cardinal Newman published many articles and books expounding the teachings of the Catholic Church. Cardinal Newman died in Birmingham in 1890.

READ AND RESPOND

⊙ Work in pairs.
⊙ Read this famous hymn which Cardinal Newman wrote in 1833.
⊙ Then discuss: what Newman is asking of God; what he is afraid of; how he judges himself; what he hopes for; how his image of light/darkness helps explain what conscience is.

> **Lead, Kindly Light**
> Lead, Kindly Light, amid the encircling gloom,
> Lead Thou me on!
> The night is dark, and I am far from home,—
> Lead Thou me on!
> Keep Thou my feet; I do not ask to see
> The distant scene—one step enough for me.
>
> I was not ever thus, nor prayed that Thou
>   shouldst lead me on:
> I loved to choose and see my path, but now
>   lead Thou me on!
> I loved the garish days, and, spite of fears,
> Pride ruled my will: remember not past years.
>
> So long thy power hath blessed me, sure it still
>   will lead me on;

90 | CREDO | LIVING AND LOVING AS DISCIPLES OF CHRIST

CHAPTER 3 | WORKSHEET 4 (CONTD.)

O'er moor and fen, o'er crag and torrent, till
    the night is gone;
And with the morn those angel faces smile
Which I have loved long since, and lost awhile.

- Now read this extract in which Cardinal Newman talks more formally about conscience.
- Select and share with your partner three things Newman says about conscience that you particularly agree with.

Man has within his breast a certain commanding dictate, not a mere sentiment, not a mere opinion or impression or view of things, but a law, an authoritative voice, bidding him do certain things and avoid others. I do not say that its particular injunctions are always clear, or that they are always consistent with each other; but what I am insisting on here is this, that it commands; that it praises, blames, it threatens, it implies a future, and it witnesses of the unseen. It is more than a man's own self. The man himself has no power over it, or only with extreme difficulty; he did not make it, he cannot destroy it. . . . This is Conscience, and, from the nature of the case, its very existence carries our minds to a Being exterior to ourselves; for else, when did it come?

JOURNAL EXERCISE

Imagine that you have been asked by your younger brother or sister to explain what conscience is. Write out your explanation.

CHAPTER 3: GOD'S LAW FOR A GOOD LIFE | WORKSHEET 4 (CONTD.) | 91

CHAPTER 3 | WORKSHEET 5

NAME:

The Prophets and Social Justice

The prophets of the Old Testament were very aware of the need for a just society. They constantly reminded people that God was on the side of the poor and the oppressed and that God called all people to work to create a world based on truth, peace and justice. This worksheet invites you to examine some of the writings of the prophets of the Old Testament and to consider the relevance of their message for today's world. You will then have the opportunity to write your own prophetic message about a just society and contribute to creating a 'Justice Speaks Out' booklet with your classmates.

READ AND RESPOND
⊙ Work in small groups.
⊙ Look up and read the passages from the writings of the prophets listed below.
⊙ As you read each one, share your views on how relevant you think their message is to today's world.
  – Isaiah 1:17
  – Isaiah 58:6–12
  – Zechariah 7:9–10
  – Jeremiah 22:3
  – Jeremiah 22:13–17
  – Micah 6:8
  – Amos 5:11–15
  – Amos 5:21–24
  – Ezekiel 16:49–50

⊙ When you have completed this task, discuss these questions:
  – Which values are universal for all times?
  – What does this tell us about the natural law?
  – If this school were to take the challenges and vision of the prophets to heart, what would need to change to make this vision a reality?
  – In what practical ways could you help to bring about such change?

SOCIAL JUSTICE CHALLENGES OF TODAY
⊙ Work as a single class group.
⊙ Brainstorm the issues facing the world today that demand greater social justice—at local, national and global levels. List these issues on the chart.

92 | CREDO | LIVING AND LOVING AS DISCIPLES OF CHRIST

CHAPTER 3 | WORKSHEET 5 (CONTD.)

Local Level	National Level	Global Level

- ⊙ Now work in pairs.
- ⊙ Select one of the issues identified above. Write a statement relating to this issue that challenges young people today to become people of truth and justice. Try to write in the style of the prophets of the Old Testament that you examined earlier.
- ⊙ When you have completed this activity, the class might like to gather all the statements together and create a class 'Justice Speaks Out' booklet.

CHAPTER 3: GOD'S LAW FOR A GOOD LIFE | WORKSHEET 5 (CONTD.) | 93

CHAPTER 3 | WORKSHEET 6

NAME:

The Seven Principles of Catholic Social Teaching

The challenge to create a society based on truth and justice and the dignity of every human person is immense. Yet it is a challenge and vision of life that every baptized Christian is called to adopt and follow. This worksheet offers you the opportunity to explore the Seven Principles of Catholic Social Teaching which echo this Gospel vision.

READ AND REFLECT

Our task as disciples of Jesus Christ is constantly to seek ways to make the love, justice and compassion of God's Kingdom a reality in our world. *The United States Catholic Catechism for Adults* (325) teaches:

> Our Gospel commitment to Christ's Kingdom of love, justice, and mercy always includes advocating and supporting fairness for all. God calls us to form community and to correct both the symptoms and causes of injustice that rip apart the solidarity of a community.

⊙ Take some quiet time alone to read these seven key principles of the Social Teaching, or Social Doctrine, of the Catholic Church and to reflect on what they say to you about living out the core values of Christian morality.

1. *Life and dignity of the human person.* Human life is sacred and the dignity of the human person is the foundation of the moral life of individuals and of society.
2. *Call to family, community and participation.* The human person is social by nature and has the right to participate in family life and in the life of society.
3. *Rights and responsibilities.* The human person has the fundamental right to life and to the basic necessities that support life and human decency.
4. *Option for the poor and the vulnerable.* The Gospel commands us 'to put the needs of the poor and the vulnerable first'.
5. *Dignity of work and workers.* Work is a form of participating in God's work of Creation. 'The economy must serve people and not the other way around.'
6. *Solidarity.* God is the Creator of all people. 'We are one human family whatever our national, racial, ethnic, economic and ideological differences.'
7. *Care for God's creation.* Care of the environment is a divine command and a requirement of our faith.

GROUP ACTIVITY/PRESENTATION

⊙ Work in small groups and choose one of the above principles.
⊙ Combine your ideas and skills to represent this principle in image form. You might like to use photographs, cuttings from newspapers or magazines or your own drawings.
⊙ Then find a Scripture passage, phrase or story that reflects and affirms this principle to accompany your image.
⊙ Present your work to the class.

94 | CREDO | LIVING AND LOVING AS DISCIPLES OF CHRIST

CHAPTER 3 | WORKSHEET 7

NAME:

My Conscience-Formation Timeline

Our conscience develops and matures as we grow in emotional, religious and intellectual maturity. The people with whom we share our lives—our family, friends, teachers, neighbors, church leaders—all influence the formation and development of our conscience. How we engage with and reflect on the events of our life can also help shape our conscience and our understanding of right and wrong. This worksheet invites you to create a timeline mapping the people, events and experiences that have influenced the development of your conscience from your childhood to the present day.

MY CONSCIENCE-FORMATION TIMELINE

- On a large sheet of paper create a timeline tracing the influences on the development of your conscience from your birth to today.
- Use words, images or symbols to represent the various stages and influences.
- Be as specific as possible in naming (1) the people who influenced you; (2) the experiences or events that were particularly formative for you.
- Look back over your timeline and, where appropriate, see if you can name the particular values that you acquired at the various stages in your development as a result of specific experiences, for example, truthfulness, honesty, courage.

REVIEW AND RESPOND

Review your timeline and describe the factors that have had the greatest influence on how you make decisions today.

_____

_____

_____

_____

_____

_____

_____

_____

CHAPTER 3: GOD'S LAW FOR A GOOD LIFE | WORKSHEET 7 | 95

CHAPTER 3 | CHAPTER REVIEW

NAME:

Review of Chapter 3

I. **Fill in the blanks. Write the letter that corresponds to the correct term in the word bank in the blank space to complete each sentence. There are more terms in the word bank than you will need.**

A. Examen	**E.** Roman tradition	**I.** Stoicism
B. St. Thomas Aquinas	**F.** natural law	**J.** Steve Jobs
C. Gifts of the Holy Spirit	**G.** Sacred Scripture	**K.** The Rosary
D. Revelation	**H.** St. Thomas More	**L.** Conscience

1. The _____ is unchangeable and permanent throughout human history.

2. _____ was among the earliest philosophies of life based on following the natural law.

3. _____ is one of the Church's philosopher theologians who wrote extensively on the natural law.

4. _____ assists our discernment and decision-making.

5. The _____ dispose and strengthen us to respond knowingly and freely to God's holy will in the very circumstances of daily life.

6. _____ is a judgment of reason that allows us to know whether some concrete act is in harmony with or contrary to natural and revealed law.

7. We form our conscience correctly by using our reason and the teachings of divine law that we find in _____ and that are taught to us by the Church.

8. _____ said, 'Don't let the noise of others' opinions drown out your own inner voice.'

9. The _____ is a practice one can use to inform one's conscience.

10. The final words of _____ were, 'The king's good servant, but God's first.'

96 | CREDO | LIVING AND LOVING AS DISCIPLES OF CHRIST

CHAPTER 3 | CHAPTER REVIEW (CONTD.)

II. **True/False. Mark the true statements 'T' and the false statements 'F'. In the case of each false statement, cross out and rewrite the incorrect words to make the statement true.**

_____1.   God is the source of all just and true law.

_____2.   The Romans believed that the natural law was revealed to those who were educated.

_____3.   Scripture echoes the moral principles and precepts that we can know from the natural law.

_____4.   Scripture clarifies that we should have a special favor for those whom we like best.

_____5.   The Catholic Tradition believes that all people can agree upon a limited set of standards for moral behavior in society.

_____6.   No matter what our bad deed, our conscience always holds out a pledge of conversion and hope.

_____7.   A person cannot choose whether or not to live by the natural moral law.

_____8.   Following our conscience is always easy.

CHAPTER 3: GOD'S LAW FOR A GOOD LIFE | CHAPTER REVIEW (CONTD.) | 97

CHAPTER 3 | CHAPTER REVIEW (CONTD.)

_____ 9. The call to Christian discipleship is always by invitation.

_____ 10. Thomas More came into conflict with King Henry VIII over Henry's decision to invade Scotland.

III. Write a brief answer. Explain the teaching of the Catholic Church on 1 or 2.
   1. God has implanted the natural law in the hearts of all people.
   2. A judgment of a person's conscience can, at times, be erroneous.

_____

_____

_____

_____

_____

_____

IV. How would you respond? A non-Catholic friend says: 'I'm not Catholic so I don't have to worry about the natural law.'

_____

_____

_____

_____

_____

_____

98 | CREDO | LIVING AND LOVING AS DISCIPLES OF CHRIST

CHAPTER 3 | CHAPTER REVIEW (CONTD.)

V. Make a 'disciple decision'.

1. What is the most important wisdom for life that you discovered in this chapter?

_____

_____

_____

_____

_____

2. Name several ways you can put this wisdom into practice. Choose one of the ways you identify and describe how you will make that wisdom part of your life right now.

_____

_____

_____

_____

_____

_____

_____

CHAPTER 3: GOD'S LAW FOR A GOOD LIFE | CHAPTER REVIEW (CONTD.) | 99

CHAPTER 4

The Reality of Sin

INTRODUCTION

The 'commandment' of love is only possible because it is more than a requirement. Love can be 'commanded' because it has first been given.

—Pope Benedict XVI,
Deus Caritas Est (God Is Love)

It is in relation to others that we exist as human beings and that we come to discover the fullness of the potential that God calls us to. Pope Benedict XVI's Encyclical Letter *Deus Caritas Est* reminds us that God is the source of all love. Created in the image and likeness of God who first gifted us with love, we are invited to love in return and, through the act of loving, to grow in our relationship with God and with others.

This chapter explores the concept of sin within the context of a God who loves us unconditionally, who desires our eternal happiness and who invites us to participate in divine love.

Chapter 4 is developed under five major headings:

- ⊙ **ATTEND AND REFLECT:** Where is the evidence for sin in the world?
- ⊙ **HEAR THE STORY:** The divine plan of goodness versus sin
- ⊙ **EMBRACE THE VISION:** 'Do you reject Satan, and all his works, and all his empty promises?'
- ⊙ **THINK IT THROUGH:** The many faces of sin and our response
- ⊙ **JUDGE AND ACT:** (*Activities and exercises that encourage the young people to integrate what they have learned in the chapter into their daily lives*)

Theological Background for the Teacher

Above all, clothe yourselves with love, which binds everything together in perfect harmony.

—Colossians 3:14

We are at our best when we live in intimacy and harmony with one another and when we are at one with God and with God's dream for us. 'This happens when we consistently choose ways that are in harmony with God's plan' (*United States Catholic Catechism for Adults* [USCCA], 310).

Each of us has experienced times in our lives when we were true to ourselves and reflected the goodness that God has implanted in our hearts. However, we are also aware of times when this does not happen— times when we fail to reflect the divine in whose image we are created, times when we do not mirror God and his love in our way of being in the world. It is at times like this that we become aware of the reality of sin and of our capacity to fall short of the love with which God has gifted us.

> God calls man and woman, made in the image of the Creator 'who loves everything that exists', to share in his providence toward other creatures; hence their responsibility for the world that God has entrusted to them.
>
> —*Catechism of the Catholic Church* (CCC), no. 373

Once we truly experience and accept the depth of God's love for us, nothing can ever be the same again. When we accept the unearned love of God for us, we come to the fullest understanding of Christian morality. Morality arises out of our human need to live in harmony and with dignity and respect for others. Christian morality, however, is more than living in harmony with one another. It is deeply bound to the Creator God, the source of all life, who 'loves everything that exists' (CCC, no. 373). Sin, essentially a religious concept, is grounded in the dynamic of God's love for us and our free response to God's initiative of love.

> . . . for only in this relationship is the evil of sin unmasked in its true identity as humanity's rejection of God.
>
> —CCC, no. 386

It is within this relationship that we acknowledge our wrongdoings and seek God's healing and forgiveness.

100 | CREDO | LIVING AND LOVING AS DISCIPLES OF CHRIST

LOSS OF ORIGINAL HARMONY WITH GOD

Adam and Eve were created to reflect the image of the God who breathed life into them.

> In figurative and symbolic language, Scripture describes God's creating the first man and woman, Adam and Eve, and placing them in Paradise. They were created in friendship with God and in harmony with creation. The Church teaches that theirs was a state of original holiness and justice, with no suffering or death.
>
> —USCCA, 67

In the Garden of Eden, that wonderful symbol of intimacy, peace and unity, Adam and Eve were firmly established in friendship with their Creator God (CCC, no. 374). And 'from their friendship with God flowed the happiness of their existence in paradise' (CCC, no. 384). But, through Adam and Eve's free decision to choose 'for themselves' rather than 'for God', sin entered this world of perfect union and God's creative plan was interrupted.

> Through the Fall of Adam and Eve, the harmony of creation was also destroyed. If we continue to read the Book of Genesis, we see how Adam and Eve became aware of their sinful condition, were driven out of the garden, and were forced to live by the sweat of their brow. The beauty and harmony of God's creative plan was disrupted.
>
> —USCCA, 69

The action of Adam and Eve led to loss of the original joy and intimacy they shared with God; loss of freedom; loss of integrity and authenticity; and loss of trust in each other.

> The account of The Fall in Genesis 3 uses figurative language, but it affirms a primeval event, a sin that took place at the beginning of history.
>
> —USCCA, 73

The Garden of Eden offered Adam and Eve eternal happiness with God. However, discontent crept into their hearts and, as it did so, their capacity to embrace all that was theirs became stunted and seeds of arrogant questioning and greed took root. Adam and Eve's disquiet pushed them to search for something 'greater'—greater power, greater control and greater mastery over their own lives and over their Creator God. Succumbing to temptation, they turned away from God's divine plan and turned their backs on all that God offered. They hoped for freedom but experienced limitations. They hoped for power but experienced vulnerability and suffering. Their desire to be like God weakened them as persons, caused them inner turmoil, estranged them from each other and banished them from that place of everlasting truth and happiness.

> This was not the way it was meant to be. Once sin entered into life and into our world, all harmony with God, with self, with each other, and with the world around us was shattered.
>
> —USCCA, 69

By sinning, Adam and Eve departed from God's original vision for humanity. And because all humanity is intrinsically interconnected, each one of us is affected by that first sin. Each one of us, through free will and reason, can choose to turn away from God and choose evil over good. But God's mercy is never-ending. Like the father in the parable of the Prodigal Son, God awaits our return with compassion and forgiveness. And so, through Baptism, each one of us is redeemed to right relationship with God, through the life, Death, Resurrection and Ascension of Jesus Christ.

> It is Jesus Christ who frees us from Original Sin and our own actual sins. By Baptism, we share in the redemptive act of Jesus' death and Resurrection, are freed from Original Sin, and are strengthened against the power of sin and death. We are reconciled to God and made members of his holy people, the Church.
>
> —USCCA, 70

UNDERSTANDING SIN

> In recent times the comment frequently arises, What's happened to sin? Where has sin gone? There is a perceptible discomfort in our culture with the notion of sin as an evil for which we must give an account to God, our Creator, Redeemer, and Judge.
>
> —USCCA, 71

In the predominantly secular world of today there is little discourse about sin, and when there is, many seem ill at ease with the topic. Some of us are reluctant to name the reality of sin in our personal, everyday lives. And the same unease is seen in our reluctance to name the reality of sin in the structures of our institutions and in our culture. There is no doubt that growth in the fields of psychology and personal development has deepened our understanding of human development; however, it seems also to have led to a diminution of our need to explore what it means to 'sin' and to identify the root

CHAPTER 4: THE REALITY OF SIN | INTRODUCTION | 101

of moral evil for ourselves and for the communities in which we live. The *United States Catholic Catechism for Adults* points to the lack of understanding of Revelation as one possible reason for this lack of interest in sin.

> The origin of this attitude may be found in an underdeveloped sense of Revelation: 'Without the knowledge Revelation gives of God we cannot recognize sin clearly. . . . Only in the knowledge of God's plan . . . can we grasp that sin is an abuse of the freedom that God gives to created persons' [CCC, no. 387].
>
> —USCCA, 71, 72

Sin is a refusal to love God and to love others. It cuts us off from God, the source of life and the source of our very humanity. It prevents us from living in intimacy and harmony with ourselves, with others and with God in the manner in which God created us to live. Sin is a refusal to participate in the divine life and love. In this context sin is a failure to respond to God's love. Our relationship with the divine becomes ruptured and damaged. Sin corrupts our innate nature and 'injures human solidarity' (CCC, no. 1849). The *Catechism of the Catholic Church* teaches that sin is

> . . . an offence against reason, truth and right conscience; it is failure in genuine love for God and neighbor.
>
> —CCC, no. 1849

SIN AND THE BIBLE

In trying to come to grips with the reality of sin, the Old Testament writers turned to imagery. Their understanding of the complexity of sin is reflected in the range and depth of imagery they use to describe sin. Much of that imagery is borrowed from the configurations of human relationships. For them, sin could only be understood within the relational dynamic between God and the people of Israel. So, sin was seen as not stepping up to the mark of the relationship (Exodus 20:5); breaking of the covenant relationship, violation of the relationship (Hosea 2; Jeremiah 4:1–4); foolishness, 'folly' (Jeremiah 8:8–9); hardening of the heart (Psalm 95:7–9); rebellion against God (Isaiah 1:2–4; Jeremiah 2:29). Central to all the Old Testament images is the rupturing of the relationship with God. The prophets time and again denounced sin as an immense betrayal of, and transgression against, the God who liberated them.

> See, the Lord's hand is not too short to save, nor his ear too dull to hear. Rather, your iniquities have been barriers between you and your God, and your sins have hidden his face from you.
>
> —Isaiah 59:1–2

The people of Israel knew the love of their God, but they also knew the destructive force of sin, which destroyed their capacity to relate in fullness to their God. The *Catechism of the Catholic Church* echoes this when it teaches:

> Sin sets itself against God's love for us and turns our hearts away from it. Like the first sin, it is disobedience, a revolt against God through the will to become 'like gods', knowing and determining good and evil. Sin is thus 'love of oneself even to contempt of God'. In this proud self-exaltation, sin is diametrically opposed to the obedience of Jesus, which achieves our salvation.
>
> —CCC, no. 1850

Through Jesus' life, Death, Resurrection and Ascension, humanity is reconciled with God. Jesus re-establishes right relationships with God. He reminds his listeners of the love and inherent goodness that lies at the heart of each one of us. The heart is the very core of who we are, of our humanity and our dignity. The heart is the place from which a response to the love of God emerges. When we turn away from God, something alters in the heart. 'For out of the heart come evil intentions' (Matthew 15:19). But repentance also begins in the heart. Jesus calls people to a 'change of heart', to repent and return to God's love. Jesus uses the imagery of the heart to show us that it is with the heart that we love; it is within the heart that the seeds of compassion and forgiveness are sown; it is with the heart that we forgive; it is in the heart that our desire for God ultimately resides.

> No matter how sinful we human beings become, the desire for God never dies. . . . In Jesus Christ, we can overcome the power of sin, for it is the Lord's desire that all come to salvation.
>
> —USCCA, 72

Jesus reminds us that the desire for God is written in the hearts of all of us; that we are created in the image of God; that as children of God we are called to reflect God in our lives; that God shares divine love with us. Through his suffering and death, Jesus Christ triumphed over sin and radically changed the sinful state of all humanity, reinstating right relationship with God.

DIFFERENT KINDS OF SIN

The Catholic Church teaches that sins can be 'evaluated according to their gravity' (CCC, no. 1854).

Mortal sinfulness seriously disrupts our relationship with God. It is a full and total rejection of an option for goodness and a denial of the natural tendency for goodness and truth. It is the rejection of our very nature as human persons. We do not enter into mortal sin with ease or in haste. It is a lived choice that is reflected in a person's life orientation and way of being in the world. It is a choice about who we are at the core of our being—and so to 'be' in mortal sinfulness is always a grave affair, and is always accompanied by full awareness and knowledge and full consent.

Venial sinfulness reflects a broken but not a severed relationship with God. We become less than who we are called to be and we fail to live in accordance with the plan of God. We become less true to ourselves and distant from the humanity and dignity of those around us.

Social sinfulness produces 'unjust social laws and oppressive institutions. They are social situations and institutions contrary to divine goodness' (USCCA, 528). When we uphold the dignity of all human persons as created in God's image and likeness, we create a society that is based on truth and justice. However, when we deny that each person reflects the goodness of God and fail to uphold the dignity of all persons, we are in serious danger of creating a society that undermines human dignity through exclusion, discrimination, exploitation and oppression and we create structures that perpetuate injustice, fear and hate. In this case we create a culture of sin that often is hard to recognize because we ourselves are immersed in the structures. Through personal sin we contribute to and sustain the reality of social sin.

Our journey, then, as disciples of Jesus Christ is to reconnect with the truth that sets us free, to reconnect with God's plan for humanity and to seek once again that original state of harmony, love and justice. This is the journey we seek to help our young people to make in their own lives—the journey that brings them home to right relations with God which began on the day of their Baptism, when they became adopted sons and daughters of God and 'sharers of divine life and temples of the Holy Spirit' (USCCA, 193).

ADDITIONAL BACKGROUND READING

Catechism of the Catholic Church, nos. 369–379, 396–406, 1849–1869; *United States Catholic Catechism for Adults,* 69, 71–74, 155, 224, 226, 235, 237–338, 242, 245, 313, 331, 342–343.

Teacher Reflection

As you prepare to engage your group in a study of the reality of sin in the world, take a moment to read and reflect on these words from Peter McVerry S.J., from his book *Jesus: Social Revolutionary?,* as he comments on the challenge Jesus presented to us by reaching out to sinners.

> And all who saw it [Jesus inviting himself to a meal at Zacchaeus' house] began to grumble and said, 'He has gone to be the guest of one who is a sinner.'
>
> (Luke 19:7)

The challenge that Jesus posed by eating with sinners lay in the simple but deeply profound act of looking at a human being whom society considered of little value, of little worth, and recognizing that person's extraordinary dignity as a child of God . . . recognizing their privileged place in the mind and heart of God. That simple God-like act of reaching out and caring for someone whom most people considered of no value reflected God's vision of humanity and the compassion of God. In reaching out to them, Jesus revealed the nature of God.

REFLECT

Identify some practical ways in which you might reach out to those whom society considers to be of little worth.

CHAPTER 4: THE REALITY OF SIN | INTRODUCTION | 103

CHAPTER OUTCOMES

See general note on page 19 of this resource.

Learning Outcomes
As a result of studying this chapter and exploring the issues raised, the young people should be able to:

- see the genocide in Rwanda as one example of the reality of sin in the world;
- recognize our human tendency to 'turn a blind eye' to violence and injustice;
- understand sin to be an offense against God that wounds our human nature and injures human solidarity;
- understand that sin works against God's plan of goodness for humanity;
- know the three sources for the morality of human acts;
- appreciate that moral actions must always be measured by truth;
- recognize Jesus' response of loving the sinner but hating the sin;
- come to a deeper understanding of the teaching on sin in the Old Testament;
- recall the meaning of the Hebrew word *chesed*;
- understand the words *hattah*, *pescha* and *awon*;
- recognize that Jesus freed humanity from the power of sin and its consequences;
- become more familiar with St. Paul's teaching on sin;
- recognize forces or trends in life that blind people to the many faces of sin;
- know what actions are included among the Capital Sins;
- distinguish between sins of commission and sins of omission;
- distinguish between personal sin and social sin;
- distinguish between mortal sin and venial sin;
- recognize that Jesus overcame the power of sin and death;
- know that God offers us forgiveness in the Sacrament of Reconciliation;
- know about the life and work of St. Claudine Thévenet.

Faith-formation Outcomes
As a result of studying this chapter and exploring the issues raised, the young people should also:

- become more aware of their own struggle to choose between good and evil and to resist the effects of Original Sin;
- reassess their response to sin in light of Jesus' example of loving the sinner and hating the sin;
- reflect on how they are living up to their covenant with God;
- relate the biblical teachings on sin to their own lives;
- become more aware of their inclination to sin;
- recognize the connection between their personal sinful choices and social sin;
- identify ways in which they could work against social sin;
- be inspired by the work of St. Claudine Thévenet to reach out to the poor and vulnerable in society.

104 | CREDO | LIVING AND LOVING AS DISCIPLES OF CHRIST

Notes and Guidelines for Student Activities

ATTEND AND REFLECT

Where is the evidence for sin in the world?

Learning Outcomes

That the young people would:

⊙ see the genocide in Rwanda as one example of the reality of sin in the world;

⊙ recognize our human tendency to 'turn a blind eye' to violence and injustice;

⊙ understand sin to be an offense against God that wounds our human nature and injures human solidarity.

Faith-formation Outcome

That the young people would also:

⊙ become more aware of their own struggle to choose between good and evil and to resist the effects of Original Sin.

Overview

Chapter 1 begins with an account of a young woman's horrific experiences during the genocide in Rwanda. This provides the backdrop for our opening discussion on violence and injustice in the world today, and the tendency that people have to 'turn a blind eye' to sin and evil happening around them. We move on from this to explore the origin of sin, as revealed in Adam and Eve's rejection of God's plan of holiness and justice, and the consequences of sin. We reassure the young people that while we have a tendency to sin, our human nature has not been totally corrupted. As a consequence of Original Sin there is *an inclination* in human nature that engages every person in a spiritual battle between good and evil. We also remind the young people that God did not turn his back on humanity after the Fall. Rather, he promised to send his Son, Jesus, to save and redeem humanity. God is always faithful! The section ends with the life-giving news that through the gift of sanctifying grace in Baptism God restores us to a state of holiness. He offers us the graces we need to resist the effects of Original Sin and to live 'holy' and 'just' lives.

Supplementary Activities for 'Attend and Reflect'

Worksheet 1: 'Turning a Blind Eye' (*page 110 of this resource*) invites the young people to identify times in their lives when they were given the 'blind eye' by others, and also times when they themselves ignored the challenge of a particular moral issue and chose instead to 'turn a blind eye'.

_____

Worksheet 2: 'The Human Face of Sin' (*page 112 of this resource*) presents the young people with an extract from Elie Wiesel's famous novel *Night*, in which he recalls the pain and horror of being a prisoner in Auschwitz concentration camp during the Second World War. We invite the young people to reflect on the human capacity that is in all of us to portray and act out of our 'dark' and 'shadow' sides.

_____

Worksheet 3: 'My Multifaceted Self' (*page 114 of this resource*) presents quotations from two insightful people on the multifaceted nature of the human person. The first quotation is from Reverend Ruth Patterson, a Church of Ireland minister who ministered to both the Nationalist and the Unionist communities in Northern Ireland during the 'Troubles'. The other two short quotations are from the German Christian theologian and mystic Meister Eckhart. We invite the young people first to share their responses to these extracts and then to explore the 'shadow' and the 'light' sides of their own selves and begin to identify ways in which they can become the sort of person God calls them to be.

_____

Worksheet 4: 'Hardening the Heart' (*page 116 of this resource*) offers the young people the opportunity to explore the Old Testament image of 'hardening of the heart' as a powerful symbol for what happens when we sin and fail to live up to the goodness that God has planted in the heart of each of us.

CHAPTER 4: THE REALITY OF SIN | NOTES AND GUIDELINES | 105

HEAR THE STORY

The divine plan of goodness versus sin

Learning Outcomes

That the young people would:

⊙ understand that sin works against God's plan of goodness for humanity;

⊙ know the three sources for the morality of human acts;

⊙ appreciate that moral actions must always be measured by truth;

⊙ recognize Jesus' response of loving the sinner but hating the sin.

Faith-formation Outcome

That the young people would also:

⊙ reassess their response to sin in light of Jesus' example of loving the sinner and hating the sin.

Overview

Section two, 'Hear the Story', explores how sin impedes God's plan of goodness for humanity. We begin our discussion on the sources and the nature of sin by examining an extract from *The Hobbit* by J.R.R. Tolkien. We then outline the three sources for judging the morality of human acts and stress that the root of sin lies in the human person's abuse of the God-given gift of free will. We examine Jesus' response to sin and, through the story in John's Gospel of the woman caught in adultery, we lead the young people to see that, in condemning the sin but extending his love to the sinner, Jesus modeled how we should treat one another with compassion and forgiveness. We conclude the section by teaching that moral actions must always be measured by truth and not by the circumstances or intentions of the person committing the act. As Christians, we must not remain silent when we come face to face with evil and its consequences.

Supplementary Activities for 'Hear the Story'

Worksheet 5: 'Love the Sinner; Hate the Sin' (*page 118 of this resource*) offers the young people the opportunity to examine Gospel stories that highlight Jesus' capacity to look beyond sinful behavior and wrongdoing and reach out to the person who has committed the sin. Following on from this, we invite the young people to role-play or describe a modern scenario in which a young person confronts a situation of sin and is challenged to put Jesus' response to sin into practice.

Worksheet 6: 'The Morality of Human Acts' (*page 119 of this resource*) offers the young people the opportunity to apply the Church's teaching on the three sources of the morality of human acts to real-life situations.

Worksheet 7: 'Making Rash Judgments' (*page 121 of this resource*) uses some words of wisdom from St. Ignatius of Loyola to engage the young people in reviewing their inclination to rush quickly into judgment of others. We invite them to recall a recent judgment they made and to look at it anew in light of the advice offered by Ignatius.

Worksheet 8: 'Tolerance versus Truth' (*page 123 of this resource*) invites the young people to identify situations in which a person might be challenged to compromise on truth for the sake of tolerance or a desire not to offend the feelings and sensitivities of others.

Worksheet 9: 'Jesus' Compassion, Love and Forgiveness' (*page 125 of this resource*) invites the young people to examine the story of Jesus' encounter with Zacchaeus for evidence of how Jesus reached out with love, compassion and forgiveness to those who were marginalized and socially isolated.

EMBRACE THE VISION

'Do you reject Satan, and all his works, and all his empty promises?'

Learning Outcomes

That the young people would:

⊙ come to a deeper understanding of the teaching on sin in the Old Testament;

⊙ recall the meaning of the Hebrew word *chesed*;

⊙ understand the words *hattah*, *pescha* and *awon*;

⊙ recognize that Jesus freed humanity from the power of sin and its consequences;

⊙ become more familiar with St. Paul's teaching on sin.

106 | CREDO | LIVING AND LOVING AS DISCIPLES OF CHRIST

Faith-formation Outcomes

That the young people would also:

⊙ reflect on how they are living up to their covenant with God;

⊙ relate the biblical teachings on sin to their own lives.

Overview

Section three, 'Embrace the vision', begins with an exploration of the teaching on sin in the Old Testament. The heart of the Old Testament is the story of the mutual covenant between God and his people, and God's fidelity to his people when they turned their backs on him and on the Covenant We remind the young people of the Hebrew word *chesed* which the inspired sacred authors used to describe God's steadfast love. We guide them to see a correlation between the false gods of the ancient Israelites and modern gods such as money and power, fame and pleasure. We introduce them to three of the many words the Old Testament uses to describe the harm brought about by sin; namely, *hattah*, *pescha* and *awon*. We then turn to the New Testament teaching on sin and reiterate that Jesus Christ, our Savior and Redeemer, by his Death, Resurrection and Ascension, has freed humanity from the power of sin and from its consequence, death. We look at the parable of the Prodigal Son and see that the younger son's gravest sin was not his dissolute living but his rupturing of the relationship of love with his parent and family. We conclude the chapter by looking at St. Paul's portrayal of sin within the context of the old self and the new self.

Supplementary Activities for 'Embrace the Vision'

Research Activity

Invite the young people to choose a daily newspaper and, over the course of a week, to find articles or stories that they will 'categorize' under the biblical titles of 'Hattah', 'Awon', 'Pescha' and 'Chesed'. They may work in groups for this activity. At the end of the week they will write a formal report on their findings and share the insights they have gained.

'False Gods' Survey

Encourage the young people to work in groups and compile a questionnaire that seeks to identify the 'false gods' that young people are tempted to follow today. The questions should also invite responses in relation to why these 'false gods' are so tempting in today's culture. The young people could present their questionnaires to students of different age groups. Afterward, you might encourage them to share their findings with the class and then follow up with a whole-class discussion on the implications of the findings for society today.

Creative Exercise

Taking the Letters of St. Paul as a template, invite the young people to write a letter to the youth of their local parish encouraging them to seek good and to avoid evil in their daily lives.

THINK IT THROUGH

The many faces of sin and our response

Learning Outcomes

That the young people would:

⊙ recognize forces or trends in life that blind people to the many faces of sin;

⊙ know what actions are included among the Capital Sins;

⊙ distinguish between sins of commission and sins of omission;

⊙ distinguish between personal sin and social sin;

⊙ distinguish between mortal sin and venial sin;

⊙ recognize that Jesus overcame the power of sin and death;

⊙ know that God offers us forgiveness in the Sacrament of Reconciliation.

Faith-formation Outcomes

That the young people would also:

⊙ become more aware of their inclination to sin;

⊙ recognize the connection between their personal sinful choices and social sin;

⊙ identify ways in which they could work against social sin.

Overview

Section four, 'Think It Through', begins with an exploration of a passage from William Golding's *Lord of the Flies*, which highlights the human capacity for denying wrongdoing and evading taking responsibility for one's actions. We then examine the range and varying degrees of sin and explain the Church's teaching in relation to Capital Sins; sins of commission and omission; personal sin and social sin; mortal sins and venial sins. We conclude the section with a discussion around Christ's victory over sin

CHAPTER 4: THE REALITY OF SIN | NOTES AND GUIDELINES | 107

and God's offer of forgiveness and love through the Sacrament of Reconciliation.

Supplementary Activities for 'Think It Through'

Research Activity
Invite the young people to work in groups to search through newspapers and/or the internet for words commonly used by institutions, political parties, the media and others that distort or minimize the true reality of what the words are describing; for example, 'collateral damage' to describe the killing of innocent civilians or the destruction of civilian property during armed conflict; 'reengineering' to describe the elimination of jobs. Encourage the young people to discuss the effects or consequences of using such words and to write a brief description of how the words they found can distort the reality that underlies them. They could present their findings to the class as the basis for a class discussion.

Teacher Tip: You might invite the young people to watch the film *Les Misérables*, which portrays how, when a desire for goodness persists, good can triumph over evil.

Worksheet 10: 'Sins of Omission—A Study in Poetry' (*page 126 of this resource*) presents the poem 'The Sin of Omission' by Margaret Sangster (1838–1912) as a basis for examining the human capacity to sin by failing to do or say something good.

Worksheet 11: 'A Story about Conflict' (*page 128 of this resource*) presents an ancient rabbinic story that offers valuable insights into the ultimate futility of conflict.

Worksheet 12: 'Taking a Stand' (*page 130 of this resource*) presents the campaign by Jim Keady, founder of Education for Justice and Team Sweat, for the rights of the workers in Nike's sweatshops as the basis for a discussion on our responsibility as Christians to take a stand against injustices in society.

Worksheet 13: 'Christ's Victory over Sin' (*page 132 of this resource*) provides an opportunity for the young people to explore how Jesus responded to the evil and hatred that surrounded him in the days leading up to his death and to reflect on the fact that, by his Death, Resurrection and Ascension, he overcame the power of evil and death and won redemption for humankind.

JUDGE AND ACT

Learning Outcome
That the young people would:
⊙ know about the life and work of St. Claudine Thévenet.

Faith-formation Outcome
That the young people would also:
⊙ be inspired by the work of St. Claudine Thévenet to reach out to the poor and vulnerable in society.

Overview
In section five, 'Judge and Act', the young people review the teachings of the Church that they have learned about in this chapter. They also learn about St. Claudine Thévenet (1774–1837), founder of the Congregation of Religious of Jesus and Mary at Pierres Plantees in Lyons, France, who dedicated her life to working on behalf of the poor and against the sinful structures of society.

Supplementary Activity for 'Judge and Act'

Teacher Tip: You might organize for the young people to look at the film *Erin Brockovich* (2000), in which an unemployed single mother becomes a legal assistant and almost single-handedly brings down a California power company accused of polluting a city's water supply. Afterward, invite the young people to suggest ways in which ordinary students like themselves could work against social sins and sinful structures.

108 | CREDO | LIVING AND LOVING AS DISCIPLES OF CHRIST

Additional Prayer Suggestions

You might like to use this prayer by Reverend Ruth Patterson with your class as the basis for some prayerful reflection.

A Prayer

Lord, You are the God of surprises.
Thank you that what you have in mind
for each one of us
and for all of us together
is something far greater than we could ask
for, or even imagine. . . .

Thank you
for the times when You have brought
treasures out of darkness for us;
for light that began to shine in places of
shadow;
for doorways of hope opening up
in what seemed an unending valley of
trouble.

Lord, we have been wounded and hurt by
life and by people;
we have also wounded and hurt ourselves
and others;
but thank you that you still have that
special,
unique image of each of us
in Your mind and heart.

Where part of that has been anaesthetized,
exiled, trapped,
You are calling us to awaken,
to return,
to discover the truth that will set us free.

In a world where there is so much
movement,
change
and accompanying insecurity,
thank you that the one constant
unchanging
unfaltering thing
is the way you love us.

Give us the courage, in the assurance of
that unchanging love
to truly become a pilgrim people,
to risk setting out with You on an inner
journey
that will lead to the wholeness
that You desire for each one of us. . . .

Scripture Reflection

(See instructions for the use of doodling in prayer in the 'Student Activity Tool Kit', page 394 of this resource.)

Use this psalm verse to engage the young people in prayer:

The Lord is my light and my salvation.

—PSALM 27:1

CHAPTER 4: THE REALITY OF SIN | NOTES AND GUIDELINES | 109

CHAPTER 4 | WORKSHEET 1

NAME:

Turning a Blind Eye

History is full of examples of people turning a blind eye and pretending not to notice what is happening around them. Indeed, in our own lives we have all experienced the 'blind eye' being turned to us when we were in need, and we ourselves have also turned the blind eye on others. This worksheets offers you the opportunity to examine when and why people 'turn a blind eye' and ignore the needs of others.

PAIR AND SHARE
- Work with a partner.
- List five typical 'reasons' or 'excuses' people give for 'turning a blind eye'.

1. _____
   _____
2. _____
   _____
3. _____
   _____
4. _____
   _____
5. _____
   _____

OVER TO YOU
Think of a time when you experienced 'the blind eye'—when one or more people deliberately failed to take notice of or attend to your needs.

Name the incident.

_____
_____

What happened?

_____
_____
_____

110 | CREDO | LIVING AND LOVING AS DISCIPLES OF CHRIST

CHAPTER 4 | WORKSHEET 1 (CONTD.)

What did you wish would happen?

_____

_____

_____

Why do you think the blind eye was 'given' to you?

_____

_____

_____

Now recall a time when you willfully turned the blind eye to the needs of others.

Name the incident.

_____

_____

What happened? How did you feel when you turned your attention away from the person or people involved?

_____

_____

_____

Why do you think you acted in that way?

_____

_____

_____

What might you do differently if you were faced with the same situation again?

_____

_____

_____

CLASS DISCUSSION
◉ What does it feel like to have one's needs or cry for help ignored?
◉ Are there times when it is 'appropriate' for a person to turn a blind eye to something that is happening? Explain.
◉ Are there times when communities or companies or schools/colleges or governments turn a blind eye? Share examples.
◉ What words of Jesus might challenge us when we feel inclined to turn a blind eye?

CHAPTER 4: THE REALITY OF SIN | WORKSHEET 1 (CONTD.) | 111

CHAPTER 4 | WORKSHEET 2

NAME:

The Human Face of Sin

Elie Wiesel was born in 1928 in Sighet, a town in northern Romania. He was just a teenager when he was taken captive along with his father and transported to Auschwitz concentration camp. He later spent time as a prisoner in Buna and Buchenwald concentration camps. Wiesel recalled those terrifying experiences, which brought death to his father, mother and sister, in his book called *Night*. This worksheet presents an excerpt from that book and invites you to reflect on and discuss the human capacity that is in all of us to portray and act out of our 'dark' and 'shadow' sides.

READ AND REFLECT

Take some time to read this excerpt from Elie Wiesel's *Night*, in which Wiesel tells the story of how he was forced to give up his crowned tooth—not to one of the Nazi officers but to one of his own.

> Franek, the foreman, one day noticed the gold crowned tooth in my mouth.
>   'Give me your crown, kid.
>   I told him it was impossible, that I could not eat without it.
>   'What do they give you to eat, anyway?'
>   I found another answer; the crown had been put on a list after the medical inspection. This could bring trouble on us both.
>   'If you don't give me your crown, you'll pay for it even more.'
>   This sympathetic, intelligent youth was suddenly no longer the same person. His eyes gleamed with desire. I told him I had to ask my father's advice.
>   'Ask your father, kid. But I want an answer by tomorrow.'
>   When I spoke to my father about it, he turned pale, was silent a long while, and then said, 'No, son, you mustn't do it.'
>   'He'll take it out on us!'
>   'He won't dare.'
>   But alas, Franek knew where to touch me; he knew my weak point. My father had never done military service, and he had never succeeded in marching in step. Here, every time we moved from one place to another in a body, we marched in strict rhythm. This was Franek's chance to torment my father and to thrash him savagely every day. Left, right: punch! Left, right: clout!
>   I decided to give my father lessons myself, to teach him to change step, and to keep to the rhythm. . . . But my father's progress was still inadequate, and blows continued to rain down on him. . . . These scenes were repeated for two weeks. We could not stand any more. We had to give in. When the day came, Franek burst into wild laughter.

112 | CREDO | LIVING AND LOVING AS DISCIPLES OF CHRIST

CHAPTER 4 | WORKSHEET 2 (CONTD.)

'I knew it, I knew quite well I would win. Better late than never. And because you've made me wait, that's going to cost you a ration of bread. A ration of bread for one of my pals, a famous dentist from Warsaw, so that he can take your crown out.'

'What? *My* ration of bread so that you can have *my* crown?'

Franek grinned. 'What would you like then? Shall I break your teeth with my fist?'

That same evening, in the lavatory, the dentist from Warsaw pulled out my crowned tooth, with the aid of a rusty spoon.

PAIR AND SHARE
- Share your reactions to this text with a partner.
- What stands out for you the most?
- What do you think happened within Franek, a 'sympathetic, intelligent youth', that caused him to act in such a cruel way?
- What does the piece tell us about the human capacity to become ruthless, mean and hard?
- How might this extract help us to see the effects of sin?

JOURNAL EXERCISE
The horrific experiences within the concentration camp brought out the 'shadow' side of Franek. We are all capable of acting out of our 'shadow' or 'dark' side. Sometimes we do this because we feel afraid or hurt or angry or threatened. When we behave in such a negative way we are not being the person God calls us to be.
- Recall a time when you portrayed a 'shadow' or 'dark' side. Describe what happened. Then try to identify the circumstances that brought out this shadow side in you.
- Think about and describe how you might behave or act differently if you found yourself in the same situation again.

CHAPTER 4: THE REALITY OF SIN | WORKSHEET 2 (CONTD.) | 113

CHAPTER 4 | WORKSHEET 3

NAME:

My Multifaceted Self

Dr. Reverend Ruth Patterson is a minister in the Church of Ireland. She has been involved for many years in Restoration Ministry in Northern Ireland, a ministry that works to bring about reconciliation in difficult situations. From her work Reverend Patterson has gleaned many insights into human nature and the human capacity for both good and evil. This worksheet presents an excerpt from her book *Journeying Towards Reconciliation*. The worksheet also presents two short quotations from Meister Eckhart (c. 1260–1327/8), the great German Dominican preacher, theologian, philosopher and mystic.

READ AND REFLECT
Read this extract from Reverend Ruth Patterson's book *Journeying Towards Reconciliation* in which she explores the multifaceted nature of the human person.

> . . . if you think about it, all of us have at least two sides to our natures, a light side and a shadow side. Or, to put it another way, we could say that each one of us is a multi-faceted, many-sided human being. . . . I can never say that I 'know' another person fully, because to do so would be to limit them, to label them as less than human. There is always more to discover . . . each human being is mystery. When I reach the point of daring to say 'yes' to myself, then I am stepping out in faith, saying 'yes' not only to the mystery that is me, but also to this mystery that God has created.

Now read these quotations from the well-known Christian mystic Meister Eckhart.

> A human being has so many skins inside, covering the depths of the heart. We know so many things, but we don't know ourselves! Why, thirty or forty skins or hides, as thick and hard as an ox's or bear's, cover the soul. Go into your own ground and learn to know yourself there.

> God expects but one thing of you, and that is that you should come out of yourself in so far as you are a created being and let God be God in you.

PAIR AND SHARE
⊙ Share with a partner your responses to the insights the above extracts offer in relation to
  – the multifaceted nature of every human person;
  – the 'light' and 'shadow' side of our human nature;
  – the mystery of each of us that can never be fully defined;
  – answering the call to become the person that God has created us to be.

114 | CREDO | LIVING AND LOVING AS DISCIPLES OF CHRIST

CHAPTER 4 | WORKSHEET 3 (CONTD.)

OVER TO YOU

- Take some time to think about yourself and the person that you are, with all your traits and qualities.
- On the chart, try to identify aspects of your self that reflect your 'light side' and others that represent your 'shadow side'. You may use words and/or drawings or symbols to depict the different aspects.
- Then reflect on what you might do to bring some of the 'shadow' aspects of your being into the 'light'—thereby answering God's call to become the person he created you to be.

My Light Side	My Shadow Side

- Choose one aspect of your 'light' side that you are particularly proud of and one aspect of your shadow side that you would like to change. Then find a Scripture verse or passage that speaks to you about the wonderful multifaceted and unique being that is YOU.

CHAPTER 4: THE REALITY OF SIN | WORKSHEET 3 (CONTD.) | 115

CHAPTER 4 | WORKSHEET 4

NAME:

Hardening the Heart

We associate the heart with feelings of love, compassion and understanding, with openness and friendship. We often talk of someone having a 'good heart', of being 'kind hearted' or having a 'passionate heart'. Having a 'good heart' is central to our emotional and relational well-being, and it is equally important to our physical well-being. When the Old Testament writers used the stark image of 'hardening of the heart' they were telling us that when the seat of love and compassion hardens within us, that hardening of the heart blocks our capacity to love and to forgive and it has the potential to bring physical, emotional and spiritual havoc to our lives. This worksheet offers you the opportunity to identify and analyze times when you show hardness of heart and fail to live up to the goodness that God has planted within you.

REFLECT AND RESPOND

⊙ Take some time to reflect on the notion of 'hardening one's heart' as a powerful symbol for what happens to us when we sin.

⊙ Now think over your past week: the people you engaged with at home and outside of home; the activities you were involved in and so on. Identify times when you showed gentleness of heart, perhaps by being compassionate or understanding, patient or forgiving—times when you 'softened' your heart toward yourself and others. On the chart on the following page, under the heading 'My Gentle Heart', use words or symbols or images to depict these times.

⊙ Then think of the times over the past week when you might have knowingly 'hardened' your heart: perhaps you were impatient or judgmental, unforgiving or unkind, or harsh with yourself or others. Again, under the heading 'My Hard Heart', use words, symbols or images to depict these times.

116 | CREDO | LIVING AND LOVING AS DISCIPLES OF CHRIST

CHAPTER 4 | WORKSHEET 4 (CONTD.)

My Gentle Heart	My Hard Heart

PAUSE AND REVIEW

Take time to look back at the examples you gave of how you displayed both a 'gentle' and a 'hard heart' over the past week. Reflect quietly on these questions:

◉ What strikes you? Are there familiar patterns in what you have depicted?

◉ Are there some unfamiliar patterns that you are beginning to see?

◉ Are there certain people, or certain places or times that make it easier for you to have an open, compassionate heart?

◉ What causes you to harden your heart and close yourself off from others?

◉ Try to identify the people or things that might help you to 'soften' your heart—and then make a commitment to follow that course.

SCRIPTURE ACTIVITY

◉ Work with a partner.

◉ Look up ten of the Bible verses listed below and share what you think the Old Testament writers were trying to convey in using the image of the 'heart'.

Leviticus 19:17	2 Kings 22:19	Ecclesiastes 10:2
Deuteronomy 4:29	1 Chronicles 22:19	Ecclesiastes 11:9
Deuteronomy 4:39	Tobit 1:12	Sirach (Ecclesiasticus) 2:2
Deuteronomy 6:5	Psalm 16:9	Sirach (Ecclesiasticus) 7:27
Deuteronomy 10:12	Psalm 37:31	Sirach (Ecclesiasticus) 14:2
Deuteronomy 15:7	Psalm 40:8	Isaiah 51:7
Deuteronomy 30:10	Psalm 62:8	Isaiah 66:14
Joshua 24:23	Psalm 94:15	Jeremiah 4:19
1 Samuel 7:3	Psalm 139:23	Jeremiah 32:39
1 Samuel 12:24	Proverbs 2:1–2	Ezekiel 11:19–20
1 Samuel 24:5	Proverbs 3:3	Ezekiel 36:26–28
1 Kings 2:4	Proverbs 4:4	
2 Kings 10:15	Proverbs 23:17	

JOURNAL EXERCISE

Choose one of the verses from above that you think speaks clearly to young people today. Copy the verse into your journal and write a short paragraph explaining why you think it is of relevance to a young person like yourself.

CHAPTER 4: THE REALITY OF SIN | WORKSHEET 4 (CONTD.) | 117

CHAPTER 4 | WORKSHEET 5

NAME:

Love the Sinner; Hate the Sin

Jesus revealed both God's response to sin and the appropriate human response to sin and to the sinner. He taught that while we are to 'hate' and reject the sin, we are to love and welcome the sinner. This worksheet offers you the opportunity first to examine specific Gospel stories in which Jesus put this teaching into practice, and then to imagine and role-play a modern scenario in which a young person acts according to Jesus' teaching.

GROUP ACTIVITY

⊙ Work in small groups. Each group chooses one of these Gospel stories:
  – Luke 7:36–50: A sinful woman forgiven
  – Luke:19:1–10: Jesus and Zacchaeus
  – John 4:1–30: Jesus and the woman of Samaria

⊙ Read the story together and take particular note of
  – the person with whom Jesus is engaging;
  – the social status of this person;
  – the sin(s) this person has committed;
  – the manner in which Jesus relates to this person;
  – the words of affirmation and encouragement that Jesus offers.

⊙ Now work together to imagine and describe a modern scenario in which a young person confronts a situation of sin and is challenged to put Jesus' response to sin into practice.

⊙ When you are ready, either role-play the scenario for the class or have a representative of your group describe the scenario.

118 | CREDO | LIVING AND LOVING AS DISCIPLES OF CHRIST

CHAPTER 4 | WORKSHEET 6

NAME:

The Morality of Human Acts

The *Catechism of the Catholic Church* teaches that 'The object, the intention and the circumstances make up the three 'sources' of the morality of human acts' (CCC, no. 1757). The goodness of all three is required for an act to be morally good in itself. For example, a good purpose does not make an evil act good. This worksheet offers you the opportunity to apply this Church teaching to real life.

MEDIA ACTIVITY
⊙ Work in small groups.
⊙ Search newspapers or the internet for an account of a good deed. For example, you might choose a story about something good done for an individual or an organization or in response to a specific cause or issue.
⊙ Work together to analyze the action according to the Church's teaching on the sources of a morally good act, namely, the object chosen; the intention of the person acting, or the purpose of the act; and the circumstances surrounding the act.
⊙ When you have agreed on your conclusions, complete the chart on the following page.
⊙ In the 'Insights/Questions' box on the chart, note any insights you gained from this activity, or questions that may have arisen in relation to the issue you chose.

CLASS DISCUSSION
When you have completed the media activity, share your insights and questions with the class group.

JOURNAL EXERCISE
Recall a good act that you did recently. Apply the same analysis to this action as you did for the media activity. Write your analysis and conclusion in your journal.

CHAPTER 4: THE REALITY OF SIN | WORKSHEET 6 | 119

CHAPTER 4 | WORKSHEET 6 (CONTD.)

DESCRIPTION OF THE ISSUE

THE OBJECT	THE INTENTION	THE CIRCUMSTANCES

INSIGHTS/QUESTIONS

CHAPTER 4 | WORKSHEET 7

NAME:

Making Rash Judgments

Jesus said, 'Do not judge, and you will not be judged; do not condemn, and you will not be condemned. Forgive, and you will be forgiven; give, and it will be given to you'
—Luke 6:37–38

Every day of our lives we are called to make judgments. Sometimes we come to our judgments after careful and just consideration. Other times, however, we make rash judgments; we rush to quick conclusions and hasty interpretations that are often colored by our own ego, presumptions and prejudices. This worksheet offers you the opportunity first to study some words of advice from St. Ignatius of Loyola in relation to making judgments and then to see how his advice matches your own experience of making judgments.

READ AND REFLECT
Read this passage from the *Spiritual Exercises* of St. Ignatius of Loyola, in which he advocates applying understanding and love when making judgments.

> Every good Christian ought to be more ready to give a favorable interpretation to another's statement than to condemn it. But if he cannot do so, let him ask how the other understands it. And if the latter understands it badly, let the former correct him with love. If that does not suffice, let the Christian try all suitable ways to bring the other to a correct interpretation so that he may be saved.

Now recall a time in the past week when you made a judgment of someone.

What were the circumstances in which you made your judgment?

_____

_____

_____

What judgment did you make?

_____

_____

_____

CHAPTER 4: THE REALITY OF SIN | WORKSHEET 7 | 121

CHAPTER 4 | WORKSHEET 7 (CONTD.)

In forming your judgment, how did you interpret the person's thoughts, words or actions?

_____

_____

_____

_____

_____

What was the outcome?

_____

_____

_____

_____

Now review your judgment in light of the advice from St. Ignatius of Loyola. If faced with the same situation again, how might you approach your judgment differently?

_____

_____

_____

_____

_____

_____

_____

_____

122 | CREDO | LIVING AND LOVING AS DISCIPLES OF CHRIST

CHAPTER 4 | WORKSHEET 8

NAME:

Tolerance versus Truth

There is a lot of pressure in our culture today to practice tolerance toward all and not to criticize or condemn those who do not live by our standards. It can often be very difficult to express a view that is critical of others, especially when this view is not the popular or prevailing viewpoint. This worksheet invites you to identify situations in which a person might be challenged to compromise on truth for the sake of tolerance or a desire not to offend the feelings and sensitivities of others.

GROUP WORK
⊙ Form small groups.
⊙ Read this extract which you will have studied in chapter 4 of your theology text:

> Tolerance does not include ignoring the true moral nature of the actions of others. When those actions are contrary to moral law, to the teachings of the Gospel and of the Church, we are to name them as such. Moral actions must always be measured by truth. There are some actions that are just plain evil and contrary to the moral law by nature. The nature of such acts is not changed by the circumstances surrounding the act or by the intention or purpose of the person committing the act. In other words, the end never justifies the means. We must not show by our words or actions that we agree with the 'evil act' of another person in order to avoid confronting them or hurting their feelings.

⊙ See if you can imagine and describe five situations where a person might witness wrongdoing or sinful acts but feel compelled to compromise on the truth and ignore or go along with the situation for the sake of tolerance or to avoid confrontation, embarrassment or the criticism of others.

1. _____

_____

_____

_____

CHAPTER 4: THE REALITY OF SIN | WORKSHEET 8 | 123

CHAPTER 4 | WORKSHEET 8 (CONTD.)

2. _____

_____

_____

_____

_____

_____

3. _____

_____

_____

_____

_____

4. _____

_____

_____

_____

_____

5. _____

_____

_____

_____

_____

⊙ Now take one of the situations you described and share ideas on how as a Christian you might condemn the wrongdoing while at the same time offer Christian love and concern to the wrongdoer.

JOURNAL EXERCISE
Write a summery of the insights you gained from this activity.

124 | CREDO | LIVING AND LOVING AS DISCIPLES OF CHRIST

CHAPTER 4 | WORKSHEET 9

NAME:

Jesus' Compassion, Love and Forgiveness

This worksheet invites you to take a closer look at the story of Jesus' encounter with Zacchaeus for evidence of how Jesus reached out with love, compassion and forgiveness to those who were marginalized and socially isolated.

READ AND REFLECT

⊙ Read the story of Jesus' encounter with Zacchaeus in Luke 19:1–10.

⊙ As you read it, look out for evidence of Jesus displaying the characteristics of love, compassion, understanding and forgiveness that were his hallmark.

⊙ Then see if you can identify and give the biblical reference for specific incidences in the story that point to the following actions of Jesus:

Jesus' desire to connect and engage with Zacchaeus:

_____

Jesus showing respect for Zacchaeus through his words:

_____

Jesus seeking to be part of Zacchaeus' life:

_____

Jesus separating the act from the person:

_____

Jesus listening attentively to Zacchaeus:

_____

Jesus supporting and encouraging Zacchaeus:

_____

Jesus affirming Zacchaeus and offering him hope for the future:

_____

CHAPTER 4: THE REALITY OF SIN | WORKSHEET 9 | 125

CHAPTER 4 | WORKSHEET 10

NAME:

Sins of Omission—A Study in Poetry

This worksheet presents the poem 'The Sin of Omission' by Margaret Sangster (1838–1912) as a basis for examining the human capacity to sin by failing to do or say something good.

READ AND RESPOND

⦿ Read this poem which names specific ways in which a person might have acted for the good but neglected to do so.

⦿ Then read it again, this time calling to mind any examples in the poem that resonate with your own experience.

The Sin of Omission

It isn't the thing you do, dear;
It's the thing you leave undone,
Which gives you a bit of heartache
At the setting of the sun.
The tender word forgotten,
The letter you did not write,
The flower you might have sent, dear,
Are your haunting ghosts to-night.

The stone you might have lifted
Out of brother's way,
The bit of heartsome counsel
You were hurried too much to say;
The loving touch of the hand, dear,
The gentle and winsome tone,
That you had no time nor thought for,
With troubles enough of your own.

The little acts of kindness,
So easily out of mind;
Those chances to be angels
Which every one may find
They come in night and silence
Each chill, reproachful wraith
When hope is faint and flagging
And a blight has dropped on faith.

126 | CREDO | LIVING AND LOVING AS DISCIPLES OF CHRIST

CHAPTER 4 | WORKSHEET 10 (CONTD.)

For life is all too short, dear,
And sorrow is all too great;
To suffer our great compassion
That tarries until too late;
And it's not the thing you do, dear,
It's the thing you leave undone,
Which gives you the bit of heartache
At the setting of the sun.

—Margaret Sangster

JOURNAL EXERCISE
Reflect upon and describe some good works you may have neglected to do in the past
that you would now like to return to and not 'leave undone'.

CHAPTER 4: THE REALITY OF SIN | WORKSHEET 10 (CONTD.) | 127

CHAPTER 4 | WORKSHEET 11

NAME:

A Story about Conflict

This worksheet presents an ancient rabbinic story about a conflict between two men over a piece of land and what happens when they seek the advice of a rabbi. The story offers valuable insight into the ultimate futility of conflict.

READ AND REFLECT
Read the story and take some time to reflect on what you think is its underlying message.

Down to Earth
There were two neighbors who had adjoining fields. There was one part there that they had a violent feud over. Each one claimed that the part was his and refused to listen to the other one's arguments. Finally they agreed to approach Rabbi Chaim Volozhiner for a judgment. Each one stated his claims to the rabbi. The rabbi heard their arguments and suggested that he wanted to see the piece of the field that was in question. Maybe that would help him understand their individual points of view. The rabbi studied the layout of the land and its boundaries. Then he heard their arguments again.

All of a sudden, the rabbi bent down and placed his ear to the soil. The two men were astounded. 'What are you doing there on the ground?' one of them asked.

'I have heard your points of view about this piece of property,' answered Rav Chaim, 'but now I would like to hear what the ground has to say for itself.'

The men thought he was joking, so one man said in a humorous tone, 'All right, so indeed tell us—what does the ground say?'

Rav Chaim smiled at them and said, 'The ground finds it hard to understand the anger and short-sightedness of both of you. It says, "This one claims that I belong to him, then the other one claims that no, I belong to him. The truth, though, is that eventually they will both belong to me!"'

PAIR AND SHARE
⊙ Pair up with a partner and share your initial response to this story.
⊙ What do you think is the main message? Share your interpretations.
⊙ What do you think the ground represents?
⊙ Does this story remind you of any stories from the Bible, or teachings of Jesus? If so, name those stories or teachings and explain the connection you see between them and the rabbinic story.

128 | CREDO | LIVING AND LOVING AS DISCIPLES OF CHRIST

CHAPTER 4 | WORKSHEET 11 (CONTD.)

OVER TO YOU

◎ Think about a specific conflict that you have been involved in, where you or another party stuck rigidly to the initial viewpoint and wouldn't budge.

◎ Imagine yourself back in the middle of that conflict.

◎ Who could you have turned to for advice—to help you see the situation from a different perspective?

◎ Can you recall any words of wisdom that you have heard or studied in your theology class that you could bring to the situation?

◎ Write your thoughts on the best path you now see for resolving that conflict.

_____

_____

_____

ADVICE FROM SCRIPTURE

Locate and write out a Scripture verse or passage that will remind you to stand back and look at the broader picture when you find yourself in a conflict situation in the future.

_____

_____

_____

Then find and write out three examples of words from the Bible that could help you in such situations to focus on what is really important in life, and so help you to keep things in their proper perspective.

_____

_____

_____

_____

_____

_____

_____

CHAPTER 4: THE REALITY OF SIN | WORKSHEET 11 (CONTD.) | 129

CHAPTER 4 | WORKSHEET 12

NAME:

Taking a Stand

This worksheet presents the campaign by Jim Keady, founder of Education for Justice and Team Sweat, for the rights of the workers in Nike's sweatshops as the basis for a discussion on our responsibility as Christians to take a stand against injustices in society.

READ AND REFLECT

For more than a decade Jim Keady has focused much of his time and energy on improving the living and working conditions of Nike's overseas factory workers. Read these excerpts from an article in *The Huffington Post* in which Keady speaks of his work.

In 1997, I was in my first season as a graduate assistant coach with the Men's Soccer Team at St. John's University, the defending NCAA Division I National Champions. Along with my coaching, I was pursuing a Masters degree in Theology. For one of my first classes, I was charged with writing a research paper linking moral theology and sports. I researched Nike's sweatshops in light of Catholic Social Teaching. Simultaneously, the SJU Athletic Department was negotiating a $3,500,000.00 million dollar endorsement contract with Nike.

Within six months I was at the center of a campus-wide debate over whether SJU should ink the deal. Within ten months I was given an ultimatum by my head coach, 'Wear Nike and drop this issue, or resign.' I resigned in protest and became the first (and still the only) athlete or coach in the world to say 'no' to taking part in a Nike endorsement deal because of their sweatshop abuses.

. . . My critics charged that those were 'great jobs for those poor people' and that 'you can live like a king on a sweatshop wage in places like Indonesia'. I knew from my research that they were wrong, but I wanted to prove it.

In July 2000 I lived with Nike factory workers in Indonesia. I lived in conditions they lived in and on the wages they were paid—$1.25 a day. I lost 25lbs in a month in a rat-infested slum in Tangerang, Indonesia, home to tens of thousands of the women and men who produce the Nike sneakers adored by so many athletes and consumers.

. . . I conducted field research in 2001, 2002, 2008 and 2009; I took part in demonstrations on three continents; I met with an Indonesian President (Wahid) and members of the U.S. Congress; I led workshops and listening sessions with Nike workers from a dozen factories in Bekasi, Bogor, Bandung, Balaraja, Tangerang, and Jakarta; I lobbied Nike shareholders and was escorted by police from at least one shareholder meeting; I produced a short documentary, 'Behind the Swoosh', and am

130 | CREDO | LIVING AND LOVING AS DISCIPLES OF CHRIST

CHAPTER 4 | WORKSHEET 12 (CONTD.)

currently producing a feature documentary and writing a book, both under the title, SWEAT; I lectured at more than 400 schools in 39 states and in three different countries; and I met with representatives from Nike at all levels, including Nike founder and chairman, Phil Knight.

Has there been any progress? Has anything changed? Yes. For example, because of the pressure that was placed on Nike by consumers, women workers no longer have to prove they are menstruating to get their legally guaranteed leave. Also, workers are no longer beaten with machetes or threatened at gunpoint for union organizing activity. However . . . Nike workers are still being paid a poverty wage and Nike still refuses to bargain with their workers in good faith. . . .

I was in Indonesia as recently as August 2009 and in my meetings with workers I heard all too familiar stories of inadequate wages, forced overtime, illegal firings for union organizing, workers being cheated out of pay, etc. In part, what made this trip slightly different was that Caitlin Morris, Nike's Director of Sustainable Business and Innovation, accompanied me. So now, when I put forth a charge about Nike's sweatshop abuses, Nike cannot say it isn't true as Ms. Morris was in the room with me when the latest round of videotaped allegations were made. . . .

So, what do we do to get Nike to take action on the wage and collective bargaining issues? The same stuff we did to get them to move on the other human rights violations. We engage, we demonstrate, we publicly embarrass, and we organize, organize, organize!

CLASS DISCUSSION

⊙ Do you agree or disagree with the stance Jim Keady has taken? Share your views.

⊙ How does his campaign reflect the principles of Catholic Social Teaching?

⊙ Do you know of anyone else who has taken a strong stance in defense of justice—at a local or national level? Perhaps you have taken a stance yourself on some issue? If so, share that story.

⊙ What might be the implications of standing up for justice in this way?

CHAPTER 4: THE REALITY OF SIN | WORKSHEET 12 (CONTD.) | 131

CHAPTER 4 | WORKSHEET 13

NAME:

Christ's Victory over Sin

During his Passion Jesus experienced sin in many forms. *The Catechism* reminds us:

> It is precisely in the Passion, when the mercy of Christ is about to vanquish it, that sin most clearly manifests its violence and its many forms: unbelief, murderous hatred, shunning and mockery by the leaders and the people, Pilate's cowardice and the cruelty of the soldiers, Judas' betrayal—so bitter to Jesus, Peter's denial and the disciples' flight.
>
> —CCC, no. 1851

This worksheet offers you the opportunity to explore how Jesus responded to the evil and hatred that surrounded him in the days leading up to his death and to reflect on the fact that, by his Death, Resurrection and Ascension, he overcame the power of sin and death and gave birth to new life.

READ AND RESPOND

⊙ Work alone or with a partner.

⊙ Read one of the Passion Narratives: Matthew 26–27; Mark 14–15; Luke 22–23; John 18–19.

⊙ Take note of where sin is reflected in the words, deeds or, indeed, the inaction of the people. Write the Scripture references for the instances of sin listed on the chart, along with a brief description of the context.

Sin	Scripture Reference	Context
Unbelief		
Hatred		
Mockery		
Cowardice		

132 | CREDO | LIVING AND LOVING AS DISCIPLES OF CHRIST

CHAPTER 4 | WORKSHEET 13 (CONTD.)

Sin	Scripture Reference	Context
Cruelty		
Betrayal		
Denial		
Flight		

- It was because of Jesus' capacity to love, to have compassion and to forgive in the face of the evil that surrounded him that the good finally triumphed.
- Look again at one of the Passion Narratives and this time take note of where Jesus responded to the evil around him with compassion, truth, love, forgiveness, integrity, forbearance, serenity and mercy. As you identify each instance, add the reference and a brief description to the chart.

Jesus' Response	Scripture Reference	Context
Compassion		
Truth		
Love		
Forgiveness		
Integrity		
Forbearance		
Serenity		
Mercy		

PAIR AND SHARE

Work in pairs and share a story from your own life or from the life of someone you know where good persisted in the face of evil and eventually triumphed.

CHAPTER 4: THE REALITY OF SIN | WORKSHEET 13 (CONTD.) | 133

CHAPTER 4 | CHAPTER REVIEW

NAME:

Review of Chapter 4

I. **Fill in the blanks. Write the letter that corresponds to the correct term in the word bank in the blank space to complete each sentence. There are two more terms in the word bank than you will need.**

A. sin	**E.** healthcare	**I.** *Awon*
B. *Hattah*	**F.** freedom	**J.** racism
C. Original Sin	**G.** fidelity	**K.** education
D. Capital Sins	**H.** venial sins	**L.** *Protoevangelium*

1. Scripture reveals that human beings can misuse and abuse their God-given gift of _____.

2. As a consequence of _____ there is an inclination in human nature that engages every person in a spiritual battle between good and evil.

3. The _____ is the first announcement of the Messiah and Redeemer.

4. _____ corrodes our character and undermines our integrity.

5. The Old Testament reveals God's _____ to his people even when they turned their backs on him and on the mutual covenant.

6. _____ is the quality of people who are so distracted that they make erroneous judgments.

7. _____ describes the burden of guilt that a person experiences through sinning.

8. Anger and envy are two of the _____.

9. The *Catechism* describes _____ as 'a violation of human dignity, and a sin against justice'.

10. The main aim of the Congregation of the Religious of Jesus and Mary was the Christian _____ of all social classes.

134 | CREDO | LIVING AND LOVING AS DISCIPLES OF CHRIST

CHAPTER 4 | CHAPTER REVIEW (CONTD.)

II. **True/False. Mark the true statements 'T' and the false statements 'F'. In the case of each false statement, cross out and rewrite the incorrect words to make the statement true.**

_____1. The Gospel commands that we remain silent in the face of violence and injustice.

_____2. The Catholic Church teaches that the human person is intrinsically good.

_____3. God turned his back on Adam and Eve after the Fall.

_____4. Jesus taught us to hate and reject the sinner and to hate the sin.

_____5. *Pescha* describes the attitude that leads people to make good decisions.

_____6. St. Paul often portrays sin within the context of the old self and the new self.

_____7. A person who knowingly and freely chooses to do or say something that is contrary to God's law and will commits a sin of omission.

_____8. A person who knowingly and freely chooses not to do something good that he or she has the responsibility to do and can do commits a sin of commission.

CHAPTER 4: THE REALITY OF SIN | CHAPTER REVIEW (CONTD.) | 135

CHAPTER 4 | CHAPTER REVIEW (CONTD.)

_____9. Every society has the fundamental responsibility to defend the dignity and rights of its members.

_____10. St. Claudine Thévenet worked to relieve suffering caused by the American Revolution.

III. Write a brief answer. Explain the teaching of the Catholic Church on 1 or 2.
   1. The difference between mortal sin and venial sin
   2. Social Sin

_____

_____

_____

_____

_____

_____

IV. How would you respond? A friend argues, 'Moral rules and standards are irrelevant. No act is good or evil in and of itself. It all depends on one's individual perspective and circumstances.'

_____

_____

_____

_____

_____

_____

_____

_____

136 | CREDO | LIVING AND LOVING AS DISCIPLES OF CHRIST

CHAPTER 4 | CHAPTER REVIEW (CONTD.)

V. Make a 'disciple decision'.

1. What is the most important wisdom for life that you discovered in this chapter?

_____

_____

_____

_____

_____

_____

_____

2. Name several ways you can put this wisdom into practice. Choose one of the ways you identify and describe how you will make that wisdom part of your life right now.

_____

_____

_____

_____

_____

_____

_____

_____

_____

_____

_____

CHAPTER 4: THE REALITY OF SIN | CHAPTER REVIEW (CONTD.) | 137

CHAPTER 5

The Liberating Power of the Ten Commandments

INTRODUCTION

Moral existence is a *response* to the Lord's loving initiative. It is the acknowledgment and homage given to God and a worship of thanksgiving. It is co-operation with the plan God pursues in history.
—*Catechism of the Catholic Church* (CCC), no. 2062

The dream of Yahweh is for the world to be transformed and for the presence of God to be allowed to break through. As Christians, we are called to work toward that transformation so that God's presence becomes obvious and that 'God with us' is a reality expressed in the way we live our daily lives, in our right relations with one another, in our solidarity and in our thirst for truth and justice and peace. The Ten Commandments give us guidance as disciples of Jesus to bring about the Kingdom of God.

The gift of the Commandments is the gift of God himself and his holy will. In making his will known, God reveals himself to his people.
—CCC, no. 2059

Through the Commandments the people of Israel gradually came to know God, to love what God loves, to see as God sees and to trust in God's friendship and fidelity. In this sense, the Commandments are the Word of God. They belong to God's Revelation and teach us what it means to be truly human.

Chapter 5 is developed under five major headings:

- ⊙ **ATTEND AND REFLECT:** What good deeds must you do?
- ⊙ **HEAR THE STORY:** 'I am the LORD your God'
- ⊙ **EMBRACE THE VISION:** 'You shall have no other gods before me'
- ⊙ **THINK IT THROUGH:** Living the First Commandment
- ⊙ **JUDGE AND ACT:** (*Activities and exercises that encourage the young people to integrate what they have learned in the chapter into their daily lives*)

Theological Background for the Teacher

THE EXODUS EXPERIENCE

The Decalogue must first be understood in the context of the Exodus, God's great liberating event at the center of the Old Covenant.
—CCC, no. 2057

As the *Catechism of the Catholic Church* reminds us, the Decalogue must be seen in the context of the Exodus. In the Book of Deuteronomy we are given a vivid account of God's involvement in the lives of the people of Israel. The God of the Israelites is a God of freedom—a God who intervened in human history to set the oppressed free.

The Exodus narrative tells us of the suppression of the Israelites after the death of Abraham, when for many, many years they experienced great hardship at the hands of the Egyptians. It tells us about a people who knew what it was like not to be free, to be prisoners, to be slaves, to be at the receiving end of the repressive powers of a dominant force that inflicted pain and suffering, despair and death.

The Israelites knew at first hand the humiliation of being worthless, the ignominy of being stripped of everything they had in life, the loss of human dignity. They understood what it was like to be terrified, powerless and vulnerable, to be without hope, without a future for themselves or for their children. The Exodus account tells us how the Israelites over the years became downcast, dejected and despondent. They resigned themselves to the hopelessness of their misfortune and became dispirited and disunited as a people.

Imprisoned in a foreign land, they became disconnected from one another and powerless to unite themselves as a group or sustain themselves as a community. In the depths of their anguish they also became separate from their God, the God of their ancestors, who promised always to be with them. Their suffering blinded them to the presence of God in their midst. They forgot their roots and who they

138 | CREDO | LIVING AND LOVING AS DISCIPLES OF CHRIST

were as a People of God. However, throughout it all, God's love remained a constant.

The Israelites groaned under their slavery, and cried out. Out of their slavery their cry for help rose up to God. God heard their groaning, and God remembered his covenant with Abraham, Isaac, and Jacob. God looked upon the Israelites, and God took notice of them.

—Exodus 2:23–25

GOD THE LIBERATOR

Deuteronomy tells us about God's graciousness and powerful redemptive action for the people of Israel. God always remains faithful. God's desire was for their liberation from the misery and captivity of Egypt and to lead them to hope and freedom, to the Promised Land.

Then God spoke all these words: I am the LORD your God, who brought you out ofw the land of Egypt, out of the house of slavery.

— Exodus 20:1–2

God choose Moses to be the leader of the Israelites. Moses was to liberate them from their bondage and idols, mould them into a people and lead them to the Promised Land. Through Moses God entered into a mutual covenant with the descendants of Abraham. On Mount Sinai God made known to them the terms of the Covenant. God promised to lead them, to protect them and to remain faithful to them. The Israelites for their part were to remain true to their promises, to abstain from worshipping idols and to observe the law.

God's liberating action revealed his very nature: God is a Liberator who calls all people toward freedom.

Without freedom, we cannot speak meaningfully about morality or moral responsibility. Human freedom is more than a capacity to choose between this and that. It is the God-given power to become who he created us to be and so to share eternal union with him. This happens when we consistently choose ways that are in harmony with God's plan. Christian morality and God's law are not arbitrary, but are specifically given to us for our happiness.

—*United States Catholic Catechism for Adults* (USCCA), 310

GOD'S LAW: THE TEN COMMANDMENTS

The 'ten words' sum up and proclaim God's law . . . they contain the terms of the covenant concluded between God and his people.

—CCC, no. 2058

Several codes of law were in existence centuries before the Exodus experience. The most famous of these codes is the Code of Hammurabi, which dates from the second millennium BC. The Code of Hammurabi and other similar codes share some common ground with the laws of the Ten Commandments. However, one significant difference separates the codes of law that pre-dated the Ten Commandments and the Ten Commandments that God gave to Moses: that is, the context within which the Ten Commandments were framed.

The Ten Commandments possessed a religious significance and meaning for the Israelites that other laws did not. They were not just a code of law to be obeyed; rather, they were an external expression of the mutual covenant with their God. Relationship to a personal and caring God, and not mere duty and obligation, resides at the heart of the Ten Commandments. The Israelites experienced a God who desired to be with them in love and who wanted to be involved in their lives. 'Face to face at the mountain' of Horeb (Deuteronomy 5:4) God initiated a personal relationship of love with the Israelites and invited them to return that love. The context of a loving relationship with a personal God makes the Ten Commandments unique from all other pre-existing codes of law.

Hear, O Israel, the statutes and ordinances that I am addressing to you today; you shall learn them and observe them diligently. The LORD our God made a covenant with us at Horeb. Not with our ancestors did the LORD make this covenant, but with us, who are all of us here alive today. The LORD spoke with you face to face at the mountain, out of the fire.

—Deuteronomy 5:1–4

Written by the 'finger of God', the Ten Commandments communicate a people's hope in and faithfulness to a God who cares deeply about them.

The First Commandment: 'I am the LORD your God, who brought you out of the land of Egypt, out of the house of slavery; you shall have no other gods before me. You shall not make for yourself an idol, whether in the form of anything that is in heaven above, or that is on the earth beneath, or that is in the water under

CHAPTER 5: THE LIBERATING POWER OF THE TEN COMMANDMENTS | INTRODUCTION | 139 the earth. You shall not bow down to them or worship them' (Exodus 20:2–5).

'It is written, "Worship the Lord your God, and serve only him" ' (Matthew 4:10).

In speaking 'the first word', the First Commandment, God reminded the people of his liberating action on their behalf. God is 'always the same, faithful and just, without any evil. . . . He is almighty, merciful and infinitely beneficent' (CCC, no. 2086). In the face of such a God the people are challenged to acknowledge him as Lord, 'I am the Lord' (CCC, no. 2086). The First Commandment calls us to offer worship to God, both as individuals and as members of a community. Superstition, sacrilege, simony, idolatry and atheism are all contrary to the First Commandment.

JESUS—THE NEW COVENANT

'Do not think that I have come to abolish the law or the prophets; I have come not to abolish but to fulfill.'

—Matthew 5:17

Jesus in his life, Death, Resurrection and Ascension was the perfect fulfillment of the law of God. In the Sermon on the Mount Jesus presented God's law 'in light of the grace of the New Covenant' (CCC, no. 577):

'Do to others as you would have them do to you; for this is the law and the prophets.'

—Matthew 7:12

The law of the Old Covenant was engraved on tablets of stone. The law of the New Covenant is engraved on the heart of Jesus Christ, the Servant who became 'a covenant to the people' (CCC, no. 580).

The story of the meeting between the rich young man and Jesus, narrated in Matthew's Gospel account, gives us a wonderful insight into the new light Jesus sheds on the Old Covenant. The young man gives expression to a fundamental question that lies at the heart of many of us: What exactly must we do to be true and faithful Christians? It is hard to imagine what the young man, sincere in his question, might have anticipated Jesus' response to be. But we can guess that the answer he heard: 'You shall love your neighbor as yourself' (Matthew 19:19) was not what he expected. In giving this answer, Jesus shifts the focus of obeying the law from 'doing' to a 'way of being'. If love, compassion and respect—for ourselves and for others—form the center of who we are as human persons, then our actions, our 'doing', will inevitably become a reflection of this 'golden rule' that resides in our hearts.

This 'Golden Rule' taught by Jesus in his Sermon on the Mount is a golden thread that weaves its way through the moral life of the Christian. It is a behavior that flows from life in Christ and in the Holy Spirit.

— USCCA, 324

This is our challenge as disciples of Jesus Christ. This is the New Covenant that we are being called to—a new love that fulfills and perfects the Old Law and that seeks to make God's providential plan for a world of peace and justice a reality.

Our Gospel commitment to Christ's Kingdom of love, justice, and mercy always includes advocating and supporting fairness for all. . . . We also are invited to experience God's love for us and to return that love to God and to our neighbor. Our love of neighbor includes our solidarity with the human community and a commitment to social justice for all.

—USCCA, 325

The Christian is called upon to act justly, to resist oppression, to take social action rather than just subscribing to a belief and knowledge system. The Ten Commandments form the basis of all true society because they tell us that we must live in love, harmony and peace with God and with all people. The values underlying the Commandments must be observed by people in private and in community, as well in their exploration of the world and in the development and application of science and technology. These values apply to all people at all times. As baptized Christians, we are aided in the living out of these values by God, who 'assists us in living our moral life through the divine gift of grace . . . the free and undeserved assistance God offers us so that we might respond to his call to share in his divine life and attain eternal life' (USCCA, 328–329).

ADDITIONAL BACKGROUND READING

Catechism of the Catholic Church, nos. 1803–1829, 2011, 2052–2074, 2083, 2196; *United States Catholic Catechism for Adults,* 87, 309, 315–316, 324–325, 327–328, 342–343.

140 | CREDO | LIVING AND LOVING AS DISCIPLES OF CHRIST

CHAPTER OUTCOMES

See general note on page 19 of this resource.

Learning Outcomes

As a result of studying this chapter and exploring the issues raised, the young people should be able to:

- know the origins and context of the Ten Commandments;
- understand that the Ten Commandments reflect the natural law;
- recognize that we are to interpret the Ten Commandments in light of Jesus' Greatest Commandment;
- understand the Exodus narrative as the story of God's liberating action on behalf of the Israelites;
- understand Moses' role as prophet and liberator of God's people;
- understand the Ten Commandments in the context of the Covenant and God's liberating love;
- know that the First Commandment calls us to worship God alone;
- identify some of the many forms idolatry can take in our lives;
- understand that obedience to God's Word in the Commandments will keep us on the path to true freedom;
- identify some of the things that ensnare young people today;
- know how the Theological Virtues help them to live their faith;
- understand what the First Commandment requires and what it forbids;
- know of how Moses led his people to the freedom that God had promised them.

Faith-formation Outcomes

As a result of studying this chapter and exploring the issues raised, the young people should also:

- value the wisdom that the Ten Commandments bring to their lives;
- recognize that the Ten Commandments are an expression of God's love for them;
- recognize the many idols that strive for their allegiance;
- take to heart Jesus' words, 'Worship the Lord your God, and serve only him';
- profess their faith in acts of adoration and prayer;
- look to Mary, the Mother of Jesus, as a model for their faith;
- be inspired by Moses' fidelity to God and by his commitment to fighting injustice.

Teacher Reflection

As you prepare to engage your group in a study of the liberating power of the Ten Commandments, take a moment to read and reflect on these words from Pope Francis.

The Ten Commandments are a gift from God. The word 'commandment' isn't fashionable. To today's persons, it recalls something negative, someone's will that imposes limits, that places obstacles to our lives. Unfortunately history, even recent history, is marked by tyranny, ideologies, mindsets that have been imposed and oppressive, that haven't sought the good of humanity but rather power, success, and profit.

The Ten Commandments, however, come from a God who created us out of love, from a God who established a covenant with humanity, a God who only wants the good of humanity. Let us trust in God. The Ten Commandments show us a path to travel and also constitute a sort of 'moral code' for building just societies that are made for men and women.

How much inequality there is in the world! How much hunger for food and for truth! How much moral and material poverty resulting from the rejection of God and from putting so many idols in his place! Let us be guided by these Ten Words that enlighten and guide those seeking peace, justice, and dignity.

—Pope Francis, quoted in *The Catholic Herald*,
12 June 2013

Notes and Guidelines for Student Activities

ATTEND AND REFLECT

What good deeds must you do?

Learning Outcomes

That the young people would:

⊙ know the origins and context of the Ten Commandments;

⊙ understand that the Ten Commandments reflect the natural law;

⊙ recognize that we are to interpret the Ten Commandments in light of Jesus' Greatest Commandment.

Faith-formation Outcome

That the young people would also:

⊙ value the wisdom that the Ten Commandments bring to their lives.

Overview

Section one, 'Attend and Reflect', begins by recalling the story of the meeting between the rich young man and Jesus, narrated in Matthew's Gospel account, and then invites the young people to identify laws that promote true freedom in society and allow people to flourish. This leads into our discussion on the Ten Commandments, which we situate within the context of God's relationship and covenant with the Israelites. We examine how the Ten Commandments reflect the natural law and how Jesus, by his life and his preaching, attested to their permanent validity. We explain that Jesus interpreted the Law of the Commandments in the Sermon on the Mount, unfolding its spirit and true meaning. Thus, as disciples of Jesus, we are to interpret the Ten Commandments and live them in light of the threefold yet single 'Greatest' Commandment of love for God, for neighbor and for ourselves. We remind the young people that this is our pathway to the fullness of life God created us to have, both here and now and in the life everlasting.

Supplementary Activities for 'Attend and Reflect'

Research Activity

Invite the young people to work in small groups to research the Code of Hammurabi, which dates from the second millennium BC, and to compare its laws to the Ten Commandments. In doing their research, they should pay particular attention to:

⊙ The historical context of the Code

⊙ The content of the laws: the principles and practices

⊙ The type of society/lifestyle that is reflected in the laws

The young people should also comment on how the personal relationship between God and the people of Israel make the Ten Commandments a very different type of covenant to the Code of Hammurabi.

The young people might like to present their research in PowerPoint or chart form for the class.

You may choose to follow the presentations with a general class discussion around the similarities and differences between the Code of Hammurabi and the Ten Commandments.

_____

Worksheet 1: 'Jesus Demonstrates the Spirit of the Law' (*page 146 of this resource*) invites the young people to examine how Jesus' words and actions in the story of the woman caught in adultery (John 8:1–11) challenged the scribes and Pharisees' understanding of the true spirit of the law underlying the Ten Commandments.

HEAR THE STORY

'I am the LORD your God'

Learning Outcomes

That the young people would:

⊙ understand the Exodus narrative as the story of God's liberating action on behalf of the Israelites;

⊙ understand Moses' role as prophet and liberator of God's people;

⊙ understand the Ten Commandments in the context of the Covenant and God's liberating love.

142 | CREDO | LIVING AND LOVING AS DISCIPLES OF CHRIST

Faith-formation Outcome

That the young people would also:
- recognize that the Ten Commandments are an expression of God's love for them.

Overview

Section two, 'Hear the Story', focuses on the Exodus narrative, on the leadership of Moses and on the Israelites' experience of being liberated from slavery, oppression and misery by God. We help the young people to see how the Exodus experience defined the Israelites as a people, formed them into a community and drew them into a free and mutual covenant with God. We recall how, at Mount Sinai, God invited the Israelites to enter into a relationship of trust and love, of promise and hope. We guide the young people to understand that God's liberating love was at the very center of this covenant. The Ten Commandments, which summarize the Law of the Covenant, give explicit expression to that relationship and covenant.

Supplementary Activities for 'Hear the Story'

Worksheet 2: 'The Concept of Freedom' (*page 148 of this resource*) presents a poem entitled 'Freedom is. . .' as the basis for a discussion and an activity on the topic of freedom.

Worksheet 3: 'Understanding Freedom' (*page 150 of this resource*) explores how our understanding of the meaning of freedom changes and develops as we move through the different stages of our life and as we reflect on our own experiences and relationships and on our engagement with the world around us.

Worksheet 4: 'Covenants of Old' (*page 151 of this resource*) invites the young people to research the other covenants that God made with his people prior to the Exodus covenant and to identify the signs, the promises and the obligations relating to each covenant.

EMBRACE THE VISION

'You shall have no other gods before me'

Learning Outcomes

That the young people would:
- know that the First Commandment calls us to worship God alone;
- identify some of the many forms idolatry can take in our lives;
- understand that obedience to God's word in the Commandments will keep us on the path to true freedom.

Faith-formation Outcomes

That the young people would also:
- recognize the many idols that strive for their allegiance;
- take to heart Jesus' words, 'Worship the Lord your God, and serve only him'.

Overview

Section three, 'Embrace the Vision', begins with a discussion on idolatry and the many idols that strive for our allegiance today. We guide the young people to see that when people pursue idols in place of God they travel deeper and deeper into a self-imposed slavery. On the other hand, when we respond to God's invitation to love and serve him above all else, we discover what it means to be free and truly 'alive'. We remind the young people that Jesus' whole life was one of obedience to his Father—an obedience rooted in love. The challenge for us is to choose to make God the center of our life too.

Supplementary Activities for 'Embrace the Vision'

Worksheet 5: 'God Loved Us First' (*page 152 of this resource*) takes its title from 1 John 4:10. In this worksheet the young people explore the concept of God's unconditional love for each one of them and God's desire that they allow the divine goodness planted in their hearts to be reflected in their lives.

Worksheet 6: 'The Lure of False Gods' (*page 153 of this resource*) offers the young people the opportunity to examine the attraction and power of today's 'false gods', which can tempt people away from worshiping God alone.

CHAPTER 5: THE LIBERATING POWER OF THE TEN COMMANDMENTS | NOTES AND GUIDELINES | 143

THINK IT THROUGH

Living the First Commandment

Learning Outcomes
That the young people would:
- identify some of the things that ensnare young people today;
- know how the Theological Virtues help them to live their faith;
- understand what the First Commandment requires and what it forbids.

Faith-formation Outcomes
That the young person would also:
- profess their faith in acts of adoration and prayer;
- look to Mary, the Mother of Jesus, as a model for their faith.

Overview
Section four, 'Think It Through', begins by reminding the young people of God's constant and never-ending invitation to come to know, love and serve him. We explain that the First Commandment calls us to be a people of faith and a faithful people and we introduce the three Theological Virtues of faith, hope and love (charity) which enable us to live out this invitation. We encourage the young people to look to Mary, the Mother of Jesus, and to the saints as models for their faith and as witnesses to how lives lived in obedience to God bring true freedom. We extol the virtue of religion and emphasize how adoration of God frees us from the slavery of sin and leads us toward holiness of life. Finally, we explain the concepts of polytheism, superstition, irreligion, atheism and agnosticism, all of which are forbidden by the First Commandment.

Supplementary Activities for 'Think It Through'

Worksheet 7: 'Bringing God's Compassion to Others'
(*page 155 of this resource*) offers the young people the opportunity to explore and identify (1) people in society today who are in distress and crying out for help; (2) examples of people who respond to these cries for help, and (3) ways in which they themselves can bring God's compassion to others by responding to the cries for help that they hear in the course of their daily lives.

Worksheet 8: 'Fighting the Thoughts That Enslave Us'
(*page 156 of this resource*) invites the young people to identify (1) any negative thoughts or beliefs that may be holding them back from being the person God created them to be; (2) the people and things that help them to be the person they feel God is calling them to be.

Worksheet 9: 'Living the Virtues of Faith, Hope and Charity'
(*page 158 of this resource*) invites the young people to identify the greatest challenges to their living of these virtues in their everyday lives.

Worksheet 10: 'Right Relationship with God'
(*page 160 of this resource*) invites the young people to create an imaginary chat show in which various biblical characters discuss their relationship with God.

JUDGE AND ACT

Learning Outcome
That the young people would:
- know of how Moses led his people to the freedom that God had promised them.

Faith-formation Outcome
That the young people would also:
- be inspired by Moses' fidelity to God and by his commitment to fighting injustice.

Overview
In section five, 'Judge and Act', the young people review the teachings of the Church that they have studied in this chapter. They also learn about Moses' perseverance and commitment in leading the Israelites out of slavery and on to freedom in the land that God had promised them.

Supplementary Activities for 'Judge and Act'

Research Activity 1
Encourage the young people to work in groups to identify popular movies or television programs that reflect either directly or implicitly the teaching that the Ten Commandments are pointers or paths to true freedom. Invite each group to prepare a presentation on one specific program or movie, outlining why they chose it and how it reflects this teaching.

144 | CREDO | LIVING AND LOVING AS DISCIPLES OF CHRIST

Research Activity 2

Encourage the young people to work in groups to research and explore media documentaries that portray inequalities and injustices in the world today. Invite each group to choose one example and (1) explain the nature of the injustice(s) highlighted; (2) summarize the findings and conclusions that the documentary presented; and (3) outline any suggestions or insights that were offered for how the injustice(s) might be redressed. The young people could present their findings to the class and invite the students' response.

Additional Prayer Suggestions

Guided Meditation: 'Living Each Day as Disciples of Jesus Christ'
(*See 'Student Activity Tool Kit', pages 394-6 of this resource, for further helpful suggestions in relation to conducting guided meditations.*)

Leader
Today, for our meditation, we are going to think about how we live as disciples of Jesus Christ in and through the ordinary, everyday moments of each day. It is through those everyday moments that we shape and form ourselves into the person we seek to be.

Sit comfortably in your seat.
Close your eyes and allow your body and mind to become quiet and still.
Become aware of your breath as it moves gently in and out of your body.
With every in-breath, draw into your body and mind a sense of stillness and calm.
As you breathe out, release any tension or anxiety or worries you may have.
Breathe in . . . and out. . . .
In . . . and out. . . .

Now think back over your day so far. (*Pause*)
Think of the people you have met in the course of the day. (*Pause*)
　　– people you met at home;
　　– people you met on your way to school.
　　– people you met while in school.
Allow the image of each person to come into your consciousness. (*Pause*)

Now, taking each person you have recalled one by one, become aware of how you were with that person today.

How did you engage with them?
Did you respond to them?

Allow a few moments for the young people to reflect.

Leader
Lord, you love us. You teach us. (*Pause*)
We try our best to listen to your guidance in our lives. (*Pause*)
We know you are with us always. (*Pause*)
We know you hear our prayer. (*Pause*)

Leader
To you, O LORD, I lift up my soul.
O my God, in you I trust.
All
To you, O LORD, I lift up my soul.
O my God, in you I trust.

Leader
Make me know your ways, O LORD.
All
To you, O LORD, I lift up my soul.
O my God, in you I trust.

Leader
Lead me in your truth. . . .
All
To you, O LORD, I lift up my soul.
O my God, in you I trust.

Leader
All the paths of the LORD are steadfast love and faithfulness.
All
To you, O LORD, I lift up my soul.
O my God, in you I trust.

—Based on Psalm 25:1–2, 4–5, 10

Allow a few moments for the young people to reflect. Then invite them to open their eyes.

Scripture Reflection
(*See instructions for the use of doodling in prayer in the 'Student Activity Tool Kit', page 394 of this resource.*)

Use this psalm verse to engage the young people in prayer:

O my God, in you I trust.

PSALM 25:2

CHAPTER 5: THE LIBERATING POWER OF THE TEN COMMANDMENTS | NOTES AND GUIDELINES | 145

CHAPTER 5 | WORKSHEET 1

NAME:

Jesus Demonstrates the Spirit of the Law

This worksheet offers you the opportunity to examine how Jesus' words and actions in the story of the woman caught in adultery (John 8:1–11) challenged the scribes and Pharisees' understanding of the true spirit of the law underlying the Ten Commandments.

READ AND REFLECT

Read this story from St. John's account of the Gospel and then pair up with a partner to discuss the questions below.

> Early in the morning [Jesus] came again to the temple. All the people came to him and he sat down and began to teach them. The scribes and the Pharisees brought a woman who had been caught in adultery; and making her stand before all of them, they said to him, 'Teacher, this woman was caught in the very act of committing adultery. Now in the law Moses commanded us to stone such women. Now what do you say?' They said this to test him, so that they might have some charge to bring against him. Jesus bent down and wrote with his finger on the ground. When they kept on questioning him, he straightened up and said to them, 'Let anyone among you who is without sin be the first to throw a stone at her.' And once again he bent down and wrote on the ground. When they heard it, they went away, one by one, beginning with the elders; and Jesus was left alone with the woman standing before him. Jesus straightened up and said to her, 'Woman, where are they? Has no one condemned you?' She said, 'No one, sir.' And Jesus said, 'Neither do I condemn you. Go your way, and from now on do not sin again.'

◉ What understanding of the Law of Moses were the scribes and Pharisees operating from? What might have shaped their particular understanding of the Law?

◉ Do you think the woman might have had a different understanding of the same Law? Explain.

◉ The men would have felt that it was within their right to stone the woman. How did Jesus challenge them? What did he ask them to do?

◉ How might taking to heart Jesus' Great Commandment—that we should love God with our whole heart, soul and mind and love others as ourselves because of our love for God—have changed the men's way of thinking—and, ultimately, their way of acting and reacting?

◉ How do you think the woman would have felt after this episode: about Jesus? About the scribes and Pharisees? About herself and her own life and behavior?

146 | CREDO | LIVING AND LOVING AS DISCIPLES OF CHRIST

CHAPTER 5 | WORKSHEET 1 (CONTD.)

ROLE-PLAY ACTIVITY

⊙ Divide into three groups, with each group taking one of the following scenarios to act out:
  – The dialogue between the woman and Jesus
  – The dialogue between the men and Jesus
  – The dialogue between the woman and the men.
⊙ Share your ideas first about how the dialogue might run. Recall any insights or observations you gained from your previous discussions on the story.
⊙ When you are ready, role-play your dialogue for the class.

JOURNAL EXERCISE

Write your own description of the spirit underlying the Ten Commandments, in light of what Jesus taught in the Great Commandment.

CHAPTER 5: THE LIBERATING POWER OF THE TEN COMMANDMENTS | WORKSHEET 1 (CONTD.) | 147

CHAPTER 5 | WORKSHEET 2

NAME:

The Concept of Freedom

This worksheet offers you the opportunity to read a poem about freedom as the basis for a discussion and an activity on the topic of freedom.

READ AND SHARE
- Work in pairs.
- Take turns to read the poem out loud to one another. Read it slowly. As each person reads the poem aloud, the other listens.

Freedom is . . .
Freedom is when the mind, the body or the spirit
is released from its chains
    to soar to the heights
    and dip and dive
    and wander or wonder
    and taste or feel,
no longer bound or restrained
    by obligation or fear
    by oppression or subjugation
    by hunger or cold
    by despair or doubt,
but led now by a vision
    of endless possibilities
    opportunities
    openings
for LIFE and LOVE and HOPE.

- Now read the poem alone and write down words, reactions, insights or questions that spring to mind.
- Share your insights with your partner and discuss:
  – What is the poem saying about freedom?
  – What difference would it make to your life and to the lives of others if you looked upon freedom in this way?
  – How does the poem connect with your own experience of freedom?
  – What are some of the things that bind or restrain you—that limit your freedom?
  – Does your faith impact upon your experience of freedom? Why or why not?

CHAPTER 5 | WORKSHEET 2 (CONTD.)

OVER TO YOU

In the space provided below, write your own word cloud or poem to depict what freedom means to you.

CLASS ACTIVITY

You might like to assemble some of the word clouds or poems to create a class collage.

CHAPTER 5: THE LIBERATING POWER OF THE TEN COMMANDMENTS | WORKSHEET 2 (CONTD.) | 149

CHAPTER 5 | WORKSHEET 3

NAME:

Understanding Freedom

This worksheet invites you to reflect on and articulate how your understanding of freedom has changed and developed during the various stages of your life, from early childhood to the present day, and to identify the experiences and relationships that have influenced that development.

REFLECT AND RESPOND

⊙ Before filling in the chart, spend some time thinking about what the concept of freedom means to you in your life right now.

⊙ Also, consider these questions:
　– What helped to shape your understanding of freedom?
　– What people, events or experiences stand out for you as significant in influencing the development of your concept of freedom from childhood to the present day?
　– How influential were your parents or other family members, your teachers, your friends and your faith in helping to form your understanding?

⊙ Then complete the chart, identifying how your understanding of freedom has changed and developed over the different stages of your life.

When I was about _____ years old	I thought of freedom in terms of	I was influenced in my thinking by
When I was about _____ years old	I thought of freedom in terms of	I was influenced in my thinking by
When I was about _____ years old	I thought of freedom in terms of	I was influenced in my thinking by
Now. . . .	I think of freedom in terms of	I have been influenced in thinking this way by

150 | CREDO | LIVING AND LOVING AS DISCIPLES OF CHRIST

CHAPTER 5 | WORKSHEET 4

NAME:

Covenants of Old

The Covenant that God made with the ancient Israelites on Mount Sinai sealed the relationship between God and the people of Israel. However, God had entered into other covenants with his people prior to the Exodus covenant. This worksheet offers you the opportunity to research these covenants and identify the signs, obligations and promises relating to each one.

RESEARCH AND RESPOND
⊙ Work in pairs.
⊙ Read the accounts of God's covenants with Noah (Genesis 6:18–22 and 9:1–17) and Abraham (Genesis 12:3, 15:1–18, 17:9–10 and 22:17–18).
⊙ Identify on the chart the particular signs, obligations and promises that were part of each covenant.

Covenant	Sign of the covenant	Obligations of the Covenant	Promises of the Covenant
Covenant with Noah			
Covenant with Abraham			

JOURNAL EXERCISE
Read the account of God's covenant with Moses and the Israelites on Mount Sinai (Exodus 20:1–21) and describe any differences between it and the covenants God made with Noah and Abraham.

CHAPTER 5: THE LIBERATING POWER OF THE TEN COMMANDMENTS | WORKSHEET 4 | 151

CHAPTER 5 | WORKSHEET 5

NAME:

God Loved Us First

In this is love, not that we loved God but that he loved us. . . .

—1 JOHN 4:10

God loved us first. God desires that we allow the divine goodness that he planted in our hearts to be reflected in our lives. God's love is always there for each one of us. God invites us to return that love and he awaits our response. This worksheets offers you the opportunity to explore what God's invitation of love means for your life.

PAIR AND SHARE
- Work with a partner.
- Divide a sheet of paper into two columns: the first column titled 'What it means to love unconditionally'; the second titled 'What it means to receive unconditional love'.
- Brainstorm with your partner what unconditional love means—for the person giving the love and the person who receives it. Mention the feelings and expectations that accompany such giving and receiving of love. Jot down your responses in the appropriate columns.
- Look for a moment at the two lists you have drawn up. Think about how God's unconditional love matches up with the feelings and expectations you identified in the first column. Think also about how receiving this love matches up with the feelings and expectations you identified in the second column.
- Then look up and read these Scripture passages and share what each one reveals about God and his love for us: Jeremiah 31:3; Hosea 11:1; Hosea 11:4; 1 John 4:16; 1 John 4:19.
- Finally, share with your partner what God's love means for you at this time in your life. Share also what you think God desires from you.

REFLECTIVE EXERCISE
- Identify a person from whom you experienced 'being loved first'.
- Write a letter to him or her saying what 'being loved first' has meant to you.
- If you feel comfortable doing so, send or give the letter to the person in question.

152 | CREDO | LIVING AND LOVING AS DISCIPLES OF CHRIST

CHAPTER 5 | WORKSHEET 6

NAME:

The Lure of False Gods

This worksheet offers you the opportunity to examine the attraction and power of today's 'false gods', which can tempt people away from worshiping God alone.

Media Search

⊙ Work in small groups.

⊙ Search through magazines that are directed at young men and young women and take note of the things they propose for happiness and fulfillment; for example, in the areas of fashion, image, youth, beauty and the acquisition of material goods.

⊙ You might also examine TV advertisements for similar items.

⊙ List the top five attractions that are being presented to young people as highly desirable and recipes for happiness.

1. _____

2. _____

3. _____

4. _____

5. _____

⊙ Identify three strategies that are used to attract young people into believing that these things are necessary and worth striving for.

1. _____
   _____

2. _____
   _____

3. _____
   _____

CHAPTER 5: THE LIBERATING POWER OF THE TEN COMMANDMENTS | WORKSHEET 6 | 153

CHAPTER 5 | WORKSHEET 6 (CONTD.)

⊙ List three ways in which young people show that they believe in and take to heart many of the messages they receive from the media.

1. _____

   _____

2. _____

3. _____

   _____

⊙ Identify three reasons why the prescriptions for happiness and fulfillment offered in the media might seem more attractive to young people than the prescription for happiness and fullness of life that is offered through serving God alone.

1. _____

   _____

2. _____

   _____

3. _____

   _____

CLASS DISCUSSION

⊙ Share the insights you gained from this activity.
⊙ What surprised you?
⊙ What happens when people get drawn into accepting what the TV ads and popular magazines propose as recipes for happiness? In what way could these lures be seen as 'false gods'?
⊙ How might the promises made through the media be seen as limitations to our freedom? How might young people in particular become slaves to their promises?

JOURNAL EXERCISE

⊙ Write the First Commandment into your journal.
⊙ In the light of your explorations and the class discussion, reflect on and name any false god(s) in your life at present.
⊙ Write a prayer asking God to help you to remember that true happiness can only be found by placing God at the center of your life.

154 | CREDO | LIVING AND LOVING AS DISCIPLES OF CHRIST

CHAPTER 5 | WORKSHEET 7

NAME:

Bringing God's Compassion to Others

In the Exodus story we are told that the Israelites were in distress; that they cried out to God; that God heard their pleas and had compassion on them; that God, working through Moses, brought the Israelites out of slavery and into freedom. This worksheet offers you the opportunity to identify (1) people in our society today who are in distress and crying out for help; (2) examples of people who respond to these cries for help, and (3) ways in which you can bring God's compassion to others by responding to their cries for help.

BRAINSTORM EXERCISE

Brainstorm: Who are the people crying out in distress in our world today? Think of the people in our families; in our schools and colleges; in our local communities; in the global community.

RESEARCH ACTIVITY

◉ Work in small groups.
◉ Look up newspapers, magazines and the internet for:
  – words, phrases, statements or stories that express the afflictions of some of the people you identified in the brainstorm exercise above;
  – images or photographs that give expression to those who feel that they have no voice.
◉ Then look through the same sources for evidence of people who hear and respond to the pleas and cries of those in distress.
◉ Choose the best three examples of people responding to cries for help in society and share their stories with the class.

JOURNAL EXERCISE

Reflect on and describe concrete ways in which you could respond with compassion to some of the cries for help that you hear in your daily life.

CHAPTER 5: THE LIBERATING POWER OF THE TEN COMMANDMENTS | WORKSHEET 7 | 155

CHAPTER 5 | WORKSHEET 8

NAME:

Fighting the Thoughts That Enslave Us

Sometimes we can be a slave to patterns of thought that keep us from flourishing and reaching our full potential. These thoughts can poison our mind and harden our heart and damage our capacity for growth and change. They can enslave us and deepen our sense of isolation, pain, fear, hate or anger. This worksheet offers you the opportunity to identify (1) any negative thoughts or beliefs that may be holding you back from being the person God created you to be; (2) the people and things that help you to be the person you feel God is calling you to be.

REFLECT AND RESPOND
Think about the person God created you to be. Name some of the qualities you feel you should have in order to live up to being an image of God who created you.

_____

_____

_____

Identify any negative beliefs or thoughts you have *about yourself* that may be holding you back from being the person God created you to be.

_____

_____

_____

Identify any negative beliefs or thoughts you have *about others* that may be holding you back from being the person God created you to be.

_____

_____

_____

_____

156 | CREDO | LIVING AND LOVING AS DISCIPLES OF CHRIST

CHAPTER 5 | WORKSHEET 8 (CONTD.)

Now identify the people in your life who support you to grow and change, and mention briefly how they help you.

_____

_____

_____

_____

Identify the places where you find peace in times of distress, and mention how these places help you.

_____

_____

_____

_____

Write about how your faith helps you to become the person God created you to be. Mention any prayers that you find helpful.

_____

_____

_____

_____

_____

_____

_____

_____

_____

_____

_____

CHAPTER 5: THE LIBERATING POWER OF THE TEN COMMANDMENTS | WORKSHEET 8 (CONTD.) | 157

CHAPTER 5 | WORKSHEET 9

NAME:

Living the Virtues of Faith, Hope and Charity

As you learned in your theology text, the *Compendium of the Catechism of the Catholic Church* summarizes the centrality of the Theological Virtues of faith, hope and love for our living our life in Christ. The *Compendium* teaches that the First Commandment means:

> . . . that the faithful must guard and activate the three theological virtues and must avoid sins which are opposed to them. **Faith** believes in God and rejects everything that is opposed to it, such as, deliberate doubt, unbelief, heresy, apostasy and schism. **Hope** trustingly awaits the blessed vision of God and his help, while avoiding despair and presumption. **Charity** loves God above all things and therefore repudiates indifference, ingratitude, lukewarmness, sloth or spiritual indolence, and that hatred of God which is born of pride.
>
> —*Compendium*, no. 442

This worksheet offers you the opportunity to reflect on what is the greatest challenge to your living each of the Theological Virtues in your life right now.

REFLECT AND RESPOND

The greatest challenges to my faith right now are:

_____

_____

_____

_____

_____

_____

_____

_____

158 | CREDO | LIVING AND LOVING AS DISCIPLES OF CHRIST

CHAPTER 5 | WORKSHEET 9 (CONTD.)

The greatest challenges to hope in my life right now are:

_____

_____

_____

_____

_____

_____

_____

The greatest challenges to love (charity) in my life right now are:

_____

_____

_____

_____

_____

_____

_____

THINK IT THROUGH

⊙ See if you notice any patterns or similarities in what you have written for each of the virtues.

⊙ Think about what might need to happen in your life right now to help you with the challenges you have identified.

⊙ If there are people whom you feel you could talk to who might support you in addressing any of these challenges, make a firm commitment to seek them out.

JOURNAL EXERCISE

Write a prayer, poem or song asking God to increase within you the virtues of faith, hope and love.

CHAPTER 5: THE LIBERATING POWER OF THE TEN COMMANDMENTS | WORKSHEET 9 (CONTD.) | 159

CHAPTER 5 | WORKSHEET 10

NAME:

Right Relationship with God

Imagine that you are a member of a TV team that produces a weekly relationship-focused chat show. This worksheet offers you the opportunity to work with others in your class to create this week's show. The topic will be: 'Maintaining a good relationship with God.' The panel of 'experts' will be made up of characters from the Bible.

PREPARATION
◉ Form three groups.
◉ Each group appoints a **Presenter**, who will interview the participants and take questions from the audience.
◉ Each group invites volunteers (perhaps three or four) to play the roles of the **biblical characters**, who will be questioned about their relationship with God.
◉ The groups must then select their biblical characters. Some suggestions: Isaiah, Abraham, Moses, Adam, Eve, a psalmist, St. Paul—the list of possibilities is endless. (*Check in with the other groups to ensure that no character is chosen by more than one group.*)
◉ When each group has made its selection, the group members should share ideas on how the characters will describe their relationship with God.
◉ Review the material in your theology text, and perhaps in previous *Credo* texts, in relation to the biblical characters your group has chosen. The characters' responses should mention how they nurture and sustain their relationship with God; the characteristics or features of the relationship; the challenges they face in maintaining the relationship— from outside and from within themselves—and how they deal with such challenges; how their relationship with God impacts their lives and the lives of others, and so on.
◉ Ideally, the participants will back up their arguments with reference to events and quotations from the Scriptures. All the members of the group should contribute to coming up with ideas in this regard.
◉ The students who will take on the roles of the biblical characters may also need to do some research of their own so as to get into the mindset of the characters they will represent.
◉ The Presenter of each group needs to prepare the interview questions to ensure that the interviews run smoothly and that the questions elicit good responses from the participants.

THE CHAT SHOWS IN PROGRESS
◉ Each group takes it in turn to present its chat show.
◉ The Presenter introduces the panel with a brief description of who each biblical character is.
◉ The Presenter then interviews each participant in turn.
◉ When all the interviews have been conducted, the Presenter invites responses and comments from the audience.
◉ The Presenter may then summarize the key points made by the participants.

160 | CREDO | LIVING AND LOVING AS DISCIPLES OF CHRIST

CHAPTER 5 | CHAPTER REVIEW

NAME:

Review of Chapter 5

I. **True/False. Mark the true statements 'T' and the false statement 'F'. In the case of each false statement, cross out and rewrite the incorrect words to make the statement true.**

_____1. The Ark of the Covenant was the revered chest made to contain the Holy Grail.

_____2. The first three of the Ten Commandments pertain to our love of ourselves.

_____3. The Exodus was God's great liberating action on behalf of his people.

_____4. The ancient Israelites remembered and celebrated the Exodus during Hanukah.

_____5. When the Israelites were only a month and a half out of Egypt, they turned around and went back.

_____6. Jesus' whole life was one of obedience to his Father.

_____7. Mary, the Mother of Jesus, is a model for our faith.

_____8. Superstition is in keeping with the worship due to the true God.

CHAPTER 5: THE LIBERATING POWER OF THE TEN COMMANDMENTS | CHAPTER REVIEW | 161

CHAPTER 5 | CHAPTER REVIEW (CONTD.)

_____9. Sacrilege consists in profaning, stealing or treating unworthily something sacred.

_____10. The Romans rescued baby Moses from the River Nile.

II. **Matching. Write the letter of the term or phrase from column 2 next to its best match in column 1. There are two more items in column 2 than you need.**

COLUMN 1	COLUMN 2
_____ 1. Adoration and honor given to God	A. Decalogue
_____ 2. Mount Horeb	B. The Greatest Commandment
_____ 3. Acknowledgement of God as the Lord and Master of everything that exists	C. Agnosticism
	D. 'You have heard that it was said. . . . But I say to you...'
_____ 4. Faith, hope and love	E. Theological Virtues
_____ 5. 'Ten words'	F. Simony
_____ 6. Involves the buying or selling of spiritual things	G. Mount Sinai
_____ 7. Rejection of the existence of God	H. Moses
	I. Worship
_____ 8. Jesus repeated this phrase six times during the Sermon on the Mount	J. Adoration
	K. Spiritual Works of Mercy
_____ 9. Love of God, of neighbor and of self	L. Atheism
_____ 10. Prophet of freedom and liberator of God's people	

162 | CREDO | LIVING AND LOVING AS DISCIPLES OF CHRIST

CHAPTER 5 | CHAPTER REVIEW (CONTD.)

III. Write a brief answer. Explain the teaching of the Catholic Church on 1 or 2
  1. Idolatry
  2. The Decalogue and the Natural Law

_____

_____

_____

_____

_____

_____

_____

_____

_____

_____

IV. How would you respond? A friend tells you that she thinks the Ten Commandments do nothing more than stifle a person's freedom to live their own life. The Fifth through the Tenth Commandments are all about what 'not' to do.'

_____

_____

_____

_____

_____

_____

_____

_____

_____

_____

_____

_____

CHAPTER 5: THE LIBERATING POWER OF THE TEN COMMANDMENTS | CHAPTER REVIEW (CONTD.) | 163

CHAPTER 5 | CHAPTER REVIEW (CONTD.)

V. Make a 'disciple decision'.

1. What is the most important wisdom for life that you discovered in this chapter?

_____

_____

_____

_____

_____

_____

_____

_____

2. Name several ways you can put this wisdom into practice. Choose one of the ways you identify and describe how you will make that wisdom part of your life right now.

_____

_____

_____

_____

_____

_____

_____

_____

_____

_____

_____

164 | CREDO | LIVING AND LOVING AS DISCIPLES OF CHRIST

CHAPTER 6

Love the Lord your God
—The Second and Third Commandments

INTRODUCTION

God is omnipresent and life itself is the primal sacrament, namely, *the* visible sign of the invisible grace. The structures of our experience are the windows into the divine. When we are true to the call of experience, we are true to God.
—John O'Donohue, *Benedictus: A Book of Blessings*

What does it mean to be true to God? How do we allow the 'structures of our experience' to become windows into the divine in whose image we have been forged? Imagine for a moment a world where God was the focal point of our life, a world where God's love seeped into every thought we had, every word we spoke and every action we performed. If God were our overarching priority, what would happen—to us and to the world we inhabit? Would our engagement with others be different? Would we increase our efforts to create a world of truth and justice? Would we participate more fully in bringing God's plan for all humanity to fruition?

In chapter 6 we focus on the demands of the Second and Third Commandments and their challenge to us to put God first! Putting God first in our lives is the key to the very best of everyday living, offering us the promise that 'all things work together for good for those who love God' (Romans 8:28). The Ten Commandments are premised on having a loving relationship with a loving God. Having the Lord as our God has implications, however, for how we are to be—with ourselves, with others, with all of creation and with our God. If the Lord our God is the pivotal point of our life, then there can be no place for diminishing God, for disrespecting God or for not worshiping God. The way we hold the name of God in our hearts and on our lips is fundamental to our relationship with God. The Third Commandment, 'Remember to keep holy the Lord's Day', reinforces the importance of setting aside one day each week to worship God and to acknowledge God's place in our lives.

Chapter 6 is developed under five major headings:

- **ATTEND AND REFLECT:** What does a name tell us?
- **HEAR THE STORY:** You shall not take the name of the LORD, your God, in vain
- **EMBRACE THE VISION:** Remember to keep holy the LORD's Day
- **THINK IT THROUGH:** Love the Lord your God with your whole mind
- **JUDGE AND ACT:** (*Activities and exercises that encourage the young people to integrate what they have learned in the chapter into their daily lives*)

Theological Background for the Teacher

GOD OF THE ISRAELITES

Thus says the LORD of hosts: Return to me, says the LORD of hosts, and I will return to you, says the LORD of hosts.
—Zechariah 1:3

In the Ten Commandments God called the Israelites into a real and reciprocal relationship based on love and trust. This was not a distant, uninterested God but a personal God who addressed them directly and in the first person: the 'I' of the First Commandment speaks to each individual and issues an invitation: 'You shall. . . .' This, then, is a God who desires a response to the love that he has initiated. It is difficult for us today to understand the original impact of this Revelation for the Israelites. But Scripture affirms for us that the Israelites came to see this God as being apart from all other gods and to recognize his code of law as apart from all other codes of law known at the time.

We get glimpses of the uniqueness of the God of the Israelites in the Second Commandment: 'You shall not take the name of the LORD your God in vain.' The naming process is significant across all cultures: it connects us with our ancestors; reinforces personal characteristics; expresses the hopes of parents and families; denotes a change of direction in someone's life. The Scriptures contain many examples of where the change of a name signified the beginning of a new life, as in the case of St. Paul. In the Sacrament of Baptism we are named as children of God. In the Sacrament of Confirmation, when we affirm

CHAPTER 6: LOVE THE LORD YOUR GOD | INTRODUCTION | 165

our commitment to be a disciple of Christ, we may adopt a new name. The Israelites believed that a person's name encapsulated the very mystery of their personhood. They placed great store on honoring the name of a person and knew the power of defiling a person's name. The *Catechism of the Catholic Church* teaches:

> The gift of a name belongs to the order of trust and intimacy.
>
> —CCC, no. 2143

RESPECTING GOD'S NAME

To respect a person's name is to show respect for one's relationship with that person. The Second Commandment urges us to respect the divine name of God, who is the source of all love and life.

We explore with the young people how they are challenged in today's world to maintain their relationship with God and to reflect that relationship in the manner in which they talk about God. If God does not remain the focal point of our lives, then it can become easy to slip into the habit of diminishing the name of God. We do this when we willingly or unconsciously take God's name in vain; when we make false and rash promises using God's name; when we blaspheme the name of God in anger or in jest; when we speak ill of God or of Jesus Christ. Christians are called always to respect the name of God and his Incarnate Son, Jesus Christ.

KEEPING THE LORD'S DAY HOLY

> The third commandment of the Decalogue recalls the holiness of the sabbath: 'The seventh day is a sabbath of solemn rest, holy to the LORD.'
>
> —CCC, no. 2168

Scripture reminds us that the Sabbath has its origins in the account of God resting on the seventh day of creation (Exodus 20:11); that it is a memorial of Israel's liberation from bondage (Deuteronomy 5:15), and that it is a sign of the mutual covenant between God and his people (Exodus 31:16).

> Therefore the Israelites shall keep the sabbath, observing the Sabbath throughout their generations, as a perpetual covenant. It is a sign forever between me and the people of Israel that in six days the LORD made heaven and earth, and on the seventh day he rested, and was refreshed.
>
> —Exodus 31:16–17

The Third Commandment asks us to worship God on the Sabbath Day. The Christian Sabbath remembers that Jesus rose from the dead on the first day of the week. The Resurrection of Jesus recalls the first creation. And so, Christians celebrate the Sabbath on the first day of the week, Sunday, the Lord's Day.

> Jesus rose from the dead 'on the first day of the week'. Because it is the 'first day', the day of Christ's Resurrection recalls the first creation. Because it is the 'eighth day' following the sabbath, it symbolizes the new creation ushered in by Christ's Resurrection. For Christians it has become the first of all days, the first of all feasts, the Lord's Day—Sunday.
>
> —CCC, no. 2174

For Christians, Sunday is a day of grace and rest from work. The parish gathers the Christian community together, it teaches Christ's saving doctrine and practices charity in good works and brotherly love.

> Just as God 'rested on the seventh day from all his work which he had done', human life has a rhythm of work and rest. The institution of the Lord's Day helps everyone enjoy adequate rest and leisure to cultivate their familial, cultural, social and religious lives.
>
> —CCC, no. 2184

At the time of Jesus a very legalistic approach governed Sabbath observance. Thirty-nine different types of work were prohibited on the Sabbath; for example: 'You shall kindle no fire in all your [buildings] on the Sabbath Day' (Exodus 35:3). Jesus' approach was different. He contended that in God's eyes the needs of the people were more important than a legalistic observance of Sabbath law.

> The Gospel reports many incidents when Jesus was accused of violating the sabbath law. But Jesus never fails to respect the holiness of this day. He gives this law its authentic and authoritative interpretation: 'The sabbath was made for man, not man for the sabbath.' With compassion, Christ declares the sabbath for doing good rather than harm, for saving life rather than killing. The Sabbath is the day of the Lord of mercies and a day to honor God. 'The Son of Man is lord even of the sabbath' [see Matthew 12:5; John 7:23].
>
> —CCC, no. 2173

166 | CREDO | LIVING AND LOVING AS DISCIPLES OF CHRIST

In this chapter we seek to deepen the young people's relationship with and reverence for God, in whose image they are created. We encourage them to recognize the importance of taking time out from the busyness of their day to feel God's presence and to continue to seek ways to safeguard the centrality of God in their lives. By helping them deepen their sense of awe and reverence for God through reflecting on the Second and Third Commandments, we hope that they will continue to grow as persons of faith and come to know for themselves the sustaining graces of the Eucharist as they gather with other members of the Christian community to give praise and thanks to God on the Sabbath day.

ADDITIONAL BACKGROUND READING
Catechism of the Catholic Church, nos. 2052–2074, 2142–2155, 2168–2176, 2180–2188, 2744–2745; *United States Catholic Catechism for Adults,* 351– 371.

CHAPTER OUTCOMES

See general note on page 19 of this resource.

Learning Outcomes
As a result of studying this chapter and exploring the issues raised, the young people should be able to:

- understand the significance of names and naming;
- understand how the names of some key biblical figures point to their role in God's plan for humanity;
- understand that the Second Commandment calls us to reverence the holy name of God and forbids the abuse of God's name;
- know that we honor and respect God when we honor and respect his holy name;
- appreciate that all Christians are called to show the same respect for the name of Jesus;
- know that the Second Commandment also forbids blasphemy, false promises and false oaths;
- understand the biblical origins of keeping the seventh day of the week as the Sabbath day;
- understand that Christians fulfill the Third Commandment on Sunday, the day of the Lord's Resurrection;
- understand the wisdom of Jesus on the true meaning of Sabbath law;
- know what the first and third precepts of the Church command;
- understand why the Church calls us to come together for the celebration of the Eucharist on Sundays;
- know how the first and third precepts of the Church relate to the Third Commandment;
- understand what the term 'praying without ceasing' means;
- know about the life and spirituality of St. Ignatius of Loyola.

Faith-formation Outcomes
As a result of studying this chapter and exploring the issues raised, the young people should also:

- come to know God better by exploring the many names he has used to reveal himself;
- reflect on their use of the holy names of God, Jesus, Mary and the saints and commit to using them with reverence and respect;
- observe the Third Commandment by faithfully keeping the Sabbath day;
- come to a deeper appreciation of the value of the Sunday Eucharist;
- grow as people of prayer;
- be inspired by St. Ignatius of Loyola to 'slow down' and see God in all people and all things.

CHAPTER 6: LOVE THE LORD YOUR GOD | INTRODUCTION | 167

Teacher Reflection

As you prepare to engage your group in a study of the Second and Third Commandments, take a moment to read and reflect on this poem by John Shea.

Magnificat

All that I am
sings of the God
who brings his life
to birth in me.
My spirit soars
on the wings of my Lord.
He has smiled on me
and the blaze of his smile
no woman or man
shall ever forget.

My God is a gentle strength
who has caught me up
and carried me to greatness.
His love
space cannot hold
nor time age
and all quicken to his touch.

My God is a torrent of justice.
He takes the straight paths
in the minds of the proud
and twists them to labyrinth.
The boot of the oppressor
he pushes aside
and raises the lowly,
whom he loves,
from the ground.
With his own hands
he sets a table for the hungry
but the unfeeling rich
suffer the cold eye
of his judgment.

Our mothers and our fathers
he has held in his arms
and the future grows
like this child within me
for the God of whom I sing
bears us his son.

REFLECT
Reflect on how in your everyday life you are called to sing of the God who brings his life and goodness to birth in you.

168 | CREDO | LIVING AND LOVING AS DISCIPLES OF CHRIST

Notes and Guidelines for Student Activities

ATTEND AND REFLECT

What does a name tell us?

Learning Outcomes
That the young people would:
⊙ understand the significance of names and naming;
⊙ understand how the names of some key biblical figures point to their role in God's plan for humanity.

Faith-formation Outcome
That the young people would also:
⊙ come to know God better by exploring the many names he has used to reveal himself.

Overview
Section one, 'Attend and Reflect', begins by discussing the significance of names and identifies how the 'names' of a number of key figures from the Old Testament point to the role God willed them to have in his divine plan for humanity. The section moves on to explore how God, gradually and over time, revealed himself by making his name known. We examine two of these names in detail: 'YHWH' and 'Jesus'. We conclude the section by explaining Jesus' revelation that the name of the one God is Father, Son and Holy Spirit.

Supplementary Activities for 'Attend and Reflect'

Worksheet 1: 'I Have Called You by Name' (*page 174 of this resource*) offers the young people an opportunity to reflect on what it means to them to know that God has called them by name. You might like to play some quiet background music while they engage in this activity.

Worksheet 2: 'The Name of God' (*page 175 of this resource*) provides a framework for the young people to research some of the names for God that are found in the Old Testament. We then invite them to think of some new names for God.

Worksheet 3: 'What's in a name?' (*page 177 of this resource*) invites the young people to study a selection of biblical passages in which God or Jesus changed a person's name.

Worksheet 4: 'My Names' (*page 178 of this resource*) invites the young people to recall the different names they have been given and to explore the significance behind each of these names. We also invite them to compose a prayer thanking God for their names.

Worksheet 5: 'The Seven "I Am" Statements of Jesus' (*page 180 of this resource*) offers the young people an opportunity to recall these statements of Jesus and to choose one for closer study. We then invite them to write their own 'I am' statement—to reveal something of their own identity.

HEAR THE STORY

You shall not take the name of the LORD, your God, in vain

Learning Outcomes
That the young people would:
⊙ understand that the Second Commandment calls us to reverence the holy name of God and forbids the abuse of God's name;
⊙ know that we honor and respect God when we honor and respect his holy name;
⊙ appreciate that all Christians are called to show the same respect for the name of Jesus;
⊙ know that the Second Commandment also forbids blasphemy, false promises and false oaths.

Faith-formation Outcome
That the young people would also:
⊙ reflect on their use of the holy names of God, Jesus, Mary and the saints and commit to using them with reverence and respect.

Overview
Section two, 'Hear the Story', emphasizes the respect and reverence that Christians are called to show for God and for his name. We remind the young people that reverence is an expression of piety, which is one of the seven Gifts of the Holy Spirit. We recall how

CHAPTER 6: LOVE THE LORD YOUR GOD | NOTES AND GUIDELINES | 169 the ancient Israelites had such respect for the divine name that God had revealed to Moses that they never spoke or wrote it; in its place they most often used Adonai or Lord. We teach that Christians must have the same honor and respect for the name of Jesus as we have for the name of God. Our reverence for the name 'Jesus' is an expression of our belief that Jesus is God. Our reverence for God moves us to bless, praise and glorify God and to thank him for all that is associated with him, and so we also honor and respect the name of Mary and the saints and everything else that we associate with God. We conclude this section by identifying ways in which the name of God may be abused through blasphemy, through false promises made in the name of God and through perjury.

Supplementary Activities for 'Hear the Story'

Research Activity
Invite the young people to research one or both of the following: the naming process across different cultures; naming rituals or ceremonies in the major religions. They could present their findings to the class.

or

Invite the young people to choose a particular biblical name and research its source in the Bible and its meaning. They might also research famous people or saints who have this name. Afterward, encourage them to share their findings with the class.

Classroom ritual
Invite each young person to represent in poetry, music or art the name they prefer to be called by. Then have the young people use these materials to prepare a classroom ritual that honors the name of each person in the class.

or

Invite the young people to look up and read the *Magnificat*, Mary's wonderful prayer in praise of God, in Luke 1:46–55. Then have them work together in small groups to compose a 'Young Person's Magnificat'. They could then incorporate these prayers into a classroom ritual in praise of God.

Worksheet 6: 'Name-Calling' (*page 182 of this resource*) presents the poem 'Names Never Hurt' by Michelle Harper Davis as the basis for a reflection on the implications of name-calling and bullying.

Worksheet 7: 'Titles and Forms of Address' (*page 184 of this resource*) invites the young people to contrast some titles used in society today with titles and forms of address used in Sacred Scripture.

Worksheet 8: 'In Praise of God' (*page 186 of this resource*) presents Psalm 100 and invites the young people to work in pairs to create their own poem in praise of God using the lune pattern.

Teacher Tip in relation to Worksheet 8: Create a quiet space and invite each pair of students to present their poem to the class. You might also encourage the young people to gather all their poems together and create a display of poetry in honor of God.

EMBRACE THE VISION

Remember to keep holy the Lord's Day

Learning Outcomes
That the young people would:
⊙ understand the biblical origins of keeping the seventh day of the week as the Sabbath day;
⊙ understand that Christians fulfill the Third Commandment on Sunday, the day of the Lord's Resurrection;
⊙ understand the wisdom of Jesus on the true meaning of Sabbath law.

Faith-formation Outcome
That the young people would also:
⊙ observe the Third Commandment by faithfully keeping the Sabbath day.

Overview
Section three, 'Embrace the Vision', focuses on the command to keep the Lord's Day holy. The section begins by recalling the biblical origins in the account of Creation of Israel's practice of keeping the seventh day of the week as the Sabbath day. We explain to the young people that keeping the Sabbath day holy was and continues to be a concrete sign of the irrevocable covenant binding God and his people. The Sabbath day is a day of total rest for everyone to

170 | CREDO | LIVING AND LOVING AS DISCIPLES OF CHRIST

acknowledge and honor God as the center of their life. We explain that in Jesus' time there were many man-made 'laws' detailing the celebration of the Sabbath Commandment, which often blurred the true meaning of the Sabbath. We then present three Gospel accounts of Jesus celebrating and teaching on the Sabbath, actions that the Pharisees judged to be in contravention of Sabbath law, and we guide the young people to understand that obeying the Sabbath *includes* spending time with the sick, in reflection and helping those in need, as Jesus demonstrated.

Supplementary Activities for 'Embrace the Vision'

Drama Activity

Invite the young people to form small groups and act out the scenes described in Mark 2:23–28 and Luke 13:10–17. Alternatively, they might prefer to write modern versions of these Gospel stories and dramatize them. The groups could present their dramas to the class and then discuss the insights gained through this activity.

_____

Worksheet 9: 'Keeping the Sabbath Commandment'

(*page 187 of this resource*) invites the young people to study a selection of Gospel passages that reveal Jesus' attitude to keeping the Sabbath Commandment. We then invite the young people to compose 'Six Directives for Keeping the Sabbath' that reflect Jesus' understanding of what it means to keep the Lord's Day holy.

_____

Worksheet 10: 'Work to be Avoided on the Sabbath'

(*page 188 of this resource*) lists the thirty-nine categories of labor that Jewish Law forbids on the Sabbath as a starting point for the young people to reflect on the sort of activities that Christians should avoid on the Sabbath Day.

_____

Worksheet 11: 'Making Sunday Special' (*page 190 of this resource*) invites the young people to review how they treat Sunday, the Lord's Day, and to identify practical ways in which they could make Sunday a special day for rest and reflection.

THINK IT THROUGH

Love the Lord your God with your whole mind

Learning Outcomes

That the young people would:

- ⊙ know what the first and third precepts of the Church command;
- ⊙ understand why the Church calls us to come together for the celebration of the Eucharist on Sundays;
- ⊙ know how the first and third precepts of the Church relate to the Third Commandment;
- ⊙ understand what the term 'praying without ceasing' means.

Faith-formation Outcomes

That the young people would also:

- ⊙ come to a deeper appreciation of the value of the Sunday Eucharist;
- ⊙ grow as people of prayer.

Overview

Section four, 'Think It Through', explores the obligation Catholics have to gather together on the Lord's Day to give adoration, praise and thanks to God through their celebration of the Eucharist. We explain the first and third precepts of the Church and how these connect with the Third Commandment. We conclude the section by guiding the young people to understand that their prayer should not be limited to the celebration of Mass, and we explain the term 'praying without ceasing', a practice that is vital to living the Great Commandment.

Supplementary Activities for 'Think It Through'

Creative Activity

Invite the young people to imagine that they have been asked to speak to a group of children who are preparing for First Communion about their own best Eucharist experience and why they think it is important to participate in the Sunday celebration of the Mass. Invite them to write out the talk they would like to give in such a scenario.

Teacher Tip in relation to the 'Creative Activity':
Should the opportunity arise, you might invite a number of students to present their 'talk' to children in your parish who are preparing for First Communion.

CHAPTER 6: LOVE THE LORD YOUR GOD | NOTES AND GUIDELINES | 171

Worksheet 12: 'The First Precept of the Church' (*page 191 of this resource*) invites the young people to take a closer look at the elements and structure of the celebration of the Eucharist and to reflect on how they can live the Eucharist in their daily lives.

Worksheet 13: 'The Lord's Prayer' (*page 193 of this resource*) offers the young people the opportunity to review the components of this great prayer and to reflect on how it helps them to be 'people of prayer'.

JUDGE AND ACT

Learning Outcome
That the young people would:
⊙ know about the life and spirituality of St. Ignatius of Loyola.

Faith-formation Outcome
That the young people would also:
⊙ be inspired by St. Ignatius of Loyola to 'slow down' and see God in all people and all things.

Overview
In section five, 'Judge and Act', the young people review the teachings of the Church that they have studied in this chapter. We also introduce them to the life and spirituality of St. Ignatius of Loyola.

Supplementary Activities for 'Judge and Act'

Research Activity
Encourage the young people to search various media for stories, reports or images of Christians throughout the world who place God at the center of their lives.

Media Watch
Sometimes the Mass is broadcast on TV and on radio. You might suggest to the young people that they watch or listen to such a broadcast and observe the different elements of the celebration of the Eucharist. If possible, they should pause the live TV or radio during the broadcast to give them time to take note of the various elements. Invite them to share any insights they gain from this activity with the class.

Worksheet 14: 'Learn from St. Ignatius of Loyola' (*page 194 of this resource*) presents a selection of quotations from St. Ignatius of Loyola for the young people to reflect on in light of their everyday lives as disciples of Jesus Christ.

Additional Prayer Suggestions

Litany in Praise of God
(**Note:** *Pause between each blessing to allow the young people a moment for reflection. Alternatively, you might like to substitute a hand/movement gesture instead of the pause between each blessing.*)

Leader
Let us praise God.

Leader	**All:**
Creator of the Universe	Blessed be God.
Mystery of Love	Blessed be God.
Holy of Holies	Blessed be God.
Keeper of Promises	Blessed be God.
Liberator of the Oppressed	Blessed be God.
Breath of Life	Blessed be God.
Compassionate Heart	Blessed be God.
Loving Father	Blessed be God.
Fountain of Mercy	Blessed be God.
Guiding Spirit	Blessed be God.
Gracious Giver	Blessed be God.

Leader
Blessed be the name of God.
Blessed are we who gather today
in praise
in gratitude
in thanksgiving
in hope.

172 | CREDO | LIVING AND LOVING AS DISCIPLES OF CHRIST

Leader raises hand in blessing gesture:

May the Lord bless you and keep you always,
in the name of the Father
and of the Son
and of the Holy Spirit.

As it was in the beginning
is now
and ever shall be.

All
Amen.

Scripture Reflection
(*See instructions for the use of doodling in prayer in the 'Student Activity Tool Kit, page 394 of this resource.*)

Use this Scripture verse to engage the young people in prayer:

> **See, I have inscribed you on the palms of my hands.**
>
> **ISAIAH 49:16**

CHAPTER 6 | WORKSHEET 1

NAME:

I Have Called You by Name

The title of this worksheet comes from the Book of Isaiah, where we read: 'I have called you by name, you are mine' (Isaiah 43:1). This worksheet offers you an opportunity to reflect on what it means to you to know that God has called you by name.

READ AND REFLECT

'I have called you by name, you are mine.'

—Isaiah 43:1

The Catechism of the Catholic Church reiterates this message:

God calls each one by name. Everyone's name is sacred. The name is the icon of the person. It demands respect as a sign of the dignity of the one who bears it.

—CCC, no. 2158

- ⊙ Think of the many official names you have been given: your birth name, your baptismal name, your Confirmation name. Think of the many less formal names your family and friends know you by; for example, a pet name, nickname, name used by a younger sibling or a special friend and so on.
- ⊙ Take a few moments now to reflect on what it means for you to know that God has called you personally by name.
- ⊙ Select the name that you would like God to call you. (You might like to create a new name.)
- ⊙ Now insert your chosen name in the blank space alongside this verse from Isaiah:

_____, I have called you by name, you are mine.

RESPOND
Imagine that God is calling you by name right now. Write your response.

_____

_____

_____

_____

_____

_____

CHAPTER 6 | WORKSHEET 2

NAME:

The Name of God

Respect for God's name is reflected time and again in the many different ways the Old Testament refers to the mystery of God. The *Catechism of the Catholic Church* teaches: 'The second commandment *prescribes respect for the Lord's name.* . . . The gift of a name belongs to the order of trust and intimacy. "The Lord's name is holy" ' (CCC, no. 2142–2143). This worksheet invites you to explore some of the names for God found in the Old Testament.

GROUP ACTIVITY
⊙ Work in small groups.
⊙ The names on the chart are some of the names for God found in the Old Testament. Look up these biblical references and complete the chart by matching each of the names for God with the appropriate reference(s) from Scripture:

Genesis 14:20; 16:13; 17:1; 21:33; 35:11; **Numbers** 24:16; **Deuteronomy** 7:9; 10:17; **Ruth** 1:20; **Nehemiah** 9:32; **Psalms** 9:2; 29:3; 31:5; 90:1–3; 93:2; **Isaiah** 7:14; 9:6; 26:4; 45:21; **Ezekiel** 1:24; **Zechariah** 14:9; **Malachi** 2:7

Names for God	Scripture References
One	
Faithful God	
Righteous God	
Savior	
Almighty	
Prince of Peace	
Most High	
Everlasting God	
El-roi	
Lord of Hosts	
Wonderful Counselor	
God of Glory	
Immanuel	
Awesome God	

CHAPTER 6: LOVE THE LORD YOUR GOD | WORKSHEET 2 | 175

CHAPTER 6 | WORKSHEET 2 (CONTD.)

CLASS DISCUSSION
◉ What does the range of names for God in the Old Testament reveal about God?

PAIR AND SHARE
◉ Work with a partner.
◉ Think of some new names that would express the wonder and mystery of God.
◉ Think also of names that would be particularly relevant to the lives of young people.
◉ Share these names with the class.

JOURNAL EXERCISE
Describe how young people today can honor the mystery of God by honoring God's name.

176 | CREDO | LIVING AND LOVING AS DISCIPLES OF CHRIST

CHAPTER 6 | WORKSHEET 3

NAME:

What's in a Name?

This worksheet offers you the opportunity to study a selection of biblical passages in which God the Father or Jesus changed a person's name. We invite you to consider the significance of name-changing in biblical times and today.

SCRIPTURE ACTIVITY

⊙ With a partner, look up and read each of these Scripture passages, paying special attention to the names given to the various characters:

Genesis 17:1–8

Genesis 32:22–28

John 1:35–42

Acts 13:9

⊙ Answer these questions in relation to any <u>two</u> of the above Scripture passages.

What did the change of name signify?

_____

_____

_____

_____

_____

When and why might people change their names nowadays?

_____

_____

_____

What connections do you see between the biblical name-changing in the examples you chose and modern name-changing practices?

_____

_____

_____

CHAPTER 6: LOVE THE LORD YOUR GOD | WORKSHEET 3 | 177

CHAPTER 6 | WORKSHEET 4

NAME:

My Names

Names are important. We name children, cities, countries, planets, animals, houses, streets, teams, websites . . . the list goes on. This worksheet offers you the opportunity to recall the different names you have been given and to explore the significance behind each of these names.

RECALL AND RESPOND
You may have to do some research in order to answer some of these questions.

My first Christian name is: _____

My second Christian name is: _____

My Confirmation name is: _____

My family name (surname) is: _____

My first Christian name means: _____

It was chosen for me because: _____

_____

My second Christian name means: _____

It was chosen for me because: _____

_____

My Confirmation name means: _____

It was chosen for me because: _____

_____

The origin of my family name is: _____

_____

_____

178 | CREDO | LIVING AND LOVING AS DISCIPLES OF CHRIST

CHAPTER 6 | WORKSHEET 4 (CONTD.)

I am connected by name to _____

_____

_____

If I could, I would change my name to: _____

The reason I would/would not change my name is: _____

_____

_____

GET CREATIVE!
Compose a prayer thanking God for your names. Write your prayer in the box.

CHAPTER 6: LOVE THE LORD YOUR GOD | WORKSHEET 4 (CONTD.) | 179

CHAPTER 6 | WORKSHEET 5

NAME:

The Seven 'I Am' Statements of Jesus

This worksheet offers you an opportunity to focus on one of Jesus' 'I am' statements and to consider the message(s) that Jesus was seeking to convey through this statement. We will then invite you to write your own 'I am' statement—revealing something of your own identity.

READ AND RESPOND
⊙ Slowly and attentively read these seven 'I am' statements of Jesus from St. John's account of the Gospel.

'I am the bread of life. Whoever comes to me will never be hungry, and whoever believes in me will never be thirsty.' (John 6:35)

'I am the light of the world. Whoever follows me will never walk in darkness but will have the light of life.' (John 8:12)

'I am the gate. Whoever enters by me will be saved, and will come in and go out and find pasture.' (John 10:9)

'I am the good shepherd. The good shepherd lays down his life for the sheep.' (John 10:11)

'I am the resurrection and the life. Those who believe in me, even though they die, will live.' (John 11:25)

'I am the way, and the truth, and the life. No one comes to the Father except through me.' (John 14:6)

'I am the vine, you are the branches. Those who abide in me and I in them bear much fruit, because apart from me you can do nothing.' (John 15:5)

⊙ Choose one statement to examine more closely.
⊙ Think for a few moments about what Jesus might have meant when he made this statement.
⊙ Now pair up with a partner and discuss the statement (or statements, if your partner has chosen a different one). Share your thoughts on the message(s) you think Jesus was seeking to convey.

180 | CREDO | LIVING AND LOVING AS DISCIPLES OF CHRIST

CHAPTER 6 | WORKSHEET 5 (CONTD.)

◉ Compose your own 'I am' statement for Jesus based on your reading and understanding of the four accounts of the Gospel. Write this statement on the lines provided below.

_____

_____

_____

_____

OVER TO YOU

Compose an 'I am' statement for yourself. Before you do so, spend a little while thinking about what you want to convey about your identity in your 'I am' statement.

_____

_____

_____

_____

CHAPTER 6: LOVE THE LORD YOUR GOD | WORKSHEET 5 (CONTD.) | 181

CHAPTER 6 | WORKSHEET 6

NAME:

Name-Calling

Sometimes people are not shown the respect and dignity that they deserve. One of the simplest and easiest ways to disrespect or bully another person is to name-call. Belittling and making fun of a person by calling them names strikes at the very core of the person's identity. The taunts and mocking can resonate deeply within them and can be extraordinarily destructive. This worksheet offers you the opportunity to explore the impact of such behavior.

READ, REFLECT AND RESPOND
Read and reflect on this poem by Michelle Harper Davies and then complete the exercise below.

> **Names Never Hurt**
> Sticks and stones break bones,
> Names never hurt
> Or so they say.
> But it's the names that stick in the mind,
> Like leeches sucking away
> At what's left of the confidence and pride inside you,
> Leaving a slimy trail of hurt
> And fear.
> The sticks and the stones
> And the punches and the kicks
> Leave the painful, purple marks,
> But none are as wounding
> As the razor-sharp remarks,
> That hit like stones
> And sting like sticks
> And scar for life.

List the imagery the poet uses to describe the effects of name-calling.

_____

_____

_____

182 | CREDO | LIVING AND LOVING AS DISCIPLES OF CHRIST

CHAPTER 6 | WORKSHEET 6 (CONTD.)

What is the impact of name-calling, according to the poet?

_____

_____

_____

_____

Identify ways in which the poem echoes reality for some young people today:

In school or college:

_____

_____

At home:

_____

_____

In the community/neighborhood:

_____

_____

_____

_____

OVER TO YOU

◉ Sometimes people are denigrated and abused because they look different or speak in a different way or come from a different place or background. There may have been times when you found yourself at the receiving end of such behavior and attitudes. Or there may have been times when you participated in such destructive activity. Reflect on those times.

◉ Write a prayer in your journal asking God either to forgive you for those times when you hurt others in this way, or asking God to forgive those who hurt you.

CHAPTER 6: LOVE THE LORD YOUR GOD | WORKSHEET 6 (CONTD.) | 183

CHAPTER 6 | WORKSHEET 7

NAME:

Titles and Forms of Address

Titles and various forms of address are used to demonstrate respect and to indicate attainment or position in society. Such titles are often sought after by people and they are bestowed by those in power. This worksheet offers you an opportunity to identify some of the titles used in society today and to contrast them with some titles and forms of address used in Sacred Scripture.

BRAINSTORM AND RESPOND

◉ Brainstorm all the titles and forms of address you can think of that are used in society today.

◉ Do any of these titles stir up positive or negative reactions in you? If so, explain why.

TITLES IN SCRIPTURE

◉ Look up each of the Scripture references in column 1 below and write the title or form of address used in that reference in column 2.

Column 1	Column 2
Matthew 1:23	
Mark 1:11	
Mark 14:61	
Mark 15:18	
John 1:1	
John 1:29	
John 8:12	
John 11:27	
John 20:16	
Romans 10:9	

184 | CREDO | LIVING AND LOVING AS DISCIPLES OF CHRIST

CHAPTER 6 | WORKSHEET 7 (CONTD.)

⊙ Choose three of the biblical titles from the previous activity and write a brief description of what each one represents.

Title:

_____

_____

Title:

_____

_____

Title:

_____

_____

COMPARE AND CONTRAST

Describe how the biblical titles listed in column 2 of the chart compare with any of the titles you identified in the brainstorm exercise. Mention how they are similar or different.

_____

_____

_____

_____

_____

_____

_____

_____

CHAPTER 6: LOVE THE LORD YOUR GOD | WORKSHEET 7 (CONTD.) | 185

CHAPTER 6 | WORKSHEET 8

NAME:

In Praise of God

Our reverence and awe for God moves us to bless, praise and glorify God and to thank him for everything he has created. This worksheet presents a psalm of praise from the Book of Psalms and invites you to write your own psalm.

READ AND REFLECT

Take some time to read and reflect on this psalm of thanksgiving. It is Psalm 100 from the Book of Psalms.

Make a joyful noise to the Lord, all the earth.
Worship the Lord with gladness;
come into his presence with singing.

Know that the Lord is God.
It is he that made us, and we are his;
we are his people, and the sheep of his pasture.

Enter his gates with thanksgiving,
and his courts with praise.
Give thanks to him, bless his name.

For the Lord is good;
his steadfast love endures forever,
and his faithfulness to all generations.

BRAINSTORM

On a single page, brainstorm all the things for which you feel thankful.

PAIR AND SHARE

⊙ Share your thoughts on Psalm 100 with a partner.
⊙ Then work together to compose your own poem of thanksgiving using the poetry pattern known as lune, which is the American version of the Japanese haiku.
⊙ One way of writing lune poetry is to count the words in each line rather than the syllables. Each verse contains three lines, with the word count as follows:
Line 1: three words
Line 2: five words
Line 3: three words

CHAPTER 6 | WORKSHEET 9

NAME:

Keeping the Sabbath Commandment

In your theology text you explored three Gospel accounts of Jesus celebrating and teaching on the Sabbath, namely, Mark 2:23–28, Luke 4:16–21 and 13:10–17. This worksheet offers you the opportunity first to study some more Gospel passages that reveal Jesus' attitude to keeping the Sabbath Commandment, and then to compose 'Six Directives for Keeping the Sabbath' that reflect Jesus' understanding of what it means to keep the Lord's Day holy.

READ AND RESPOND

⊙ Work with a partner.

⊙ Read each of these passages and note what they reveal about Jesus' attitude to the Sabbath. Then complete the exercise below.

Matthew 12:9–14: The Man with a Withered Hand
Matthew 15:1–9: The Tradition of the Elders
Mark 3:1–6: The Man with a Withered Hand
Mark 7:1–13: The Tradition of the Elders
Luke 6:1–5: The Question about the Sabbath
Luke 11:37–41: Jesus Denounces Pharisees and Lawyers
John 5:1–18: Jesus Heals on the Sabbath
John 9:13–17: The Pharisees Investigate a Healing

In light of the above passages from Scripture, compose six directives for keeping the Sabbath Commandment.

1. _____

2. _____

3. _____

4. _____

5. _____

6. _____

CHAPTER 6: LOVE THE LORD YOUR GOD | WORKSHEET 9 | 187

CHAPTER 6 | WORKSHEET 10

NAME:

Work to Be Avoided on the Sabbath

This worksheet offers you the opportunity to reflect on and identify the sort of activities that Christians should avoid on the Sabbath Day.

READ AND RESPOND

According to Jewish Law, thirty-nine categories of labor are forbidden on the Sabbath. These are known as the thirty-nine melachot. They are:

1. Carrying
2. Burning
3. Extinguishing
4. Finishing
5. Writing
6. Erasing
7. Cooking
8. Washing
9. Sewing
10. Tearing
11. Knotting
12. Untying
13. Shaping
14. Plowing
15. Planting
16. Reaping
17. Harvesting
18. Threshing
19. Winnowing
20. Selecting

21. Sifting
22. Grinding
23. Kneading
24. Combing
25. Spinning
26. Dyeing
27. Chain-stitching
28. Warping
29. Weaving
30. Unraveling
31. Building
32. Demolishing
33. Trapping
34. Shearing
35. Slaughtering
36. Skinning
37. Tanning
38. Smoothing
39. Marking

188 | CREDO | LIVING AND LOVING AS DISCIPLES OF CHRIST

CHAPTER 6 | WORKSHEET 10 (CONTD.)

PAIR AND SHARE

Pair up with a partner and share your responses to the following:

◉ From your study of the Gospel accounts, which of the above-named activities was Jesus accused of doing on the Sabbath day?

◉ Which of these activities do you think Christians would find it acceptable to do on Sundays?

◉ List five activities that you think Christians should avoid doing on the Lord's Day.

1. _____

2. _____

3. _____

4. _____

5. _____

CHAPTER 6: LOVE THE LORD YOUR GOD | WORKSHEET 10 (CONTD.) | 189

CHAPTER 6 | WORKSHEET 11

NAME:

Making Sunday Special

Our lives tend to be filled with frenzied activity, with little 'quiet time' left over for peace and reflection. Deliberately choosing to make Sunday a day of rest, away from the concerns and preoccupations that have come to characterize our daily lives, is a spiritual stance that witnesses eloquently to the fundamental nature of our relationship with God. Such a stance views Sunday as a 'lilies of the field' day (see Luke 12:22–32). This worksheet offers you the opportunity to review your approach to Sunday, the Lord's Day.

REFLECT AND RESPOND

Identify three things that you would typically do on Sundays that you might choose to avoid doing from here on in order to keep the Lord's Day holy.

_____

_____

_____

Identify three things that you could choose to do *on your own* on Sundays in order to keep the Lord's Day holy.

_____

_____

_____

Identify three things that you could choose to do *with others* on Sundays in order to keep the Lord's Day holy.

_____

_____

_____

JOURNAL EXERCISE

Write a prayer to the Holy Spirit asking for support and guidance to keep the Lord's Day holy.

CHAPTER 6 | WORKSHEET 12

NAME:

The First Precept of the Church

The first precept of the Church (You shall attend Mass on Sundays and holy days of obligation and rest from service labor) 'requires the faithful to participate in the Eucharistic celebration when the Christian community gathers together on the day commemorating the Resurrection of the Lord' (*Catechism of the Catholic Church*, no. 2042). This worksheet offers you the opportunity to take a closer look at the elements and structure of the celebration of the Eucharist and to reflect on how you can live the Eucharist in your daily life.

PAIR AND SHARE
- Work with a partner.
- Read through list A. On the lines provided, identify what each major part of the Mass involves; use a missal to check if you are unsure.
- Read through list B. On the lines provided, identify how the various 'elements' of the celebration of the Eucharist connect with the major 'parts' of the Mass.

List A: The Major Parts of the Mass

Introductory Rite

_____

Liturgy of the Word

_____

Liturgy of the Eucharist

_____

Communion Rite

_____

Concluding Rites

_____

CHAPTER 6: LOVE THE LORD YOUR GOD | WORKSHEET 12 | 191

CHAPTER 6 | WORKSHEET 12 (CONTD.)

List B: The Fundamental Elements of the Mass

The Christian community gathers together

_____

Listening to the Word of God

_____

Remembering Jesus' love for us

_____

Giving thanks

_____

Celebrating the forgiveness of God our Father

_____

Sharing the Bread of Life

_____

Going in peace to live like Jesus

_____

OVER TO YOU

Describe three ways in which your celebration of Sunday Eucharist influences (or, perhaps, should influence) the remainder of your week.

_____

_____

_____

_____

_____

_____

_____

192 | CREDO | LIVING AND LOVING AS DISCIPLES OF CHRIST

CHAPTER 6 | WORKSHEET 13

NAME:

The Lord's Prayer

Jesus is the model for our prayer. By his preaching and the example of his life Jesus showed us that prayer is essential to our daily life. Jesus taught us how to pray by giving us the Our Father (see Matthew 6:9–13). This worksheet offers you the opportunity to review the components of this great prayer and to reflect on how it helps you to be a person of prayer.

REVIEW THE LORD'S PRAYER

We begin the Our Father by placing ourselves in the presence of God and acknowledging that he is our Father by saying:

_____

Then follows the first three of seven petitions. The first three petitions are theological in nature. In these petitions we give praise and glory to God. We put ourselves at God's service and pray that we will glorify his name and serve the Kingdom and his divine will. These three petitions are:

1. _____

2. _____

3. _____

_____

The final four petitions ask God to give us and all people the graces to live as his faithful children. These final four petitions are:

1. _____

2. _____

3. _____

4. _____

JOURNAL EXERCISE

Reflect on what the Lord's Prayer means to you. Mention some typical thoughts that come to your mind when you pray this prayer.

CHAPTER 6: LOVE THE LORD YOUR GOD | WORSHEET 13 | 193

CHAPTER 6 | WORKSHEET 14

NAME:

Learn from St. Ignatius of Loyola

This worksheet offers you the opportunity to read and reflect on a selection of inspirational quotations from St. Ignatius of Loyola.

READ AND REFLECT

⊙ Take some time alone to read these quotations from St. Ignatius of Loyola.

⊙ Choose one that you think might provide inspiration to young people today.

'Go forth and set the world on fire.'

'Act as if everything depended on you; trust as if everything depended on God.'

'God freely created us so that we might know, love, and serve him in this life and be happy with him forever. God's purpose in creating us is to draw forth from us a response of love and service here on earth, so that we may attain our goal of everlasting happiness with him in heaven.'

'All the things in this world are gifts of God, created for us, to be the means by which we can come to know him better, love him more surely, and serve him more faithfully. As a result, we ought to appreciate and use these gifts of God insofar as they help us toward our goal of loving service and union with God. But insofar as any created things hinder our progress toward our goal, we ought to let them go.'

'Love is shown more in deeds than in words.'

'Laugh and grow strong.'

'*Ad majorem Dei gloriam*' (The Latin motto of the Jesuits, meaning 'For the greater glory of God')

'O my God, teach me to be generous,
teach me to serve you as I should,
to give without counting the cost,
to fight without fear of being wounded,
to work without seeking rest,
to labor without expecting any reward,
but the knowledge that I am doing your most holy will.'

194 | CREDO | LIVING AND LOVING AS DISCIPLES OF CHRIST

CHAPTER 6 | WORKSHEET 14 (CONTD.)

'[L]ove ought to manifest itself in deeds rather than in words. . . . [L]ove consists in a mutual sharing of goods, for example, the lover gives and shares with the beloved what he possesses, or something of that which he has or is able to give; and vice versa, the beloved shares with the lover. Hence, if one has knowledge, he shares it with the one who does not possess it; and so also if one has honors, or riches. Thus, one always gives to the other.'

'If God causes you to suffer much, it is a sign that He has great designs for you, and that He certainly intends to make you a saint. And if you wish to become a great saint, entreat Him yourself to give you much opportunity for suffering; for there is no wood better to kindle the fire of holy love than the wood of the cross, which Christ used for His own great sacrifice of boundless charity.'

PAIR AND SHARE
Share your chosen quotation with a partner and explain why you chose it.

JOURNAL EXERCISE
Read through the quotations again and choose one that speaks in a particular way to you today. Explain why you find it inspirational and relevant to your life.

CHAPTER 6: LOVE THE LORD YOUR GOD | WORKSHEET 14 (CONTD.) | 195

CHAPTER 6 | CHAPTER REVIEW

NAME:

Review of Chapter 6

I. **Fill in the blanks. Write the letter that corresponds to the correct term in the word bank in the blank space to complete each sentence. There are two more terms in the word bank than you will need.**

A. *Israel*	**F.** LORD	**K.** pray
B. bowing slightly	**G.** *Abraham*	**L.** *shabbath*
C. YHWH	**H.** theophany	**M.** Jesuits
D. Blasphemy	**I.** ADONAI	
E. pausing briefing	**J.** Precepts of the Church	

1.   The Hebrew name _____ means 'father of many'.

2.   _____ is the name God revealed to Moses and to the people of ancient Israel.

3.   The word _____ means a revelation or visible appearance of God.

4.   The Israelites used the name _____ or _____ in place of the divine name that God had revealed to Moses.

5.   One way Catholics show reverence for the name of Jesus is by _____ when the name is spoken or heard.

6.   _____ is speech, thought or action involving contempt for God or the Church, or persons or things dedicated to God.

7.   The Hebrew word _____ means 'end', 'cease' or 'rest'.

8.   The _____ are Church laws that indicate basic requirements for her members.

9.   St. Paul taught: 'Rejoice always, _____ without ceasing.'

10.   With a small group of friends, St. Ignatius founded the _____.

196 | CREDO | LIVING AND LOVING AS DISCIPLES OF CHRIST

CHAPTER 6 | CHAPTER REVIEW (CONTD.)

II. **True/False. Mark the true statements 'T' and the false statements 'F'. In the case of each false statement, cross out and rewrite the incorrect words to make the statement true.**

_____1.   The Hebrew name *Mary* means 'God is salvation'.

_____2.   Gradually and over time God has revealed himself by making his name known.

_____3.   The Hebrew letters YHWH can be translated 'You Have Wealth Here'.

_____4.   Jesus, the Incarnate Son of God, most fully reveals the name and identity of God.

_____5.   When Jesus commissioned the Apostles to baptize all nations, he told them to baptize in his name.

_____6.   Veneration of Mary and the other saints is contrary to both the First and the Second Commandment.

_____7.   A person commits perjury when he or she lies under oath.

_____8.   The Sabbath day is a day of rest for priests to acknowledge and honor God as the center of their lives.

_____9.   Catholics are required to take part in the celebration of Mass on Holy Days of Obligation.

_____10. St. Ignatius of Loyola collected his insights, prayers and suggestions in his *Mindfulness Exercises*.

CHAPTER 6: LOVE THE LORD YOUR GOD | CHAPTER REVIEW (CONTD.) | 197

CHAPTER 6 | CHAPTER REVIEW (CONTD.)

III. Write a brief answer. Explain the teaching of the Catholic Church on 1 or 2.
   1. The obligation to attend Mass on Sundays and Holy Days of Obligation.
   2. Reverence for the name of God.

_____

_____

_____

_____

_____

_____

_____

_____

IV. How would you respond? A friend tells you that going to Mass on Sunday is a waste of time and you can honor God by praying at home as a family.

_____

_____

_____

_____

_____

_____

_____

_____

_____

_____

198 | CREDO | LIVING AND LOVING AS DISCIPLES OF CHRIST

CHAPTER 6 | CHAPTER REVIEW (CONTD.)

V. Make a 'disciple decision'.

1. What is the most important wisdom for life that you discovered in this chapter?

_____

_____

_____

_____

_____

_____

2. Name several ways you can put this wisdom into practice. Choose one of the ways you identify and describe how you will make that wisdom part of your life right now.

_____

_____

_____

_____

_____

_____

_____

_____

CHAPTER 6: LOVE THE LORD YOUR GOD | CHAPTER REVIEW (CONTD.) | 199

CHAPTER 7

Honor Your Father and Your Mother

—The Fourth Commandment

INTRODUCTION

> How very good and pleasant it is
>> when kindred live together in unity!
>
> — Psalm 133:1

In this chapter the young people explore the teachings of the Catholic Church on how best to live out the Fourth Commandment. In light of their own experience of *being* family, we lead them to an appreciation of the Christian family as a communion of persons who are called to reflect the spirit of communion that exists between God the Father, God the Son and God the Holy Spirit. We address not only parental and family-based relationships but also relationships with those external to the family who have legitimate authority over the young people. We explore the duty of civil authorities to promote the common good of all citizens and the right and duty of all citizens to contribute to the life of the society in which they live. We encourage the young people to embody discipleship of Jesus in their everyday lives— in their homes, in school, in their interactions with the local community and with the wider world.

Chapter 7 is developed under five major headings:
- ⊙ **ATTEND AND REFLECT:** Why is 'family' important?
- ⊙ **HEAR THE STORY:** The heart and foundation of healthy family life
- ⊙ **EMBRACE THE VISION:** Responding to the fundamental rights of every person
- ⊙ **THINK IT THROUGH:** Living as faithful citizens
- ⊙ **JUDGE AND ACT:** (*Activities and exercises that encourage the young people to integrate what they have learned in the chapter into their daily lives.*)

Theological Background for the Teacher

THE FAMILY

The family is one of the most significant units in our lives. We are shaped and formed by the relationships and interactions we experience within our family.

As adults, we often return to the town or the city or country of our birth to explore our roots and identity. As educators, when we need to find out more about a young person entrusted to our care, we frequently seek out the help of the young person's family.

> For the common good of its members and of society, the family necessarily has manifold responsibilities, rights and duties.
>
> —*Catechism of the Catholic Church* (CCC), no. 2203

The family is the place where core values are inculcated, where our primary identity takes shape. It is within the family that we first learn about attachment and love and where from a young age we begin to learn how to deal with disappointments and worries, sadness and anger, and how to negotiate the everyday challenges that living with others brings. For some of us the experience of belonging to a family will be positive, but for others it will be negative—for most of us, it is probably a mixture of both. The same will be true for the young people you teach. Each family is unique. Each family is akin to a rich tapestry intricately woven over countless generations with the fragile threads of people's lives.

LIVING AS A 'CHRISTIAN' FAMILY

Blessed Pope John Paul II taught:

> The family finds in the plan of God the Creator and Redeemer not only its identity, what it is, but also its mission, what it can and should do. The role that God calls the family to perform in history derives from what the family is; its role represents the dynamic and existential development of what it is. Each family finds within itself a summons that cannot be ignored, and that specifies both its dignity and its responsibility: family, become what you are.
>
> —Pope John Paul II, *Familiaris Consortio (On the Role of the Christian Family in the Modern World)*, no. 17

200 | CREDO | LIVING AND LOVING AS DISCIPLES OF CHRIST

God created us to be interdependent beings. The human person cannot develop and flourish in isolation from others. We need the encouragement and the challenge, the love and the support of other people to assist us in making the goodness that God has planted in our hearts shine through in our everyday lives.

For the Christian who is seeking to live according to the Fourth Commandment, the key questions are: how can we *be* family more fully, more generously and more meaningfully? As faith-filled disciples of Jesus Christ, how can we give expression to our faith as mother, as father, as brother, as sister, as grandparent? How can we *be* family in a way that is life-giving for ourselves, for the other members of the family and, ultimately, for the society in which we live?

> It is impossible seriously to subscribe to the Christian story, to celebrate the Christian memory, or engage in the praxis of the Christian community, without experiencing the overarching demand of love for others.
>
> —Vincent MacNamara, *The Call to be Human*

Jesus' words in John 15:4 should offer some guidance for those striving to live as a Christian family:

> Abide in me as I abide in you. Just as the branch cannot bear fruit by itself unless it abides in the vine, neither can you unless you abide in me.

The *Catechism* speaks of the family unit as the 'domestic church':

> The Christian family constitutes a specific revelation and realization of ecclesial communion and for this reason it can and should be called a *domestic church*. It is a community of faith, hope and charity.
>
> —CCC, no. 2204

The process of parenting has the capacity to be wonderfully empowering and life-giving. Becoming a parent reshapes the heart and molds it to grow and to adapt so that it beats in harmony with the rhythm of another little being. Being a parent teaches us to love and to trust, challenges us to forgive, opens our eyes to wonder and, ultimately, shows us how to let go. Parenting shifts the focus from a self-centered to an other-centered one. It challenges us to face our personal vulnerabilities and to broaden the landscape of our hopes and dreams beyond ourselves. Being family then has the capacity to transform. And when family becomes a community of love, we glimpse something of the divine goodness of the Triune God

who loves us infinitely—and more than any parent ever could.

> When a family becomes a school of virtue and a community of love, it is an image of the loving communion of the Father, Son, and Holy Spirit. It is then an icon of the Trinity.
>
> —*United States Catholic Catechism for Adults (USCCA)*, 377

THE FOURTH COMMANDMENT

> God has willed that, after him, we should honor our parents to whom we owe life and who have handed on to us the knowledge of God.
>
> —CCC, no. 2197

The Fourth Commandment is the foundational expression of how we are to live the second part of the Great Commandment, 'You shall love your neighbor as yourself.' It calls us to put the Great Commandment into practice in a very specific way— by honoring our parents and by upholding their dignity through filial love and respect.

> Respect for parents derives from a grateful heart toward those who gave us the gift of life and nourished, loved, and supported us throughout all our stages of growth. Filial love is shown by genuine obedience from children to their parents while living in their parents' home and by responsible concern of grown children toward their elderly parents.
>
> —USCCA, 377

The Fourth Commandment encourages children to embody a disposition of gratitude, just obedience and assistance toward their parents. It asks that children give thanks to their parents who brought them into the world: '*remember that it was of your parents you were born*' (Sirach 7:28); that they listen to the wisdom and advice that parents offer: '*A wise child loves discipline*' (Proverbs 13:1); that they obey parents' just commands: '*Children, obey your parents in everything, for this is your acceptable duty in the Lord*' (Colossians 3:20; cf. Ephesians 6:1). Such a disposition does not happen automatically but must be fostered over time.

> It is only if we experience ourselves as loved and valued by others that we can feel good about ourselves, feel worthy. The hope always is that this will happen for us in the intimate relations of childhood, that the recognition we need to flourish will occur there.
>
> —Vincent MacNamara, *The Call to Be Human*

Children who experience love and a sense of self-worth in the home are more likely to reflect filial respect for those with whom they live. The Fourth Commandment urges parents to give the time and the commitment to nurture their children and to care for all aspects of 'their physical, spiritual, intellectual, emotional, and moral needs' (USCCA, 378). It calls them to 'regard their children as *children of God* and respect them as *human persons*' (CCC, no. 2222).

> Filial respect promotes harmony in all of family life; it also concerns *relationships between brothers and sisters*. Respect toward parents fills the home with light and warmth. 'Grandchildren are the crown of the aged' [Proverbs 17:6]. 'With all humility and meekness, with patience, [support] one another in charity [Ephesians 4:2].'
> —CCC, no. 2219

Genuine respect within the family spills over into all of one's relationships; it even extends beyond the family unit to our duties to external authorities:

> . . . to the duties of pupils to teachers, employees to employers, subordinates to leaders, citizens to their country and to those who administer or govern it.
> —CCC, no. 2199

Filial respect promotes harmony and encourages in us virtues of patience and understanding. As teens, young people may be at a point in their development where they are beginning to 'pull away' from family in order to discover their own sense of self. This is a natural part of growing up. As their perspective and dependency on family changes, it can cause disquiet and discomfort for some young people. So this may be an opportune time to lead the young people in an exploration of what 'being family' means for them and to support them in their personal growth while reaffirming for them the wisdom and life-giving truth of the Fourth Commandment.

BEING A FAITH-FULL CITIZEN

> God's fourth commandment also enjoins us to honor all who for our good have received authority in society from God.
> —CCC, no. 2234

The *Catechism of the Catholic Church* recognizes that civil authority has the right and responsibility to promote the common good of all citizens and that citizens have a right and, indeed, a duty to participate in the life of society. As disciples of Jesus Christ we have an obligation to help shape our society and to endeavor to live our lives as faithful citizens in the light of the Gospel. As the *Catechism* teaches:

> It is the *duty of citizens* to contribute along with the civil authorities to the good of society in a spirit of truth, justice, solidarity and freedom.
> —CCC, no. 2239

To be a faith-full citizen is to strive to find ways to give voice to God's dream for the world. Blessed Pope John Paul II reminded us that this is a responsibility for all Christian families.

> Families therefore, either singly or in association, can and should devote themselves to manifold social service activities, especially in favor of the poor, or at any rate for the benefit of all people and situations that cannot be reached by the public authorities' welfare organization.
> —Pope John Paul II, *Familiaris Consortio*, no. 44

The Church, in turn, has a mission to challenge civil laws that might diminish the dignity of any person in society.

> The Church, too, has the mission and obligation to critique and challenge any civil laws, societal organizations, or political structures that infringe upon or deny the fundamental rights of human persons and communities.
> —USCCA, 379–380

This chapter offers you the opportunity to explore with the young people the Christian call and duty to help create a society built on love rather than hate; on trust rather than distrust; on cooperation rather than competition; on justice for the poor, the weak and the vulnerable; on integrity and honesty. Through open discussion and honest dialogue you can help these young people begin to discover how best to live as faithful citizens so that their deeds and actions reflect the vision of Jesus Christ and the Gospel.

ADDITIONAL BACKGROUND READING
Catechism of the Catholic Church, nos. 2196–2257; *United States Catholic Catechism for Adults,* 375–385; **Vincent MacNamara**, *The Call To Be Human: Making Sense of Morality* (Dublin: Veritas Publications, 2010, chapters 8 and 9; **Pope John Paul II,** *Familiaris Consortio*.

202 | CREDO | LIVING AND LOVING AS DISCIPLES OF CHRIST

CHAPTER OUTCOMES

See general note on page 19 of this resource.

Learning Outcomes

As a result of studying this chapter and exploring the issues raised, the young people should be able to:

- recognize that the human family is an image of God the Trinity;
- understand that God is Father in a way that goes far beyond any human father;
- know how children fulfill the duties and responsibilities of the Fourth Commandment;
- know how parents fulfill the duties and responsibilities of the Fourth Commandment;
- know that the Fourth Commandment extends to all who have legitimate authority over us;
- understand that citizens and those who exercise legitimate authority have rights and responsibilities;
- know the Church's teaching in relation to the fundamental rights of all people;
- understand the obligation not to obey directives that are contrary to the rights of persons and the moral order;
- know the Church's teaching in relation to civil disobedience and armed resistance;
- know the meaning of the Christian calling to be 'lights in the world';
- understand what being a faithful citizen involves;
- be familiar with the United States' Bishops' guidelines for living as faithful citizens;
- know the story of St. Monica.

Faith-formation Outcomes

As a result of studying this chapter and exploring the issues raised, the young people should also:

- be more open to the love and wisdom of their parents, which is a reflection of the divine love of God;
- strive to adopt the attitudes and actions that will foster harmony and healthy relationships within their family;
- be more aware of the fundamental rights and duties of all citizens;
- recognize how their living as faithful disciples of Jesus supports the building of a just and compassionate society;
- come to a clearer understanding of how they can be 'lights in the world';
- apply the wisdom they have learned from the story of Monica and Augustine to their own relationship with their parent(s)/guardian(s).

Teacher Reflection

As you prepare to engage your group in a study of the Fourth Commandment, take a moment to reflect on these excerpts from the 'Preamble' to the 'Charter of Rights of the Family', presented by the Holy See to all persons, institutions and authorities concerned with the mission of the family in today's world, October 22, 1983.

> The rights of the person, even though they are expressed as rights of the individual, have a fundamental social dimension which finds an innate and vital expression in the family.

> The family constitutes, much more than a mere juridical, social and economic unit, a community of love and solidarity, which is uniquely suited to teach and transmit cultural, ethical, social, spiritual and religious values, essential for the development and well-being of its own members and of society.

> The family is the place where different generations come together and help one another to grow in human wisdom and to harmonize the rights of individuals with other demands of social life.

> The family and society, which are mutually linked by vital and organic bonds, have a complementary function in the defense and advancement of the good of every person and of humanity.

CHAPTER 7: HONOR YOUR FATHER AND YOUR MOTHER | INTRODUCTION | 203

Notes and Guidelines for Student Activities

ATTEND AND REFLECT

Why is 'family' important?

Learning Outcomes
That the young people would:
⊙ recognize that the human family is an image of God the Trinity;
⊙ understand that God is Father in a way that goes far beyond any human father.

Faith-formation Outcome
That the young people would also:
⊙ be more open to the love and wisdom of their parents, which is a reflection of the divine love of God.

Overview
Section one, 'Attend and Reflect', opens with a summary of the 2003 Disney film *Finding Nemo*, which provides a basis for discussing the parent–child relationship and young people's openness to learning from the wisdom of their parents. We move from this to explore how, just as each human being is created in the image and likeness of God, the family is created in the image of God the Trinity and is 'a sign and image of the communion of the Father and the Son in the Holy Spirit' (CCC, no. 2205). We guide the young people to come to see that God is infinitely and unconditionally loving and faithful, generous and forgiving. God is far beyond the limits of any 'human' characteristic that we use to describe him.

Supplementary Activities for 'Attend and Reflect'

Wisdom-Sharing Activity
You might like to invite a group of parents/guardians of young adults (but *not* the parents/guardians of the young people in your class) to come and talk to the young people about what it is like to be a parent or guardian today, especially in relation to the challenge of imparting wisdom and advice to young people. The young people could respond by sharing their own perspectives on this topic.

Reflective Activity
The Catholic Church teaches that the human family is an image of the Trinity, of the community of love who is Father, Son and Holy Spirit. Invite the young people first to brainstorm a list of attributes they associate with the Trinity and then to share specific examples of how their families reflect some of these divine characteristics. As an extension of this activity, you might encourage the young people to create a class collage titled 'The Human Family/The Divine Family' showing all the attributes they identified as being common to both.

Worksheet 1: 'A Parent Is Like. . . .' (*page 209 of this resource*) presents some quotations from famous people about parents as a basis for encouraging the young people to reflect on and describe what 'parents' mean to them. We then invite them to articulate how they see God in terms of a divine parent.

Worksheet 2: 'Speak to Us of Children' (*page 210 of this resource*) takes its name from Kahlil Gibran's *The Prophet*. The worksheet focuses on the uniqueness of every person and guides the young people to identify ways in which they can work in tandem with their parents to grow and develop into the person God calls them to be. We present an excerpt from Gibran's famous work as a starting point for reflection and discussion.

Worksheet 3: 'Pope Francis Speaks about Motherhood' (*page 213 of this resource*) provides excerpts from an address Pope Francis delivered on May 4, 2013 in the Papal Basilica of St. Mary Major, on Mary, the Mother of Jesus, as our mother and exemplar of motherhood. We invite the young people to reflect on and discuss the qualities of motherhood that Mary portrayed and modeled, as well as on the advice Pope Francis offers in this address that has particular relevance for young people.

204 | CREDO | LIVING AND LOVING AS DISCIPLES OF CHRIST

HEAR THE STORY

The heart and foundation of healthy family life

Learning Outcomes

That the young people would:

- ⊙ know how children fulfill the duties and responsibilities of the Fourth Commandment;
- ⊙ know how parents fulfill the duties and responsibilities of the Fourth Commandment.

Faith-formation Outcome

That the young people would also:

- ⊙ strive to adopt the attitudes and actions that will foster harmony and healthy relationships within their family.

Overview

Section two, 'Hear the Story', explores the values and responsibilities underlying the Fourth Commandment. We begin our discussion with reference to Pope Benedict XVI's statement that 'The family is the privileged setting where every person learns to give and receive love'. We guide the young people to understand that children fulfill the Fourth Commandment by showing filial respect, gratitude, just obedience and assistance to their parents. We then look at how parents fulfill their vocation and the duties of the Fourth Commandment by providing for their children's education, for their physical and spiritual needs, and by respecting and encouraging their children's vocation. We also examine the role of grandparents within the family.

Supplementary Activities for 'Hear the Story'

'Spirit of Gratitude' Ritual

Encourage the young people to think of ways in which they could express their gratitude to their parents/guardians in writing, with a view to using these written materials in a simple class 'Gratitude to Parents' ritual or blessing service, to which the young people would invite their parents/guardians. For example, they might write a note or letter of gratitude to their parent(s)/guardian(s), or write a personal tribute or testimonial to parents/guardians, or compose a tribute poem. During the ritual each young person would bless his/her parent(s)/guardian(s) and present their personal tribute.

Research Activity

Invite the young people to work in groups to research how grandparents and other elders of families or communities are honored and respected across diverse cultures. They could create PowerPoint presentations based on their findings.

'Learning from Our Elders' Activity

Invite the young people to ask a grandparent or older person in their family or close community to share some positive stories about their life. The class could gather the stories together into a book, which they could share with the school community through a series of storytelling or story reading sessions.

Worksheet 4: 'Letter to Daniel' (*page 215 of this resource*) presents excerpts from a letter written by journalist and BBC (British Broadcasting Corporation) foreign correspondent Fergal Keane to his newborn son in 1996, in which he reflects on the world his son has just entered. We would hope that this letter will help the young people to appreciate the love and the dreams, the fears and the joys, the challenges and the hopes of parents for their children.

EMBRACE THE VISION

Responding to the fundamental rights of every person

Learning Outcomes

That the young people would:

- ⊙ know that the Fourth Commandment extends to all who have legitimate authority over us;
- ⊙ understand that citizens and those who exercise legitimate authority have rights and responsibilities;
- ⊙ know the Church's teaching in relation to the fundamental rights of all people;
- ⊙ understand the obligation not to obey directives that are contrary to the rights of persons and the moral order;
- ⊙ know the Church's teaching in relation to civil disobedience and armed resistance.

Faith-formation Outcomes

That the young people would also:

- ⊙ be more aware of the fundamental rights and duties of all citizens;

CHAPTER 7: HONOR YOUR FATHER AND YOUR MOTHER | NOTES AND GUIDELINES | 205

⊙ recognize how their living as faithful disciples of Jesus supports the building of a just and compassionate society.

Overview
Section three, 'Embrace the Vision', examines how the Fourth Commandment extends to all who have legitimate authority over us. For the young, this includes teachers, coaches, employers and others. In the broadest sense, this Commandment applies to our duty to obey the civil authorities as citizens of society. We remind the young people that the home and family are the foundation of society. Likewise, the family is the foundation of the Church community; it is 'the domestic church' or 'the church of the home'. When the 'domestic church' is strong, the whole Church and society is stronger. We reiterate that all authority ultimately comes from God and that the fundamental rights of every person flow from the dignity of their being 'images of God'. The primary duty of civil authorities is to lead society in ways that best serve the common good of all the citizens and respect the fundamental rights of all. Thus, civil authority exercises its authority legitimately *only when* it protects and fosters these rights. We explain the Church's teaching in relation to the right to life, the right to human dignity and the right to religious freedom and we introduce the young people to the principle of solidarity. We also discuss the obligation not to obey directives of civil authorities that we judge to be contrary to the rights of the person and the moral order and we explain how people may exercise civil disobedience. The section ends with an explanation of the Church's teaching in relation to armed resistance and the conditions that must exist for such an action to be legitimate.

Supplementary Activities for 'Embrace the Vision'

Research Activity 1
Invite the students to work in groups to research a selection of people who have received the 'Outstanding American by Choice Award' and to analyze and evaluate the type of achievements that have been recognized by this award. The young people could present their findings to the class. This would be a good starting point for a discussion around welcoming immigrants and the principle of solidarity.

Research Activity 2
There are numerous internet sites that list and name American women and men who have committed their lives to helping to create a fairer and more just society. Invite the young people to work in groups to research a selection of such people (from past and present) and to examine the influences of their lives and work on American society today. The young people could present their findings to the class. This could form the basis of a discussion around active and responsible citizenship.

Worksheet 5: 'What Kind of Citizen Am I?' (*page 218 of this resource*) invites the young people to explore different perspectives on citizenship and to begin to identify the kind of citizens they would like to become as disciples of Jesus Christ.

THINK IT THROUGH

Living as faithful citizens

Learning Outcomes
That the young people would:
⊙ know the meaning of the Christian calling to be 'lights in the world';
⊙ understand what being a faithful citizen involves;
⊙ be familiar with the United States' Bishops' guidelines for living as faithful citizens.

Faith-formation Outcome
That the young people would also:
⊙ come to a clearer understanding of how they can be 'lights in the world'.

Overview
Section four, 'Think It Through', focuses on the obligation of all Christians to live as disciples of Jesus in every arena of life, personal and social. We introduce the young people to the guidelines that the Bishops of the Catholic Church in the United States have provided for living as faithful citizens and faithful disciples of Christ and we list the 'Top 10 Ways' the bishops propose for how young people may be faithful citizens and 'lights in the world'.

Supplementary Activities for 'Think It Through'

Worksheet 6: 'Tips for Good Citizenship' (*page 220 of this resource*) invites the young people (1) to identify practical ways in which people can be good citizens

206 | CREDO | LIVING AND LOVING AS DISCIPLES OF CHRIST

by living as faithful disciples of Jesus and (2) to write their own 'Faithful Citizenship Code' for young people.

_____

'Lights in the World' Activity

In Matthew 5:14–16 Jesus uses the image of 'light' as a way of describing faithful discipleship. Invite the young people to come up with their own images for faithful discipleship that would speak in particular to young people today. They could present their images using drawings, photographs, clip art, paintings and so on. They could then create a large wall collage of the different images under the heading 'Lights in the World' and display it in a prominent place in the school.

_____

Role-Play Activity

Invite the young people to work in pairs or small groups to prepare a role-play in which two people discuss the issue of paying taxes. One person in the scenario believes that, as a dutiful citizen, one should always pay one's taxes. The other person believes that it is up to the individual to choose when, if and how taxes should be paid.

In developing the role-play, the young people should pay particular attention to:
– the scene and the context (who? what? where?);
– the flow of the dialogue;
– the development of the arguments on both sides;
– the manner in which the characters express their points of view;
– the conclusions drawn.

The young people will then role-play their sketches for the class, and you might allow a few moments after each presentation for feedback from the other students.

JUDGE AND ACT

Learning Outcomes

That the young people would:
⊙ review the teachings of the Church that they have learned about in this chapter;
⊙ know the story of St. Monica.

Faith-formation Outcome

That the young people would also:
⊙ apply the wisdom they have learned from the story of Monica and Augustine to their own relationship with their parent(s)/guardian(s).

Overview

In section five, 'Judge and Act', the young people review the teachings of the Church that they have studied in this chapter. They also learn about St. Monica, mother of St. Augustine of Hippo, who persevered in love for her wayward child.

Supplementary Activities for 'Judge and Act'

Project 1

Invite the young people to look up Pope John Paul II's 'Charter of Family Rights' in *Familiaris Consortio* and to prepare a presentation on each aspect of the rights that are outlined using a range of creative media. They will find this document on the Vatican website: *www.vatican.va*.

_____

Project 2

The United States Bishops teach that living as faithful citizens and disciples of Jesus Christ should stem from an attitude of prayer and prayerful reflection. The USCCB website (*www.usccb.org*) outlines nine ways in which we can make prayer more central to our lives. Invite the young people first to look up and read these guidelines and then to create and develop a prayer practice or ritual suitable for young people using some of the ideas suggested by the Bishops.

Additional Prayer Suggestions

Guided Meditation: 'Being Family'

(*See 'Student Activity Tool Kit', pages 394–6 of this resource, for further helpful suggestions in relation to conducting guided meditations.*)

Note: The young people will need their Journal and a pen for this meditation. You might also play some quiet background music to create a prayerful atmosphere.

Invite the young people to form a circle.

Leader

Find a comfortable position with your feet resting gently on the ground and your back straight but relaxed.

Now close your eyes.

CHAPTER 7: HONOR YOUR FATHER AND YOUR MOTHER | NOTES AND GUIDELINES | 207

Listen to the rhythm of your breath as it flows gently in and out of your nostrils. (*Pause*)

With every in-breath, feel your whole being filling up with God's love. (*Pause*)

With every exhalation, feel your body relax as you allow your being to accept God's love. (*Pause*)

Breathing in, feel God's love fill your whole being. (*Pause*)

Breathing out, accept God's love for you right here and now. (*Pause*)

(*Repeat the last two instructions several times.*)

Now bring your attention to the people you live with. (*Pause*)

In your mind's eye, picture each person in your home. (*Pause*)

Think of each person one by one. (*Pause*)

Look at each person as if you were seeing them for the very first time. (*Pause*)

Each person in your home is an image of God. (*Pause*)

God loves you unconditionally. . . . God loves you no matter what. (*Pause*)

God loves each person in your home unconditionally. (*Pause*)

Now, in your mind's eye, one by one, take each person in your home by the hand and place them into God's open hands. Imagine God taking their hand with love, with tenderness and with forgiveness. (*Pause*)

Feel God's love fill your home and all who live there. (*Pause*)

Ask for God's continuing love for yourself . . . and for all who live in your home. (*Pause*)

Gently and slowly open your eyes.

Now move around and find yourself a quiet and private place for this part of the meditation.

In your journal draw a symbol of what 'being family' means to you at this moment.

Let your symbol give expression to whatever comes into your mind . . . this is private and just for you.

(*Allow the young people time to complete their symbols.*)

Now write a short prayer to God, who loves each one of us just as we are.

(*Conclude the meditation by praying the Our Father together.*)

_____

Scripture Reflection
(*See instructions for the use of doodling in prayer in the 'Student Activity Tool Kit, page 394 of this resource.*)

Use the following Scripture verse to engage the young people in prayer:

And now bless the God of all, who everywhere works great wonders, who fosters our growth from birth.

SIRACH (ECCLESIASTICUS) 50:22

CHAPTER 7 | WORKSHEET 1

NAME:

A Parent is Like. . . .

This worksheet offers you the opportunity to explore the mystery and complexity of what it means to be a parent, and what God as divine parent means for you.

READ, REFLECT AND SHARE

⊙ Take a few moments to read and reflect on these statements:

'Parents are the bones on which children sharpen their teeth.'
—George Santayana (1863–1952), American philosopher and poet

'You [parents] are the bows from which your children as living arrows are sent forth.'
—Kahlil Gibran, Lebanese mystic and poet

'A father's goodness is higher than the mountain, a mother's goodness deeper than the sea.'

—Japanese proverb

⊙ Now pair up with a partner and share the meaning you take from each of these statements.
⊙ If you feel comfortable in doing so, share stories of how your parent(s) nurture, guide and support you, and how you respond to their wisdom and care.

GET CREATIVE!
In the box provided draw some simple sketches to reflect what 'a parent' means to you.

JOURNAL EXERCISE
Try to describe how you see God as your divine parent. Mention any similarities between the way you experience God's unconditional love and guidance and the way you experience the love and guidance of your human parent(s) or guardian(s).

CHAPTER 7: HONOR YOUR FATHER AND YOUR MOTHER | WORKSHEET 1 | 209

CHAPTER 7 | WORKSHEET 2

NAME:

Speak to Us of Children

Each one of us is unique. God has blessed each one of us with gifts and talents. Parents have the duty to discover and nurture the gifts and talents of their children and to provide opportunities for their children to develop those gifts. In doing so, parents help their children to discern and realize the vocation to which God is calling them. This worksheet offers you the opportunity to reflect on how you can work in tandem with your parents to develop your gifts and talents and become the person God calls you to be.

READ AND REFLECT
Read and reflect on this excerpt from *The Prophet* by Kahlil Gibran (1883–1931), in which he addresses parents on how they should relate to their children.

Your children are not your children. They are the sons and daughters of Life's longing for itself. They come through you but not from you, and though they are with you, yet they belong not to you.

You may give them your love but not your thoughts, for they have their own thoughts. You may house their bodies but not their souls, for their souls dwell in the house of tomorrow, which you cannot visit, not even in your dreams. You may strive to be like them, but seek not to make them like you. For life goes not backward nor tarries with yesterday.

You are the bows from which your children as living arrows are sent forth. The Archer sees the mark upon the path of the infinite, and He bends you with His might that His arrows may go swift and far.
Let your bending in the Archer's hand be for gladness; for even as He loves the arrow that flies, so He loves also the bow that is stable.

PAIR AND SHARE
⊙ Share with a partner what you agree or disagree with in this excerpt.
⊙ You might also like to share it with your parents/guardians and invite them to respond.

210 | CREDO | LIVING AND LOVING AS DISCIPLES OF CHRIST

CHAPTER 7 | WORKSHEET 2 (CONTD.)

OVER TO YOU
Name some of the gifts and talents that you see in yourself.

_____

_____

_____

_____

Name three ways in which you work at developing your gifts and talents.

1. _____

_____

2. _____

_____

3. _____

_____

Name three ways in which your parents/guardians guide or support you in developing your gifts and talents.

1. _____

_____

2. _____

_____

3. _____

_____

_____

CHAPTER 7 | WORKSHEET 2 (CONTD.)

Identify three ways in which you and your parents/guardians could cooperate to nurture your gifts and talents so that you would live your life as a faithful disciple of Jesus.

1. _____

   _____

   _____

2. _____

   _____

   _____

3. _____

   _____

   _____

Identify one ambition or desire for your life that you would like to share with your parents/guardians. Then consider sharing it with them!

_____

_____

_____

_____

212 | CREDO | LIVING AND LOVING AS DISCIPLES OF CHRIST

CHAPTER 7 | WORKSHEET 3

NAME:

Pope Francis Speaks About Motherhood

This worksheet offers you the opportunity to read some excerpts from an address Pope Francis delivered on May 4, 2013 in the Papal Basilica of St. Mary Major, on Mary, the Mother of Jesus, as our mother and exemplar of motherhood. We invite you to reflect on the qualities of motherhood that Mary portrayed and modeled as well as on the advice Pope Francis offers in this address that has particular relevance for young people.

READ AND REFLECT

Read the following excerpts from Pope Francis' sermon on motherhood and how Mary the Mother of Jesus is our Mother and model of motherhood.

> Mary is the mother, and a mother worries above all about the health of her children, she knows how to care for them always with great and tender love. Our Lady guards our health . . . she helps us grow, to confront life, to be free.
>
> 1. A mother helps her children grow up and wants them to grow strong; that is why she teaches them not to be lazy. . . . The mother takes care that her children develop better, that they grow strong, capable of accepting responsibilities, of engaging in life, of striving for great ideals. The Gospel of St Luke tells us that, in the family of Nazareth, Jesus 'grew and became strong, filled with wisdom; and the favor of God was upon him' (Luke 2:40). Our Lady does just this for us, she helps us to grow as human beings and in the faith, to be strong and never to fall into the temptation of being human beings and Christians in a superficial way, but to live responsibly, to strive ever higher.
>
> 2. A mother then thinks of the health of her children, teaching them also *to face the difficulties of life*. You do not teach, you do not take care of health by avoiding problems, as though life were a motorway with no obstacles. The mother helps her children to see the problems of life realistically and not to get lost in them, but to confront them with courage, not to be weak, and to know how to overcome them, in a healthy balance that a mother 'senses' between the area of security and the area of risk. . . . A mother knows how to balance things. A life without challenges does not exist and a boy or a girl who cannot face or tackle them is a boy or girl with no backbone! . . .
>
> Jesus from the Cross says to Mary, indicating John: 'Woman, behold your son!' and to John: 'Here is your mother!' (cf. John 19:26–27). In that disciple, we are all represented: the Lord entrusts us to the loving and tender hands of the [M]other, that we might feel her support in facing and overcoming the difficulties of our human and Christian journey; to never be afraid of the struggle, to face it with the help of the [M]other.

CHAPTER 7: HONOR YOUR FATHER AND YOUR MOTHER | WORKSHEET 3 | 213

CHAPTER 7 | WORKSHEET 3 (CONTD.)

3. Lastly, a good mother not only accompanies her children in their growth, without avoiding the problems and challenges of life; a good mother also helps them *to make definitive decisions with freedom.* This is not easy, but a mother knows how to do it. But what does freedom mean? It is certainly not doing whatever you want, allowing yourself to be dominated by the passions, to pass from one experience to another without discernment, to follow the fashions of the day; freedom does not mean, so to speak, throwing everything that you don't like out the window. No, that is not freedom! Freedom is given to us so that we know how to make good decisions in life! Mary as a good mother teaches us to be, like her, capable of making definitive decisions; definitive choices, at this moment in a time controlled by, so to speak, a philosophy of the provisional. . . .

PAIR AND SHARE

Reread Pope Francis' message with a partner. Combine your insights and observations to respond to the following tasks.

List the characteristics of Mary as mother that Pope Francis highlights, or implies, in his sermon.

_____

_____

_____

Identify three important things Pope Francis is saying in this excerpt to mothers today.

1. _____

_____

2. _____

_____

3. _____

_____

Identify three important things Pope Francis is saying in this excerpt that are particularly relevant to young people today.

1. _____

_____

2. _____

_____

3. _____

_____

214 | CREDO | LIVING AND LOVING AS DISCIPLES OF CHRIST

CHAPTER 7 | WORKSHEET 4

NAME:

Letter to Daniel

This worksheet presents excerpts from a letter written by journalist Fergal Keane to his newborn son in which he reflects on the world his son has just entered. Keane wrote this letter while working as a foreign correspondent for the British BBC TV station in Hong Kong in February 1996.

READ AND REFLECT

Read and reflect on this letter from a father to his newborn son.

My dear son, it is six o'clock in the morning on the island of Hong Kong. You are asleep cradled in my left arm and I am learning the art of one-handed typing. Your mother, more tired yet more happy than I've ever known her, is sound asleep in the room next door and there is a soft quiet in our apartment. . . .

Outside the window, below us on the harbor, the ferries are ploughing back and forth to Kowloon. Millions are already up and moving about and the sun is slanting through the tower blocks and out on to the flat silver waters of the South China Sea.

Your coming has turned me upside down and inside out. So much that seemed essential to me has, in the past few days, taken on a different color. Like many foreign correspondents I know, I have lived a life that, on occasion, has veered close to the edge: war zones, natural disasters, darkness in all its shapes and forms.

In a world of insecurity and ambition and ego, it's easy to be drawn in, to take chances with our lives, to believe that what we do and what people say about us is reason enough to gamble with death. Now, looking at your sleeping face, inches away from me, listening to your occasional sigh and gurgle, I wonder how I could have ever thought glory and prizes and praise were sweeter than life.

And it's also true that I am pained, perhaps haunted is a better word, by the memory, suddenly so vivid now, of each suffering child I have come across on my journeys. . . . Ten-year-old Andi Mikail dying from napalm burns on a hillside in Eritrea, how his voice cried out, growing ever more faint when the wind blew dust on to his wounds. The two brothers, Domingo and Juste, in Menongue, southern Angola. Juste, two years old and blind, dying from malnutrition, being carried on seven-year-old Domingo's back. And Domingo's words to me, 'He was nice before, but now he has the hunger.'

Last October, in Afghanistan, when you were growing inside your mother, I met Sharja, aged twelve. Motherless, fatherless, guiding me through the grey ruins of her home, everything was gone, she told me. And I knew that, for all her tender years, she had learned more about loss than I would likely understand in a lifetime.

CHAPTER 7: HONOR YOUR FATHER AND YOUR MOTHER | WORKSHEET 4 | 215

CHAPTER 7 | WORKSHEET 4 (CONTD.)

There is one last memory, of Rwanda, and the churchyard of the parish of Nyarubuye where, in a ransacked classroom, I found a mother and her three young children huddled together where they'd been beaten to death. The children had died holding on to their mother, that instinct we all learn from birth and in one way or another cling to until we die.

Daniel, these memories explain some of the fierce protectiveness I feel for you, the tenderness and the occasional moments of blind terror when I imagine anything happening to you. But there is something more, a story from long ago that I will tell you face to face, father and son, when you are older. It's a very personal story but it's part of the picture. It has to do with the long lines of blood and family, about our lives and how we can get lost in them and, if we're lucky, find our way out again into the sunlight.

It begins thirty-five years ago in a big city on a January morning with snow on the ground and a woman walking to the hospital to have her first baby. . . . She's walking because there is no money and everything of value has been pawned to pay for the alcohol to which her husband has become addicted.

On the way, a taxi driver notices her sitting, exhausted and cold, in the doorway of a shop and he takes her to hospital for free. Later that day, she gives birth to a baby boy and, just as you are to me, he is the best thing she has ever seen. Her husband comes that night and weeps with joy when he sees his son. He is truly happy. Hungover, broke, but in his own way happy, for they were both young and in love with each other and their son.

But, Daniel, time had some bad surprises in store for them. The cancer of alcoholism ate away at the man and he lost his family. This was not something he meant to do or wanted to do, it just was. When you are older, my son, you will learn about how complicated life becomes, how we can lose our way and how people get hurt inside and out. By the time his son had grown up, the man lived away from his family, on his own in a one-roomed flat, living and dying for the bottle.

He died on the fifth of January, one day before the anniversary of his son's birth, all those years before in that snowbound city. But his son was too far away to hear his last words, his final breath, and all the things they might have wished to say to one another were left unspoken.

Yet now, Daniel, I must tell you that when you let out your first powerful cry in the delivery room of the Adventist Hospital and I became a father, I thought of your grandfather and, foolish though it may seem, hoped that in some way he could hear, across the infinity between the living and the dead, your proud statement of arrival. For if he could hear, he would recognize the distinct voice of family, the sound of hope and new beginnings that you and all your innocence and freshness have brought to the world.

PAIR AND SHARE

Share your responses to this letter with a partner.

216 | CREDO | LIVING AND LOVING AS DISCIPLES OF CHRIST

CHAPTER 7 | WORKSHEET 4 (CONTD.)

OVER TO YOU

Describe three insights into parenthood that you gained from this letter.

1. _____

_____

_____

2. _____

_____

_____

3. _____

_____

_____

CHAPTER 7: HONOR YOUR FATHER AND YOUR MOTHER | WORKSHEET 4 (CONTD.) | 217

CHAPTER 7 | WORKSHEET 5

NAME:

What Kind of Citizen Am I?

This worksheet invites you to examine some different perspectives on citizenship so that you may begin to identify the kind of citizen you would like to become as a disciple of Jesus Christ.

READ AND RESPOND

⊙ Carefully examine the descriptions on the chart opposite for three different types of citizen, or three different perspectives on citizenship, namely, the personally responsible citizen, the participatory citizen and the justice-oriented citizen.

⊙ Pair up with a partner and identify two specific examples for each category of individuals or members of organizations or institutions who reflect that type of citizenship.

Examples of responsible citizens

1. _____

2. _____

Examples of participatory citizens

1. _____

2. _____

Examples of justice-oriented citizens

1. _____

2. _____

JOURNAL EXERCISE

⊙ Take some time to think about the kind of citizen you are. Is there anything you would like to change or improve upon?

⊙ Write about the kind of citizen you would like to become in light of the example that Jesus modeled for us.

218 | CREDO | LIVING AND LOVING AS DISCIPLES OF CHRIST

CHAPTER 7 | WORKSHEET 5 (CONTD.)

KINDS OF CITIZENS			
	Personally Responsible Citizen	**Participatory Citizen**	**Justice-oriented Citizen**
Description	Acts responsibly in his/her community Works and pays taxes Obeys laws Recycles, gives blood Volunteers to lend a hand in times of crisis	Active member of community organizations and/or improvement efforts Organizes community efforts to care for those in need, promote economic development, or clean up environment Knows how government agencies work Knows strategies for accomplishing collective tasks	Critically assesses social, political and economic structures to see beyond surface causes Seeks out and addresses areas of injustice Knows about social movements and how to effect systemic change
Sample Action	Contributes food to a food drive	Helps to organize a food drive	Explores why people are hungry and acts to solve root causes
Core Assumptions	To solve social problems and improve society, citizens must have good character; they must be honest, responsible and law-abiding members of the community	To solve social problems and improve society, citizens must actively participate and take leadership positions within established systems and community structures	To solve social problems and improve society, citizens must question and change established systems and structures when they reproduce patterns of injustice over time

CHAPTER 7: HONOR YOUR FATHER AND YOUR MOTHER | WORKSHEET 5 (CONTD.) | 219

CHAPTER 7 | WORKSHEET 6

NAME:

Tips for Good Citizenship

This worksheet invites you to identify practical ways in which people can be good citizens by living as faithful disciples of Jesus.

PAIR AND SHARE

⊙ Work with a partner. You will need two sheets of paper for this activity.

⊙ Brainstorm *values* that you regard as important for a just, fair and stable society. Recall the values that Jesus lived by and modeled for us. Jot down your suggestions on a sheet of paper.

⊙ Now brainstorm *actions* of people that support and reinforce these values and that contribute to a healthy and just society. Once again, bring to mind the actions of Jesus and how he related to people from all walks of life. Record your suggestions on a separate sheet of paper.

⊙ Choose your best suggestions from each sheet and complete the chart. An example has been provided.

⊙ Afterward, share your 'tips' with the class.

TIPS FOR GOOD CITIZENSHIP

Good Values	Actions that promote these values	Outcomes for society
Honesty	Being truthful in one's dealings with others	An atmosphere of trust

220 | CREDO | LIVING AND LOVING AS DISCIPLES OF CHRIST

CHAPTER 7 | WORKSHEET 6 (CONTD.)

FAITHFUL CITIZENSHIP CODE
- Read again the 'Top 10 Ways That You Can Be A Faithful Citizen' in the 'Think It Through' section of chapter 7 of your theology text.
- Now, with your partner, write out what you believe would be a good 'Faithful Citizenship Code' for young people of your age.

Faith for Citizenship Code

Review of Chapter 7

I. True/False. Mark the true statements 'T' and the false statements 'F'. In the case of each false statement, cross out and rewrite the incorrect words to make the statement true.

_____1.   After the creation of Adam, God said, 'It is good that the man should be alone.'

_____2.   The attitudes and actions that flow from the respect we owe our parents derive from the honor and respect we owe God.

_____3.   A child is obliged to obey a parent, or any person in authority, who asks them to do something even if it is contrary to God's law or to civil law.

_____4.   The Catholic Church teaches that parents have a right to choose a school for their children that corresponds to the parents' own convictions.

_____5.   The *Catechism of the Catholic Church* teaches that work is a duty.

_____6.   Welcoming immigrants is an expression of the principle of solidarity.

_____7.   Even when a person, in good conscience, judges the directives of civil authorities to be contrary to the rights of persons and the moral order, the person is still obliged to obey those directives.

_____8.   Examples of civil disobedience include non-violent acts of refusal, such as protests, sit-ins and marches.

CHAPTER 7 | CHAPTER REVIEW (CONTD.)

_____9. The Catholic Church teaches that armed resistance to unjust laws and oppressive political authority is legitimate in all circumstances.

_____10. St. Monica and her family lived in North America in the fourth century.

II. Matching. Write the letter of the term or phrase from column 2 next to its best match in column 1. There are two more items in column 2 than you need.

COLUMN 1	COLUMN 2
_____ 1. A man and a woman united in marriage, together with their children	A. To follow Jesus
	B. Society
_____ 2. US Bishops' guidelines for living as faithful citizens and faithful disciples of Christ	C. _Lumen Gentium_
	D. Solidarity
	E. August 27
_____ 3. A small silver Roman coin	F. Family
_____ 4. How the Second Vatican Council described the family	G. _Forming Consciences for Faithful Citizenship_
_____ 5. The quality by virtue of which persons or institutions make laws	H. The domestic church
_____ 6. On this day the Church remembers and celebrates the life of St. Monica	I. April 27
	J. Authority
_____ 7. The habit of listening and responding to our parents' guidance on how we can live a just and holy life	K. Denarius
	L. Just obedience
_____ 8. A group of persons bound together organically by a principle of unity that goes beyond each one of them	
_____ 9. The principle that respects the needs of others and the common good in an interdependent world	
_____ 10. The first vocation of all Christians	

CHAPTER 7: HONOR YOUR FATHER AND YOUR MOTHER | CHAPTER REVIEW (CONTD.) | 223

CHAPTER 7 | CHAPTER REVIEW (CONTD.)

III. Write a brief answer. Explain the teaching of the Catholic Church on 1 or 2.

    1. Catholic youth are obliged to be faithful citizens

    2. The human family as the image of the divine family

_____

_____

_____

_____

_____

_____

_____

_____

IV. How would you respond? A friend says to you, 'My parents sometimes ask me to do things that I know are wrong, but the Church tells me I have to obey them.'

_____

_____

_____

_____

_____

_____

_____

_____

_____

224 | CREDO | LIVING AND LOVING AS DISCIPLES OF CHRIST

CHAPTER 7 | CHAPTER REVIEW (CONTD.)

V. Make a 'disciple decision'.

1. What is the most important wisdom for life that you discovered in this chapter?

_____

_____

_____

_____

_____

_____

2. Name several ways you can put this wisdom into practice. Choose one of the ways you identify and describe how you will make that wisdom part of your life right now.

_____

_____

_____

_____

_____

_____

_____

_____

_____

_____

CHAPTER 7: HONOR YOUR FATHER AND YOUR MOTHER | CHAPTER REVIEW (CONTD.) | 225

CHAPTER 8

Living the 'Way' of Life and Truth

—The Fifth and Eighth Commandments

INTRODUCTION

'I came that they may have life, and have it abundantly.'

—John 10:10

Many people today meander through life with a lack of purpose. Some people only come to a full realization about the meaning of life when death comes to their door, when they discover, perhaps for the very first time, that life is a precious gift to be embraced. However, there are people for whom life has deep and significant meaning, who believe in God as the source of all life and who acknowledge life as a precious gift that comes from God. They experience the presence of God in their lives and 'hear' God inviting them to embody faith and hope, truth and justice, love and compassion in their everyday experiences.

In this chapter we explore with the young people the implications of living our lives in a God-filled and meaningful way. We focus on the Fifth Commandment 'You shall not kill' and on the Eighth Commandment 'You shall not bear false witness against your neighbor' and we lead the young people to understand that respecting all life and living by the truth is the best way to live as disciples of Jesus Christ.

Chapter 8 is developed under five major headings:

- ⊙ **ATTEND AND REFLECT:** How are you being true to yourself?
- ⊙ **HEAR THE STORY:** Living truthful lives
- ⊙ **EMBRACE THE VISION:** Choose life so that you may live
- ⊙ **THINK IT THROUGH:** Love and respect for ALL human life—even those who call themselves your enemy
- ⊙ **JUDGE AND ACT:** (*Activities and exercises that encourage the young people to integrate what they have learned in the chapter into their daily lives*)

Theological Background for the Teacher

LIVING LIFE TO THE FULL

Somebody should tell us, right at the start of our lives, that we are dying. Then we might live life to the limit, every minute of every day.

—Pope Paul VI

What does it mean to live life to the full? What does it mean to live every moment of our lives to the limit? Sometimes this question arises when our own life or the life of someone we hold dear is threatened. In the book *Tuesdays with Morrie* by Mitch Album (Sphere, London, 1997), the central character Morrie, who is dying, explains, 'When you learn how to die, you learn how to live.'

Our human capacity to think, to imagine, to reason and to reflect marks us apart from all other creatures. We have the capacity to wonder about the meaning of life and death. Down through the ages, philosophers, artists, writers, musicians and others have struggled with this question and have sought answers from many different sources. For the Christian, however, the answer to the meaning of life and death, and the path to happiness, is found in God the Father, God the Son and God the Holy Spirit. The *Catechism of the Catholic Church* teaches:

The desire for God is written in the human heart, because man is created by God and for God.

—CCC, no. 27

For Christians, life is a living response of love to God, who created us out of love and who sustains us by that same love.

In this chapter we guide the young people to examine what gives meaning to their lives right now; what helps them to flourish and grow; what it means to put God at the center of their world and how that shapes their everyday lives; how to live with dignity and respect, and what values they should hold.

226 | CREDO | LIVING AND LOVING AS DISCIPLES OF CHRIST

Jesus spoke to the hearts of his disciples when he said: 'I am the way, and the truth, and the life' (John 14:6). Jesus showed us how to live a life of truth, how to engage in truthful relationships and how to live in love of God, neighbor and self. Made in God's image and likeness, we are invited to reflect God in our lives. This is the thrust of the Fifth and the Eighth Commandments. The more loving and respectful we are, the more clearly we reflect God, in whose image we are created.

LIVING THE WAY OF TRUTH AND LIFE

It is not always easy to respect the gift of life that God has given us and to live truthful lives. It is not always easy to speak truthfully, to bear witness to the truth and to be 'true in deeds and truthful in words' (CCC, no. 2468). The members of the early Church also knew what it meant to be tested in faith and they understood the difficulties of bearing witness to the truth of Christ.

My brothers and sisters, whenever you face trials of any kind, consider it nothing but joy, because you know that the testing of your faith produces endurance. . . . If any of you is lacking in wisdom, ask God, who gives to all generously and ungrudgingly, and it will be given to you.

—Letter of James 1:2–3, 5

Christian faith demands that we stand up for truth. Jesus tells us that 'the truth will make you free' (John 8:32). Our faith demands that we embrace a 'culture of life' and uphold the mystery of life because God is the source of all life. Living the truth that honors the sacredness and dignity of all human persons will liberate us to grow more fully into the sort of people God desires us to be.

Human life is sacred because from its beginning it involves the creative action of God and it remains for ever in a special relationship with the Creator, who is its sole end. God alone is the Lord of life from its beginning until its end.

—CCC, no. 2258

As Christians we are called to protect and respect all life and to do what is necessary to sustain and nourish human life at all times. The Fifth Commandment mandates us to peaceful and healthy living. It heightens our awareness of the importance of life and asks us to become champions for the dignity of the human person. It calls each one of us to safeguard human life, especially the life of the most vulnerable—those growing in the womb; those who are suffering and dying; those who are

sad and depressed; those who are tortured, in prison and condemned to death. The Fifth Commandment demands that we seek to create a culture of life that is expressed in the structures of families and communities, governments and institutions, and in the values of world leaders. The Fifth Commandment demands that we work tirelessly to build a world founded on reconciliation rather than on hate and lack of forgiveness; on peace rather than on war; on giving life rather than on the taking of life; on integrity rather than on deceit; on love rather than on fear; on community rather than on isolation.

You have heard that it was said to those of ancient times, 'You shall not murder'; and 'whoever murders shall be liable to judgment'. But I say to you that if you are angry with a brother or sister, you will be liable to judgment; and if you insult a brother or sister, you will be liable to the council.

—Matthew 5:21–22

Here, Jesus warns his listeners against murder and states clearly that such action is wrong. In the same breath he teaches about the dangers of unjustified anger and insults against a 'brother or sister'. Jesus was a storyteller *par excellence*, so we can probably take it for granted that he knew the power of words to heal and affirm and the power of words to destroy and damage. The Eighth Commandment asks us to pay attention to our use of words, especially in relation to others. It commands us not to bear false witness, not to lie, not to be deceitful, not to gossip and not to spread untrue rumors. It calls on us to be witnesses to the truth within ourselves and in our relationships with others. As disciples of Jesus, we are mandated to create a society based on justice and truth.

The duty of Christians to take part in the life of the Church impels them to act as *witnesses of the Gospel* and of the obligations that flow from it. This witness is a transmission of the faith in words and deeds. Witness is an act of justice that establishes the truth or makes it known.

—CCC, no. 2472

In our modern age of internet and electronic social networking, young people need help to apply the Eighth Commandment to their lives and to realize the damage and hurt that can be caused by gossip and calumny, by ridicule and detraction, by the spreading of false rumors and the dissemination of misleading information.

Truth or truthfulness is the virtue which consists in showing oneself true in deeds and truthful in words, and in guarding against duplicity, dissimulation and hypocrisy.

—CCC, no. 2468

The Eighth Commandment demands that we use words with care and show respect for the dignity of ourselves and others; that we choose our words with honesty and articulate them from a standpoint of fairness and justice. This can be a difficult task, but we are not alone. Through the love of God the Father, the example of his Son Jesus, of his life, Death, Resurrection and Ascension, and the gift of the Holy Spirit, we are supported in our efforts to respect life and to live the truth.

Speaking to young people, Pope John Paul II addressed the challenges of today, affirmed the young people in their capacity to be true disciples of Christ, and offered them hope and encouragement when he said:

Ask yourselves, young people, about the love of Christ. Acknowledge His voice resounding in the temple of your heart. Return His bright and penetrating glance which opens the paths of your life to the horizons of the Church's mission. It is a taxing mission, today more than ever, to teach men the truth about themselves, about their end, their destiny, and to show faithful souls the unspeakable riches of the love of Christ. Do not be afraid of the radicalness of His demands, because Jesus, who loved us first, is prepared to give Himself to you, as well as asking of you. If He asks much of you, it is because He knows you can give much.

—Pope John Paul II, *The Meaning of Vocation*

ADDITIONAL BACKGROUND READING
Catechism of the Catholic Church, nos. 2258–2329, 2464–2513; *United States Catholic Catechism for Adults,* 387–401; 429–438.

CHAPTER OUTCOMES

See general note on page 19 of this resource.

Learning Outcomes
As a result of studying this chapter and exploring the issues raised, the young people should be able to:
- understand that living as our 'true selves' is about living as images of God, who is Love;
- know that God's gift of sanctifying grace enables us to live the way of Jesus and thus give glory to God;
- understand the power of words to cause harm as well as good;
- recognize attitudes and actions that are contrary to the Eighth Commandment;
- recognize attitudes and actions that dishonor the reputation of others;
- appreciate the responsibility of the media and art to present information truthfully and with respect for the rights and dignity of the individual;
- know the Catholic Church's teaching on the sacredness of all human life;
- understand the Church's teaching on abortion, embryonic stem cell research, euthanasia, suicide and intentional disregard of our bodily and mental health;
- know the Church's teaching on legitimate self-defense;
- know the strict conditions the Church requires for war to be justifiable;
- know the Church's teaching on capital punishment;
- understand the meaning of 'retributive justice' and 'restorative justice';
- know about Sister Helen Prejean and her work and writings against the death penalty.

Faith-formation Outcomes
As a result of studying this chapter and exploring the issues raised, the young people should also:
- value their life as a precious gift from God;
- know that they give glory to God just by being alive, in the divine image and likeness;
- value the importance of being truthful;
- recognize the power their words have to cause harm as well as good;
- make choices that show love and respect for all human life;
- favor and advocate non-violence and the peaceful resolution of conflict;
- find inspiration from Sister Helen Prejean to promote and pursue at all times a culture of life.

228 | CREDO | LIVING AND LOVING AS DISCIPLES OF CHRIST

Teacher Reflection

As you prepare to engage your group in a study of the Fifth and the Eighth Commandments, which guide us in living the way of truth and life, take a moment to read this reflection from the poet and mystic Kahlil Gibran (1883–1931).

Words to Live: Don't Live A Half Life

Do not love half lovers
Do not entertain half friends
Do not indulge in works of the half talented
Do not live half a life and do not die a half death
If you choose silence, then be silent
When you speak, do so until you are finished
Do not silence yourself to say something
And do not speak to be silent
If you accept, then express it bluntly
Do not mask it
If you refuse then be clear about it
for an ambiguous refusal
is but a weak acceptance
Do not accept half a solution
Do not believe half truths
Do not dream half a dream
Do not fantasize about half hopes
Half a drink will not quench your thirst
Half a meal will not satiate your hunger
Half the way will get you no where
Half an idea will bear you no results
Your other half is not the one you love
It is you in another time yet in the same space
It is you when you are not
Half a life is a life you didn't live
A word you have not said
A smile you postponed
A love you have not had
A friendship you did not know
To reach and not arrive
Work and not work
Attend only to be absent
What makes you a stranger to them closest to you
and they strangers to you
The half is a mere moment of inability
but you are able for you are not half a being
You are a whole that exists
to live a life not half a life

CHAPTER 8: LIVING THE 'WAY' OF LIFE AND TRUTH | INTRODUCTION | 229

Notes and Guidelines for Student Activities

ATTEND AND REFLECT

How are you being true to yourself?

Learning Outcomes

That the young people would:

◉ understand that living as our 'true selves' is about living as images of God, who is Love;

◉ know that God's gift of sanctifying grace enables us to live the way of Jesus and thus give glory to God.

Faith-formation Outcomes

That the young people would also:

◉ value their life as a precious gift from God;

◉ know that they give glory to God just by being alive, in the divine image and likeness.

Overview

Section one, 'Attend and Reflect', opens with the last words of advice from Polonius to his son Laertes in Shakespeare's *Hamlet*: 'To thine own self be true', and the question 'How are you being true to yourself?' We recall with the young people that Jesus Christ, the Incarnate Son of God, clearly revealed that striving to live as our 'true selves' is not about being selfish and doing what we want, regardless of how that impacts other people; rather, it is about living as people who are created in the image of God, who is Love. Our challenge as Christians is to love God, to love others and to love our self, as Jesus did. When we do this, we act in the best interests of our 'true self' and in the best interests of other people. We guide the young people to recognize their capacity as rational, social and free human beings to come to know God, to live in right relationship with other people, to choose to love rather than to hate, to tell the truth rather than to lie, to be life-givers rather than life-takers. It is in this context that we explore the Fifth and the Eighth Commandments in this chapter.

Supplementary Activities for 'Attend and Reflect'

Teacher Tip: You might like to show the film *Tuesdays with Morrie* in class, or excerpts from it, and discuss Morrie's reflections on living life to the full.

Worksheet 1: 'My Tree of Life' (*page 235 of this resource*) is a reflective exercise that provides a framework and guidance to enable the young people to reflect on and identify how they are living their life right now. Through an activity centered around the tree as a symbol of life, we guide them to identify the people and things that help them to live life to the full and to become aware of the visible signs in their lives that they are living in a life-giving and meaningful way, as God desires for them.

———————

Worksheet 2: 'Made in the Image of the Triune God' (*page 237 of this resource*) invites the young people to reflect on the fact that they have been created in the image of the Triune God and to name ways in which this might be different from being made in the image of a one-dimensional God.

———————

Worksheet 3: 'What does it mean to be human?' (*page 239 of this resource*) offers the young people the opportunity to explore the key aspects of our humanity that differentiate us from other creatures and to identify the responsibilities and the challenges that stem from these differences.

HEAR THE STORY

Living truthful lives

Learning Outcomes

That the young people would:

◉ understand the power of words to cause harm as well as good;

◉ recognize attitudes and actions that are contrary to the Eighth Commandment;

◉ recognize attitudes and actions that dishonor the reputation of others;

230 | CREDO | LIVING AND LOVING AS DISCIPLES OF CHRIST

◉ appreciate the responsibility of the media and art to present information truthfully and with respect for the rights and dignity of the individual.

Faith-formation Outcomes

That the young people would also:
◉ value the importance of being truthful;
◉ recognize the power their words have to cause harm as well as good.

Overview

Section two, 'Hear the Story', examines how the Eighth Commandment calls us to live truthful lives and forbids us from misrepresenting the truth in our relations with others. We begin by exploring the power of words and how they can give truthful witness to or betray our true identity. We identify attitudes and actions that are contrary to the Eighth Commandment, such as lying and other forms of self-serving deception, and the consequences for our relationships with others when we engage in these actions. We then examine what it means to respect the reputation and honor of 'neighbors' and how we dishonor the reputation of others when we engage in gossip, calumny and detraction, rash judgment, irony and sarcasm. Finally, we explore the responsibility of the communications media and art to present information truthfully and with full respect for the laws of morality and for the rights and dignity of the individual.

Supplementary Activities for 'Hear the Story'

Worksheet 4: 'My Words' (*page 240 of this resource*) invites the young people to take a close look at the words they use and the manner in which they use them.

_____

Worksheet 5: 'Jesus' Words' (*page 243 of this resource*) offers the young people the opportunity to recall and reflect on words of Jesus that they find meaningful and relevant to their lives right now.

Research Activity

Invite the young people to find cuttings from newspapers and magazines of stories that reflect people not adhering to the teaching of the Church which urges 'respect for the reputation of persons' and 'forbids every attitude and word likely to cause [people] unjust injury' (CCC, no. 2477). Encourage

them to share their stories and then to discuss the negative consequences of disrespecting the reputation of others.

Worksheet 6: 'Witnesses to the Truth' (*page 245 of this resource*) tells the story of Bishop Juan Gerardi of Guatemala City, a human rights campaigner who was brutally murdered in April 1998 and who inspired Auxiliary Bishop Mario Rios of Guatamala to continue Gerardi's work for human rights in Guatemala.

_____

Worksheet 7: 'Living and Witnessing to the Truth' (*page 246 of this resource*) invites the young people to reflect on what it means to live a life based on truth and integrity.

_____

Worksheet 8: 'Testimonies to Truth' (*page 248 of this resource*) invites the young people to recall and write about times when they and others stood up for the truth.

_____

Worksheet 9: 'Pope John Paul II's Letter to Artists' (*page 249 of this resource*) presents excerpts from Pope John Paul II's famous Letter in which he extols the role artists play in the world today and affirms the artist as a creator of beauty who reflects the image of God, the Creator, in a unique manner.

Teacher Tip: You might like to invite the young people to think of a visual work of art that resonates with them in some way. Alternatively, they could choose a piece of music or a song or dance that they find particularly beautiful. Ask them to write a prayer of praise and thanks to God for the creative capacity of the artist who created the art work they chose.

Media Watch

Invite the young people to select and watch a TV documentary and examine whether or not it conforms to the ideals underlying the T.H.I.N.K. rule that they have encountered in their text; in other words, is the message that the program transmits True, Helpful, Inspiring, Necessary, Kind?

Teacher Tip: You might like to share with the young people this comment from Pope John Paul II on the media's responsibility to communicate its messages truthfully: 'Television is often required to deal with serious themes: with human weakness and sin, and their consequences for individuals and society;

CHAPTER 8: LIVING THE 'WAY' OF LIFE AND TRUTH | NOTES AND GUIDELINES | 231 with the failings of social institutions, including government and religion; with weighty questions about the meaning of life. It should treat these subjects responsibly—without sensationalism and with a sincere concern for the good of society, as well as with scrupulous regard for the truth. "The truth shall make you free" (John 8:32), Jesus said, and ultimately all truth has its foundation in God, who is also the source of our freedom and creativity' ('Television and Family: Guidelines for Good Viewing', a message from Pope John Paul II for the 28th World Communications Day, 1994).

Worksheet 10: 'The Transmission of Truth' (*page 251 of this resource*) provides guidelines to help the young people to critically analyze an article from the media in order to test the reliability and truthfulness of the content.

EMBRACE THE VISION

Choose life so that you may live

Learning Outcomes
That the young people would:
⊙ know the Catholic Church's teaching on the sacredness of all human life;
⊙ understand the Church's teaching on abortion, embryonic stem cell research, euthanasia, suicide and intentional disregard of our bodily and mental health.

Faith-formation Outcome
That the young people would also:
⊙ make choices that show love and respect for all human life.

Overview
Section three, 'Embrace the Vision', focuses on the Fifth Commandment's demand that we embrace a 'culture of life' and respect the right to life of every person. Beyond condemning murder, the Fifth Commandment mandates choosing life over all forms of death-bearing attitudes and actions. We guide the young people to appreciate that reverence for the sacredness of every human life is not only the best antidote to a culture of death; it is the only way to the fullness of life that God promised for all people.

We explain the Catholic Church's teaching on acts that are contrary to the Fifth Commandment, such as direct abortion, embryonic stem cell and

other scientific research that does not respect the sacredness of the embryo, intentional euthanasia, suicide and intentional disregard of our bodily and mental health. Throughout the section we stress that human life is sacred because God is the source of all life.

Supplementary Activities for 'Embrace the Vision'

Teacher Tip: In March 2009 President Obama signed an order to lift restrictions on federal funding for embryonic stem cell research. You might invite the young people to look up President Obama's 'stem cell order' and analyze the arguments in relation to the Catholic Church's teaching on stem cell research.

Research Activity
Invite the young people to look up the USCCB website (*www.usccb.org*) to find and summarize what the Bishops have to say about respect for human life, justice, anti-trafficking and migrant refugees.

Worksheet 11: 'The Sacredness of Human Life' (*page 253 of this resource*) presents statements made by some American Catholic bishops on the sacredness of human life, and invites the young people's response.

Worksheet 12: 'Papal Messages on Social Justice' (*page 255 of this resource*) presents a selection of quotations on respect for life and social justice from different Popes down through the ages and invites the young people to work in groups to write a presentation on one of them.

Worksheet 13: 'Loving Ourselves' (*page 257 of this resource*) seeks to help the young people to be aware that we cannot love others unless we have a deep love and respect for ourselves. We invite the young people to think about ways in which they take care of themselves and to identify how they might sustain a sense of responsibility and care for their own selves.

Research Activity
There are many organizations that offer services and support to people who are dying and to their families; to people with disabilities; to victims of crime, violence or bullying; to people who feel depressed

232 | CREDO | LIVING AND LOVING AS DISCIPLES OF CHRIST

or suicidal and so on. Invite the young people to find out what caring organizations are available in their school or community or city. They could choose one organization and, if appropriate, arrange to meet with some of the people who either access or provide the service. They could then share what they have learned with the class.

THINK IT THROUGH

Love and respect for ALL human life—even those who call themselves your enemy

Learning Outcomes
That the young people would:
⊙ know the Church's teaching on legitimate self-defense;
⊙ know the strict conditions the Church requires for war to be justifiable;
⊙ know the Church's teaching on capital punishment;
⊙ understand the meaning of 'retributive justice' and 'restorative justice'.

Faith-formation Outcome
That the young people would also:
⊙ favor and advocate non-violence and the peaceful resolution of conflict.

Overview
Section four, 'Think It Through', examines the Church's teaching on legitimate self-defense and capital punishment. We begin with an extract from the film *Dead Man Walking*, a film in which Sister Helen Prejean describes her insights and experiences of ministering to men facing execution, and, later, to the families of murder victims. We then examine the Church's teaching on legitimate self-defense and how this teaching is in keeping with the Fifth Commandment. We outline the strict conditions that must exist in order for war to be deemed justifiable and we stress that the Church always favors the non-violent resolution of differences. We move on from this to discuss how torture and gun violence contribute to a culture of death. The section ends with a discussion on the Church's position in relation to capital punishment. While the Church's teaching on capital punishment has evolved and changed over time, the Church today is very clearly opposed to the death penalty in all but the rarest of circumstances. She teaches strongly that punishment for crime should be oriented toward the rehabilitation of the

offender, even in the case of those who commit capital crimes.

Supplementary Activities for 'Think It Through'

Teacher Tip: Amnesty International works extensively against the death penalty, conducting campaigns in individual countries and working in cooperation with civil society. You might invite the young people to look up Amnesty International's website to find out more about their work.

Worksheet 14: 'The Sinner and the Sin' (*page 259 of this resource*) focuses on Jesus' capacity to separate the sinner from the sin. We invite the young people first to identify Gospel stories that show Jesus' love and compassion for the 'sinner', and then to rewrite one of these stories in a modern context.

JUDGE AND ACT

Learning Outcomes
That the young people would:
⊙ review the teachings of the Church that they have learned about in this chapter;
⊙ know about Sister Helen Prejean and her work and writings against the death penalty.

Faith-formation Outcome
That the young people would also:
⊙ find inspiration from Sister Helen Prejean to promote and pursue at all times a culture of life.

Overview
In section five, 'Judge and Act', the young people review the teachings of the Church that they have studied in this chapter. They also learn about Sister Helen Prejean and her work and writings against the death penalty.

Supplementary Activity for 'Judge and Act'

Research Activity
We live in a world where people do not always show respect for human life. On the other hand, there are people who work tirelessly to uphold the dignity and rights of all human persons. Divide the class into two groups: the first group will choose a local or national

CHAPTER 8: LIVING THE 'WAY' OF LIFE AND TRUTH | NOTES AND GUIDELINES | 233 daily newspaper and, over the course of a week, find reports in it of situations where respect for human life is not being upheld; the second group will conduct similar research to find examples of situations where respect for human life is valued and honored. This could be followed by a class discussion and/or presentations from the students.

Additional Prayer Suggestions

Guided Meditation: 'Living the Truth'
(*See 'Student Activity Tool Kit', pages 394–6 of this resource, for further helpful suggestions in relation to conducting guided meditations.*)

Leader
Let us ask God to be with us as we seek to respect life and live the truth in our everyday lives as God calls us to.
Let us sit in stillness. (*Pause*)

Feel your breath as it moves in and out of your body.
As you inhale, feel your breath flow through you, bringing life to every part of your body. (*Pause*)
As you exhale, breathe out all that blocks your ability to live your life to the full. (*Pause*)

Inhale . . . God is the source of your life. (*Pause*)
Exhale . . . God is always with you, helping you to live a respectful and truthful life, right here and now. (*Pause*)

Let us pray.

May we live the truth God calls us to live.
All
Within our hearts

Leader
May we live the truth God calls us to live.
All
In our dealings with others

Leader
May we live the truth God calls us to live.
All
In the words we speak

Leader
May we live the truth God calls us to live.
All
In the promises we make

Leader
May we live the truth God calls us to live.
All
In the judgments we hold

Leader
May we live the truth God calls us to live.
All
In our respect for all life

Leader
May we live the truth God calls us to live.
All
In bearing witness

Leader
May we live the truth God calls us to live.
All
In championing the oppressed

Leader
May we live the truth God calls us to live.
All
In seeking justice for all

Leader
Let us think of the times when we have failed to live as God asks us. (*Pause*)
We now ask God's forgiveness as we say the Confiteor together.

All
I confess to almighty God. . . .

Amen.

_____

Scripture Reflection
(*See instructions for the use of doodling in prayer in the 'Student Activity Tool Kit', page 394 of this resource.*)

Use the following Scripture verse to engage the young people in prayer:

Choose life so that you and your descendants may live.

DEUTERONOMY 15:19

234 | CREDO | LIVING AND LOVING AS DISCIPLES OF CHRIST

CHAPTER 8 | WORKSHEET 1

NAME:

My Tree of Life

Living life to the full is about reaching the full potential that God desires for us. It is about allowing the goodness with which God has gifted us to become visible in who we are and in our relationship with God, with other people and with the world around us. We are called to live in the image of the Holy Trinity, a community of Persons rooted in love, and thus to give glory to God by our lives and bring the abundance of life that God wills for us (life to the full) to ourselves and others. This worksheet uses the symbol of a tree as a framework to enable you to reflect upon and describe how you are living your life as God desires, and to identify the people and things that help you to live in a way that is life-giving for yourself and others.

MY TREE OF LIFE

- You will need a large sheet of paper for this activity.
- On the paper, draw the outline of a tree—with roots, trunk, branches and fruit—under the title 'My Tree of Life'. Allow plenty of space to write around the edges of the page.
- The tree represents your life. Just as a tree will flourish and bear fruit if it is rooted in the earth, has sufficient light from the sun and can draw nourishment from the rain and the soil, so will your life flourish if it receives the right supports and nourishment. The fruits of the tree are the visible signs that it is flourishing; your life also bears fruit that is visible for all to see.
- The notes that follow will guide you to reflect on your life and to identify what nourishes and supports you to live your life to the full as God desires. As you reflect on the questions, write the responses that come to your mind in the form of labels pointing to the different parts of your 'Tree of Life'.

The **ROOTS** represent the foundations of your life, from which you derive stability and support.
- What influences have shaped and formed you since your birth?
- What have you absorbed from your family, friends and community?
- What values have you retained from your childhood?
- What dreams do you have for the future?

The **TRUNK** represents how you live your life right now.
- How do you relate to family, friends and community?
- What kind of person do you strive to be?
- How involved are you in the world around you; for example, projects, interests.
- How do you go about achieving your dreams?
- What values do you live by?

CHAPTER 8: LIVING THE 'WAY' OF LIFE AND TRUTH | WORKSHEET 1 | 235

CHAPTER 8 | WORKSHEET 1 (CONTD.)

The **BRANCHES** represent the supports that help you to live your life to the full.
- Where do you find nourishment and support—both physical and spiritual?
- What people help and support you to live your life well?
- What places offer you comfort or inspiration?
- What activities or projects or events enable you to express your true self and to live to your full potential?

The **FRUITS** represent the visible signs of the person you are and of the life you are living.
- How do you think people see you?
- What personal qualities or traits of yours are visible to the world?
- What values of yours are evident to others?
- Which of your achievements, successes and fulfilled dreams are visible to others?

REVIEW AND REFLECT
- ⊙ Take some time to reflect on your 'Tree of Life'.
- ⊙ How did this exercise help you see the shape of your life at this moment more clearly?
- ⊙ Do you think you are living to your fullest potential right now?
- ⊙ What would need to happen or to change for you to live your life more fully—to live as God desires?
- ⊙ If God were always at the center of your life, how would that change anything that you have added to your 'Tree of Life'?

236 | CREDO | LIVING AND LOVING AS DISCIPLES OF CHRIST

CHAPTER 8 | WORKSHEET 2

NAME:

Made in the Image of the Triune God

Each one of us has been created in the image of the Triune God, who is a community of Persons rooted in love—equal, united and intimately interconnected. Through the Sacraments of Baptism and Confirmation we are invited, by name, to share in the love of God the Father, God the Son and God the Holy Spirit. This worksheet invites you to reflect on this fact and to name ways in which being created in the image of the Triune God might be different from being made in the image of a one-dimensional God.

REFLECT AND RESPOND

- Think about what each Person of the Trinity means to you; for example, how each Person of the Trinity represents a different dimension of the one God.
- Think about how you relate in different ways to each of the Persons of the Trinity; for example, in your prayer; in times of difficulty; when you need inspiration and so on.
- Think about how you mirror each Person of the Trinity in the unique person that you are.
- Now describe three ways in which being created in the image of the Triune God might be different from being created in the image of a one-dimensional God.

1. _____

   _____

   _____

2. _____

   _____

   _____

3. _____

   _____

   _____

CHAPTER 8: LIVING THE 'WAY' OF LIFE AND TRUTH | WORKSHEET 2 | 237

CHAPTER 8 | WORKSHEET 2 (CONTD.)

GET CREATIVE!

In the box below, draw an image/symbol to represent how the human person reflects the love and vitality of the Triune God.

JOURNAL EXERCISE

Write a prayer expressing what each Person of the Triune God means to you.

238 | CREDO | LIVING AND LOVING AS DISCIPLES OF CHRIST

CHAPTER 8 | WORKSHEET 3

NAME:

What does it mean to be human?

Classically, philosophers and theologians have identified three key aspects of what it means to be human, namely, (1) we are *rational* beings, with the ability to reason and think; (2) we are *social* beings, created to live in relationship with others; and (3) we are *free* beings, capable of choosing how we will live. This worksheet offers you the opportunity to explore these three aspects of our humanity.

PAIR AND SHARE
- Work with a partner.
- Name four ways in which you show that you are **rational** beings.

1. _____
2. _____
3. _____
4. _____

- Name four ways in which you show that you are **social** beings.

1. _____
2. _____
3. _____
4. _____

- Name four ways in which you show that you are **free** beings.

1. _____
2. _____
3. _____
4. _____

NOW PROBE DEEPER
- With your partner, discuss and identify the responsibilities and the challenges that come with each of these human attributes in terms of our relationships with other people, with other creatures and with the world around us.
- Share your conclusions with another pair of students.

CHAPTER 8: LIVING THE 'WAY' OF LIFE AND TRUTH | WORKSHEET 3 | 239

CHAPTER 8 | WORKSHEET 4

NAME:

My Words

Often we do not pay sufficient attention to the sort of words we use or to the manner in which we use words. Words have incredible power—to affirm and nourish; to negate and put down; to influence for good or bad; to challenge and encourage; to harm and destroy, and the list goes on. This worksheet offers you an opportunity to heighten your awareness of the power of words.

REFLECT AND RESPOND

Recall some words people have said to you or that you have heard over the years that have stayed with you. These words can be positive or negative.

Words from parents/guardians/family members:

_____

_____

_____

Words from teachers:

_____

_____

_____

Words from music:

_____

_____

_____

Words from literature:

_____

_____

240 | CREDO | LIVING AND LOVING AS DISCIPLES OF CHRIST

CHAPTER 8 | WORKSHEET 4 (CONTD.)

Words from poetry:

_____

_____

_____

Take one example from the list above that stands out for you. Describe how those words have affected, shaped or influenced you, either positively or negatively.

_____

_____

_____

Recall some words (positive and negative) that you have spoken over past week. Take one example of your positive words and one example of your negative words to examine in more detail.

1. What **positive** words did you use?

_____

_____

To whom did you speak these words and in what context?

_____

_____

_____

Describe the effect or response that these positive words evoked.

_____

_____

_____

CHAPTER 8: LIVING THE 'WAY' OF LIFE AND TRUTH | WORKSHEET 4 (CONTD.) | 241

CHAPTER 8 | WORKSHEET 4 (CONTD.)

2. What **negative** words did you use?

_____

_____

_____

To whom did you speak these words and in what context?

_____

_____

_____

Describe the effect or response that these negative words evoked.

_____

_____

JOURNAL EXERCISE
Describe the insights you have gained from this activity in relation to the power of words.

242 | CREDO | LIVING AND LOVING AS DISCIPLES OF CHRIST

CHAPTER 8 | WORKSHEET 5

NAME:

Jesus' Words

Jesus was a storyteller and communicator *par excellence*. He knew the power of words to affirm, to challenge, to encourage. He knew the power of words to express emotion—anger, hope, love, hate, compassion. Jesus' words were life-giving for those who took them to heart; his words showed the way to live life to the full with integrity and authenticity. This worksheet offers you the opportunity to recall and reflect on words of Jesus that you find meaningful and relevant to your life.

RECALL AND REFLECT

Make a list of Jesus' words that have special meaning for you or that come into your mind when you think about Jesus and who he was and the message he preached and lived. Include, for example, words of Jesus that you call to mind in times of need or anxiety, or words of Jesus that help you to pray, or words of Jesus that you find challenging or unsettling and so on.

_____

_____

_____

_____

_____

_____

_____

_____

_____

_____

CHAPTER 8: LIVING THE 'WAY' OF LIFE AND TRUTH | WORKSHEET 5 | 243

CHAPTER 8 | WORKSHEET 5 (CONTD.)

SCRIPTURE ACTIVITY

⊙ Choose one of the four accounts of the Gospel from which to gather a range of words or phrases of Jesus that you find meaningful and that speak to your life right now.

⊙ As you come upon the words, write the Gospel reference and the words on the chart. You may write just a part of a Gospel verse or the whole verse; for example:

Matthew 4:19 'Follow me. . . .'

Matthew 5:13 'You are the salt of the earth. . . .'

Matthew 6:34 'So do not worry about tomorrow. . . .'

Matthew 18:4 'Whoever becomes humble like this child is the greatest in the kingdom of heaven.'

Gospel Reference	Words of Jesus

JOURNAL EXERCISE

Take two of the examples of words of Jesus that you chose above and write about how they speak to your life now as a young person.

244 | CREDO | LIVING AND LOVING AS DISCIPLES OF CHRIST

CHAPTER 8 | WORKSHEET 6

NAME:

Witnesses to the Truth

There have been countless martyrs in the Catholic Church down through the ages—women and men, lay and religious—who have courageously taken a stance against injustice and have paid the ultimate price. Their example is an inspiration and a challenge to all of us to witness to the truth. They remind us that opposing evil in the world and confronting the institutions in society that fail to uphold the dignity of all human persons is a duty of all disciples of Jesus Christ. This worksheet tells the story of Bishop Juan Gerardi of Guatemala City, a human rights campaigner who was brutally murdered in April 1998 and who inspired Auxiliary Bishop Mario Rios of Guatamala to continue his work for human rights in Guatemala.

READ AND REFLECT

Read and reflect on this article about lives lived in witness to the truth, despite the personal cost of so doing.

Catching the Spirit

In almost any setting Auxiliary Bishop Mario Rios of Guatemala City would stand out as a person of courage, one who speaks his mind and devotes his days to creating a new and better day for his fellow Guatemalans. But add to it the fact that his predecessor was martyred in April 1998 for exhibiting the very same qualities.

The brutal slaying of Auxiliary Bishop Juan Gerardi occurred two days after the veteran human-rights campaigner issued a damning report of abuses committed during Guatemala's long civil war in which 200,000 people died. The report blamed most of the atrocities on the military. Although the murder remains unsolved, members of the country's security forces are thought to be responsible.

'I'm convinced he was a martyr,' Bishop Rios said of his longtime friend who founded the Human Rights Office in Guatemala City, an office Bishop Rios now heads. The path Bishop Rios pursues as head of the Social Ministry Office in Guatemala City (which includes the Human Rights Office), is an arduous one. His country's 36-year civil war has ended, 'but the violence is worse than ever,' he says. 'The human rights of the poor are continually violated. My greatest hope,' he continues, 'is that everyone from the oldest person to the youngest recognizes his dignity and does not resign himself to a life that is not humane. This history of the culture of death we have lived has to be transformed into a true culture of life and peace.'

Whatever the risks, Bishop Rios continues to walk in the footsteps of his predecessor in pursuit of 'a different Guatemala,' a better Guatemala.

—Judy Ball

RESEARCH ACTIVITY

Research the life and times of Bishop Gerardi, who worked and died for the poor of Guatemala City. You might also like to find out more about Auxiliary Bishop Mario Rios, who retired as Auxiliary Bishop of Guatemala City in 2010.

CHAPTER 8 | WORKSHEET 7

NAME:

Living and Witnessing to the Truth

God is the source of all truth.

—Catechism of the Catholic Church (CCC), no. 2465

Living and witnessing to the truth involves being true to God, to others and to one's self. Jesus proclaimed that he 'came into the world to testify to the truth' (John 18:37). We, as disciples of Jesus Christ, are called to do the same. This worksheet offers you the opportunity to explore how you live and witness to the truth in your daily life; in other words, how you live a life based on truth and integrity.

RECALL AND REFLECT

Recall some of the things you do or say that reflect how you are true to God, to others and to your self.

I am true to myself when I. . . .

_____

_____

_____

I am true to my family when I. . . .

_____

_____

_____

I am true to my friends when I. . . .

_____

_____

_____

246 | CREDO | LIVING AND LOVING AS DISCIPLES OF CHRIST

CHAPTER 8 | WORKSHEET 7 (CONTD.)

I am true to my teachers when I. . . .

_____

_____

_____

I am true to my neighbors/community when I. . . .

_____

_____

_____

I am true to God when I. . . .

_____

_____

_____

PAIR AND SHARE

> 'Men could not live with one another if there were not mutual confidence that they were being truthful to one another.'
>
> —St. Thomas Aquinas, quoted in CCC, no. 2469

⊙ Discuss with a partner what you think St. Thomas meant by this statement.
⊙ Share your thoughts on why being truthful is central to our lives in the world.
⊙ Imagine what the world would be like if nobody told the truth. What would happen?
⊙ Imagine what the world would be like if everybody told the truth. What would happen?

CHAPTER 8: LIVING THE 'WAY' OF LIFE AND TRUTH | WORKSHEET 7 (CONTD.) | 247

CHAPTER 8 | WORKSHEET 8

NAME:

Testimonies to Truth

There are times in all our lives when we are asked to stand up for the truth or to give testimony to what is true and just. This can happen in relation to big issues and involve a very public declaration. But, most of the time, challenges to give witness to the truth come in the small everyday events of our lives. This worksheet offers you the opportunity to identify and reflect upon some of those experiences.

RECALL AND DESCRIBE
Write about a time when you stood up for the truth.

_____

_____

_____

_____

_____

Write about a time when someone in your community stood up for the truth.

_____

_____

_____

_____

Write about a time when someone famous stood up for the truth.

_____

_____

_____

_____

_____

248 | CREDO | LIVING AND LOVING AS DISCIPLES OF CHRIST

CHAPTER 8 | WORKSHEET 9

NAME:

Pope John Paul II's Letter to Artists

In April 1999 Pope John Paul II wrote his famous 'Letter to Artists', in which he extoled the role artists play in the world today and affirmed the artist as a creator of beauty who reflects the image of God the Creator in a unique manner. This worksheet offers you the opportunity to read some extracts from this Letter and then to identify how works of art do not always give glory to God.

READ AND REFLECT

Take some time to read and reflect on these extracts from Pope John Paul II's 'Letter to Artists'.

> **The artist, image of God the Creator**
> God saw everything that he had made, and indeed, it was very good.
> —Genesis 1:31

None can sense more deeply than you artists, ingenious creators of beauty that you are, something of the *pathos* with which God at the dawn of creation looked upon the work of His hands. A glimmer of that feeling has shone so often in your eyes when—like the artists of every age—captivated by the hidden power of sounds and words, colors and shapes, you have admired the work of your inspiration, sensing in it some echo of the mystery of creation with which God, the sole creator of all things, has wished in some way to associate you.

That is why it seems to me that there are no better words than the text of Genesis with which to begin my Letter to you, to whom I feel closely linked by experiences reaching far back in time and which have indelibly marked my life. . . .

The opening page of the Bible presents God as a kind of exemplar of everyone who produces a work: the human craftsman mirrors the image of God as Creator. . . .

What is the difference between 'creator' and 'craftsman'? The one who creates bestows being itself, he brings something out of nothing . . . , and this, in the strict sense, is a mode of operation which belongs to the Almighty alone. The craftsman, by contrast, uses something that already exists, to which he gives form and meaning. This is the mode of operation peculiar to man as made in the image of God. In fact, after saying that God created man and woman 'in His image' (cf. Genesis 1:27), the Bible adds that He entrusted to them the task of dominating the earth (cf. Genesis 1:28). This was the last day of creation (cf. Genesis 1:28–31). On the previous days, marking as it were the rhythm of the

CHAPTER 8: LIVING THE 'WAY' OF LIFE AND TRUTH | WORKSHEET 9 | 249

CHAPTER 8 | WORKSHEET 9 (CONTD.)

birth of the cosmos, YHWH had created the universe. Finally He created the human being, the noblest fruit of His design, to whom He subjected the visible world as a vast field in which human inventiveness might assert itself.

God therefore called man into existence, committing to him the craftsman's task. Through his 'artistic creativity' man appears more than ever 'in the image of God', and he accomplishes this task above all in shaping the wondrous 'material' of his own humanity and then exercising creative dominion over the universe which surrounds him. With loving regard, the divine Artist passes on to the human artist a spark of His own surpassing wisdom, calling him to share in His creative power. . . .

That is why artists, the more conscious they are of their 'gift', are led all the more to see themselves and the whole of creation with eyes able to contemplate and give thanks, and to raise to God a hymn of praise. This is the only way for them to come to a full understanding of themselves, their vocation and their mission.

PAIR AND SHARE

◉ Re-read this statement which you will already have seen in your theology text: 'Good art reflects the truth and beauty in life. Art that is true and beautiful can uplift people, move them toward contemplation and, ultimately, lead them to worship and thankfulness to God, who is the source of all beauty and goodness.'
This statement is in keeping with Pope John Paul II's praise of artists in his 'Letter to Artists'.

◉ But not all art is good and true. Art can also be used to degrade and deny the dignity of the human person.

◉ Work with a partner. Identify how art (including photography) can be used in ways that disrespect or ignore the dignity of the human person.

◉ Finally, identify concrete ways in which art has had a positive impact on you or on others.

250 | CREDO | LIVING AND LOVING AS DISCIPLES OF CHRIST

CHAPTER 8 | WORKSHEET 10

NAME:

The Transmission of Truth

We live in a media-driven world. We rely on the media for information and news about local and world affairs. Very often we accept the information we are given in an uncritical manner. It can be useful at times to stop and analyze what we are reading in order to ascertain the reliability and truthfulness of the content. This worksheet offers guidelines to help you engage in such critical analysis.

READ AND CRITIQUE
- Work in pairs or small groups.
- Choose an article from a local or national newspaper or from a magazine or journal.
- Critically analyze the article using the steps outlined below as a guide.

1. **Read the article from beginning to end several times.**

2. **Pay particular attention to:**
   – the title
   – the tone
   – the handling of the topic
   – the target audience

3. **Check for bias**
   – What judgments are being made?
   – Are there any unsubstantiated generalizations?
   – Does the article take a particular viewpoint?
   – Does the author state his/her own views?

4. **Sources of information**
   – Are the sources cited by the author?
   – Are the sources reliable and correct?
   – Can you check the accuracy of the information/facts?

5. **Presentation**
   – How is the information presented?
   – What kind and range of words are used?
   – Is there any exaggeration, or confusing or misleading information?

6. **Images/Photographs**
   – Are there images accompanying the article?
   – Do the images accurately reflect the topic?
   – Are the images biased in any way?

CHAPTER 8: LIVING THE 'WAY' OF LIFE AND TRUTH | WORKSHEET 10 | 251

CHAPTER 8 | WORKSHEET 10 (CONTD.)

CLASS DISCUSSION

◉ Share what you learned from this exercise about the trustworthiness of the information we get from the media.

◉ What responsibilities do the media have when communicating information?

◉ What responsibilities does the reader have in relation to what he or she reads or watches?

◉ What measures might help to ensure that information is communicated with integrity and honesty?

252 | CREDO | LIVING AND LOVING AS DISCIPLES OF CHRIST

CHAPTER 8 | WORKSHEET 11

NAME:

The Sacredness of Human Life

This worksheet offers you the opportunity to read and respond to statements made by three American Catholic bishops on the sacredness of human life.

READ AND RESPOND

Read through the three statements on the sacredness of human life and then write your personal response to any two of them on the lines provided.

One need only consider the harm to our society and culture when science, technology and medicine proceed without respect for the innate and inalienable dignity of human life. A culture of death, sown by totalitarian regimes in the last century, is also sown in democratic societies when freedom's dependence on truth is denied.

—Bishop Kevin C. Rhoades, Bishop of Fort Wayne-South Bend, Message to Graduates, May 11, 2011

_____

_____

_____

_____

_____

CHAPTER 8: LIVING THE 'WAY' OF LIFE AND TRUTH | WORKSHEET 11 | 253

CHAPTER 8 | WORKSHEET 11 (CONTD.)

The founders of our country declared that each human being has certain inalienable rights that government must protect. It is no accident that they named life before liberty and the pursuit of happiness. Life itself is a basic human good, the condition for enjoying all other goods on this earth. Therefore the right to life is the most basic human right. Other valued rights—the right to vote, to freedom of speech, or to equal protection under law—lose their foundation if life itself can be destroyed with impunity.

—United States Conference of Catholic Bishops, 'To Live Each Day with Dignity: A Statement on Physician-Assisted Suicide', June 16, 2011

_____

_____

_____

_____

Assisted suicide also opens the door to putting more people into the category of those who 'would be better off dead', e.g., the mentally ill and the severely handicapped. It plays into culture's biased judgment that a person's worth is based on his or her productivity and autonomy. It also further undermines the foundational truth that human life is the inalienable right upon which our other inalienable rights depend—the basic human good, the condition for enjoying all other goods. Each life is precious and unique. As Christians, this is not only confirmed, but enhanced by the fact that the Son of God, in sharing our human nature, made each human life sacred.

—Bishop James V. Johnston, Bishop of Springfield-Cape Girardeau, 'Protecting Life in the Last Days', June 24, 2011

_____

_____

_____

_____

_____

_____

254 | CREDO | LIVING AND LOVING AS DISCIPLES OF CHRIST

CHAPTER 8 | WORKSHEET 12

NAME:

Papal Messages on Social Justice

This worksheet offers you an opportunity to read a selection of quotations on respect for life and social justice from different Popes and to write a presentation on one of them.

GROUP WORK
- Form small groups.
- Read through each of the quotations from the Popes.
- Choose one of the quotations and work together to write a presentation based on its message.
- One student from each group makes the presentation to the class and invites the students' responses.

> Some opportune remedy must be found quickly for the misery and wretchedness pressing so unjustly on the majority of the working class.
> —Leo XIII, *Rerum Novarum (Rights and Duties of Capital and Labor)*, 1891

> It is certainly most lamentable, that there have been, nay, that even now there are men who, although professing to be Catholics, are almost completely unmindful of that sublime law of justice and charity that binds us not only to render to everyone what is his but to succor brothers in need as Christ the Lord Himself, and—what is worse—out of greed for gain do not scruple to exploit the workers. Even more, there are men who abuse religion itself, and under its name try to hide their unjust exactions in order to protect themselves from the manifestly just demands of the workers. The conduct of such we shall never cease to censure gravely. For they are the reason why the Church could, even though undeservedly, have the appearance of and be charged with taking the part of the rich and with being quite unmoved by the necessities and hardships of those who have been deprived, as it were, of their natural inheritance. The whole history of the Church plainly demonstrates that such appearances are unfounded and such charges unjust.
> —Pius XI, *Quadragesimo Anno (In the 40th Year)*, 1931

> A society lacks solid foundations when, on the one hand, it asserts values such as the dignity of the person, justice and peace, but then, on the other hand, radically acts to the contrary by allowing or tolerating a variety of ways in which human life is devalued and violated, especially where it is weak or marginalized.
> —John Paul II, *Evangelium Vitae (The Gospel of Life)*, 1995

CHAPTER 8: LIVING THE 'WAY' OF LIFE AND TRUTH | WORKSHEET 12 | 255

CHAPTER 8 | WORKSHEET 12 (CONTD.)

Life in many poor countries is still extremely insecure as a consequence of food shortages, and the situation could become worse: hunger still reaps enormous numbers of victims among those who, like Lazarus, are not permitted to take their place at the rich man's table. *Feed the hungry* (cf. Mt 25: 35, 37, 42) is an ethical imperative for the universal Church, as she responds to the teachings of her Founder, the Lord Jesus, concerning solidarity and the sharing of goods.
—Benedict XVI, *Caritas in Veritate (Charity in Truth)*, 2009

256 | CREDO | LIVING AND LOVING AS DISCIPLES OF CHRIST

CHAPTER 8 | WORKSHEET 13

NAME:

Loving Ourselves

This worksheet seeks to help you to be aware that you cannot love others unless you have a deep love and respect for yourself. We invite you to think about ways in which you take care of yourself and to identify how you might sustain a sense of responsibility and care for yourself.

REFLECT

Loving ourselves is not a matter of being selfish or self-indulgent; indeed, it is quite the opposite. Loving ourselves involves appreciating that we are made in the image of God and acknowledging that God calls us to the fullest expression of our innate goodness and sanctity. To fulfill our potential as a human person means taking care of and taking responsibility for ourselves because we are precious in the eyes of God.

RATE HOW YOU LOVE YOURSELF!

Rate yourself on each of the areas listed on the chart by ticking the response that applies most accurately to you.

How well do you care for yourself?	Poor	Fair	Good	Excellent
Physically				
Emotionally				
Mentally				
Spiritually				
Socially				

CHAPTER 8: LIVING THE 'WAY' OF LIFE AND TRUTH | WORKSHEET 13 | 257

CHAPTER 8 | WORKSHEET 13 (CONTD.)

Comment on any aspect of yourself that you neglect and need to take better care of.

_____

_____

_____

_____

Identify three things you will do this week to take better care of yourself.

1. _____

_____

2. _____

_____

3. _____

_____

_____

258 | CREDO | LIVING AND LOVING AS DISCIPLES OF CHRIST

CHAPTER 8 | WORKSHEET 14

NAME:

The Sinner and the Sin

Jesus showed immense compassion and sympathy for human frailty. And when his compassion touched the hearts and minds of the people whom he met, his love enabled them to reflect on themselves and on their lives, leading them often to turn back to God. This worksheet invites you first to identify Gospel stories that show Jesus' love and compassion for the 'sinner', and then to rewrite one of these stories in a modern context.

SCRIPTURE ACTIVITY

◉ Work with a partner.

◉ Find and provide the Scripture references for four Gospel stories that demonstrate Jesus' love and compassion for the 'sinner'.

1. _____

2. _____

3. _____

4. _____

◉ Choose one of these stories and rewrite it in a modern-day context from (1) the sinner's perspective, and (2) Jesus' perspective.

The sinner tells the story:

_____

_____

_____

_____

_____

Jesus tells the story:

_____

_____

_____

_____

_____

CHAPTER 8: LIVING THE 'WAY' OF LIFE AND TRUTH | WORKSHEET 14 | 259

CHAPTER 8 | CHAPTER REVIEW

NAME:

Review of Chapter 8

I. **True/False.** Mark the true statements 'T' and the false statements 'F'. In the case of each false statement, cross out and rewrite the incorrect words to make the statement true.

_____1.   Classically, philosophers and theologians have talked about three key aspects of what it means to be human: that we are rational, social and free beings.

_____2.   The *Catechism of the Catholic Church* teaches that lying is the most direct offense against the truth.

_____3.   Flattery and adulation is a mortal sin.

_____4.   The words spoken by a confessor (penitent) to a priest may never be revealed to another person.

_____5.   Detraction is judging others before we know all the pertinent facts.

_____6.   The Fifth Commandment permits direct and intentional killing of an innocent person in certain circumstances.

_____7.   The Catholic Church teaches that the life of a human person begins at the moment of conception.

_____8.   Intentional euthanasia is also known as 'assisted suicide'.

260 | CREDO | LIVING AND LOVING AS DISCIPLES OF CHRIST

CHAPTER 8 | CHAPTER REVIEW (CONTD.)

_____9. Suicide is the intentional taking of one's own life.

_____10. According to Catholic teaching, autopsies, organ donation and cremation do not dishonor or disrespect the human body.

II. Matching. Write the letter of the term from column 2 next to its best match in column 1. There are two more items in column 2 than you need.

COLUMN 1	COLUMN 2
_____ 1. The ultimate form of commitment to living a truthful life in the Lord	A. Dissimulation
_____ 2. The act of repairing the harm we have caused	B. Truth
_____ 3. The spreading of lies about a person or group of people	C. Calumny
_____ 4. Saying one thing or acting in one way and meaning the opposite	D. Reparation
_____ 5. An act that shows complete and grave disregard for the dignity of human life	E. _Survive_
	F. Arms race
	G. Martyrdom
	H. Euthanasia
_____ 6. Book written by Sr. Helen Prejean	I. Hypocrisy
_____ 7. A form of lying in which one conceals the truth, or speaks in half-truths, in order to deceive	J. _Dead Man Walking_
	K. Torture
_____ 8. The _Catechism_ calls this 'one of the greatest curses on the human race'	L. Duplicity
_____ 9. The ending of a human life in order to end the suffering of a person	
_____ 10. The virtue which consists in showing oneself true in deeds and truthful in words	

CHAPTER 8: LIVING THE 'WAY' OF LIFE AND TRUTH | CHAPTER REVIEW (CONTD.) | 261

CHAPTER 8 | CHAPTER REVIEW (CONTD.)

III. Write a brief answer. Explain the teaching of the Catholic Church on 1 or 2.
    1. Embryonic stem cell and other scientific research
    2. Capital punishment

_____

_____

_____

_____

_____

_____

_____

_____

IV. How would you respond? A friend says to you, 'Surely the Catholic Church would allow any medical treatment or intervention that would help alleviate the suffering of a terminally ill person?'

_____

_____

_____

_____

_____

_____

_____

_____

_____

_____

262 | CREDO | LIVING AND LOVING AS DISCIPLES OF CHRIST

CHAPTER 8 | CHAPTER REVIEW (CONTD.)

V. Make a 'disciple decision'.

1. What is the most important wisdom for life that you discovered in this chapter?

_____

_____

_____

_____

_____

_____

2. Name several ways you can put this wisdom into practice. Choose one of the ways you identify and describe how you will make that wisdom part of your life right now.

_____

_____

_____

_____

_____

_____

CHAPTER 9

The Gift of Human Sexuality
—The Sixth and Ninth Commandments

INTRODUCTION

God is love and in himself he lives a mystery of personal loving communion. Creating the human race in his own image. . ., God inscribed in the humanity of man and woman the *vocation*, and thus the capacity and responsibility, of love and communion.

> —*Familiaris Consortio (On the Role of the Christian Family in the Modern World)*, no. 11

God has gifted us with the capacity to give and to receive love, to participate in the 'mystery of personal loving communion' that is God. Created in the divine image, we are to mirror God's love in our 'way of being' in the world.

> We must learn to realize that the love of God seeks us in every situation, and seeks our good. His inscrutable love seeks our awakening.
> —Thomas Merton

Love is multifaceted and may be expressed in many different forms, for example, love of a child for a parent; love for a friend; love for a spouse or a partner; love for a brother or sister. Love can be calm and reassuring and love can be passionate. We know the love that challenges us beyond our comfort zones and the love that is open and forgiving when we have done wrong. We see fresh and new love in the faces of our young people and we can recognize aged love in the faces of those who have sustained years of faithful and loyal commitment. The wisdom of our hearts tells us that love is at its best when it is founded on respect for the dignity and uniqueness of ourselves and of the other person. It is then that we truly reflect the image of our God.

In this chapter we explore the complexity and wonder of sexual love as a sacred gift from God through which we give expression to the divine love that is within us. Within this context we lead the young people to a fuller understanding of the Sixth Commandment 'You shall not commit adultery' and the Ninth Commandment 'You shall not covet your neighbor's wife or husband'.

Chapter 9 is developed under five major headings:

- ⊙ **ATTEND AND REFLECT:** What responsibilities come with our sexuality?
- ⊙ **HEAR THE STORY:** The universal vocation to live a chaste life
- ⊙ **EMBRACE THE VISION:** Self-control fosters the freedom to love
- ⊙ **THINK IT THROUGH:** The sacramental covenant of marriage—The Sacrament of Matrimony
- ⊙ **JUDGE AND ACT:** (*Activities and exercises that encourage the young people to integrate what they have learned in the chapter into their daily lives*)

Theological Background for the Teacher

TO BE HUMAN IS TO LOVE

Love is the fundamental and innate vocation of every human being.

> —*Familiaris Consortio*, no. 11

Time and again throughout the *Credo* series we have heard how each and every person is an *imago Dei*, created in the image and likeness of God, as the Book of Genesis reveals. Created in love by God who is Love, we are called to image that love in our lives and in our relationships, indeed in our very being. Love of God is carved into the human heart, and our hearts do not rest until they rest, ultimately, in God's love.

The dignity of the human person and the human heart's capacity to love are what human relationships are built on. We grow in and through our relationships. We seek out love in a way that no other creature on earth does. Other creatures take care of their young, feed and protect them, but their actions are instinctive, functional and are fundamentally about survival of the species. Humans also feed, protect and nurture those whom they love, but something more than mere survival and instinctual functioning is at work—and that 'more' is the human person's capacity to love. Engaging with others opens our hearts to give and to receive love. And the love that resonates within us finds expression in our

264 | CREDO | LIVING AND LOVING AS DISCIPLES OF CHRIST

actions, our thoughts, our hopes, our dreams and our desires. This is what God asks of us.

Each of us is capable of self-knowledge and of entering into communion with other persons through self-giving.

—*United States Catholic Catechism for Adults* (USCCA), 67

This is the wonder of what being human and growing more fully as a human person means.

SEXUALITY IS A GIFT FROM GOD

God created human beings as male and female. In so doing, he gave equal dignity to both man and woman. In this plan, men and women should respect and accept their sexual identity. God created both the body and sex as good. Hence, we do not approach sexuality with fear or with hostility to the flesh. It is a gift of God by which men and women participate in his saving plan and respond to his call to grow in holiness.

—USCCA, 404–405

Sexuality is a gift from God and it is good. In a world that sometimes appears to be obsessed with sex, it can be difficult for our young people to come to terms with a deeper understanding of their sexuality and what it means to be fully human.

In our modern-day consumerist culture, our sexuality is trivialized, packaged and presented as an appealing, and often tantalizing, commodity. It is presented as a 'thing' to be used at one's pleasure or at someone else's behest. The sexual appetite is just another appetite to be mastered and satisfied. The messages communicated to us are very powerful. And because these messages operate subliminally, their power to influence and shape our understanding of who we are is even greater. Many people, especially the young, accept these messages uncritically and unconsciously and they can be unaware of the strength these messages have to manipulate and shape how we think about the human body and human sexuality. Fr. Ronald Rolheiser puts it particularly well when writing about the media's portrayal of sex and sexuality:

… we are paying a price for this, mostly without consciously realizing it: Sex, outside of its proper containers, respect, unconditional commitment, and love, isn't bringing more joy into our lives, but is leaving us more fragmented and lonely…. There's a lot of sex in culture, but it isn't taking a lot of people home, home to that place where they feel fully respected, unconditionally safe,

able to be themselves, comfortable, and confident that the joy of their love-making is making their hearts bigger, softer, more gracious, more joyous.

Young people are immersed in a media world—a world of film and song, magazine and internet, social networking and accessibility to information—that is literally at their fingertips. It is a culture they have grown up in, with which they are familiar and at ease. And that is good. Our task is to help our young people appreciate the riches that media brings to their lives and at the same time lead them toward a critical awareness of the messages that are being directed at them. Through exploring the teachings of the Catholic Church, we seek to find creative and life-giving ways to engage them with the deeper meaning of sexuality, a meaning that will lead them to integrate the Christian message about love into their everyday lives: that God calls us to participate in divine love; that all that God creates is good; that sexuality is a gift from God and so it too is good; that through our sexuality we give expression to the image of God; that we are embodied people—unified in body and soul, heart and mind; that we are at our best when our sexual love is chaste, respectful, faithful, committed and life-giving; that all love calls us home to the deepest sense of who we are—beloved children of God.

The human body is beautiful…. It is in and through your body that your soul becomes visible and real for you. Your body is the home of your soul on earth.

—John O'Donohue, *Anam Cara*

LIVING CHRISTIAN MARRIAGE

In marriage the physical intimacy of the spouses becomes a sign and pledge of spiritual communion.

—*Catechism of the Catholic Church* (CCC), no. 2360

The Catholic Church values the institution of marriage and honors the sacredness of the intimacy between spouses. She sees in that physical intimacy a visible sign of God's covenant with us.

The Sacrament of Marriage is a covenant, which is more than a contract. Covenant always expresses a relationship between persons. The marriage covenant refers to the relationship between the husband and wife, a permanent union of persons capable of knowing and loving each other and God.

—USCCA, 281

CHAPTER 9: THE GIFT OF HUMAN SEXUALITY | INTRODUCTION | 265

The sexual love between spouses, baptized into the life and grace of God, enriches them in 'joy and gratitude' (CCC, no. 2362) and is deeply meaningful. Their conjugal love 'is not something simply biological, but concerns the innermost being of the human person' (CCC, no 2361) and offers them a wonderful expression of their humanity.

> The grace of this Sacrament perfects the love of husband and wife, binds them together in fidelity, and helps them welcome and care for children. Christ is the source of this grace and he dwells with the spouses to strengthen their covenant promises, to bear each other's burdens with forgiveness and kindness, and to experience ahead of time the 'wedding feast of the Lamb' (Revelation 19:9).
>
> —USCCA, 285

It is not easy to live up to the ideals that the Church sets before us. Today more than ever before, the vocation to marriage is a vocation that brings enormous challenges. We know the tragedy and pain, the hurt and loss of broken relationships and family separation. We also know how difficult it can be to live out the fidelity and the commitment of the wedding vows. The Church recognizes the fact that marriage can be challenging.

> Married couples have always experienced problems that threaten their union: jealousy, infidelity, conflicts, and quarrels.
>
> —USCCA, 287

Marriage can bring enormous joy and growth to couples as they mature in their love for each other and embrace new life through the birth, the fostering or the adoption of children. But marriage can also bring the sadness of infertility, the grief of miscarriage, the worry of illness, the regret of unfulfilled dreams, the hurt of conflict and disharmony. Sometimes, married couples become restless for something 'better' and can find it difficult to resist the temptations of selfish love; at such times the strength to follow the call of the Sixth and Ninth Commandments lessens. At times like that we fail to connect with the goodness God has implanted in our hearts and we turn our backs on the Triune community of Love in whose image each one of us is created.

> It can seem difficult, even impossible, to bind oneself for life to another human being. This makes it all the more important to proclaim the Good News that God loves us with a definitive

and irrevocable love, that married couples share in this love, that it supports and sustains them, and that by their own faithfulness they can be witnesses to God's faithful love.

> —CCC, no. 1648

When presenting the Catholic Church's teaching on sexuality and marriage, we must at all times be clear, faithful and realistic, bearing in mind that it is not always easy to 'have and to hold in sickness and in health till death do us part', especially in today's culture.

> Those in charge of education can reasonably be expected to give young people instruction respectful of the truth, the qualities of the heart, and the moral and spiritual dignity of man.
>
> —CCC, no. 2526

Time and again in their theology texts the young people have learned that Christ's New Commandment of love calls us to honor and respect the whole person. They have been invited to become aware of the rewards that living a life based on integrity, chastity and love brings. In this chapter we seek to develop their awareness that in living a chaste life we strive to live free from the slavery of self-centeredness; that as disciples of Jesus Christ we desire, above all, not to enter relationships for self-serving reasons that enslave us and other people, but rather that we endeavor to enter and live loving relationships that are free, faithful and life-giving. This is our call as baptized Christians. True love is the generous self-giving of one person to another. When we love in such a way, as Jesus modeled in his life, we are most like our God.

We must also affirm the young people in the knowledge that God is a God of compassion and forgiveness, a God who never abandons us, a God who is with us even in times of failure and sin. We experience the gift of God's boundless mercy in the understanding and love of others and, most especially, when we celebrate God's forgiveness in the Sacrament of Reconciliation. Like the Father in the Parable of the Prodigal Son, God waits and watches for us to return 'home' to that place of goodness within ourselves where we can enjoy, once more, right relationships with one another and with our God.

ADDITIONAL BACKGROUND READING
Catechism of the Catholic Church, nos. 2331–2400, 2514–2533; *United States Catholic Catechism for Adults,* 403–416, 439–446.

266 | CREDO | LIVING AND LOVING AS DISCIPLES OF CHRIST

CHAPTER OUTCOMES

See general note on page 19 of this resource.

Learning Outcomes

As a result of studying this chapter and exploring the issues raised, the young people should be able to:

- appreciate that human sexuality is a gift from God and integral to the divine plan for creation;
- know that the marriage partnership is the foundational human relationship that God has willed for human beings;
- know the Catholic Church's teaching on how we should value and express our sexuality;
- understand what is meant by the virtues of chastity and temperance;
- recognize how temperance, purity of heart and modesty enable us to live chaste lives;
- know the Church's teaching in relation to homosexual and lesbian persons and in relation to homosexual acts;
- appreciate that self-control gives them the freedom to love more fully;
- understand the connection between the virtue of chastity and the virtue of charity (love);
- know the difference between true love and lust;
- recognize that masturbation, pornography, fornication, prostitution, rape and homosexual acts are contrary to living a chaste life;
- remember that God's healing, grace and forgiveness is always available to us;
- understand that marriage is an image and living sign of God's Covenant with his people;
- know the elements the Church requires for a marriage to be true and valid;
- be familiar with the Church's teaching on contraception and family planning;
- know that adultery, divorce, polygamy, incest and free unions are contrary to marriage and to the Sixth and Ninth Commandments;
- know the story of Blessed Louis and Zélie Martin.

Faith-formation Outcomes

As a result of studying this chapter and exploring the issues raised, the young people should also:

- appreciate that the Christian faith offers a powerful and life-giving alternative to the destructive sexual mores prevalent in society today;
- adopt attitudes and actions that will ensure that their relationships are life-giving and love-generating;
- commit to practicing the virtues of chastity, purity and modesty;
- reaffirm their commitment to living a chaste and holy life;
- seek God's forgiveness in the Sacrament of Reconciliation when they deviate from the path of chastity and holiness;
- have a clearer view of what the sacramental covenant of marriage means;
- be inspired by the story of Blessed Louis and Zélie Martin to appreciate how Christian marriage should be lived.

CHAPTER 9: THE GIFT OF HUMAN SEXUALITY | INTRODUCTION | 267

Teacher Reflection

As you prepare to engage your group in a study of the Sixth and the Ninth Commandments, which guide us in living a chaste life and encourage us to respect our body as a gift from God the Creator, take a few moments to read and reflect on this extract which describes the body as the temple of the Holy Spirit and 'the mirror where the secret world of the soul comes to expression'.

> The body is a sacrament. The old traditional definition of sacrament captures this beautifully. A sacrament is a visible sign of invisible grace. In that definition there is a fine acknowledgment of how the unseen world comes to expression in the visible world. This desire for expression lies deep at the heart of the invisible world. All our inner life and intimacy of soul longs to find an outer mirror. It longs for a form in which it can be seen, felt and touched. The body is the mirror where the secret world of the soul comes to expression. The body is a sacred threshold; and it deserves to be respected, minded and understood in its spiritual nature. This sense of the body is wonderfully expressed in the amazing phrase from the Catholic tradition: *the body is the temple of the Holy Spirit.*
>
> The Holy Spirit holds the intimacy and distance of the Trinity alert and personified. To describe the human body as the temple of the Holy Spirit recognizes that the body is suffused with wild and vital divinity. This theological insight shows that the sensuous is sacred in the deepest sense.

—John O Donohue, *Anam Cara*

268 | CREDO | LIVING AND LOVING AS DISCIPLES OF CHRIST

Notes and Guidelines for Student Activities

ATTEND AND REFLECT

What responsibilities come with our sexuality?

Learning Outcomes

That the young people would:

◉ appreciate that human sexuality is a gift from God and integral to the divine plan for creation;

◉ know that the marriage partnership is the foundational human relationship that God has willed for human beings;

◉ know the Catholic Church's teaching on how we should value and express our sexuality.

Faith-formation Outcomes

That the young people would also:

◉ appreciate that the Christian faith offers a powerful and life-giving alternative to the destructive sexual mores prevalent in society today;

◉ adopt attitudes and actions that will ensure that their relationships are life-giving and love-generating.

Overview

Section one, 'Attend and Reflect', opens with an excerpt from *Mere Christianity* by C.S. Lewis, in which he defends and explains the Christian teaching on marriage and sexual relationships. Following on from this we reiterate that human sexuality is a gift from God which is integral to our human nature and to the divine plan for creation. We explain that the marriage partnership revealed in Genesis is the foundational human relationship that God has willed for human beings. We guide the young people to understand that sexual pleasure and intimacy is in itself a 'created good', but it cannot be separated from the totality of who God creates the human person to be—an integrated unity of body and spirit. Sexual intercourse and the seeking of other sexual pleasures need to honor and respect the 'wholeness' and 'oneness' of the human person. We introduce the young people to Blessed Pope John Paul II's 'Theology of the Body' and we outline the guiding moral principles, revealed in Scripture and taught by the Catholic Church, for our striving to grow into mature sexual persons.

Supplementary Activities for 'Attend and Reflect'

Worksheet 1: 'Healthy Relationships' (*page 274 of this resource*) offers the young people the opportunity to reflect on and evaluate how their relationships are healthy, life-giving and love-generating.

Worksheet 2: 'Made in God's Image' (*page 276 of this resource*) invites the young people to identify the male and female attributes in human beings that best reflect God's image.

Worksheet 3: 'St. Paul Speaks of Love' (*page 278 of this resource*) is a reflective activity based on a famous passage about love from St. Paul's First Letter to the Corinthians (1 Corinthians 13:1–13), which is often used at marriage ceremonies.

Worksheet 4: 'Kahlil Gibran Speaks of Marriage' (*page 280 of this resource*) presents an extract about married love from *The Prophet*, Gibran's much acclaimed work, and invites the young people to reflect on its meaning and wisdom.

HEAR THE STORY

The universal vocation to live a chaste life

Learning Outcomes

That the young people would:

◉ understand what is meant by the virtues of chastity and temperance;

◉ recognize how temperance, purity of heart and modesty enable us to live chaste lives;

◉ know the Church's teaching in relation to homosexual and lesbian persons and in relation to homosexual acts.

Faith-formation Outcome

That the young people would also:

◉ commit to practicing the virtues of chastity, purity and modesty.

CHAPTER 9: THE GIFT OF HUMAN SEXUALITY | NOTES AND GUIDELINES | 269

Overview

Section two, 'Hear the Story', explores the call to all the faithful to live chaste lives in line with the life of holiness that God desires for all people. We explore what the virtue of chastity means and how it fosters in us the appropriate attitudes and behavior that enable us to honor and respect our own dignity and the dignity of other people as sexual persons. We explain how the virtue of chastity works hand in glove with the virtue of temperance, leading to self-mastery, or self-control, which can be particularly difficult to accomplish during adolescence, as changing bodies and hormones ignite powerful feelings. We also introduce the concept of purity of heart which, strengthened by the virtue of temperance, enables us to live a life of modesty and chastity. We present the Church's teaching in relation to homosexuals and lesbians, emphasizing that all people are children of God, deserving of respect, understanding and love, irrespective of our sexual orientation. We explain that while it is not a sin to be attracted to persons of the same gender, the Catholic Church regards homosexual acts as intrinsically disordered. Finally, we provide a list of practical tips for young people on living a chaste life.

Supplementary Activities for 'Hear the Story'

Relationship-Monitoring Activity
Invite the young people to select one person in their lives with whom they have a loving and significant relationship (this person could be a family member or friend) and, over the course of a few days or a week, to 'monitor' the ways in which they relate to this person. They might like to carry a notebook to write down their observations. This activity, which should be done in a non-judgmental manner, is intended simply to heighten the young people's awareness of how they relate to those whom they love. When they have completed the activity, the young people might like to discuss with the class or with a partner what they observed or learned.

Media Study
Ask the young people to take note, while watching TV during the week, of the different ways in which women's and men's bodies and their sexuality are used as a commodity for commercial purposes.

You could follow this up with a class discussion, to include these questions: What sort of message is communicated through the use of men's and women's bodies as a commodity? Who benefits from the portrayal of women and men in this manner? What or who suffers as a result of these types of advertisements?

You might also suggest that the young people write to the Advertising Authorities to challenge or query their advertising philosophies and strategies.

Worksheet 5: 'Living the Virtue of Chastity' (*page 282 of this resource*) offers the young people the opportunity to explore what the virtue of chastity means for young people today and to compose 'Top Ten Tips for Living a Chaste Life' that would help young people like themselves to live this virtue.

Worksheet 6: 'Listening to Our Bodies' (*page 284 of this resource*) offers the young people the opportunity to tune into what their body is saying to them at this time in their life; in other words, to listen to the wisdom their body is communicating to them.

Teacher Tip in relation to Worksheet 6: You might like to play some quiet background music as the young people complete this activity.

EMBRACE THE VISION

Self-control fosters the freedom to love

Learning Outcomes
That the young people would:
- appreciate that self-control gives them the freedom to love more fully;
- understand the connection between the virtue of chastity and the virtue of charity (love);
- know the difference between true love and lust;
- recognize that masturbation, pornography, fornication, prostitution, rape and homosexual acts are contrary to living a chaste life;
- remember that God's healing, grace and forgiveness is always available to us.

Faith-formation Outcomes
That the young people would also:
- reaffirm their commitment to living a chaste and holy life;
- seek God's forgiveness in the Sacrament of Reconciliation when they deviate from the path of chastity and holiness.

270 | CREDO | LIVING AND LOVING AS DISCIPLES OF CHRIST

Overview

Section three, 'Embrace the Vision', begins with an explanation of how the virtue of chastity is driven by the virtue of charity, or love, which is the central force behind our living a moral life. We probe deeper into what it means to be a chaste person and then discuss how true love, which is free, total, faithful and fruitful, differs from lust, which is the enemy of freedom, true love and living a chaste life. We also explain the term 'concupiscence'. From this we move on to identify and explore acts that are contrary to living a chaste life, namely masturbation, pornography, fornication, prostitution, rape and homosexual acts. We conclude the section by reminding the young people that God's mercy, forgiveness and healing is always available through the Sacrament of Penance and Reconciliation to those who repent, seek forgiveness and commit to changing their sinful ways and living a chaste and holy life.

Supplementary Activities for 'Embrace the Vision'

Teacher Tip: You might like to invite the young people to research the background, ethos and philosophy of organizations that work in these and similar areas: sexual abuse; trafficking for the sex trade; sex addiction; women in prostitution; violence against women in the home.

Research Activity

Invite the young people to select one song on the theme of love and relationships from popular music and to analyze what the song is telling young people about love and relationships. They should use the characteristics of true love that they have learned about in their text, namely, free, total, faithful and fruitful, as a yardstick against which to critique the song's definition of love.

Worksheet 7: 'Characteristics of True Love' (*page 286 of this resource*) offers the young people an opportunity to explore the characteristics of true love and to identify how these characteristics manifest themselves in loving, life-giving relationships.

Media Watch

Invite the young people to watch a popular TV soap for a week. Ask them to focus on one of the relationships portrayed in the program and to take note of: relationship context; dialogue; hopes/fears; conflict and conflict resolution; physical expression of love; sources of relationship support. This would be an ideal activity for group work and could be followed by presentations and a class discussion.

THINK IT THROUGH

The sacramental covenant of marriage—the Sacrament of Matrimony

Learning Outcomes

That the young people would:

- ◉ understand that marriage is an image and living sign of God's Covenant with his people;
- ◉ know the elements the Church requires for a marriage to be true and valid;
- ◉ be familiar with the Church's teaching on contraception and family planning;
- ◉ know that adultery, divorce, polygamy, incest and free unions are contrary to marriage and to the Sixth and Ninth Commandments.

Faith-formation Outcome

That the young people would also:

- ◉ have a clearer view of what the sacramental covenant of marriage means.

Overview

Section four, 'Think It Through', begins by explaining that the covenant of marriage is an image and living sign of the Covenant that God and his people have freely and irrevocably entered, and that Christ raised the marriage between a baptized woman and a baptized man to the dignity of a Sacrament that signifies the love uniting Christ and his Church. From this we move on to explain the elements the Catholic Church requires for a sacramental marriage to be true and valid, namely, total unity freely entered, faithful and indissoluble, and openness to the gift of children. We present the Catholic Church's teaching on family planning and explain the rationale behind her approval of the refined methods of self-observation and Natural Family Planning (NFP). We outline the Church's opposition to all artificial means of contraception, which separate the conjugal act from its procreative potential and block the total self-giving of the husband and wife. We explain the Church's opposition to artificial insemination and fertilization but stress that the Church has great sympathy with and compassion for couples who are unable to conceive. In this regard, we explore

CHAPTER 9: THE GIFT OF HUMAN SEXUALITY | NOTES AND GUIDELINES | 271

adoptive parenting and foster parenting, both of which are supported by the Church. We conclude the section by exploring how attitudes and actions such as adultery, divorce, polygamy, incest and free unions are contrary to marriage and to the Sixth and Ninth Commandments.

Supplementary Activities for 'Think It Through'

Teacher Tip: You might like to invite a married couple to come and talk to the class about their marriage. The young people could prepare some questions for the couple in advance of the visit.

Research Activity

Invite the young people to research the Catholic services that offer support and help to couples struggling with infertility or with the grief of miscarriage.

Debate

Invite the young people to prepare for a class sharing of ideas on the topic 'Marriage is for life'.

Worksheet 8: 'Ideal versus Real Marriage' (*page 288 of this resource*) invites the young people to explore how popular beliefs about what the 'ideal' marriage constitutes contrast with the Christian view of a loving and life-giving marriage.

Worksheet 9: 'A Blessing for Married Couples' (*page 289 of this resource*) presents a poem of blessing by the Irish spiritual poet and philosopher John O'Donohue (1956–2008).

Worksheet 10: 'C.S. Lewis Speaks about Love' (*page 290 of this resource*) presents an extract from *Mere Christianity* by C.S. Lewis (1898–1963) in which Lewis compares the excitement and thrill of 'being in love' with the real, down-to-earth love between two people that develops and grows over time.

JUDGE AND ACT

Learning Outcomes
That the young people would:
- ⊙ review the teachings of the Church that they have learned about in this chapter;
- ⊙ know the story of Blessed Louis and Zélie Martin.

Faith-formation Outcome
That the young people would also:
- ⊙ be inspired by the story of Blessed Louis and Zélie Martin to appreciate how Christian marriage should be lived.

Overview
In section five, 'Judge and Act', the young people review the teachings of the Church that they have studied in this chapter. They also hear the story of Blessed Louis and Zélie Martin, the parents of St. Thérèse of Lisieux, who throughout their lives exemplified how Christian marriage should be lived. They are a model of Christian marriage for the world today.

Supplementary Activities for 'Judge and Act'

Creative Activity
Invite the young people to work in small groups to create a presentation on Christian marriage. The content should reflect the characteristics of married love: free, faithful, total and fruitful. The young people might interview married couples and use some quotations from the interviews for their presentation; or they might include images, words of songs, poems and so on that promote the qualities of Christian marriage; they might even consider writing their own songs or poetry for the project. They would then present the material to the class in a format of their choice.

Worksheet 11: 'The Story of Ruth' (*page 292 of this resource*) offers the young people the opportunity to hear the biblical story of Ruth, a story of love, loyalty and solidarity.

272 | CREDO | LIVING AND LOVING AS DISCIPLES OF CHRIST

Additional Prayer Suggestions

Leader
Listen carefully to these words from Psalm 103.

Bless the Lord, O my soul,
  and all that is within me,
  bless his holy name.
Bless the Lord, O my soul,
  and do not forget all his benefits. . . .
The Lord is merciful and gracious,
  slow to anger and abounding in steadfast love.
He will not always accuse,
  nor will he keep his anger forever.
He does not deal with us according to our sins,
  nor repay us according to our iniquities.
For as the heavens are high above the earth,
  so great is his steadfast love toward those who fear him;
as far as the east is from the west,
  so far he removes our transgressions from us.
As a father has compassion for his children,
  so the Lord has compassion for those who fear him.
For he knows how we were made;
  he remembers that we are dust.

—Psalm 103:1–2, 8–14

Leader
Now quietly recall a time when you experienced God's love for you.
Remember the people or place that you associate with this experience.

Allow the young people a few moments for reflection.

Now give thanks to God for his constant care.
Finally, think of someone for whom you can make God's love real . . . and resolve to do that.

Scripture Reflection
(*See instruction for the use of doodling in prayer in the 'Student Activity Tool Kit', page 394 of this resource.*)

Use the following Scripture verse to engage the young people in prayer:

Do you not know that you are God's temple and that God's Spirit dwells in you?

1 CORINTHIANS 3:16

CHAPTER 9: THE GIFT OF HUMAN SEXUALITY | NOTES AND GUIDELINES | 273

CHAPTER 9 | WORKSHEET 1

NAME:

Healthy Relationships

Healthy relationships bring out what is best in us. This worksheet offers you the opportunity to reflect on and evaluate how your relationships are healthy, life-giving and love-generating.

REFLECT AND RESPOND

◉ Think of one relationship you have at the moment. This may be with a family member, a friend, a boyfriend or girlfriend, a neighbor or a person from your school or local community . . . any relationship that is important to you.

◉ Describe three ways in which this relationship brings out the best in you.

1. _____

_____

2. _____

_____

3. _____

_____

◉ Describe three ways in which you think this relationship brings out the best in the other person.

1. _____

_____

2. _____

_____

3. _____

_____

274 | CREDO | LIVING AND LOVING AS DISCIPLES OF CHRIST

CHAPTER 9 | WORKSHEET 1 (CONTD.)

⊙ Now think of a relationship you have had or still have that has brought out the worst in you. Name three ways in which this negative situation has manifested itself.

1. _____

   _____

2. _____

   _____

3. _____

   _____

JOURNAL EXERCISE
Describe any insights you have gained from the above activity that may be helpful for your relationships in the future.

CHAPTER 9 | WORKSHEET 2

NAME:

Made in God's Image

God created humankind in his image . . . male and female he created them.

—Genesis 1:27

This worksheet invites you to identify the male and female attributes in human beings that best reflect God's image.

REFLECTIVE ACTIVITY

⊙ Work in pairs for this activity. (A mixed class might like to work in same-sex pairs.)

⊙ Name female attributes that you feel best reflect how human beings are images of God. Write your choices in the box.

⊙ Name male attributes that you feel best reflect how human beings are images of God. As before, write your choices in the box.

276 | CREDO | LIVING AND LOVING AS DISCIPLES OF CHRIST

CHAPTER 9 | WORKSHEET 2 (CONTD.)

REVIEW AND EVALUATE
- Review your lists with your partner.
- What strikes you about the attributes you chose?
- Are there any attributes common to both lists?
- What do the attributes that you chose reflect about your own image of God and how you view God's own nature?
- Share any other insights you gained from this activity.

JOURNAL EXERCISE
Choose one attribute from either list and write about a time when you portrayed this attribute and, in so doing, mirrored the image of God to others.

CHAPTER 9 | WORKSHEET 3

NAME:

St. Paul Speaks of Love

The reflective activity in this worksheet is based on a famous passage about love from St. Paul's First Letter to the Corinthians (1 Corinthians 13:1–13), which is often used at marriage ceremonies.

READ AND REFLECT
Read and reflect on this popular passage from the First Letter of St. Paul to the Corinthians in which he describes the gift of love, the essential element of all healthy and life-giving relationships.

[1] If I speak in the tongues of mortals and of angels, but do not have love, I am a noisy gong or a clanging cymbal.
[2] And if I have prophetic powers, and understand all mysteries and all knowledge, and if I have all faith, so as to remove mountains, but do not have love, I am nothing.
[3] If I give away all my possessions, and if I hand over my body so that I may boast, but do not have love, I gain nothing.
[4] Love is patient; love is kind; love is not envious or boastful or arrogant or rude.
[5] It does not insist on its own way; it is not irritable or resentful;
[6] it does not rejoice in wrongdoing, but rejoices in the truth.
[7] It bears all things, believes all things, hopes all things, endures all things.
[8] Love never ends. But as for prophecies, they will come to an end; as for tongues, they will cease; as for knowledge, it will come to an end.
[9] For we know only in part, and we prophesy only in part;
[10] but when the complete comes, the partial will come to an end.
[11] When I was a child, I spoke like a child, I thought like a child, I reasoned like a child; when I became an adult, I put an end to childish ways.
[12] For now we see in a mirror dimly, but then we will see face to face. Now I know only in part; then I will know fully, even as I have been fully known.
[13] And now faith, hope, and love abide, these three; but the greatest of these is love.

—1 Corinthians 13:1–13

278 | CREDO | LIVING AND LOVING AS DISCIPLES OF CHRIST

CHAPTER 9 | WORKSHEET 3 (CONTD.)

RESPOND

Select five statements about love from this passage that resonate with you (you may cite just the verse numbers, given in the square brackets) and state briefly why you find them meaningful or insightful or particularly relevant to you at this moment in your life.

1. _____

   _____

   _____

2. _____

   _____

   _____

3. _____

   _____

   _____

4. _____

   _____

   _____

5. _____

   _____

   _____

CHAPTER 9 | WORKSHEET 4

NAME:

Kahlil Gibran Speaks of Marriage

This worksheet presents an extract about married love from *The Prophet* by Kahlil Gibran (1883–1931) and invites you to reflect on its meaning and wisdom.

READ AND REFLECT
◉ Read and reflect on this statement about marriage from *The Prophet* by Kahlil Gibran, the famous poet, philosopher and artist.
◉ As you read it, be mindful of how it might either correspond to or contradict Catholic Church teaching in relation to the marriage partnership.

You were born together, and together you shall be for evermore. You shall be together when the white wings of death scatter your days. Aye, you shall be together even in the silent memory of God. But let there be spaces in your togetherness, and let the winds of the heavens dance between you.

Love one another, but make not a bond of love: let it rather be a moving sea between the shores of your souls. Fill each other's cup but drink not from one cup. Give one another of your bread but eat not from the same loaf. Sing and dance together and be joyous, but let each one of you be alone, even as the strings of a lute are alone though they quiver with the same music.

Give your hearts, but not into each other's keeping, for only the hand of Life can contain your hearts. And stand together yet not too near together, for the pillars of the temple stand apart, and the oak tree and the cypress grow not in each other's shadow.

RESPOND
Describe your response to Gibran's statement about marriage. What parts do you agree with or, perhaps, disagree with, and why?

_____

_____

_____

_____

_____

280 | CREDO | LIVING AND LOVING AS DISCIPLES OF CHRIST

CHAPTER 9 | WORKSHEET 4 (CONTD.)

_____

_____

_____

_____

How does Kahlil Gibran's view of love compare with St. Paul's description of love in 1 Corinthians 13:1–13?

_____

_____

_____

_____

_____

_____

CHAPTER 9: THE GIFT OF HUMAN SEXUALITY | WORKSHEET 4 (CONTD.) | 281

CHAPTER 9 | WORKSHEET 5

NAME:

Living the Virtue of Chastity

This worksheet offers you the opportunity to explore what the virtue of chastity means for young people today and to make some practical suggestions that would help young people like yourself to live this virtue.

PAIR AND SHARE

⊙ Reread these excerpts on chastity which you will already have encountered in your theology text:

Chastity is a virtue 'connected to purity of heart, . . . that moves us to love others with generous regards for them. It excludes lust and any wish to exploit them sexually. It helps us see and put into practice God's plan for the body, person, and sexuality' (*United States Catholic Catechism for Adults* [USCCA], 506).

Developing and practicing the virtue of chastity fosters in us the appropriate attitudes and behavior that enable us to honor and respect our own dignity and the dignity of other people as sexual persons.

⊙ With your partner, identify and write in the box all the characteristics, attitudes or behaviors that you would associate with the virtue of chastity.

IDENTIFY YOUR 'TOP TEN'

⊙ Review the characteristics, attitudes and behaviors that you identified.
⊙ Prioritize those that you would regard as the 'top ten' suggestions by numbering them in the order of their importance, with number 1 being the most important.
⊙ Then formulate each one into a statement that would help young people to practice the virtue of chastity. Write your statement on the chart on the opposite page.
⊙ Share your 'Top Ten Tips for Living a Chaste Life' with the class.

282 | CREDO | LIVING AND LOVING AS DISCIPLES OF CHRIST

CHAPTER 9 | WORKSHEET 5 (CONTD.)

Top Ten Tips for Living a Chaste Life

1. _____

2. _____

   _____

3. _____

   _____

4. _____

5. _____

   _____

6. _____

   _____

7. _____

   _____

8. _____

   _____

9. _____

   _____

10. _____

    _____

CHAPTER 9: THE GIFT OF HUMAN SEXUALITY | WORKSHEET 5 (CONTD.) | 283

CHAPTER 9 | WORKSHEET 6

NAME:

Listening to Our Bodies

Psychologists tell us that our bodies never lie. Scripture tells us that our body is a temple of the Holy Spirit. If we pay attention to our body it will let us know how we are within ourselves—physically, emotionally, mentally and spiritually. This worksheet offers you the opportunity to tune into what your body is saying to you at this time in your life.

REFLECT AND RESPOND
- Take some quiet time to listen to what your body is telling you right now.
- Jot down any thoughts that come into your mind in relation to each heading below. Mention how, for example, things may be going well or badly for you in each of these areas, or challenges you may be meeting in any of these areas at this time in your life.
- Remember: there are no correct answers; your body's messages to you are personal and unique.

Physically, at this moment in time, my body is telling me that I am. . . .

_____

_____

_____

_____

Emotionally, at this moment in time, my body is telling me that I am. . . .

_____

_____

_____

_____

284 | CREDO | LIVING AND LOVING AS DISCIPLES OF CHRIST

CHAPTER 9 | WORKSHEET 6 (CONTD.)

Mentally, at this moment in time, my body is telling me that I am. . . .

_____

_____

_____

_____

Spiritually, at this moment in time, my body is telling me that I am. . . .

_____

_____

_____

_____

COMPOSE A PRAYER

Write a prayer asking the Holy Spirit for the guidance you need in order to embody more fully the wonder and mystery of God.

CHAPTER 9: THE GIFT OF HUMAN SEXUALITY | WORKSHEET 6 (CONTD.) | 285

CHAPTER 9 | WORKSHEET 7

NAME:

Characteristics of True Love

You have learned in your theology text that true love is the generous self-giving (agape) of one person to another; that true love is free, total, faithful and fruitful; that true love is respectful, generous and chaste; and that when we love in such a way, as Jesus did, we are most like our God, for 'God is love' (1 John 4:8). This worksheet invites you to explore in more detail the various characteristics and attributes that constitute true love.

REFLECT AND RESPOND
- Take some time on your own to reflect on what true love means.
- Then complete the following exercise by identifying ways in which true love manifests each of the characteristics that are named.

Love that is **free** is marked by:

1. _____

2. _____

3. _____

Love that is **total** is marked by:

1. _____

2. _____

3. _____

Love that is **faithful** is marked by:

1. _____

2. _____

3. _____

286 | CREDO | LIVING AND LOVING AS DISCIPLES OF CHRIST

CHAPTER 9 | WORKSHEET 7 (CONTD.)

Love that is **fruitful** is marked by:

1. _____

2. _____

3. _____

Love that is **respectful** is marked by:

1. _____

2. _____

3. _____

Love that is **generous** is marked by:

1. _____

2. _____

3. _____

Love that is **chaste** is marked by:

1. _____

2. _____

3. _____

CHAPTER 9: THE GIFT OF HUMAN SEXUALITY | WORKSHEET 7 (CONTD.) | 287

CHAPTER 9 | WORKSHEET 8

NAME:

Ideal versus Real Marriage

This worksheet invites you to explore how popular beliefs about what the 'ideal' marriage constitutes contrast with the Christian view of a loving and life-giving marriage.

PAIR AND SHARE
- Share with a partner your ideas on what the 'ideal marriage' would be like.
- In the left column of the chart list all the qualities you can think of that would constitute the 'ideal' marriage.
- Then recall what you have learned about the Church's teaching on the covenant of marriage and what it represents.
- In the right column of the chart list the qualities you would expect to find in a good and 'real' Christian marriage as it is lived out from day to day, year to year, by millions of couples all over the world.

Ideal Marriage	Real Christian Marriage

CLASS DISCUSSION
- What were the main differences you identified between the 'ideal' of marriage and the lived reality?
- Which type of marriage might you aim for, and why?
- What insights did you gain from this activity about what is really important for a loving, healthy and life-giving marriage?

288 | CREDO | LIVING AND LOVING AS DISCIPLES OF CHRIST

CHAPTER 9 | WORKSHEET 9

NAME:

A Blessing for Married Couples

This worksheet offers you the opportunity to read and respond to a poem of blessing for married couples by the Irish spiritual poet and philosopher John O'Donohue (1956–2008).

READ AND REFLECT
Read and reflect on this blessing for a married couple.

For Marriage

As spring unfolds the dream of the earth,
May you bring each other's hearts to birth.

As the ocean finds calm in view of land,
May you love the gaze of each other's mind.

As the wind arises free and wild,
May nothing negative control your lives.

As kindly as moonlight might search the dark,
So gentle may you be when light grows scarce.

As surprised as the silence that music opens,
May your words for each other be touched with reverence.

As warmly as the air draws in the light,
May you welcome each other's every gift.

As elegant as dreams absorbing the night,
May sleep find you clear of anger and hurt.

As twilight harvests all the day's color,
May love bring you home to each other.

OVER TO YOU
⊙ The poem uses rich imagery for married love. What does the imagery point the reader toward? What view of marriage does it reflect?
⊙ The poem is a blessing for marriage. What are the sources of blessing that a couple receive on their wedding day?
⊙ In what way is the Sacrament of Marriage a blessing *par excellence*?

CHAPTER 9: THE GIFT OF HUMAN SEXUALITY | WORKSHEET 9 | 289

CHAPTER 9 | WORKSHEET 10

NAME:

C.S. Lewis Speaks About Love

This worksheet offers you the opportunity to read an extract from the book *Mere Christianity* by C.S. Lewis (1898–1963) in which Lewis compares the excitement and thrill of 'being in love' with the real, down-to-earth love between two people that develops and grows over time.

READ AND REFLECT
Read and reflect on this extract from C.S. Lewis.

What we call 'being in love' is a glorious state, and, in several ways, good for us. It helps to make us generous and courageous. It opens our eyes not only to the beauty of the beloved but to all beauty, and it subordinates (especially at first) our merely animal sexuality; in that sense, love is the great conqueror of lust. No one in his senses would deny that being in love is far better than either common sensuality or cold self-centeredness. But, as I said before, 'the most dangerous thing you can do is to take any one impulse of our own nature and set it up as the thing you ought to follow at all costs'. Being in love is a good thing, but it is not the best thing. There are many things below it, but there are also things above it. You cannot make it the basis of a whole life. It is a noble feeling, but it is still a feeling. Now no feeling can be relied on to last in its full intensity, or even to last at all. Knowledge can last, principles can last, habits can last but feelings come and go. And in fact, whatever people say, the state called 'being in love' usually does not last. If the old fairy-tale ending 'They lived happily ever after' is taken to mean 'They felt for the next fifty years exactly as they felt the day before they were married', then it says what probably never was nor ever would be true, and would be highly undesirable if it were. Who could bear to live in that excitement for even five years? What would become of your work, your appetite, your sleep, your friendships? But, of course, ceasing to be 'in love' need not mean ceasing to love. Love in this second sense—love as distinct from 'being in love'—is not merely a feeling. It is a deep unity, maintained by the will and deliberately strengthened by habit; reinforced by (in Christian marriages) the grace which both partners ask, and receive, from God. They can have this love for each other even at those moments when they do not like each other; as you love yourself even when you do not like yourself. They can retain this love even when each would easily, if they allowed themselves, be 'in love' with someone else. 'Being in love' first moved them to promise

290 | CREDO | LIVING AND LOVING AS DISCIPLES OF CHRIST

CHAPTER 9 | WORKSHEET 10 (CONTD.)

fidelity: this quieter love enables them to keep the promise. It is on this love that the engine of marriage is run: being in love was the explosion that started it.

If you disagree with me, of course, you will say, 'He knows nothing about it, he is not married.' You may quite possibly be right. But before you say that, make quite sure that you are judging me by what you really know from your own experience and from watching the lives of your friends, and not by ideas you have derived from novels and films. This is not so easy to do as people think. Our experience is colored through and through by books and plays and the cinema, and it takes patience and skill to disentangle the things we have really learned from life for ourselves.

CLASS DISCUSSION

◉ What is your reaction to Lewis's analysis of love?

◉ Do you think it is possible to remain in the state of 'being in love' that often characterizes the early stages of a relationship? Why?/Why not?

◉ Do you agree with Lewis when he says that feelings are not permanent but that they come and go? Share how this resonates with your own experience in relation to your feelings.

◉ In what ways do you think literature, films, fairy stories and so on perpetuate the notion that when people fall in love and get married they 'live happily ever after'? What might be the implications of this for how young people today view marriage?

JOURNAL EXERCISE

Describe how you think married love might be different from the love that young people experience in their dating relationships. Mention any factors that might contribute to this difference.

CHAPTER 9: THE GIFT OF HUMAN SEXUALITY | WORKSHEET 10 (CONTD.) | 291

CHAPTER 9 | WORKSHEET 11

NAME:

The Story of Ruth

This worksheet presents a synopsis of the story of Ruth from the Book of Ruth in the Old Testament, with the events told as Ruth may have experienced them. Ruth is an immigrant who uproots herself from her own country in order to accompany her mother-in-law to a new country when life becomes difficult and Ruth's husband has died. Both women are poor, homeless and without a family. It is a story of love, loyalty and solidarity.

READ AND REFLECT
Read and reflect on this synopsis of the story of Ruth from the Book of Ruth.

There was a famine in the country where Bethlehem lies, so my parents-in-law left their home and their fields and went to a neighboring country to find work. I, Ruth, a Moabite from that country, married one of their sons. Unfortunately, my husband died while we were still childless. His brother and father died too, so only my mother-in-law, Naomi, and I were left. She decided to return to her home country, and I insisted on going with her. —Not without protests from Naomi, because she thought that a young immigrant widow wouldn't have a future in her country. But I said: 'You won't persuade me to leave you. For where you go, I will go; and where you live, I will live. Your people are my people, and your God is my God.'

We came to Bethlehem during the barley harvest. I decided to do as other poor women do: go to rich men's fields and glean the grain that falls from the sheaves that are being tied up. I happened to glean in a field belonging to Boaz, a relative of my father-in-law. He was kind, and said that I should keep close to his own women, and even eat with them. I bowed before him and asked why he was so kind to me, a foreigner. Boaz replied that he had heard of my concern for my mother-in-law, and that I had left my father and mother and my own country in order to come to a people I didn't know. 'God reward you for what you have done,' he said.

When I came home in the evening, Naomi was overwhelmed over how much I had gleaned, and when she heard that I had been in Boaz' fields, she exclaimed, 'May he be blessed by God, who does not forsake the living or the dead.'

292 | CREDO | LIVING AND LOVING AS DISCIPLES OF CHRIST

CHAPTER 9 | WORKSHEET 11 (CONTD.)

OVER TO YOU

⊙ The story of Ruth is a story about fidelity, courage, loyalty, selflessness, faithfulness, commitment, hope and trust in God. Which of these qualities would you regard as most significant for your close relationships at the moment, and why?

⊙ Which of these qualities would you regard as most important in a marriage context, and why?

⊙ Can you think of any modern-day parallels to this story?

⊙ Share any other insights about love that you took from the story of Ruth.

SCRIPTURE ACTIVITY

You might like to read the full story of Ruth in the Book of Ruth in the Old Testament.

CHAPTER 9: THE GIFT OF HUMAN SEXUALITY | WORKSHEET 11 (CONTD.) | 293

CHAPTER 9 | CHAPTER REVIEW

NAME:

Review of Chapter 9

I. **True/False. Mark the true statements 'T' and the false statements 'F'. In the case of each false statement, cross out and rewrite the incorrect words to make the statement true.**

_____1.   God created human beings as sexual beings.

_____2.   Blessed Pope John Paul II's teaching about the goodness and sacredness of the human body is called his 'Theology of the Spirit'.

_____3.   The *United States Catholic Catechism for Adults* teaches that a modest person dresses, speaks and acts in a manner that supports and encourages purity and chastity.

_____4.   The Catholic Church teaches that homosexuals and lesbians are children of God.

_____5.   Love is one of the seven Capital Sins.

_____6.   Sexual erotic love is the same as self-giving and self-sacrificing love, or agape.

_____7.   An essential part of sexual union is that the gift of self must be given freely within the context of love.

_____8.   Natural Family Planning makes use of the natural alternation of fertile and infertile days in a woman's cycle to achieve or avoid pregnancy.

294 | CREDO | LIVING AND LOVING AS DISCIPLES OF CHRIST

CHAPTER 9 | CHAPTER REVIEW (CONTD.)

_____ 9. The Catholic Church does not support research into reducing infertility.

_____10. Blessed Louis and Zélie Martin were the parents of St. Francis of Assisi.

II. Matching. Write the letter of the term or phrase from column 2 next to its best match in column 1. There are two more items in column 2 than you need.

COLUMN 1	COLUMN 2
_____ 1. The moral virtue that empowers us to put into practice God's plan for the body, person and sexuality	A. Apologist
	B. Chastity
	C. Celibacy
_____ 2. The disorder in our human appetites and desires as the result of Original Sin	D. Abstinence
	E. Temperance
	F. Concupiscence
_____ 3. Intimate relations between relatives or in-laws	G. Artificial insemination and fertilization
_____ 4. The state of those who have chosen to remain unmarried in order to give themselves entirely to God and to the service of his people	H. Adultery
	I. Annulment
	J. Adoptive parenting and foster parenting
_____ 5. Procedures that are contrary to the generative purpose of marriage	K. Incest
_____ 6. Someone who speaks or writes to defend and explain a belief, doctrine or idea	L. The practice of having more than one wife at the same time
_____ 7. Polygamy	
_____ 8. The cardinal virtue by which one moderates one's desires and provides balance in the use of created goods	
_____ 9. Sexual relations between two partners, at least one of whom is married to another party	
_____ 10. Refraining from sexual intercourse and other inappropriate expressions of intimacy until one marries	

CHAPTER 9: THE GIFT OF HUMAN SEXUALITY | CHAPTER REVIEW (CONTD.) | 295

CHAPTER 9 | CHAPTER REVIEW (CONTD.)

III. Write a brief answer. Explain the teaching of the Catholic Church on 1 or 2.
   1. The elements necessary for the Sacrament of Marriage to be true and valid
   2. Divorce

IV. How would you respond? Your local store starts to sell pornographic magazines in addition to all the other magazines and newspapers it sells. While in the store, you overhear some people say that pornography represents freedom of expression by those who wish to take part in or buy it.

296 | CREDO | LIVING AND LOVING AS DISCIPLES OF CHRIST

CHAPTER 9 | CHAPTER REVIEW (CONTD.)

V. Make a 'disciple decision'.

1. What is the most important wisdom for life that you discovered in this chapter?

_____

_____

_____

_____

_____

_____

_____

2. Name several ways you can put this wisdom into practice. Choose one of the ways you identify and describe how you will make that wisdom part of your life right now.

_____

_____

_____

_____

_____

_____

_____

_____

_____

CHAPTER 9: THE GIFT OF HUMAN SEXUALITY | CHAPTER REVIEW (CONTD.) | 297

CHAPTER 10

Building a Just and Compassionate Society

—The Seventh and Tenth Commandments

INTRODUCTION

'Be fruitful and multiply, and fill the earth and subdue it; and have dominion over the fish of the sea and over the birds of the air and over every living thing that moves upon the earth' (Genesis 1:28). Like the other living creatures, humanity is given the power to procreate and so possesses at least a reflection of the divine power to give life . . . . To be in God's image means to be blessed with the responsibility of ruling the world in such a way that it is the ordered, good, life-giving place that God intends it to be. . . . We live up to this responsibility when we make the world good, live in just nonviolence, and render the blessed life possible here.

—David Cotter, quoted in
Megan McKenna, *Harm Not the Earth*

'And God saw that it was good' (Genesis 1:25). This is the mantra that heralds the completion of the work of Creation of each day in the Creation accounts in the Book of Genesis. And because 'God saw that it was good', God's desire was that all creation would continue to be 'good'. Gifted with God's creation, which God has shared with us, we are invited to see to it that the earth and its resources are justly and fairly shared with all for the common good.

In the beginning God entrusted the earth and its resources to the common stewardship of mankind to take care of them, master them by labor and enjoy their fruits. The goods of creation are destined for the whole human race.
—*Catechism of the Catholic Church* (CCC), no. 2402

Chapter 10 focuses on the Seventh and Tenth Commandments: 'You shall not steal' and 'You shall not covet your neighbor's goods'. We lead the young people to understand that these commandments call us to treat all material things as gifts from God and to appreciate that we, the highest point of God's creation, are responsible for caring for the earth, for justly distributing the goods of the earth and for being generous with the benefits that accrue from our labor. We hope that through exploring the Catholic Church's teaching on social justice, the young people will begin to apply the principles of social justice in their own lives.

Chapter 10 is developed under five major headings:

- ◉ **ATTEND AND REFLECT:** What responsibilities come with God's gifts?
- ◉ **HEAR THE STORY:** The Seventh Commandment: much more than not stealing
- ◉ **EMBRACE THE VISION:** The Social Teaching of the Catholic Church
- ◉ **THINK IT THROUGH:** Attitudes and actions count in living the Christian moral life
- ◉ **JUDGE AND ACT:** (*Activities and exercises that encourage the young people to integrate what they have learned in the chapter into their daily lives*)

Theological Background for the Teacher

TREASURES OF THE HEART

Do not store up for yourselves treasures on earth, where moth and rust consume and where thieves break in and steal; but store up for yourselves treasures in heaven, where neither moth nor rust consumes and where thieves do not break in and steal. For where your treasure is, there your heart will be also.

—Matthew 6:19–21

Our treasure is where our heart is. This truth is constantly echoed in Jesus' teachings, in his way of being with people and in the stories he told. In the parable of the Prodigal Son, it was because the father treasured forgiveness in his heart that he was able to embrace his son and welcome him home. It was compassion treasured in the heart of the Good Samaritan that enabled this foreigner to tend to the needs of a total stranger. And it was because

298 | CREDO | LIVING AND LOVING AS DISCIPLES OF CHRIST

Zacchaeus, the dishonest tax collector, treasured an openness and wonder for new possibilities in his heart that he was capable of understanding the radical way of living that Jesus offered him.

> You shall love the Lord your God with all your heart, and with all your soul, and with all your mind.
>
> —Matthew 22:37

Jesus invites us to make God the treasure of our hearts. Jesus promises that, by keeping God at the center of our lives, we can help realize God's dream for a world that is characterized by justice and equality, by love for the vulnerable and the oppressed, by respect for all people, by generosity in sharing wealth and resources, by care for the earth and by trust-filled relationships and a spirit of solidarity.

However, there are times in all our lives when instead of treasuring love, justice and compassion we treasure avarice and resentment, bitterness and greed and our hearts harbor evil rather than good. 'Why do you think evil in your hearts?' Jesus asked the scribes (see Matthew 9:4). Jesus was aware of the human capacity to deny the innate goodness that God has planted in the hearts of all of us and to think and do evil. The ancient Israelites were also acutely aware of the human person's inclination for evil. They understood how internal attitudes and dispositions are mirrored in external behavior and actions. The Seventh and Tenth Commandments are a reminder of the consequences of harboring evil in our hearts. These Commandments prompt us to realize what happens within ourselves and within our society when we ignore the image of the divine within us and we foster instead the false gods of worldly possessions, materialism, greed and envy. The Seventh Commandment deals with 'the visible acts of stealing and injustice' and forbids them. The Tenth Commandment refers to 'interior attitudes of greed and envy' which, when fostered within us, can take root and lead us to act with selfishness and, often, with a lack of integrity, truth and justice. (See *United States Catholic Catechism for Adults* [USCCA], 449.)

THE SPIRIT OF GENEROSITY

Cautioning us against the temptation of becoming the sort of people who steal from others, who exploit the world's resources for personal profit or gain, who accumulate excessive wealth and possessions at the expense of the vulnerable, the Tenth Commandment also calls us

> . . . to practice poverty of spirit and generosity of heart. These virtues liberate us from being

slaves to money and possessions. They enable us to have a preferential love for the poor and to be witnesses of justice and peace in the world. They also enable us to adopt a simplicity of life that frees us from consumerism and helps us preserve God's creation.
>
> —USCCA, 449–450

The Tenth Commandment specifically forbids us from coveting anything that does not belong to us. It also alerts us to the virtues and interior attitudes that underpin this prohibition. So, while the Tenth Commandment says: 'You shall not covet your neighbor's goods', it is also saying, 'You shall be respectful of other people; You shall lessen your attachment to worldly goods; You shall resist the false gods of today's world that say you must compare yourself with your neighbor; You shall find true happiness in God and measure your worth by a life of truth and integrity and not by wealth and riches; You shall learn to live simply; You shall nurture a spirit of sharing and generosity; You shall rejoice in the good fortune of others; You shall acknowledge the blessings that God has bestowed on you; You shall store up treasures in your heart.'

THE SPIRIT OF JUSTICE AND SOLIDARITY

God has bestowed the world to us for our enjoyment and use. This is clear from the Genesis Creation accounts. But the gift of the world that God has bequeathed to us is for the use of all persons, not just the powerful and the strong, the rich and beautiful. Creation has been gifted to *all* humankind. God's gift to us brings with it enormous challenges and responsibilities. We are called to be stewards, loyal caretakers and faithful protectors of the world; to be just and caring, to shelter the weak and the sick, to share with equality and fairness.

> The seventh commandment forbids *theft*, that is, usurping another's property against the reasonable will of the owner. . . . Even if it does not contradict the provisions of civil law, any form of unjustly taking and keeping the property of others is against the seventh commandment: thus, deliberate retention of goods lent or of objects lost; business fraud; paying unjust wages; forcing up prices by taking advantage of the ignorance or hardship of another.
>
> —CCC, nos. 2408–2409

Obedience to the Seventh Commandment goes beyond the provisions of civil law. For the disciple of Jesus Christ the law of God is greater than civil law. The law of God demands a just way of living and

CHAPTER 10: BUILDING A JUST AND COMPASSIONATE SOCIETY | INTRODUCTION | 299 being in the world that upholds the sacredness and dignity of every person in all situations and across all spheres of life.

The Seventh Commandment also has far-reaching implications for the global Christian community. Speaking at the 2007 Gathering of Latin American Bishops, Pope Francis (then Cardinal Bergoglio), told those assembled that:

> The unjust distribution of goods persists, creating a situation of social sin that cries out to Heaven and limits the possibilities of a fuller life for so many of our brothers.

The Seventh Commandment reminds us of our responsibility to ensure that 'the goods of creation are destined for the whole human race' (CCC, no. 2402). Selfishness and greed form the root cause of the actions proscribed by the Seventh Commandment. And it is the same greed that, on an international scale, leads to the unequal distribution of the earth's wealth and resources and inflicts gross injustices on the poorest communities within our world.

The Seventh Commandment asks us not just to refrain from theft but to treasure the virtues of justice, solidarity and moderation in our hearts and to shift our focus from fulfilling our personal wants and desires to attending to the needs of others with dignity and respect—at local, national and global levels. At the core of the Seventh Commandment is our responsibility to help create a world where every human person is affirmed and honored for who they are and not for what they possess. To achieve this we are each called in our personal lives to be just, to be respectful, to be honest; and to embody

> . . . the virtues of moderation in our possessions, justice in our treatment of others, respect for their human dignity, and solidarity with all peoples.
>
> —USCCA, 419

Pope John Paul II reminded us:

> It is not wrong to want to live better; what is wrong is a style of life which is presumed to be better when it is directed towards 'having' rather than 'being', and which wants to have more, not in order to be more but in order to spend life in enjoyment as an end in itself.
>
> —Centesimus Annus, no. 36

The *United States Catholic Catechism for Adults* teaches:

> Moderation curbs our attachment to worldly goods and restrains our appetite for consumerism. Justice helps us respect our neighbor's rights and be interested in their human well-being. Solidarity opens our hearts to identifying with the whole human family, reminding us of our common humanity.
>
> —USCCA, 419

The challenges of both the Seventh and the Tenth Commandments are great. They place before us the Christian ideal, an ideal we are each called to live by as adopted children of God. As catechists we need to ask ourselves: how do we help our young people to become aware of the values they treasure in their hearts? How do we guide them to adopt values based on generosity and justice? How do we help them sustain their faith journey in a society that frequently counters such Christian values? There are no easy answers to these questions; but, as baptized Christians, we do know that

> [God] is not far from each one of us. For 'In him we live and move and have our being'. . . 'For we too are his offspring.'
>
> —Acts 17:27–28

So, when we encourage our young people to explore their own 'interior attitudes', we are guiding them to become cognizant of how the treasures in their hearts are mirrored each day in their lives and in their relationships. When we openly address the dominant philosophy of today's world that values individualism over solidarity; accumulation of goods over equal distribution; envy of others over contentment with oneself; excess over moderation; wealth over simplicity, we are providing them with the resources to name and criticize the false gods of today's world and to begin to identify for themselves ways in which they can counter these influences in their day-to-day living.

> People who want to live as Christian disciples and Christian stewards face serious obstacles. In the United States and other nations, a dominant secular culture . . . frequently encourages us to focus on ourselves and our pleasures. . . .
>
> We know what it is to struggle against selfishness and greed, and we realize that it is harder for many today to accept the challenge of being a Christian steward.
>
> —USCCA, 453–454

When we place before our young people the challenge of living the Gospel, we have an opportunity to remind them that living as a disciple of Jesus Christ and working toward the Kingdom of God is a lifelong task—a task that cannot be achieved alone. As members of the Church we have the support of others, the guidance of the teaching of the Church and the blessings and grace of God the Father, God the Son and God the Holy Spirit.

CATHOLIC SOCIAL TEACHING

The *Catechism of the Catholic Church* teaches that the human person is

> . . . the author, center, and goal of all economic and social life. The decisive point of the social question is that goods created by God for everyone should in fact reach everyone in accordance with justice and with the help of charity.
>
> —CCC, no. 2459

The Catholic Church's teaching on social justice has its foundation in the principle of the sacredness of all human life and the dignity of the human person. While the Church's teaching has changed over the centuries in line with developments in society and culture, the Church has always been very clear about the focus of her social teaching and the implications for the disciple of Jesus Christ. Through Baptism we are called to work toward the elimination of poverty, to speak out against exploitation and injustice, and to create a more caring society and a more equal world.

> The central focus of the Church's social teaching is justice for all, especially for the helpless and the poor. It involves the removal of the symptoms and causes of poverty and injustice.
>
> The Church's social doctrine addresses a wide range of issues that include the dignity of work, the need of workers to receive a salary that will enable them to care for their families, a safe working environment, and the responsibility of the state for areas such as a stable currency, public services, and protecting personal freedom and private property. Church teaching also speaks to the need of business enterprises to consider the good of the employees, not just the profit motive. Wage earners should be able to represent their needs and grievances when necessary.
>
> . . . All of the Church's social teaching is rooted in the fundamental principle of the sacredness of human life and the fundamental dignity of every single individual. Out of these truths flows the rest.
>
> —USCCA, 421

The key themes at the core of the Church's teaching that are relevant to the Seventh and Tenth Commandments are outlined by the United States Conference of Catholic Bishops as follows:

Option for the Poor and Vulnerable

A basic moral test is how our most vulnerable members are faring. In a society marred by deepening divisions between rich and poor, our tradition recalls the story of the Last Judgment (Mt 25:31–46) and instructs us to put the needs of the poor and vulnerable first.

The Dignity of Work and the Rights of Workers

The economy must serve people, not the other way around. Work is more than a way to make a living; it is a form of continuing participation in God's creation. If the dignity of work is to be protected, then the basic rights of workers must be respected—the right to productive work, to decent and fair wages, to the organization and joining of unions, to private property, and to economic initiative.

Solidarity

We are one human family whatever our national, racial, ethnic, economic, and ideological differences. We are our brothers' and sisters' keepers, wherever they may be. Loving our neighbor has global dimensions in a shrinking world. At the core of the virtue of solidarity is the pursuit of justice and peace. Pope Paul VI taught that if you want peace, work for justice. The Gospel calls us to be peacemakers. Our love for all our sisters and brothers demands that we promote peace in a world surrounded by violence and conflict.

Care for God's Creation

We show our respect for the Creator by our stewardship of creation. Care for the earth is not just an Earth Day slogan; it is a requirement of our faith. We are called to protect people and the planet, living our faith in relationship with all of God's creation. This environmental challenge has fundamental moral and ethical dimensions that cannot be ignored.

ADDITIONAL BACKGROUND READING

Catechism of the Catholic Church, nos. 2401–2463, 2534–2557; *United States Catholic Catechism for Adults*, 417–428, 447–457.

Teacher Reflection

As you prepare to engage your group in a study of the Seventh and the Tenth Commandments, which remind us to treat all material things as gifts from God and to use them for the good of all people, take a few moments to reflect on this story about giving and receiving.

One day a rich baker was sleeping in the synagogue. As he was half dozing, the biblical verses telling the children of Israel to place twelve loaves in the tabernacle were being read (Leviticus 24:5–6). In his sleepy state he thought that it was God who had spoken to him directly. He wasn't sure why God would need bread but he was proud to be asked and rushed home to bake the bread. When he came back to the synagogue he tucked the loaves behind the curtain next to the scrolls of the Bible. No sooner had he gone than the poorest man in the village, the synagogue cleaner, came into the sanctuary. All alone he whispered his prayer, 'O Lord. I am so poor. My family is starving. We will die unless you perform a miracle for us.' He then walked around the room to tidy it up. As he approached the scrolls he saw the loaves of bread. 'A miracle!' he exclaimed. 'I never thought you worked so quickly!' Minutes later the baker returned, curious as to what had happened. He was amazed. 'You really ate my bread, Lord! I will bring you more next week.' And he did, and this strange exchange continued for many years until the rabbi by chance was in the synagogue late one day and saw what happened. He called the two men together and told them what they had been doing. 'I see,' said the baker sadly, 'God doesn't really eat bread.' 'I understand,' said the poor man, 'God hasn't been baking bread for me after all.' They were both sad that God would no longer be a part of their lives. Then the rabbi said, 'Look at your hands. Your hands,' he said to the rich man, 'are the hands of God giving to the poor. And your hands,' he said to the poor man, 'are also the hands of God receiving gifts from the rich. So continue baking and continue taking. Your hands are the hands of God.'

Reflect

Reflect on times when your hands have been the hands of God . . . giving *and* receiving.

CHAPTER OUTCOMES

See general note on page 19 of this resource.

Learning Outcomes

As a result of studying this chapter and exploring the issues raised, the young people should be able to:

- recognize their responsibility to be stewards of creation;
- understand the Church's teaching on 'the universal destination of goods';
- appreciate how small acts of individuals and the social policies of nations can contribute to social sin;
- know that the Seventh Commandment asks us to use the gifts of creation not only for our own good but for the benefit of everyone;
- understand how the Seventh Commandment relates not only to personal possessions but also to larger economic and political dealings;
- recognize acts that are contrary to the Seventh Commandment;
- know that Christians are bound by their faith to work for a just society and to resist and work to reform societal structures that exploit or enslave human beings;
- know that the Cardinal Moral Virtues empower us to live the Seventh Commandment;
- understand the concepts of original justice, commutative justice, distributive justice, legal justice, social justice, retributive justice and restorative justice;
- know that the commitment to build a just society is rooted in the principle of solidarity;
- understand the wisdom behind the Tenth Commandment and what this Commandment asks of us;
- understand the meaning of 'covetousness';
- recognize attitudes and behaviors that are contrary to the Tenth Commandment;
- know about the life and faith of St. Martin de Porres.

Faith-formation Outcomes

As a result of studying this chapter and exploring the issues raised, the young people should also:

- develop and live the moral values of justice and generosity;
- take to heart Jesus' challenge to us to live out of a spirit of generosity and sharing;
- identify ways in which they could promote social justice;
- cultivate a lifestyle of detachment and simplicity, in accordance with the Gospel;
- be inspired by St. Martin de Porres' life of Gospel simplicity and service.

302 | CREDO | LIVING AND LOVING AS DISCIPLES OF CHRIST

Notes and Guidelines for Student Activities

ATTEND AND REFLECT

What responsibilities come with God's gifts?

Learning Outcomes

That the young people would:

⊙ recognize their responsibility to be stewards of creation;

⊙ understand the Church's teaching on 'the universal destination of goods';

⊙ appreciate how small acts of individuals and the social policies of nations can contribute to social sin.

Faith-formation Outcome

That the young people would also:

⊙ develop and live the moral values of justice and generosity.

Overview

Section one, 'Attend and Reflect', examines humanity's responsibility to care for God's gift of creation. We remind the young people that this responsibility includes stewardship of creation. As creatures, we receive the gift of life and all creation solely through God's gratuitous generosity. We have no gift of our own making to offer God in return; what we can offer is our gratitude, and we do this best when we take good care of the gifts God has given us. We guide the young people to understand that in the Seventh Commandment God directs us to know and live by his divine plan for all creation, which includes respect for people, the humane treatment of animals and the responsible use of such natural resources as air, water and earth. We explain Catholic social teaching on 'the universal destination of goods' and we encourage the young people to be diligent in developing and living the moral virtues of justice and generosity, even in the smallest details of their daily lives.

Supplementary Activities for 'Attend and Reflect'

Development Games

In recent years a variety of interactive games have been developed to heighten awareness of the unfair distribution of the world's wealth and resources. Some have been developed by educationalists, some by Christian Churches and some by development agencies. Encourage the young people to search the internet for some of these games. If appropriate, you might invite the young people to play one of the games and then follow up with a class discussion on the theme of this chapter, that is, sharing God's gifts in accordance with God's plan.

Alternatively, you could invite the young people to create their own game and to test it with a group in class. If this proves successful, the young people might introduce the game to a younger class group in the school.

Worksheet 1: 'Creating a Fruitful World' (*page 309 of this resource*) invites the young people to read an inspirational rabbinic story and to reflect on how they might contribute to creating a fair, just and fruitful world.

Worksheet 2: 'Ban Ki-moon Addresses Young People' (*page 311 of this resource*) presents excerpts from a speech given by the United Nations Secretary General Ban Ki-moon at the 2013 Fifth Global Forum of the United Nations Alliance of Civilizations in Vienna, Austria, where he was addressing a Youth Event attended by young people from all over the world. We invite the young people to reflect on the message of the speech and then to write a reply, outlining the role that young Christians can play in creating a fairer and more equal world.

Worksheet 3: 'An Alternative Philosophy on Life' (*page 313 of this resource*) invites the young people to read and respond to a story about an African tribe called the Xhosa whose philosophy on life might challenge their own approach to living in and interacting with the world.

CHAPTER 10: BUILDING A JUST AND COMPASSIONATE SOCIETY | NOTES AND GUIDELINES | 303

HEAR THE STORY

The Seventh Commandment: much more than not stealing

Learning Outcomes

That the young people would:

⊙ know that the Seventh Commandment asks us to use the gifts of creation not only for our own good but for the benefit of everyone;

⊙ understand how the Seventh Commandment relates not only to personal possessions but also to larger economic and political dealings;

⊙ recognize acts that are contrary to the Seventh Commandment.

Faith-formation Outcome

That the young people would also:

⊙ take to heart Jesus' challenge to us to live out of a spirit of generosity and sharing.

Overview

In section two, 'Hear the Story', we explore with the young people how the Seventh Commandment asks us to use the gifts of creation not only for our own good but for the benefit of everyone. As we acquire personal possessions, we must maintain a balance between our personal needs and the needs of other people, especially the poor. We outline how the responsibility to share God's gifts extends not only to personal possessions but also to our larger economic and political dealings. The moral law requires that those who oversee corporations and smaller businesses use the means at their disposal for the common good of all, even as they pursue a reasonable profit. We highlight how the violation of this moral principle is not always obvious and clear cut, for example, the making of exorbitant profits to satisfy investors and shareholders at the expense of employees and customers. We provide examples of other acts that are contrary to the Seventh Commandment, such as business fraud, paying unjust wages, doing poor work for which one is paid, breaking a legal contract that one entered freely, the unjust destruction of another person's property, and avoiding or not paying social security contributions and taxes. We conclude the chapter by recalling Jesus' words in Matthew 5:40–42, where he challenged people to live out the spirit of generosity required by the Seventh Commandment.

Supplementary Activities for 'Hear the Story'

Research Activity

In the year 2000, 189 nations made a promise to free people from extreme poverty and multiple deprivations. This pledge turned into eight 'Millennium Development Goals'. Invite the young people to check out the website of the United Nations Development Programme (UNDP) to find out what these goals are and to learn about the work that is being done to realize them. The young people could share what they learn about the work of UNDP with the class.

_____

'Blessings' Activity/Ritual

Sometimes in the frenetic world in which we live it is easy to forget about the blessings that surround us. There is a Jewish practice of saying one hundred blessings a day to thank and 'bless' God for all his gifts. You might like to invite the young people to nominate a particular day when they will gather one hundred blessings. In order to do so, they will need to be alert to the moments and the things that offer blessings to them—through the world of nature, through their interactions with other people, through their senses, through words and so on. You might like to create a class ritual to honor and give expression to the young people's blessings.

_____

Worksheet 4: 'Life in Society' (*page 315 of this resource*) invites the young people to apply what they have learned about Catholic social teaching and moral law to a series of scenarios from modern-day life.

_____

Worksheet 5: 'Actions Contrary to the Seventh Commandment' (*page 317 of this resource*) offers the young people the opportunity to explore how people commonly 'bend' the rules to justify actions and judgments that are contrary to the Seventh Commandment.

_____

Worksheet 6: 'Prayers for Social Justice' (*page 319 of this resource*) presents several prayers for justice and truth for the young people to reflect upon and pray. If the young people are doing this activity during class time, you might play some quiet background music to create a prayerful and reflective atmosphere.

_____

304 | CREDO | LIVING AND LOVING AS DISCIPLES OF CHRIST

Worksheet 7: 'Stone Soup: An Old Tale Retold' (*page 322 of this resource*) offers the young people the opportunity to read a famous and inspirational story about sharing with those in need. There are many different versions of this story found across Europe.

EMBRACE THE VISION

The Social Teaching of the Catholic Church

Learning Outcomes
That the young people would:
⊙ know that Christians are bound by their faith to work for a just society and to resist and work to reform societal structures that exploit or enslave human beings;
⊙ know that the Cardinal Moral Virtues empower us to live the Seventh Commandment;
⊙ understand the concepts of original justice, commutative justice, distributive justice, legal justice, social justice, retributive justice and restorative justice;
⊙ know that the commitment to build a just society is rooted in the principle of solidarity.

Faith-formation Outcome
That the young people would also:
⊙ identify ways in which they could promote social justice.

Overview
Section three, 'Embrace the Vision', focuses on the social teaching of the Catholic Church, whose founding principle is that every human being is created in the image and likeness of God. We discuss the responsibility of every person and every society to work for the good of all human beings. We teach that all systems that lead to the enslavement or exploitation of human beings or their labor are sinful social structures and Christians are bound by their faith to resist and work to reform such structures. For example, strikes that workers conduct in a moral way are a legitimate and just means of working for a more just society. We explain that the Cardinal Moral Virtues of justice, temperance, fortitude and prudence empower us to live the Seventh Commandment. We focus in particular on the virtue of justice and explain the concepts of original justice, commutative justice, distributive justice, legal justice, social justice, retributive justice and restorative justice. We conclude the section by exploring how a commitment to building a just society is rooted in the principle of solidarity.

Supplementary Activities for 'Embrace the Vision'

Research Activity
Invite the young people to search the website of the United Nations for the 'Ten stories the world should know more about'. Ask them to form ten groups, with each group choosing one of these stories to explore in detail. Afterward, the groups could present their findings to the class.

_____

Timeline Activity
You might like to invite the young people to participate in a Timeline Activity developed by the USCCB. The focus of the activity is to increase familiarity with the major social teaching documents and explore the development of the Church's social teaching since 1891.

You will need these online materials for the activity:
⊙ **Major Catholic social teaching documents activity cut-outs:** available from: *http://old.usccb. org/campus/documents/Encyclicals%20Descriptions. pdf*
⊙ **Timeline of events:** available from: *http://old. usccb.org/campus/documents/Timeline%20for%20 CST%20activity.pdf*
⊙ **Answer key:** available from: *http://old.usccb. org/campus/documents/CST%20Activity%20 Answer%20Key.pdf*

How to implement this activity with a group:

1. **Provide background information**
   An encyclical is a letter from the Holy Father that is a 'teaching document'. Its audience is every Catholic and all people of good will. A 'social encyclical' applies the consistent, traditional moral teachings of the Church to the social and economic challenges of the current day. For example, the most recent social encyclical, *Caritas in Veritate*, was written to address the current economic crisis and other issues facing the world today, and deals with moral aspects of economic life, poverty and development, human rights and duties, environmental responsibility, and other moral and economic issues.

2. **Break into small groups of 2–3 persons each**
   Provide each group with a copy of the timeline of events (you may want to provide tape to adhere the pages of the timeline together horizontally) and batches of the cut-out rectangles with the Catholic social teaching documents descriptions. Explain that we are going to see how, over the past

CHAPTER 10: BUILDING A JUST AND COMPASSIONATE SOCIETY | NOTES AND GUIDELINES | 305

120 years, these documents have helped guide Catholics' perspectives on issues and problems facing our human family.

3. **Small group activity**

Ask each group to read the events on the timelines and to try to match the cut-out rectangles describing the documents with the events timeline. If participants need help, tell them to pay attention to:
- Events mentioned in the timeline that are also mentioned in the social documents descriptions.
- The names of the popes, since documents by the same popes will follow one another.
- References to anniversaries, since some documents were written to celebrate the anniversary of a previous document.

4. **Checking answers**

When all the groups are finished, go through each of the years on the timeline one by one, mentioning some of the events that happened that year. For each year, ask participants to call out the correct social teaching document. The group leader can check answers using the answer key. When the correct document is named, ask the person who got it correct to explain how the document was responding to those issues facing the world.

5. **Discussion.** Discuss the following questions:
- What social teaching document did you find most interesting? Why?
- Name an example of how a social teaching document responded to issues facing the human family at a particular time? How did that document help Catholics see issues facing the world in the light of their faith?
- Which document(s) might you be most interested in reading in full?

Be sure to mention that students can find links to the text of all the documents at *www.usccb.org/campus!*

Worksheet 8: 'A Just World for the Next Generation' (*page 325 of this resource*) offers the young people an opportunity to imagine and articulate a world that would conform to the vision of the Kingdom of God that Jesus lived and taught.

Worksheet 9: 'Jesus Speaks About Poverty' (*page 327 of this resource*) invites the young people to read and complete an exercise based on a selection of Gospel passages that highlight Jesus' attitude to the marginalized in society.

Creative Exercise

Invite the young people to write a short story, poem, reflection or song on the theme of solidarity. They may work alone, in pairs or in groups. When they have completed the exercise they might like to read out or perform their work for the class.

THINK IT THROUGH

Attitudes and actions count in living the Christian moral life

Learning Outcomes

That the young people would:
- understand the wisdom behind the Tenth Commandment and what this Commandment asks of us;
- understand the meaning of 'covetousness';
- recognize attitudes and behaviors that are contrary to the Tenth Commandment.

Faith-formation Outcome

That the young people would also:
- cultivate a lifestyle of detachment and simplicity, in accordance with the Gospel.

Overview

Section four, 'Think It Through', focuses on the meaning and implications for our lives of the Tenth Commandment, which warns us against envy and the desire to have what others possess. We explain the concept of covetousness and that it is one of the Capital Sins. We guide the young people to see that the Tenth Commandment sets us free from addictive attitudes toward possessions, which never fully satisfy us, and we present the Church's teaching that 'Desire for true happiness frees man from his immoderate attachment to the goods of this world so that he can find his fulfillment in the vision and beatitude of God' (CCC, no. 2504). We remind the young people that it is only by putting the one true God at the center of our lives—the deepest desire of our heart—that we can live as the truly free persons God creates and desires us to be. We outline attitudes and behaviors that are contrary to the Tenth Commandment, including greed (avarice), envy, jealousy and gluttony. We conclude the section with Jesus' words in Luke 12:29, 31 and Luke 18:24–25, which call us to detach ourselves from over-indulging in material goods and, instead, to abandon ourselves to the caring presence of God.

306 | CREDO | LIVING AND LOVING AS DISCIPLES OF CHRIST

Supplementary Activities for 'Think It Through'

Praying for Justice
Invite the young people to look up the USCCB website and read the United States Bishops' nine suggestions to encourage young people to pray for justice: 'Nine Ways to Integrate Prayer and Justice' (*http://old.usccb.org/campus/prayer-ipj.shtml*).

Create a 'Prayer Box'
Creating a personal 'Prayer Box' is one of the activities suggested on the USCCB website. You might like to invite the young people to try this activity. They simply decorate a shoe box or another similar-sized box and put into it slips of paper on which they have written out issues that should concern faithful citizens. Encourage the young people to choose issues relating to justice and social solidarity to link in with the theme of chapter 10. As a class prayer activity each day, pick one or two slips of paper out of the box and pray together for all those who are affected by the issues, including the policymakers, and for God's guidance and help in responding to those issues.

Worksheet 10: 'God in the Margins' (*page 329 of this resource*) presents two extracts from a book titled *Encountering God in the Margins* by Dr. Aidan Donaldson (Dublin, Ireland: Veritas, 2010) in which he describes the content of a seminar on poverty that he attended. We invite the young people to read the extracts and to write their responses.

Activity: 'Fifteen Rules for Living Simply'
Invite the class to conduct a brainstorm and come up with a set of 'Fifteen Rules for Living Simply' that would be applicable to the lives of young people today who wish to live as true disciples of Jesus.

Worksheet 11: 'Prophets and Justice' (*page 332 of this resource*) offers the young people the opportunity to read and respond to some of the Old Testament prophets' words on justice and to explore their relevance for today's world. We then invite the young people to identify some modern-day prophets and the issues that concern them.

Worksheet 12: 'The Values of St. Francis of Assisi'
(*page 336 of this resource*) presents a selection of quotations from the saint that reflect his compassion for the poor and the marginalized. We invite the young people to explore the challenge for young disciples of Jesus who would wish to emulate St. Francis' example today.

JUDGE AND ACT

Learning Outcomes
That the young people would:
- ⊙ review the teachings of the Church that they have learned about in this chapter;
- ⊙ know about the life and faith of St. Martin de Porres.

Faith-formation Outcome
That the young people would also:
- ⊙ be inspired by St. Martin de Porres' life of Gospel simplicity and service.

Overview
In section five, 'Judge and Act', the young people review the teachings of the Church that they have learned about in this chapter. They also learn about the life and faith of St. Martin de Porres, who embodied what it means to be detached from earthly goods and to use one's resources for the good of others.

Supplementary Activities for 'Judge and Act'

Teacher Tip: You might invite the young people to watch the film *Slumdog Millionaire* (directed by Danny Boyle and Loveleen Tandan, 2008), which depicts poverty and its causes in India.

Actions of Service
Invite the young people to identify concrete ways in which they, individually or in groups, could reach out to the poor and vulnerable in their locality or, indeed, in the wider world. Encourage them to commit to following through on some of their suggestions. You might also agree on a date on which they will share and review the actions of service they have undertaken.

Additional Prayer Suggestions

Invite the young people to close their eyes as you pray this prayer of St. Francis.

The Divine Praises of St. Francis of Assisi

You are holy, Lord,
the only God,
and your deeds are wonderful.
You are strong,
you are great,
you are the Most High,
you are the almighty King.
You, holy Father, are King of the heaven and earth.
You are Three and One,
God above all gods.
You are good, all good, supreme good,
Lord God, living and true.
You are love,
You are wisdom,
You are humility,
You are endurance,
You are beauty,
You are gentleness,
You are security,
You are rest,
You are joy.
You are our hope and happiness,
You are justice and moderation,
You are all our riches,
You are beauty,
You are gentleness,
You are our protector,
You are our guardian and defender.
You are strength,
You are consolation,
You are our hope,
You are our faith,
You are our charity,
You are all our sweetness,
You are our eternal life,
great and admirable Lord,
God almighty,
merciful Savior.

Scripture Reflection

(See instructions for the use of doodling in prayer in the 'Student Activity Tool Kit', page 394 of this resource.)

Use the following Scripture verse to engage the young people in prayer:

If you desire wisdom, keep the commandments.

**SIRACH
(ECCLESIASTICUS) 1:26**

308 | CREDO | LIVING AND LOVING AS DISCIPLES OF CHRIST

CHAPTER 10 | WORKSHEET 1

NAME:

Creating a Fruitful World

The goods of creation are destined for the whole human race.
—*Catechism of the Catholic Church*, no. 2402

God gave humanity 'dominion' over creation so that all people can have a decent and dignified life. It is up to us—as individuals and as members of the wider society—to take care of the gifts that God has bestowed on us and to share the fruits of creation. This worksheet offers you the opportunity to read an inspirational story and to reflect on how you might contribute to creating a fair, just and fruitful world.

READ AND REFLECT
⊙ Read this rabbinic tale and take some time to reflect on its message and how it might apply to you personally before answering the questions below.
⊙ Think especially about how the story might apply to your role in helping to create a just and 'fruitful' world.

A wise rabbi was walking along a road when he saw a man planting a tree. The rabbi asked him, 'How many years will it take for this tree to bear fruit?' The man answered that it would take seventy years. The rabbi asked, 'Are you so fit and strong that you expect to live that long and eat its fruit?' The man answered, 'I found a fruitful world because my ancestors planted for me. So I will do the same for my children.'

What does this story say to you about the power of individuals to contribute to creating a better world for all? What message of hope does it offer you?

_____

_____

_____

_____

_____

_____

CHAPTER 10: BUILDING A JUST AND COMPASSIONATE SOCIETY | WORKSHEET 1 | 309

CHAPTER 10 | WORKSHEET 1 (CONTD.)

What you 'plant' now has implications not only for the present but also for future generations. With this in mind, what could you 'plant'—in other words, what contributions could you make—that would 'bear fruit' both for yourself and for the generations to come? And who would you wish to benefit in particular from your efforts?

_____

_____

_____

_____

_____

Where might you find the support and inspiration you would need to work toward the goals you outlined above?

_____

_____

_____

_____

_____

COMPOSE A PRAYER
Write a prayer to the Holy Spirit for inspiration and support with your efforts to create a fruitful, just and fair world.

_____

_____

_____

_____

_____

CHAPTER 10 | WORKSHEET 2

NAME:

Ban Ki-moon Addresses Young People

This worksheet presents excerpts from a speech given by the United Nations Secretary General Ban Ki-moon at the 2013 Fifth Global Forum of the United Nations Alliance of Civilizations in Vienna, Austria, where he was addressing a Youth Event attended by young people from all over the world.

READ AND REFLECT

Read and reflect on these excerpts from UN Secretary General Ban Ki-moon's address to young people about their role in the creation of a fairer and more equal world.

> You have already demonstrated that you are willing and able to take on the responsibility of leadership. The world will rely on you to speak the language of tolerance and respect. Your voices need to drown out those that preach division and hatred.

> You come from some 100 countries. . . . You bring a wealth of diversity—some of you in this hall have first-hand experience of the damage that can come from irresponsible leaders who preach the language of division and hatred for their own selfish ends. The world will rely on your courage and principled actions to lead us on the path of harmony and sustainable development. . . .

> You represent the largest generation of young people the world has ever known. That is why we are deepening the youth focus of our existing programs on employment and entrepreneurship; political inclusion and human rights; education and reproductive health. . . . Our youth volunteer program is already producing results. . . .

> The world is going through a period of transition—economic, demographic, political and environmental. The challenges are profound, but so are the opportunities—provided we are able to turn our backs on extremism and divisiveness.

> Conflict is one of the greatest obstacles to development. . . .

> We must aim to eradicate extreme poverty and hunger and improve the well-being of people and the planet.

CHAPTER 10: BUILDING A JUST AND COMPASSIONATE SOCIETY | WORKSHEET 2 | 311

CHAPTER 10 | WORKSHEET 2 (CONTD.)

PAIR AND SHARE

⊙ Work with a partner.

⊙ Slowly, reread the excerpts from Ban Ki-moon's speech, this time noting on the chart below the problems and challenges facing the world that Ban Ki-moon refers to and the qualities of young people that he feels can make a huge contribution to bringing about a fairer and more just world.

Problems/Challenges	Qualities young people can bring to these situations

⊙ Taking a Christian understanding of justice and recalling the Church's social teaching on the 'universal distribution of goods', work with your partner to construct a reply to Ban Ki-moon, outlining the role that young Christian people can (and already do) play in the creation of a world of peace and justice.

⊙ Share your work with the class.

⊙ Consider sending your reply to Ban Ki-moon at the United Nations headquarters in New York!

312 | CREDO | LIVING AND LOVING AS DISCIPLES OF CHRIST

CHAPTER 10 | WORKSHEET 3

NAME:

An Alternative Philosophy on Life

This worksheet invites you to read and respond to a story about an African tribe called the Xhosa whose philosophy on life might challenge your approach to living in and interacting with the world.

READ, REFLECT AND RESPOND
Read and reflect on this story and then answer the questions below.

An anthropologist suggested a game to the children of the tribe.

He placed a basket of fruit near a tree and told them that whoever reached the basket first, would win the fruit.

When it was time for the kids to run, they all joined hands and arrived at the basket simultaneously.

As they were all enjoying their reward, the anthropologist asked them why they all ran together when one child could have had all the fruit. A child replied, '*Ubuntu*. How can one of us be happy if all the other ones are sad?'

[*'Ubuntu' in the Xhosa language means 'I am because we are'.*]

Describe the principles and values upon which the children's action was based.

_____

_____

_____

_____

CHAPTER 10: BUILDING A JUST AND COMPASSIONATE SOCIETY | WORKSHEET 3 | 313

CHAPTER 10 | WORKSHEET 3 (CONTD.)

In teaching about the universal destination and the private ownership of goods, the Vatican II document *Constitution on the Church in the Modern World* states: '*In their use of things people should regard the external goods they lawfully possess as not just their own but common to others as well, in the sense that they can benefit others as well as themselves*' (paragraph 49).

In what ways might the Xhosa children's actions mirror the social teaching of the Catholic Church in the above statement?

_____

_____

_____

How would your life be different if you lived according to this social teaching?

_____

_____

_____

_____

How would the world be different if everybody lived by this social teaching?

_____

_____

_____

_____

314 | CREDO | LIVING AND LOVING AS DISCIPLES OF CHRIST

CHAPTER 10 | WORKSHEET 4

NAME:

Life in Society

This worksheet invites you to apply what you have learned about Catholic social teaching and moral law to a series of scenarios from modern-day life.

GROUP ACTIVITY
- Form six groups.
- Each group chooses <u>one</u> of these scenarios, each of which depicts the consequences of a trust that has been broken:
  1. An employee steals some materials from his or her employer.
  2. A student plagiarizes or copies information for a school project.
  3. A person burgles a house.
  4. A migrant worker discovers that he is being paid well below the average wage.
  5. In a developing country, big machines are cutting down the forests and leaving the locals landless.
  6. Someone is being sold into a form of slavery (for example, to work in the sex trade or for child labor).
- Discuss the following questions within your group before writing your answers.

What trust has been broken in the situation you chose?

_____

_____

Name some of the consequences of such a betrayal of trust—for all the parties involved.

_____

_____

_____

What consequences might such a betrayal of trust have for society in general?

_____

_____

_____

CHAPTER 10: BUILDING A JUST AND COMPASSIONATE SOCIETY | WORKSHEET 4 | 315

CHAPTER 10 | WORKSHEET 4 (CONTD.)

How might civil law respond to such a situation?

_____

_____

What might be a Christian response to such a situation?

_____

_____

_____

PAIR AND SHARE

⊙ We live in an imperfect world. We have to work constantly to help create a fair and just world based on trust and solidarity.

⊙ Share ideas with your partner in order to come up with a list of three things at the individual/personal level and three things at the societal/world level that you think would need to happen to create and sustain a world built on trust and on respect for the dignity of all human persons.

⊙ Enter your final choices on the chart and then share your ideas with another pair of students.

At an individual/personal level	At the societal/world level
1.	1.
2.	2.
3.	3.

JOURNAL EXERCISE

Describe the best insights you have gained from the activities on this worksheet.

316 | CREDO | LIVING AND LOVING AS DISCIPLES OF CHRIST

CHAPTER 10 | WORKSHEET 5

NAME:

Actions Contrary to the Seventh Commandment

We are all aware of times when we 'bend' the rules to suit our circumstances and to justify our actions and judgments. The teaching of the Catholic Church urges us to be responsible and just in our dealings at all times. This worksheet offers you the opportunity to consider some actions that are contrary to the Seventh Commandment but which are a regular occurrence in modern society.

GROUP ACTIVITY
⊙ Work in small groups.
⊙ Read this statement from the *Catechism of the Catholic Church*, paragraph 2409:

> Even if it does not contradict the provisions of civil law, any form of unjustly taking and keeping the property of others is against the seventh commandment: thus, deliberate retention of goods lent or of objects lost; business fraud; paying unjust wages; forcing up prices by taking advantage of the ignorance or hardship of another.

⊙ In relation to each of the actions listed on the chart opposite, where the temptation to break the Seventh Commandment can be an attractive option, come up with as many reasons as you can think of that people commonly use to justify following through with such actions.
⊙ Write these 'justifications' as speech bubbles extending from each action.

PAUSE, REFLECT AND PRAY
⊙ When you have completed the activity, take some time alone to look back over the speech bubbles.
⊙ Are there any statements that resonate with you? Perhaps you made some of these statements yourself at times in defense of something 'wrong' that you did, or in an attempt to justify any of the actions named?
⊙ Think about how such 'justifications' contravene the Seventh Commandment.
⊙ Now say a short prayer asking God for the help you need to change this way of thinking.

CLASS DISCUSSION
Share any insights you gained from this exercise.

CHAPTER 10: BUILDING A JUST AND COMPASSIONATE SOCIETY | WORKSHEET 5 | 317

CHAPTER 10 | WORKSHEET 5 (CONTD.)

Actions Contrary to the Seventh Commandment

Breaking a contract

Avoiding taxes

Paying unfair wages

Business fraud

Avoiding social security payments

'Squashing' fines

Availing of social security payments
that one is not entitled to

Keeping stolen or lost money or goods

Plagiarizing someone's work

318 | CREDO | LIVING AND LOVING AS DISCIPLES OF CHRIST

CHAPTER 10 | WORKSHEET 6

NAME:

Prayers for Social Justice

The values of generosity of spirit, solidarity with others, respect for the dignity of all human persons, trust and justice underpin the Seventh and Tenth Commandments. To nurture these values in our minds and in our hearts and to live them in our daily lives is rarely easy. We need the support of the Christian community and the teaching of the Church to guide and direct us. We also need God's grace and blessings. As disciples of Jesus Christ we must take the time to turn to the Triune God, to acknowledge our dependence on God and, in a spirit of openness and trust, to ask for God's help. This worksheet presents several prayers for justice and truth for you to reflect upon and pray.

READ AND PRAY
Allow the sincerity and rhythm of the words to speak to you as you reflect on and pray these prayers.

> **Prayer for Social Justice**
> Almighty and eternal God,
> may your grace enkindle in all persons
> a love of the many unfortunate people
> whom poverty and misery reduce
> to a condition of life
> unworthy of human beings.
> Arouse in the hearts
> of those who call you God
> a hunger and thirst for social justice
> and for fraternal charity
> in deeds and in truth.
> Grant, O Lord, peace in our days,
> peace to souls, peace to our community
> and peace among nations.
> Amen.
>
> —Pope Pius XII

CHAPTER 10: BUILDING A JUST AND COMPASSIONATE SOCIETY | WORKSHEET 6 | 319

CHAPTER 10 | WORKSHEET 6 (CONTD.)

Justice and Peace Prayer
God of Justice and Peace,
mold our consciences
according to justice,
and shape our hearts
according to peace,
that we may recognize the talents
that you have given us
to secure the rights of the poor,
the oppressed, the sick
and the marginalized.
God, we are Your children.
Grant us the courage and strength
to work for justice,
and in this way
live out our call
to be peacemakers.
—Jane Deren

For Those in Poverty
God of justice and compassion,
We ask forgiveness for the widening gulf between rich and poor,
For the use of money as a measure of all things,
For the culture of self-gratification,
For the continuing disparities between those that have so much
and those who have so little.
And for the suffering of those people who are excluded
from the table of abundance.
Forgive us for our focus on material goods,
And our part in the worship of economic growth
In a world where resources are limited.
— Education for Justice

Justice Prayer
O God, we pray for all those in our world
who are suffering from injustice:
For those who are discriminated against
because of their race, color or religion;
For those imprisoned
for working for the relief of oppression;
For those who are hounded
for speaking the inconvenient truth;
For those tempted to violence
as a cry against overwhelming hardship;
For those deprived of reasonable health and education;

320 | CREDO | LIVING AND LOVING AS DISCIPLES OF CHRIST

CHAPTER 10 | WORKSHEET 6 (CONTD.)

For those suffering from hunger and famine;
For those too weak to help themselves
and who have no one else to help them;
For the unemployed who cry out
for work but do not find it.
We pray for anyone of our acquaintance
who is personally affected by injustice.
Forgive us, Lord, if we unwittingly share in the conditions
or in a system that perpetuates injustice.
Show us how we can serve your children
and make your love practical by washing their feet.

—Mother Teresa

Prayer to Make Poverty History

Lord of Life,
Open our eyes to make us:
Aware of the poverty suffered by others;
Aware of the immorality of allowing that suffering to take place;
Aware of our rights as citizens to be heard;
Aware of the men, women and children dying as we speak;
Aware that our solidarity gives us strength;
Aware that our leaders may turn a deaf ear but Almighty God hears our cry;
And aware that only together can we: Make Poverty History.
Give us the strength and determination to work toward solutions
and policy changes that can free our sisters and brothers
around the world from the chains of poverty.
Inspire us to challenge our leaders to make debt relief
and fighting poverty a priority,
and make our voices loud and clear.
Amen.

—Cardinal O'Brien

JOURNAL EXERCISE

Write your own Prayer for Justice.

CHAPTER 10: BUILDING A JUST AND COMPASSIONATE SOCIETY | WORKSHEET 6 (CONTD.) | 321

CHAPTER 10 | WORKSHEET 7

NAME:

Stone Soup: An Old Tale Retold

The Seventh Commandment 'You shall not steal' goes beyond what is prohibited by civil law. Civil laws are necessary for the efficient functioning of society. However, the law of God demands a much higher standard from us. God desires that we not just tolerate one another in society but that we seek to love and to share with all others as we would love and share with our brothers and sisters.

In the Old Testament Book of Deuteronomy we read: 'Since there will never cease to be some in need on the earth, I therefore command you, "Open your hand to the poor and needy neighbor in your land" ' (Deuteronomy 15:11).

This worksheet offers you the opportunity to read a famous and inspirational old tale about sharing with those in need.

READ AND REFLECT
Read this well-known traditional tale, which is retold here by Marcia Brown.

Stone Soup
Three soldiers trudged down a road in a strange country. They were on their way home from the wars. Besides being tired, they were hungry. In fact, they had eaten nothing for two days.

'How I would like a good dinner tonight,' said the first.

'And a bed to sleep in,' said the second.

'But all that is impossible,' said the third. 'We must march on.'

On they marched. Suddenly, ahead of them they saw the lights of a village.

'Maybe we'll find a bite to eat there,' said the first.

'And a loft to sleep in,' said the second.

'No harm in asking,' said the third.

Now the peasants of that place feared strangers. When they heard that three soldiers were coming down the road, they talked among themselves.

'Here come three soldiers. Soldiers are always hungry. But we have little enough for ourselves.' And they hurried to hide their food.

They pushed the sacks of barley under the hay in the lofts. They lowered buckets of milk down the wells.

They spread old quilts over the carrot bins. They hid their cabbages and potatoes under the beds. They hung their meat in the cellars.

They hid all they had to eat. Then—they waited.

The soldiers stopped first at the house of Paul and Francoise.

'Good evening to you,' they said. 'Could you spare a bit of food for three hungry soldiers?'

'We have had no food for ourselves for three days,' said Paul. Francoise made a sad face. 'It has been a poor harvest.'

322 | CREDO | LIVING AND LOVING AS DISCIPLES OF CHRIST

CHAPTER 10 | WORKSHEET 7 (CONTD.)

The three soldiers went on to the house of Albert and Louise.

'Could you spare a bit of food? And have you some corner where we could sleep for the night?'

'Oh no,' said Albert. 'We gave all we could spare to soldiers who came before you.'

'Our beds are full,' said Louise.

At Vincent's and Marie's the answer was the same. It had been a poor harvest and all the grain must be kept for seed.

So it went all through the village. Not a peasant had any food to give away. They all had good reasons. One family had used the grain for feed. Another had an old sick father to care for. All had too many mouths to fill.

The villagers stood in the street and sighed. They looked as hungry as they could.

The three soldiers talked together.

Then the first soldier called out, 'Good people!' The peasants drew near.

'We are three hungry soldiers in a strange land. We have asked you for food and you have no food. Well then, we'll have to make stone soup.'

The peasants stared.

Stone soup? That would be something to know about.

'First, we'll need a large iron pot,' the soldiers said.

The peasants brought the largest pot they could find. How else to cook enough?

'That's none too large,' said the soldiers. 'But it will do. And now, water to fill it and a fire to heat it.'

It took many buckets of water to fill the pot. A fire was built on the village square and the pot was set to boil.

'And now, if you please, three round, smooth stones.'

Those were easy enough to find.

The peasants' eyes grew round as they watched the soldiers drop the stones into the pot.

'Any soup needs salt and pepper,' said the soldiers, as they began to stir.

Children ran to fetch salt and pepper.

'Stones like these generally make good soup. But oh, if there were carrots, it would be much better.'

'Why, I think I have a carrot or two,' said Francoise, and off she ran.

She came back with her apron full of carrots from the bin beneath the red quilt.

'A good stone soup should have cabbage,' said the soldiers as they sliced the carrots into the pot. 'But no use asking for what you don't have.'

'I think I could find a cabbage somewhere,' said Marie and she hurried home. Back she came with three cabbages from the cupboard under the bed.

'If we only had a bit of beef and a few potatoes, this soup would be good enough for a rich man's table.'

The peasants thought that over. They remembered their potatoes and the sides of beef hanging in the cellars. They ran to fetch them.

A rich man's soup—and all from a few stones. It seemed like magic!

CHAPTER 10: BUILDING A JUST AND COMPASSIONATE SOCIETY | WORKSHEET 7 (CONTD.) | 323

CHAPTER 10 | WORKSHEET 7 (CONTD.)

'Ah,' sighed the soldiers as they stirred in the beef and potatoes, 'if we only had a little barley and a cup of milk! This would be fit for the king himself. Indeed he asked for just such a soup when last he dined with us.'

The peasants looked at each other. The soldiers had entertained the king! Well!

'But—no use asking for what you don't have,' the soldiers sighed.

The peasants brought their barley from the lofts, they brought their milk from the wells. The soldiers stirred the barley and milk into the steaming broth while the peasants stared.

At last the soup was ready.

'All of you shall taste,' the soldiers said. 'But first a table must be set.'

Great tables were placed in the square. And all around were lighted torches.

Such a soup! How good it smelled! Truly fit for a king!

But then the peasants asked themselves, 'Would not such a soup require bread—and a roast—and cider?' Soon a banquet was spread and everyone sat down to eat.

Never had there been such a feast. Never had the peasants tasted such soup. And fancy, made from stones!

They ate and drank and ate and drank. And after that they danced.

They danced and sang far into the night.

At last they were tired. Then the three soldiers asked, 'Is there not a loft where we could sleep?'

'Let three such wise and splendid gentlemen sleep in a loft? Indeed! They must have the best beds in the village.'

So the first soldier slept in the priest's house.

The second soldier slept in the baker's house.

And the third soldier slept in the mayor's house.

In the morning, the whole village gathered in the square to give them a send-off.

'Many thanks for what you have taught us,' the peasants said to the soldiers. 'We shall never go hungry, now that we know how to make soup from stones.'

'Oh, it's all in knowing how,' said the soldiers, and off they went down the road.

CLASS DISCUSSION
- ◉ What is your reaction to this story?
- ◉ Why do you think the people hoarded what they had and were reluctant to share with others?
- ◉ Why do you think they responded to the strangers?
- ◉ Share examples of where and when this might happen in real life:
  - – in your home or school,
  - – in your community,
  - – globally.
- ◉ Who in today's world might the soldiers represent?

PAUSE AND REFLECT
- ◉ Are you ever like the soldiers?
- ◉ Has anyone or any organization ever encouraged you to be more generous with your gifts/ resources?

JOURNAL EXERCISE
Rewrite the story from a modern perspective.

324 | CREDO | LIVING AND LOVING AS DISCIPLES OF CHRIST

CHAPTER 10 | WORKSHEET 8

NAME:

A Just World for the Next Generation

In chapter 10 of your theology text you have been exploring the Christian obligation and responsibility to help create a just and compassionate world for all God's people. This worksheet invites you to imagine such a world in light of Jesus' vision of the Kingdom of God.

PAUSE AND REFLECT
- Take some time alone for reflection.
- Think of a young child whom you know *personally* and like—it could be a sister or brother, a cousin, a niece or nephew, a godchild, a friend's or neighbor's child.
- Imagine *this child* growing up over the next five years, then ten years, then twenty years.
- Imagine the world that *this child* might inhabit.
- Imagine how *this child* will deal with the world of the future.
- As you imagine, you might like to jot down in the box below any random words or thoughts that come to your mind.

IMAGE A FUTURE WORLD
- Now imagine the world you would really like this child to inhabit and, in the box on the following page, write a letter to the child describing your image of that ideal world. Call to mind as you do so the world that Jesus envisioned for us.
- Remember that you are writing to a child, so feel free to be as creative as you need to be to explain your vision to the child.
- You might like to finish the letter by offering encouragement and blessings for the child as he or she grows up.

CHAPTER 10: BUILDING A JUST AND COMPASSIONATE SOCIETY | WORKSHEET 8 | 325

CHAPTER 10 | WORKSHEET 8 (CONTD.)

Dear...

326 | CREDO | LIVING AND LOVING AS DISCIPLES OF CHRIST

CHAPTER 10 | WORKSHEET 9

NAME:

Jesus Speaks About Poverty

Jesus challenged his disciples by his words, his deeds and his interaction and friendship with the most impoverished people in society. The Gospel provides many insights into Jesus' attitude toward the poor, the socially outcast and those living on the edge. This worksheet invites you to read and respond to a selection of Gospel passages in which Jesus' message continues to challenge us to review our personal stance toward the disadvantaged within our society today.

PAIR AND SHARE
- Work with a partner.
- Look up and read these Gospel passages, noting five that you will examine in more detail.
  - Luke 4:16–19
  - Luke 6:20–21
  - Luke 11:39–42
  - Luke 12:16–21
  - Luke 14:12–14
  - Luke 16:19–25
  - Mark 10:21–22
  - Mark 12:41–44
  - Matthew 25:34–36
- Complete the chart on the next page in relation to the five Gospel passages that you chose.

CHAPTER 10: BUILDING A JUST AND COMPASSIONATE SOCIETY | WORKSHEET 9 | 327

CHAPTER 10 | WORKSHEET 9 (CONTD.)

Gospel reference	To whom was Jesus speaking?	In your own words, what was Jesus' message?	What was/might have been the outcome?

CHAPTER 10 | WORKSHEET 10

NAME:

God in the Margins

This worksheet offers you the opportunity to read and respond to some challenging content from a seminar on poverty.

READ AND REFLECT

Read and reflect on the following extract from a book titled *Encountering God in the Margins*, in which volunteer worker Dr. Aidan Donaldson recalls listening to a lecture on poverty delivered by a Presentation Sister from India.

Sr. Prema started her talk by asking us to reflect for a moment on the various campaigns that have hit the media, such as the 'Make Poverty History' coalition, and to recall events such as the 'Live Aid' concert of 13 July 1985 ('the day', we were told, 'when rock and roll changed the world') and the 'Live 8' concert of 2 July 2005 ('the day', we were told, 'when rock began the long walk to justice'). We were then urged to think of the many famous people who wear the white wristband bearing the Make Poverty History logo. Prema then asked us to consider whether or not there is a link between poverty and opulence or greed. I smiled smugly to myself. Of course there is. The problem is blindingly simple: poverty is created by greed. While some sections of our world live in opulence and wealth, the vast majority of humankind struggles to survive. And at least two-thirds of people in the world today—some two billion people—are condemned to live in such abject poverty that they are denied access to clean water, medicine, education and, even, food beyond one simple meal a day, if they are able to get even that. Sr. Prema then went on to outline the solution, which is equally blindingly simple and obvious—and challenging.

'All right', Prema said, 'we all accept that there is a link between richness and poverty. The affluent lifestyle of the rich and powerful necessitates the poverty and disempowerment of those on the margins. How can we change this unjust world . . . if we really want to change this world?' She paused for a moment. . . . Yes, let's make poverty history', she said, 'but let's be clear on the implications and means of achieving this.' Sr. Prema went on to point out that, if there is a direct causal link between the opulent and obscene wealth in the Western world and the dire crushing poverty in the Third World, then the overcoming of this situation will require a massive redistribution of wealth and resources. 'Perhaps, instead of talking about making poverty history, let's look at making greed and excess wealth history', she suggested. 'If we did that then we would abolish poverty. I wonder how many of the fabulously wealthy celebrities and personalities would agree to give up their riches? Perhaps many of them might look to support a different (and much safer) cause.'

CHAPTER 10: BUILDING A JUST AND COMPASSIONATE SOCIETY | WORKSHEET 10 | 329

CHAPTER 10 | WORKSHEET 10 (CONTD.)

PAUSE, REFLECT AND COMMENT
Describe any reaction or comment you may have on what you have read so far. What do you agree or disagree with?

_____

_____

_____

_____

_____

_____

Now read on....

The young Indian Sister . . . urged us to forget about the super rich and, instead, look at our own personal role in issues of justice and poverty. It is all too easy to look at governments, G8/G20, multi-national corporations, the globalization agenda and the fabulously wealthy and, in so doing, absolve ourselves of all blame and responsibility for the way the world is. We can all too easily fall into the trap of thanking God for not making us like those others! You and I didn't create the injustices of the world, they did. We don't perpetuate poverty and peddle misery on countless millions in the world today, they do. We are innocent, they are guilty—or so we thought.

Sr. Prema invited us to consider that almost every action we engage in is a social and, indeed, political action that affects other people. How we live our lives has profound effects on others, be it our friends, work colleagues, neighbors or people who we do not know but whose lives are, nevertheless, hugely affected by our actions and choices. Every time we walk into a supermarket and buy a jar of coffee, a banana, a bar of chocolate, an avocado or almost any commodity on the shelves, we are engaged in a moral action. Similarly, when we enter a sports shop and buy a pair of trainers or a replica football shirt, or go to a clothes store to buy a tee shirt or a pair of shoes, we are involved in an action that affects other people. Do we ask ourselves if we are contributing to the plight of landless peasants, promoting sweatshop production and the exploitation of child labor by buying products that are produced in unjust conditions? . . . Do we consider that by going to one of the outlets of any multi-national fast food chain we are contributing to the destruction of the environment and indigenous cultures? . . . Are we prepared to radically change our lifestyles in order to help bring justice to the marginalized—in both the Third World and at home—or do we prefer to point to the rich and the wealthy while not doing anything ourselves? Are we like the rich young man who wished to follow Jesus but was not prepared to give up his wealth and affluent lifestyle? Sometimes it's easier and safer to blame others.

330 | CREDO | LIVING AND LOVING AS DISCIPLES OF CHRIST

CHAPTER 10 | WORKSHEET 10 (CONTD.)

PAUSE, REFLECT AND COMMENT

Once again, describe any reaction or comment you may have to the extract. What new insights or challenges have you found in this second piece?

_____

_____

_____

_____

_____

PAIR AND SHARE

Share your insights and thoughts on these extracts with a partner.

CHAPTER 10: BUILDING A JUST AND COMPASSIONATE SOCIETY | WORKSHEET 10 (CONTD.) | 331

CHAPTER 10 | WORKSHEET 11

NAME:

Prophets and Justice

The prophets of Old Testament times did not mince their words when it came to challenging people on issues of justice. They reminded the Israelites of God's command to live lives of truth and justice. This worksheet offers you the opportunity to read and respond to some of the Old Testament prophets' words on justice and to explore their relevance for today's world. We then invite you to identify some modern-day prophets and the issues that concern them.

READ AND REFLECT

Read and reflect on these words from the prophets of the Old Testament before completing the exercises below.

From Prophet Isaiah (61:1–4):

The Spirit of the Lord GOD is upon me,
because the LORD has anointed me;
he has sent me to bring good news to the oppressed,
    to bind up the brokenhearted,
to proclaim liberty to the captives,
    and release to the prisoners;
to proclaim the year of the LORD's favor,
    and the day of vengeance of our God;
    to comfort all who mourn;
to provide for those who mourn in Zion—
    to give them a garland instead of ashes,
the oil of gladness instead of mourning,
    the mantel of praise instead of a faint spirit.
They will be called oaks of righteousness,
    the planting of the LORD, to display his glory.
They shall build up the ancient ruins,
    they shall raise up the former devastations;
they shall repair the ruined cities,
    the devastations of many generations.

From Prophet Amos (5:21–24):

I hate, I despise your festivals,
    and I take no delight in your solemn assemblies.
Even though you offer me your burnt offerings and grain offerings,
    I will not accept them;
and the offerings of well-being of your fattened animals

332 | CREDO | LIVING AND LOVING AS DISCIPLES OF CHRIST

CHAPTER 10 | WORKSHEET 11 (CONTD.)

I will not look upon.
Take away from me the noise of your songs;
    I will not listen to the melody of your harps.
But let justice roll down like waters,
    and righteousness like an ever-flowing stream.'

From Prophet Isaiah (1:10–17):

Hear the word of the LORD,
    you rulers of Sodom!
Listen to the teaching of our God,
    you people of Gomorrah!
 What to me is the multitude of your sacrifices?
    says the LORD;
I have had enough of burnt offerings of rams
    and the fat of fed beasts;
I do not delight in the blood of bulls,
    or of lambs, or of goats.

When you come to appear before me,
    who asked this from your hand?
    Trample my courts no more;
 bringing offerings is futile;
    incense is an abomination to me.
New moon and sabbath and calling of convocation—
    I cannot endure solemn assemblies with iniquity.
 Your new moons and your appointed festivals
    my soul hates;
they have become a burden to me,
    I am weary of bearing them.
 When you stretch out your hands,
    I will hide my eyes from you;
even though you make many prayers,
    I will not listen;
    your hands are full of blood.
 Wash yourselves; make yourselves clean;
    remove the evil of your doings
    from before my eyes;
cease to do evil,
    learn to do good;
seek justice,
    rescue the oppressed,
defend the orphan,
    plead for the widow.

From Prophet Jeremiah (22:13–17):

Woe to him who builds his house by unrighteousness,
    and his upper rooms by injustice;
who makes his neighbors work for nothing,

CHAPTER 10: BUILDING A JUST AND COMPASSIONATE SOCIETY | WORKSHEET 11 (CONTD.) | 333

CHAPTER 10 | WORKSHEET 11 (CONTD.)

and does not give them their wages;
who says, 'I will build myself a spacious house
   with large upper rooms',
and who cuts out windows for it,
   paneling it with cedar,
   and painting it with vermilion.
Are you a king
   because you compete in cedar?
Did not your father eat and drink
   and do justice and righteousness?
      Then it was well with him.
He judged the cause of the poor and needy;
   then it was well.
Is not this to know me?
   says the LORD.

OVER TO YOU

Identify three ways in which the words of the prophets in any of these verses are still relevant to our world today.

1. _____

   _____

   _____

2. _____

   _____

   _____

3. _____

   _____

   _____

Name three present-day prophets and say why you regard them as prophets. They could be people you know personally or they could be public figures.

1. _____

   _____

   _____

334 | CREDO | LIVING AND LOVING AS DISCIPLES OF CHRIST

CHAPTER 10 | WORKSHEET 11 (CONTD.)

2. _____

_____

3. _____

_____

Name five concerns of today's prophets.

1. _____

_____

2. _____

_____

3. _____

_____

4. _____

_____

5. _____

_____

What would happen if we truly listened to the challenges of our prophets?

_____

_____

_____

_____

_____

CHAPTER 10: BUILDING A JUST AND COMPASSIONATE SOCIETY | WORKSHEET 11 (CONTD.) | 335

CHAPTER 10 | WORKSHEET 12

NAME:

The Values of St. Francis of Assisi

This worksheet offers you the opportunity to read a selection of quotations from St. Francis of Assisi that reflect his compassion for the poor and the marginalized and to explore the challenge for young disciples of Jesus who would wish to emulate his example today.

READ AND REFLECT
Read and reflect on the values underlying these quotations from St. Francis.

'It would be considered a theft on our part if we didn't give to someone in greater need than we are.'

'I should be accounted a thief by the great Almsgiver were I to withhold that which I wear from him who has greater need of it than I.'

'If we can enter the church day and night and implore God to hear our prayers, how careful we should be to hear and grant the petitions of our neighbors in need.'

'Poverty is the way to salvation, the nurse of humility, and the root of perfection. Its fruits are hidden, but they multiply themselves in infinite ways.'

'Whoever curses a poor man does an injury to Christ, whose noble image he wears—the image of Him who made Himself poor for us in this world.'

'We should have no more use or regard for money in any of its forms than we have for dust. Those who think it is worth more, or who are greedy for it, expose themselves to the danger of being deceived by the devil.'

'If we had any possessions, we would be forced to have arms to protect them, since possessions are a cause of disputes and strife, and in many ways we would be hindered from loving God and our neighbor. Therefore in this life we wish to have no temporal possessions.'

PAIR AND SHARE
◉ Work with a partner to complete the following assignments.
◉ Then share your answers with another pair of students.

336 | CREDO | LIVING AND LOVING AS DISCIPLES OF CHRIST

CHAPTER 10 | WORKSHEET 12 (CONTD.)

Describe what you find most challenging about St. Francis' words and the values they reflect.

_____

_____

_____

_____

Give some reasons why St. Francis' words are still relevant today.

_____

_____

_____

_____

Identify the kinds of people who could be described as needy, poor or marginalized in the world today.

_____

_____

_____

Describe some of the challenges you face as a young person in trying to respond to needy, poor and marginalized people in the world today.

_____

_____

_____

_____

JOURNAL EXERCISE
Write about any new insights you gained from this activity.

CHAPTER 10: BUILDING A JUST AND COMPASSIONATE SOCIETY | WORKSHEET 12 (CONTD.) | 337

CHAPTER 10 | CHAPTER REVIEW

NAME:

Review of Chapter 10

I. **True/False.** Mark the true statements 'T' and the false statements 'F'. In the case of each false statement, cross out and rewrite the incorrect words to make the statement true.

_____1. It is the plan and will of God that we use the goods of creation for both the glory of God and the benefit of human beings.

_____2. God's generosity involves no responsibility on our part.

_____3. The *Catechism of the Catholic Church* teaches that giving alms to the poor is a work of justice pleasing to God.

_____4. Catholic Social Teaching rests upon the foundational principle that most human beings are created in the 'image and likeness' of God.

_____5. Commutative justice ensures that we deal fairly and honestly with those who deserve it.

_____6. Legal justice refers to the ordering of society that promotes 'respect for the fundamental rights that flow from the intrinsic dignity of the person'.

_____7. The *Catechism of the Catholic Church* describes avarice as 'sadness at the sight of another's goods and the immoderate desire to have them for oneself'.

_____8. The *United States Catholic Catechism for Adults* describes sloth as 'eating and drinking more than what is necessary'.

338 | CREDO | LIVING AND LOVING AS DISCIPLES OF CHRIST

CHAPTER 10 | CHAPTER REVIEW (CONTD.)

_____9.   Jesus told his disciples, 'Do not keep striving for what you are to eat and what you are to drink, . . . Instead, strive for his kingdom, and these things will be given to you as well.'

_____10.   Juan Martin de Porres was born in Argentina.

II. **Fill in the blanks. Write the letter that corresponds to the correct term in the word bank in the blank space to complete each sentence. There are more terms in the word bank than you will need.**

A. Covetousness	**E.** Jesuit	**I.** Social sins
B. Distributive justice	**F.** Justice	**J.** Divine Providence
C. Dominican	**G.** Original justice	**K.** Stewardship
D. greedy	**H.** money	**L.** searching

1.   _____ means caring for goods and possessions that have been entrusted to a person or group by their rightful owner.

2.   _____ is God's loving care and concern for all he has made.

3.   _____ produce unjust social laws and oppressive institutions.

4.   Pope Francis stated that _____ has to serve, not rule.

5.   The *Catechism* teaches that _____ is the 'cardinal moral virtue which consists in the constant and firm will to give their due to God and to neighbor'.

6.   _____ is God's plan and will for all creation.

7.   The *Catechism* teaches that _____ 'regulates what the community owes its citizens in proportion to their contributions and needs'.

8.   The *Catechism* describes _____ as 'a disordered inclination or desire for pleasure or possessions'.

9.   The Book of Proverbs warns, 'Those who are _____ for unjust gain make trouble for their households.'

10.   St. Martin de Porres was a _____ lay brother.

CHAPTER 10: BUILDING A JUST AND COMPASSIONATE SOCIETY | CHAPTER REVIEW (CONTD.) | 339

CHAPTER 10 | CHAPTER REVIEW (CONTD.)

III. Write a brief answer. Explain the teaching of the Catholic Church on 1 or 2.
1. Retributive justice and restorative justice
2. The principle of solidarity

_____

_____

_____

_____

_____

_____

_____

_____

_____

IV. How would you respond? You are in a corporate office waiting for an interview for a summer job. You overhear the chief executive saying, 'We don't have any responsibilities beyond making money for our shareholders.'

_____

_____

_____

_____

_____

_____

_____

_____

_____

_____

340 | CREDO | LIVING AND LOVING AS DISCIPLES OF CHRIST

CHAPTER 10 | CHAPTER REVIEW (CONTD.)

V. Make a 'disciple decision'.

1. What is the most important wisdom for life that you discovered in this chapter?

_____

_____

_____

_____

_____

2. Name several ways you can put this wisdom into practice. Choose one of the ways you identify and describe how you will make that wisdom part of your life right now.

_____

_____

_____

_____

_____

_____

_____

_____

_____

_____

CHAPTER 10: BUILDING A JUST AND COMPASSIONATE SOCIETY | CHAPTER REVIEW (CONTD.) | 341

CHAPTER 11

Living New Life in Christ Jesus

INTRODUCTION

Chapter 11 explores the call to every Christian to live as a disciple of Jesus Christ, the Incarnate Son of God, by living the 'way' that he preached and taught and modeled for us. We learn how in Baptism we were joined to Christ, we received the gift of sanctifying grace and we were restored to the holiness of life that was lost as a consequence of Original Sin. We reflect on the many ways in which people choose to follow the 'way' of Christ and we explore how we too might respond to that call to holiness of life.

Chapter 11 is developed under five major headings:

⊙ **ATTEND AND REFLECT:** What is your vocation?
⊙ **HEAR THE STORY:** A Christian's vocation is good news
⊙ **EMBRACE THE VISION:** Seeking the Kingdom of God in the world
⊙ **THINK IT THROUGH:** Leaven in the world
⊙ **JUDGE AND ACT:** (*Activities and exercises that encourage the young people to integrate what they have learned in the chapter into their daily lives*)

Theological Background for the Teacher

We should always be conscious of our inherent dignity as persons created by God in God's own image. 'Incorporated into *Christ* by Baptism' (*Catechism of the Catholic Church* [CCC], no. 1694), our dignity is enhanced as we become disciples of Jesus and follow a way of life that 'leads to life' (CCC, no. 1696). Our calling or vocation to be disciples is thus a dignified calling, with an ultimate destiny worth pursuing and treasuring.

> Endowed with 'a spiritual and immortal' soul, the human person is 'the only creature on earth that God has willed for its own sake'. From his conception, he is destined for eternal beatitude.
> —CCC, no. 1703, quoting *Gaudium et Spes* (*Constitution on the Church in the Modern World*), nos. 14 and 24

Gifted with free will, we have the freedom and the ability to make choices. We can, unfortunately, make bad choices and stray from the path of holiness to which God calls us. We must become alert and discerning in order to discover our own specific vocation.

> The human person participates in the light and power of the divine Spirit. By his reason, he is capable of understanding the order of things established by the Creator. By free will, he is capable of directing himself toward his true good. He finds his perfection 'in seeking and loving what is true and good'.
> —CCC, no 1704, quoting *Gaudium et Spes*, no. 15

As disciples of Jesus we are called to work for the Kingdom, or reign, of God. We are reminded of this constantly when we say the Lord's Prayer —'Thy Kingdom come'.

> In the Lord's Prayer, 'thy kingdom come' refers primarily to the final coming of the reign of God through Christ's return. But, far from distracting the Church from her mission in this present world, this desire commits her to it all the more strongly.
> —CCC, no 2818

As we pursue our vocation to eternal life we must not turn our back on earthly society. Rather, our work for the Kingdom must make us attentive to the needs of others, especially those who are vulnerable and marginalized, and give us new purpose and motivation in our work for justice.

> Christians have to distinguish between the growth of the Reign of God and the progress of the culture and society in which they are involved. This distinction is not a separation. Man's vocation to eternal life does not suppress, but actually reinforces, his duty to put into action in this world the energies and means received from the Creator to serve justice and peace.
> —CCC, no. 2820

342 | CREDO | LIVING AND LOVING AS DISCIPLES OF CHRIST

We are also called to the work of evangelization. As disciples of Jesus we will inevitably want to share his good news, his Gospel, with others. We need courage and wisdom to carry out the work of evangelization with conviction and respect.

Being a disciple of Jesus has an essential community dimension. Our vocation is not a solo run to God, an ego trip that ignores our fellow disciples. The Church is the 'Body of Christ', and we proclaim his Gospel in unity and solidarity.

Three aspects of the Church as the Body of Christ are to be more specifically noted: the unity of all her members with each other as a result of their union with Christ; Christ as head of the Body; and the Church as bride of Christ.

—CCC, no. 789

Like the different parts of the body, the disciples of Jesus have different and complementary roles in the life of the Church and in the work of evangelization. Some become ordained ministers, and some of those ordained ministers become part of the hierarchy of the Church, whether as Pope or as bishops. Others join the religious life and live in community, some join a variety of ecclesial communities, while others opt for the consecrated life. Most live out their vocation as laypeople and they also play crucial roles.

Since, like all the faithful, lay Christians are entrusted by God with the apostolate by virtue of their Baptism and Confirmation, they have the right and duty, individually or grouped in associations, to work so that the divine message of salvation may be known and accepted by all men throughout the earth. This duty is the more pressing when it is only through them that men can hear the Gospel and know Christ. Their activity in ecclesial communities is so necessary that, for the most part, the apostolate of the pastors cannot be fully effective without it.

—CCC, no. 900

The evangelical counsels of poverty, chastity and obedience apply in specific ways to those who have chosen the consecrated life—in the ordained ministry and in religious life.

Christ proposes the evangelical counsels, in their great variety, to every disciple. The perfection of charity, to which all the faithful are called, entails for those who freely follow the call to consecrated life the obligation of practicing chastity in celibacy for the sake of the Kingdom, poverty and obedience. It is the profession of these counsels,

within a permanent state of life recognized by the Church, that characterizes the life consecrated to God.

—CCC, no. 915

The Church is always conscious of her apostolic nature, and she encourages all the faithful to be involved wholeheartedly in apostolic work, in continuity with the work of the Apostles.

The whole Church is apostolic, in that she remains, through the successors of St. Peter and the other apostles, in communion of faith and life with her origin; and in that she is 'sent out' into the whole world. All members of the Church share in this mission, though in various ways. 'The Christian vocation is, of its nature, a vocation to the apostolate as well.' Indeed, we call an apostolate 'every activity of the Mystical Body' that aims 'to spread the Kingdom of Christ over all the earth'.

—CCC, no. 863, quoting *Apostolicam Actuositatem (Decree on the Apostolate of the Laity)*, no. 2

The Church, the Body of Christ, makes Christ present in the world, and so she can rightly be called the 'sacrament of Christ'. Those in the consecrated life do this work of making Christ present in a particularly public way, giving strong visible witness to the Gospel of Jesus in local and global contexts. They are supported and complemented in this work by all other parts of the Body of Christ, in particular by the lay faithful.

In the Church, which is like the sacrament—the sign and instrument—of God's own life, the consecrated life is seen as a special sign of the mystery of redemption. To follow and imitate Christ more nearly and to manifest more clearly his self-emptying is to be more deeply present to one's contemporaries, in the heart of Christ. For those who are on this 'narrower' path encourage their brethren by their example, and bear striking witness 'that the world cannot be transfigured and offered to God without the spirit of the Beatitudes'.

—CCC, no. 932, quoting *Lumen Gentium (Constitution on the Church)*, no. 31

ADDITIONAL BACKGROUND READING
Catechism of the Catholic Church, nos. 781–945, 1699–2051, 2816–2821; *Youth Catechism of the Catholic Church (YOUCAT),* nos. 121–128, 286–289, 520; *Compendium of the Catechism of the Catholic Church,* nos. 153–193; *United States Catholic Catechism for*

Adults, 111–139, 307–321; **Code of Canon Law,** Cann. 204–297, 607–755; **John Paul II, On the Consecrated Life and Its Mission in the Church and in the World; Apostolicam Actuositatem (Decree on the Apostolate of the Laity); Gaudium et Spes (Constitution on the Church in the Modern World).**

CHAPTER OUTCOMES

See general note on page 19 of this resource.

Learning Outcomes

As a result of studying this chapter and exploring the issues raised, the young people should be able to:

⊙ understand the concept of 'vocation';
⊙ identify role models of Christian discipleship;
⊙ know how Jesus articulated his own vocation (in Luke 4:18–19);
⊙ understand that the essence of our Christian vocation is to seek the Kingdom of God;
⊙ recognize how Jesus' parables reveal the nature of the Kingdom of God;
⊙ understand the Christian responsibility of evangelization;
⊙ know what it means to be 'apprentices of the Master';
⊙ understand the implications of the Church being the Body of Christ;
⊙ recognize the three states of life in the Church;
⊙ know how the ordained and the laity fulfill their vocations;
⊙ know about lay associations and movements in the Catholic Church;
⊙ understand the meaning of the evangelical counsels;
⊙ recognize the various expressions of the consecrated life;
⊙ understand how the Church is the sacrament of Christ;
⊙ know the story of Simon Peter.

Faith-formation Outcomes

As a result of studying this chapter and exploring the issues raised, the young people should also:

⊙ consider what their own Christian vocation in life might be;
⊙ be inspired by role models of Christian discipleship, including saints;
⊙ envisage the world God calls us to work for;
⊙ be inspired by the Kingdom parables of Jesus;
⊙ have a 'preferential love for the poor';
⊙ identify ways in which they can carry out the work of evangelization;
⊙ value the community aspect of their life in the Church;
⊙ identify moments when God's grace might have been at work in their lives;
⊙ take on board the responsibilities that flow from their Baptism;
⊙ grow in their commitment to their Christian vocation;
⊙ find inspiration from Christians who are living the consecrated life;
⊙ consider the relevance of the evangelical counsels for their own lives;
⊙ reflect on the demands and hopes of their Christian discipleship;
⊙ be inspired by the discipleship of St. Peter.

344 | CREDO | LIVING AND LOVING AS DISCIPLES OF CHRIST

Teacher Reflection

As you prepare to engage your group in a study of the Christian call to discipleship, reflect on your own vocation as a theology teacher and on the wonderful influence you can have on your students as you guide and encourage them on the road of discipleship. Here is a prayer that you might pray.

Dear God,
Help me always to be reflective in my teaching and practice.

Help me to appreciate what a great privilege it is to teach young people, to lead them to you.

May my example to them be like a shining light to their faith in you,
but help me not to get discouraged when things don't seem to be going well.

Don't allow me be a slave to tangible results,
but guide me to realize that while the seeds I sow may grow in abundance,
I may never see that growth.

Let me be guided by a spirit of gratitude—both to you for this opportunity and to the young people for what I learn from them.

May my work be guided by patience, as Jesus was patient in beginning his public ministry.

CHAPTER 11: LIVING NEW LIFE IN CHRIST JESUS | INTRODUCTION | 345

Notes and Guidelines for Student Activities

ATTEND AND REFLECT

What is your vocation?

Learning Outcomes

That the young people would:
⊙ understand the concept of 'vocation';
⊙ identify role models of Christian discipleship.

Faith-formation Outcomes

That the young people would also:
⊙ consider what their own Christian vocation in life might be;
⊙ be inspired by role models of Christian discipleship, including saints.

Overview

Section one, 'Attend and Reflect', explores the concept of 'vocation'. What to do with one's life is the ultimate question for all of us. For Christians, all of life is about responding to our vocation from God that began with our Baptism. Following 'the Way', who is Jesus, must give heart and substance to our life. It must lie behind every other decision we make. We guide the young people to search their hearts in order to discern their particular vocation as disciples of Jesus. We also remind them of the many role models who can help and inspire them in living their vocation of discipleship.

Supplementary Activities for 'Attend and Reflect'

Teacher Tip: Invite the young people to listen to vocation-themed songs, such as 'Here I am Lord' by Dan Schutte of the St. Louis Jesuits, or 'Christ Has No Body Now But Yours' by Liam Lawton, from his album *Eternal*.

Worksheet 1: 'Vocation Stories' (*page 349 of this resource*) offers the young people the opportunity to compare and contrast the vocation stories of four people who have lived, or are living, the Christian call to discipleship.

Worksheet 2: 'Vocations of Discipleship' (*page 351 of this resource*) invites the young people to consider and comment upon a range of vocations through which people live out the Christian call to discipleship.

Creative Exercise

Design a poster that would encourage a young person to consider a particular Christian vocation.

HEAR THE STORY

A Christian's vocation is good news

Learning Outcomes

That the young people would:
⊙ know how Jesus articulated his own vocation (in Luke 4:18–19);
⊙ understand that the essence of our Christian vocation is to seek the Kingdom of God;
⊙ recognize how Jesus' parables reveal the nature of the Kingdom of God;
⊙ understand the Christian responsibility of evangelization;
⊙ know what it means to be 'apprentices of the Master'.

Faith-formation Outcomes

That the young people would also:
⊙ envisage the world God calls us to work for;
⊙ be inspired by the Kingdom parables of Jesus;
⊙ have a 'preferential love for the poor';
⊙ identify ways in which they can carry out the work of evangelization.

Overview

Section two, 'Hear the Story', guides the young people to develop their understanding of the concept of the Kingdom, or reign, of God. We recall how Jesus described his own vocation and how he taught us to do God's will on earth in order to bring about God's Kingdom. We explore how the parables of Jesus reveal much about the nature of the Kingdom. We explain the Christian call to evangelization and our role as apprentices of Jesus, the Master, and we remind the young people that we are strengthened to live this new life in Christ through the graces of

346 | CREDO | LIVING AND LOVING AS DISCIPLES OF CHRIST

the Sacraments, through prayer and through the development of the virtues.

Supplementary Activities for 'Hear the Story'

Worksheet 3: 'Kingdom Parables' (*page 352 of this resource*) invites the young people to either illustrate or write a dialogue on one of the Kingdom parables mentioned in the 'Hear the Story' section of chapter 11.

Teacher Tip: Invite the students to listen to the song 'Behold Now the Kingdom' by John Michael Talbot.

Worksheet 4: 'Discipleship Commitments' (*page 353 of this resource*) invites the young people to plan five practical ways in which they will show their commitment to discipleship.

EMBRACE THE VISION

Seeking the Kingdom of God in the world

Learning Outcomes
That the young people would:
- understand the implications of the Church being the Body of Christ;
- recognize the three states of life in the Church;
- know how the ordained and the laity fulfill their vocations;
- know about lay associations and movements in the Catholic Church.

Faith-formation Outcomes
That the young people would also:
- value the community aspect of their life in the Church;
- identify moments when God's grace might have been at work in their lives;
- take on board the responsibilities that flow from their Baptism;
- grow in their commitment to their Christian vocation.

Overview
Section three, 'Embrace the Vision', explores how the Church is the Body of Christ, the community of Jesus' disciples, in the world. We remind the young people of how, as disciples, united in solidarity with

the Father and the Son and the Holy Spirit, and with one another, we learn, celebrate, pray and live the new life in Christ that we first received in Baptism. We outline the essential responsibilities that flow from Baptism and we identify the three states of life, or three primary vocations, through which God invites the baptized to live out their discipleship, namely, the ordained ministry, the consecrated life and the vocation of the laity. We examine the vocation to ordained ministry and the vocation of the laity in detail, with a special feature on the example of the community of Sant'Egidio; the vocation to the consecrated life is treated in 'Think It Through'.

Supplementary Activities for 'Embrace the Vision'

Teacher Tip: Invite the young people to listen to the song 'We Are One Body' by Dana Scallon.

Worksheet 5: 'Lay Religious Movement Profile' (*page 355 of this resource*) provides a template for the young people to research a Catholic lay religious movement or organization of their choice.

THINK IT THROUGH

Leaven in the world

Learning Outcomes
That the young people would:
- understand the meaning of the evangelical counsels;
- recognize the various expressions of the consecrated life;
- understand how the Church is the sacrament of Christ.

Faith-formation Outcomes
That the young people would also:
- find inspiration from Christians who are living the consecrated life;
- consider the relevance of the evangelical counsels for their own lives.

Overview
Section four, 'Think It Through', explores the vocation to the consecrated life. We explain the evangelical counsels of poverty, chastity and obedience and their importance to the life of the Church. We then examine some of the formal ways of living the consecrated life that are part of the spiritual tradition of the Church,

including the eremitic life, the contemplative life, living as consecrated virgins, or consecrated widows and widowers, or living as members of secular institutes or of societies of apostolic life. Finally, we look at how the Church is the sacrament of Christ and the seed of the Kingdom of God.

Supplementary Activities for 'Think It Through'

Worksheet 6: 'Religious Order Profile' (*page 356 of this resource*) provides a template for the young people to research a Catholic religious order of their choice.

Worksheet 7: 'Evangelical Counsels for Young People' (*page 357 of this resource*) offers the young people an opportunity to consider the advantages and the challenges of the evangelical counsels for young people today.

Worksheet 8: 'Choosing an Apostolate' (*page 359 of this resource*) identifies a variety of apostolates and invites the young people to consider whether they would be suited to any of these.

JUDGE AND ACT

Learning Outcomes

That the young people would:

⊙ review the teachings of the Church that they have learned about in this chapter;

⊙ know the story of Simon Peter.

Faith-formation Outcomes

That the young people would also:

⊙ reflect on the demands and hopes of their Christian discipleship;

⊙ be inspired by the discipleship of St. Peter.

Overview

In section five, 'Judge and Act', the young people review the teachings of the Church that they have studied in this chapter. They also learn about the life of Simon Peter and how he met the challenges of his Christian discipleship.

Supplementary Activities for 'Judge and Act'

Creative Exercise

Create a word cloud of some of the characteristics of Simon Peter that you think might provide inspiration for young people today.

Worksheet 9: 'Betrayal, Repentance and Reconciliation' (*page 361 of this resource*) invites the young people to imagine the conversation between Jesus and Simon Peter at their first meeting after the Resurrection and after Simon Peter's betrayal of Jesus.

Worksheet 10: 'The Call to Discipleship' (*page 362 of this resource*) presents a selection of quotations on the subject of discipleship and invites the young people's responses.

Additional Prayer Suggestion

Scripture Reflection

(*See instructions for the use of doodling in prayer in the 'Student Activity Tool Kit', page 394 of this resource.*)

Use the following psalm verse to engage the young people in prayer:

Let the hearts of those who seek the Lord rejoice.

PSALM 105:3

348 | CREDO | LIVING AND LOVING AS DISCIPLES OF CHRIST

CHAPTER 11 | WORKSHEET 1

NAME:

Vocation Stories

No two vocation stories are quite the same. This worksheet invites you to compare and contrast the vocation stories of four people who have lived, or are living, the Christian call to discipleship.

RESEARCH AND REPORT

⊙ Research the vocation stories of four people who have lived, or are living, the Christian call to discipleship. These may be people you know personally, perhaps from your parish, or people from public life or, indeed, saints of the Church.

⊙ Complete the charts below and then share your findings with the class group.

Example 1:

Name:
Vocation:
Summary of vocation story:

CHAPTER 11: LIVING NEW LIFE IN CHRIST JESUS | WORKSHEET 1 | 349

CHAPTER 11 | WORKSHEET 1 (CONTD.)

Example 2:

Name:
Vocation:
Summary of vocation story:

Example 3:

Name:
Vocation:
Summary of vocation story:

Example 4:

Name:
Vocation:
Summary of vocation story:

350 | CREDO | LIVING AND LOVING AS DISCIPLES OF CHRIST

CHAPTER 11 | WORKSHEET 2

NAME:

Vocations of Discipleship

This worksheet identifies a range of vocations through which people live out the Christian call to discipleship. We invite you to give your opinion on these vocations and to comment on whether you could see yourself living any of these vocations.

OVER TO YOU

⊙ The chart below names possible vocations in life, both religious and non-religious, through which a person may serve God and others. For each one, state briefly what you think about the nature of the vocation, how it contributes to the work of the Church and whether or not you could see yourself living out this or a similar vocation.

⊙ The last two panels have been left blank so that you may add examples of your own.

Lay teacher in a Catholic school:
Priest in a parish:
Director or member of church choir:
Monk or religious sister in a monastery or convent:
Religious or lay chaplain in a school, prison or hospital:
Worker for a Christian charity/relief organization:
Other:
Other:

CHAPTER 11: LIVING NEW LIFE IN CHRIST JESUS | WORKSHEET 2 | 351

CHAPTER 11 | WORKSHEET 3

NAME:

Kingdom Parables

Many of the parables of Jesus reveal something important about the nature of the Kingdom, or reign, of God. This worksheet invites you to either illustrate or write a dialogue on one of the Kingdom parables mentioned in the 'Hear the Story' section of chapter 11 of your theology text.

READ, REFLECT AND CREATE
⊙ Choose one of the Kingdom parables from the Gospel according to Matthew mentioned in the 'Hear the Story' section of chapter 11.
⊙ Read the parable from the Bible.
⊙ Then, in the box below, either create a mini poster highlighting the message of the parable in images and words, or draw speech bubbles containing the dialogue or reflections of a character or characters in the parable.

352 | CREDO | LIVING AND LOVING AS DISCIPLES OF CHRIST

CHAPTER 11 | WORKSHEET 4

NAME:

Discipleship Commitments

It is easy to give lip-service to the idea of discipleship without thinking through the implications of such a commitment. This worksheet offers you the opportunity to identify five practical ways in which you will show your commitment to discipleship.

REFLECT AND RESPOND
◉ Reread the section 'Disciples: Apprentices of the Master' in 'Hear the Story' of chapter 11.
◉ Think about your own commitment to discipleship.
◉ Describe five practical things you will do to be an effective disciple of Jesus.

Commitment 1:

_____

_____

_____

_____

Commitment 2:

_____

_____

_____

_____

Commitment 3:

_____

_____

_____

_____

CHAPTER 11: LIVING NEW LIFE IN CHRIST JESUS | WORKSHEET 4 | 353

CHAPTER 11 | WORKSHEET 4 (CONTD.)

Commitment 4:

_____

_____

_____

_____

Commitment 5:

_____

_____

_____

_____

PAIR AND SHARE
- Share your commitments with a partner.
- Perhaps you might decide to carry out some of your plans together, or invite other students to join you in some of the activities.

354 | CREDO | LIVING AND LOVING AS DISCIPLES OF CHRIST

CHAPTER 11 | WORKSHEET 5

NAME:

Lay Religious Movement Profile

There are many dedicated people involved in lay religious movements and organizations in the Church. This worksheet provides a template for you to research a lay Catholic religious movement or organization of your choice.

RESEARCH AND REPORT
- Work alone or with a partner.
- Research a lay religious movement or organization in the Catholic Church and complete the chart.
- Share your findings in small groups or with the class group.

Name of movement or organization and location of headquarters:
Mission:
Founder/Founding story:
Current work or initiatives:
Other information:

CHAPTER 11: LIVING NEW LIFE IN CHRIST JESUS | WORKSHEET 5 | 355

CHAPTER 11 | WORKSHEET 6

NAME:

Religious Order Profile

There is a huge variety of religious orders in the Church, from those enclosed orders for whom prayer and contemplation is central, to orders that do valuable works of service in the community. This worksheet provides a template for you to research a Catholic religious order of your choice.

RESEARCH AND REPORT

- Work alone or with a partner.
- Research a religious order in the Catholic Church and complete the chart.
- Share your findings in small groups or with the class group.

Name of movement or organization and location of headquarters:
Mission:
Founder/Founding story:
Current work or initiatives:
Other information:

356 | CREDO | LIVING AND LOVING AS DISCIPLES OF CHRIST

CHAPTER 11 | WORKSHEET 7

NAME:

Evangelical Counsels for Young People

Poverty, chastity and obedience are not the most popular concepts in the world today, and so they present many challenges to young people. Yet these evangelical counsels have a very positive history in the life of the Church. This worksheet offers you the opportunity to consider the advantages and the challenges of the evangelical counsels for young people today.

REFLECT AND RESPOND
- Work with a partner.
- Reread together the section titled 'The Evangelical Counsels' in 'Think It Through' of chapter 11.
- Share your views about the power of the evangelical counsels to transform lives. Discuss in particular how they might transform the lives of young people.
- Identify the challenges that young people might face in trying to live by these principles.
- Now complete the charts.

POVERTY

Advantages for young people:

Challenges for young people:

CHAPTER 11: LIVING NEW LIFE IN CHRIST JESUS | WORKSHEET 7 | 357

CHAPTER 11 | WORKSHEET 7 (CONTD.)

CHASTITY

Advantages for young people:

Challenges for young people:

OBEDIENCE

Advantages for young people:

Challenges for young people:

358 | CREDO | LIVING AND LOVING AS DISCIPLES OF CHRIST

CHAPTER 11 | WORKSHEET 8

NAME:

Choosing an Apostolate

Faithful Catholics become involved in all sorts of apostolic activities, according to their talents, abilities, interests and circumstances. This worksheet identifies a variety of apostolates and invites you to consider whether you would be suited to any of them. The choices presented are all possible ways in which you could become involved right now in making the values of the Gospel come alive in your own life and in the lives of others.

REFLECT AND RESPOND
- Review what you have learned about the apostolic life in 'Think It Through' of chapter 11.
- Think about the kind of apostolic works you might be willing to get involved in.
- The chart below lists some apostolic works through which a person may serve God and others. For each one, state what you think you could bring to such an apostolate and whether you feel you would suit such work or not, and why.
- The last two panels have been left blank so that you may add examples of your own.

Working with disadvantaged young people:

Working with the elderly:

Bringing the Gospel to your friends and acquaintances:

CHAPTER 11: LIVING NEW LIFE IN CHRIST JESUS | WORKSHEET 8 | 359

CHAPTER 11 | WORKSHEET 8 (CONTD.)

Promoting the Gospel through music and the arts:

Promoting prayer groups:

Spreading the Gospel through the internet:

CHAPTER 11 | WORKSHEET 9

NAME:

Betrayal, Repentance and Reconciliation

This worksheet invites you to imagine the conversation between Jesus and Simon Peter at their first meeting after the Resurrection and after Simon Peter's betrayal of Jesus.

REFLECT AND IMAGINE
⊙ Reread the account of Peter's betrayal and repentance in Matthew 26:69–75.
⊙ Imagine a short dialogue between Jesus and Simon Peter when they first meet after the Resurrection.

Peter: _____

_____

Jesus: _____

_____

_____

Peter: _____

_____

Jesus: _____

_____

Peter: _____

_____

Jesus: _____

_____

Peter: _____

_____

CHAPTER 11: LIVING NEW LIFE IN CHRIST JESUS | WORKSHEET 9 | 361

CHAPTER 11 | WORKSHEET 10

NAME:

The Call to Discipleship

This worksheet presents a selection of quotations on the subject of discipleship and invites your response.

REFLECT AND RESPOND
Read and reflect on each of the quotations before writing your personal responses.

'Where does Jesus send us? There are no borders, no limits: he sends us to everyone. The Gospel is for everyone, not just for some. It is not only for those who seem closer to us, more receptive, more welcoming. It is for everyone. Do not be afraid to go and to bring Christ into every area of life, to the fringes of society, even to those who seem farthest away, most indifferent. The Lord seeks all, he wants everyone to feel the warmth of his mercy and his love.'

—Pope Francis at World Youth Day, Rio de Janeiro, 2013

_____

_____

_____

_____

'I know the power obedience has of making things easy which seem impossible.'

—St. Teresa of Ávila

_____

_____

_____

_____

362 | CREDO | LIVING AND LOVING AS DISCIPLES OF CHRIST

CHAPTER 11 | WORKSHEET 10 (CONTD.)

'The future is in your hearts and in your hands. God is entrusting to you the task, at once difficult and uplifting, of working with him in the building of the civilization of love.'
—Pope John Paul II at World Youth Day, Toronto, 2002

'If you are what you should be you will set the whole world on fire.'
—St. Catherine of Sienna

CHAPTER 11 | CHAPTER REVIEW

NAME:

Review of Chapter 11

I. **True/False. Mark the true statements 'T' and the false statements 'F'. In the case of each false statement, cross out and rewrite the incorrect words to make the statement true.**

_____1.   God calls us to use our gifts and talents to bring about his will for creation, the Kingdom, or reign, of God.

_____2.   The Blessed Virgin Mary is the greatest among the saints of the Church.

_____3.   The Kingdom, or reign, of God is a particular place or territory.

_____4.   God's love for the rich is a major theme in Sacred Scripture.

_____5.   St. Paul described the Church as the Home of Christ.

_____6.   The term 'hierarchy' refers to laypeople who have a vocation to serve the Church full time.

_____7.   In the Sacrament of Holy Orders a baptized man is ordained to serve the People of God as bishop, priest or deacon.

_____8.   Those who live in 'chosen poverty' are living reminders of God's preferential option for the poor.

_____9.   Consecrated virgins vow or promise to live a life of virginity until marriage.

364 | CREDO | LIVING AND LOVING AS DISCIPLES OF CHRIST

CHAPTER 11 | CHAPTER REVIEW (CONTD.)

_____10. Simon Peter, like his brother Andrew, worked as a tax collector.

II. **Fill in the blanks. Write the letter that corresponds to the correct term in the word bank in the blank space to complete each sentence. There are more terms in the word bank than you will need.**

A. consecrate	**E.** Evangelization	**I.** St. Anthony of the Desert
B. Chrism	**F.** The Kingdom of God	**J.** to call
C. disciple	**G.** parables	**K.** to listen well
D. eremitic	**H.** Peter	**L.** Catechumen

1. The word 'vocation' comes from the Latin verb _vocare_, which means '_____'.

2. _____ is 'the actualization of God's will for human beings proclaimed by Jesus Christ as a community of justice, peace, mercy and love'.

3. In his _____ Jesus used ordinary examples from the daily lives of his listeners to reveal the mystery of the Kingdom of God.

4. _____ is 'the ministry and mission of proclaiming and witnessing Christ and his Gospel'.

5. The root of the word _____ is the Greek _mathetes_, which can have the meaning 'apprentice'.

6. In the Sacrament of Baptism the newly baptized are anointed with the consecrated oil of sacred _____.

7. The Latin verb _obedire_, which means '_____', is the root of the English word 'obedience'.

8. The term _____ means 'one who lives in the desert'.

9. The Latin verb _consecrare_, which means 'to dedicate or set apart for a holy purpose', is the root of the word _____.

10. According to ancient tradition, _____ requested to be crucified upside down because he declared himself to be unworthy to die in the same manner as Jesus.

CHAPTER 11 | CHAPTER REVIEW (CONTD.)

III. Write a brief answer. Explain the teaching of the Catholic Church on 1 or 2.
   1. The three essential responsibilities that flow from Baptism
   2. The evangelical counsels

_____

_____

_____

_____

_____

_____

_____

_____

IV. How would you respond? A friend who is not a Catholic says that he sees no point in laypeople being part of the Church as 'they have no real role'.

_____

_____

_____

_____

_____

_____

_____

_____

_____

_____

_____

_____

366 | CREDO | LIVING AND LOVING AS DISCIPLES OF CHRIST

CHAPTER 11 | CHAPTER REVIEW (CONTD.)

V. Make a 'disciple decision'.

1. What is the most important wisdom for life that you discovered in this chapter?

_____

_____

_____

_____

_____

2. Name several ways you can put this wisdom into practice. Choose one of the ways you identify and describe how you will make that wisdom part of your life right now.

_____

_____

_____

_____

_____

_____

_____

_____

_____

_____

CHAPTER 11: LIVING NEW LIFE IN CHRIST JESUS | CHAPTER REVIEW (CONTD.) | 367

CHAPTER 12

Sustaining the Moral Life as Disciples of Jesus

INTRODUCTION

In this chapter we see how living the moral life as a disciple of Jesus Christ is an invitation to live the New Law of the Gospel. We explore the role of the Theological Virtues of faith, hope and charity (love) and the four Cardinal Virtues of prudence, justice, fortitude and temperance which are central to living the New Law. We discover that participating in the celebration of the Sacraments, especially the Eucharist, and living a life of prayer bring us the grace and strength to live a virtuous life. Finally, we come to some decisions about how best to sustain ourselves as we take up Jesus' invitation to live as his disciples.

Chapter 12 is developed under five major headings:

- ⊙ **ATTEND AND REFLECT:** What sustains your moral life?
- ⊙ **HEAR THE STORY:** Striving to live a virtuous life
- ⊙ **EMBRACE THE VISION:** We live by the Spirit; we walk by the Spirit
- ⊙ **THINK IT THROUGH:** The 'way' of Christian prayer
- ⊙ **JUDGE AND ACT:** (*Activities and exercises that encourage the young people to integrate what they have learned in the chapter into their daily lives*)

Theological Background for the Teacher

DISCIPLESHIP: A LIFE OF VIRTUE

True discipleship includes relating to others in a moral way. The true disciple will build good relationships with God and with other people. Jesus' 'New Commandment' to love God and other people is an integral whole, and we are misguided if we think we can love God while ignoring others, or love people while ignoring God.

Allowing our lives to be actively guided by the Theological Virtues of faith, hope and charity (love) and by the Cardinal Virtues of justice, prudence, temperance and fortitude will safeguard us against extremes and imbalances.

A virtue is an habitual and firm disposition to do the good. It allows the person not only to perform good acts, but to give the best of himself. The virtuous person tends toward the good with all his sensory and spiritual powers; he pursues the good and chooses it in concrete actions.
—*Catechism of the Catholic Church* (CCC), no. 1803

In a very real way the Theological Virtues are focused on our relationship with God—as we believe in God and in what he has revealed, as we put our hope and trust in God for now and the future, as we do our best to love God. Yet, if we truly live these virtues and listen to what God is saying to us, we will inevitably be driven to love other people, our fellow children of God.

The theological virtues are the foundation of Christian moral activity; they animate it and give it its special character. They inform and give life to all the moral virtues. They are infused by God into the souls of the faithful to make them capable of acting as his children and of meriting eternal life.
—CCC, no. 1813

Faith leads us 'to know and do God's will' (CCC, no. 1814), and even a passing acquaintance with Scripture will reveal that God's will is that we treat other people in a just and loving way as we try to live a moral life.

Hope in God and in the fulfillment of his promise of things to come springs from what, in faith, we believe about God. The theological virtue of hope is firmly rooted in our humanity. People may feel that hope is in short supply in the modern world, and yet it is all the more desired, even if people fail to see its true source in God.

The virtue of hope responds to the aspiration to happiness which God has placed in the heart of every man; it takes up the hopes that inspire men's activities and purifies them so as to order them to the Kingdom of heaven; it keeps man from discouragement; it sustains him during times of abandonment; it opens up his heart in

368 | CREDO | LIVING AND LOVING AS DISCIPLES OF CHRIST

expectation of eternal beatitude. Buoyed up by hope, he is preserved from selfishness and led to the happiness that flows from charity.

—CCC, no. 1818

Of all the virtues, 'the greatest of these is love' (1 Corinthians 13:13). How could it be otherwise? The desire to love is in perfect harmony with Jesus' 'New Commandment'. Love characterizes God's whole relationship with us, from the gift of creation through the loving sacrifice on the Cross to the ongoing support and guidance of the Holy Spirit. In the judgment scene in Matthew 25:31–46, love is seen as crucial to our future in the Kingdom of God.

The practice of all the virtues is animated and inspired by charity, which 'binds everything together in perfect harmony'; it is the *form of the virtues*; it articulates and orders them among themselves; it is the source and the goal of their Christian practice.

—CCC, no. 1827

Pope Francis has much to say on love in his apostolic exhortation *Evangelii Gaudium* (The Joy of the Gospel). He teaches:

Loving others is a spiritual force drawing us to union with God; indeed, one who does not love others 'walks in the darkness' (1 John 2:11), 'remains in death' (1 John 3:14) and 'does not know God' (1 John 4:8).

—*Evangelii Gaudium*, no. 272

And in the same document we read:

Saint Thomas Aquinas taught that the Church's moral teaching has its own 'hierarchy', in the virtues and in the acts which proceed from them. [cf. Summa Theologiae, I–II, q. 66, a. 4–6]. What counts above all else is 'faith working through love' (Galatians 5:6). Works of love directed to one's neighbor are the most perfect external manifestation of the interior grace of the Spirit: 'The foundation of the New Law is in the grace of the Holy Spirit, who is manifested in the faith which works through love' [S. Th., I–II, q. 108, a. 1].

—*Evangelii Gaudium*, no. 37

As we live lives that are infused with these Theological Virtues, we practice, develop and activate the 'human virtues', those 'firm attitudes, stable dispositions, habitual perfections' (CCC, no. 1804) that govern our lives and help guide us on the path of discipleship. The Book of Wisdom (Wisdom 8:7) names four of these human virtues that are so crucial and central—temperance, prudence, justice and fortitude. These are called the Cardinal Virtues, as they 'play a pivotal role and . . . all the others are grouped around them' (CCC, no. 1805).

The wisdom of *prudence* has never been more evident—how much suffering could be avoided in our world if people acted prudently. If we lived more in line with the demands of *justice*, the many conflicts born of injustice would never arise. If we practiced *fortitude* more consistently, we would stand up for our faith and challenge injustice more effectively and confidently. If we lived in a spirit of temperance, we would love God and others without resort to extremism, intolerance or addiction.

Given our human weakness and the reality of Original Sin, it takes much effort, perseverance and courage to practice these virtues consistently and with integrity. Through our human efforts we can develop good habits and practices but we can also be assured that God is always with us, offering us the grace we need to live these virtues.

Christ's gift of salvation offers us the grace necessary to persevere in the pursuit of the virtues. Everyone should always ask for this grace of light and strength, frequent the sacraments, cooperate with the Holy Spirit, and follow his calls to love what is good and shun evil.

—CCC, no. 1811

God's gift of grace includes the special sanctifying grace of the Sacraments and the 'actual graces' for our day-to-day living.

Intimately related to our living of the virtues and our gifted life of grace are the gifts and fruits of the Holy Spirit.

The seven *gifts* of the Holy Spirit are wisdom, understanding, counsel, fortitude, knowledge, piety, and fear of the Lord. They belong in their fullness to Christ, Son of David. They complete and perfect the virtues of those who receive them.

—CCC, no. 1831

We can also see in the list of the fruits of the Holy Spirit how closely related they are to living a virtuous life.

The tradition of the Church lists twelve of them: 'charity, joy, peace, patience, kindness, goodness, generosity, gentleness, faithfulness, modesty, self-control, chastity.'

—CCC, no. 1832

CHAPTER 12: SUSTAINING THE MORAL LIFE AS DISCIPLES OF JESUS | INTRODUCTION | 369

In our life of discipleship the Holy Spirit helps us not just in a personal way, but dwells in a supportive way in the Church as community, institution and Body of Christ. Guided by the Holy Spirit, the Church, through the Magisterium, has a duty and a right to teach in God's name on faith and morals. The Holy Spirit keeps the Church free from error in its formal teaching, an attribute we call 'infallibility'.

In order to preserve the Church in the purity of the faith handed on by the apostles, Christ who is the Truth willed to confer on her a share in his own infallibility. By a 'supernatural sense of faith' the People of God, under the guidance of the Church's living Magisterium, 'unfailingly adheres to this faith' [*Lumen Gentium (Constitution on the Church), no. 12*].

—CCC, no. 889

The Holy Spirit is not the only assistance God gives us. We also have the example and ongoing support of Mary, the Mother of Jesus and, indeed, our Mother and excellent role model for our path of discipleship.

Jesus is Mary's only son, but her spiritual motherhood extends to all men whom indeed he came to save: 'The Son whom she brought forth is he whom God placed as the first-born among many brethren, that is, the faithful in whose generation and formation she co-operates with a mother's love' [*Lumen Gentium*, no. 63].

—CCC, no. 501

THE 'WAY' OF CHRISTIAN PRAYER

How appropriate that one of the two most common prayers Catholics say is the Hail Mary or Ave Maria. The other prayer, of course, is the Lord's Prayer, the prayer that Jesus himself taught us. We might call these 'formal' prayers in that they follow a formula of words provided for us, but that doesn't imply that they can't be intensely personal, even though we might say them daily.

Prayer types may be categorized for convenience and clarity, but whether we practice formal, vocal, communal, contemplative, meditative or any other kind of prayer, our prayer should always be marked by sincerity, integrity, reflection, attention to meaning and openness. Our lives can lead into prayer and grow out of prayer. We can take refuge in prayer and be inspired to go forth renewed after prayer.

The Lord leads all persons by paths and in ways pleasing to him, and each believer responds according to his heart's resolve and the personal expressions of his prayer. However, Christian tradition has retained three major expressions of prayer: vocal, meditative, and contemplative. They have one basic trait in common: composure of heart. This vigilance in keeping the Word and dwelling in the presence of God makes these three expressions intense times in the life of prayer.

—CCC, no. 2699

ADDITIONAL BACKGROUND READING

Catechism of the Catholic Church, nos. 487–507, 874–896, 963–972, 1803–1833, 2697–2724; *YOUCAT,* nos. 299–301, 343–347, 479–481, 499–527; *Compendium of the Catechism of the Catholic Church,* nos. 182–185, 196–199, 377–390, 568–571, 577–598; *United States Catholic Catechism for Adults,* 111–124, 141–150, 315–321, 470–495; **Pope Francis,** *Lumen Fidei (The Light of Faith);* **Benedict XVI,** *Spe Salvi (Saved in Hope);* **Benedict XVI,** *Deus Caritas Est (God Is Love).*

370 | CREDO | LIVING AND LOVING AS DISCIPLES OF CHRIST

CHAPTER OUTCOMES

See general note on page 19 of this resource.

Learning Outcomes

As a result of studying this chapter and exploring the issues raised, the young people should be able to:

- understand the context and meaning of the New Law and New Commandment of Jesus;
- recognize that the Theological Virtues of faith, hope and love play a central role in our living the moral life;
- understand the function and value of the four Cardinal Virtues of prudence, justice, fortitude and temperance (self-control) for living a virtuous life;
- recognize the different types of grace;
- understand the concept of our being temples of the Holy Spirit.
- understand the Church's role and authority in providing moral guidance;
- understand the central role of prayer in the Christian life;
- recognize and understand the different expressions of Christian prayer;
- know the story of the Marian devotion to Nuestra Señora de la Caridad del Cobre (Our Lady of Charity).

Faith-formation Outcomes

As a result of studying this chapter and exploring the issues raised, the young people should also:

- strive to live and develop the Theological Virtues in their day-to-day lives;
- cultivate and practice the Cardinal Virtues in their own lives;
- become aware of and respond to God's grace in their lives;
- deepen their devotion to Mary, Mother of God and our Mother;
- try out different types of prayer;
- pray the Lord's Prayer with renewed attention to the meaning of the words;
- reflect on the insights they gained through their study of virtue and prayer;
- be inspired by the Cuban people's devotion to Our Lady of Charity.

Teacher Reflection

As you prepare to engage your group in a study of the Christian virtues and their role in discipleship, take some time to reflect on the positive portrayal of the beauty of virtue in this poem by George Herbert (1593–1633).

Virtue

Sweet day, so cool, so calm, so bright,
The bridal of the earth and sky,
The dew shall weep thy fall tonight;
For thou must die.

Sweet rose, whose hue angry and brave
Bids the rash gazer wipe his eye,
Thy root is ever in its grave,
And thou must die.

Sweet spring, full of sweet days and roses,
A box where sweets compacted lie,
My music shows ye have your closes,
And all must die.

Only a sweet and virtuous soul,
Like season'd timber, never gives;
But, though the whole world turn to coal,
Then chiefly lives.

CHAPTER 12: SUSTAINING THE MORAL LIFE AS DISCIPLES OF JESUS | INTRODUCTION | 371

Notes and Guidelines for Student Activities

ATTEND AND REFLECT

What sustains your moral life?

Learning Outcomes

That the young people would:

⊙ understand the context and meaning of the New Law and New Commandment of Jesus;

⊙ recognize that the Theological Virtues of faith, hope and love play a central role in our living the moral life.

Faith-formation Outcome

That the young people would also:

⊙ strive to live and develop the Theological Virtues in their day-to-day lives.

Overview

Section one, 'Attend and Reflect', explores the role of the Theological Virtues of faith, hope and charity (love) in our living the moral life. We guide the young people to appreciate that accepting and living these three great virtues is the source and power of our receiving the abundant life that Jesus promised to his disciples. These virtues empower Christians to partner with the Spirit of Christ to work to bring about the reign of God.

Supplementary Activities for 'Attend and Reflect'

Teacher Tip: Invite the young people to listen to the song of faith 'I Believe in the Sun' by Carey Landry and to share their responses.

Worksheet 1: 'Images of Hope' (*page 375 of this resource*) takes an Emily Dickinson poem as a starting point from which to explore the Christian virtue of hope.

_____

Worksheet 2: 'Quotations About Love' (*page 376 of this resource*) presents a range of quotations about love, especially love of God, and invites the young people's responses.

_____

Role-play Activity

Invite the young people to form into groups of three. Each person in a group will represent one of the Theological Virtues of faith, hope and charity (love). Invite them to work together to create a 'dialogue' between the three virtues, whereby each virtue explains his or her role in enabling people to live as disciples of Jesus and to attain eternal life and happiness. The young people will perform their role-plays for the class.

HEAR THE STORY

Striving to live a virtuous life

Learning Outcome

That the young people would:

⊙ understand the function and value of the four Cardinal Virtues of prudence, justice, fortitude and temperance (self-control) for living a virtuous life.

Faith-formation Outcome

That the young people would also:

⊙ cultivate and practice the Cardinal Virtues in their own lives.

Overview

Section two, 'Hear the Story', explores how the human moral virtues of prudence, justice, fortitude and temperance (self-control), known as the Cardinal Virtues, are the foundation for leading a virtuous life as a disciple of Jesus. We guide the young people to reflect upon and identify how they can cultivate and practice these virtues in their own lives.

Supplementary Activities for 'Hear the Story'

Worksheet 3: 'Living the Cardinal Virtues' (*page 378 of this resource*) invites the young people to reflect on and identify how they might incorporate the virtues of prudence, justice, fortitude and temperance into their daily lives as disciples of Jesus.

Teacher Tip: Invite the young people to listen to some songs about justice; for example, Bruce Springsteen's versions of 'We Shall Overcome' and 'Eyes on the Prize' from his *Seeger Sessions* album.

372 | CREDO | LIVING AND LOVING AS DISCIPLES OF CHRIST

'In the Spotlight' Activity
Invite the young people to work in groups to prepare an 'In the Spotlight' activity based on the Cardinal Virtues. Four students from each group will sit on a panel as Prudence, Justice, Fortitude and Temperance, and the class will question them individually in relation to their role in enabling people to live virtuous lives. The preparation should involve rereading the material on the Cardinal Virtues in their theology text, envisaging the type of questions the class might put to the panel, and helping the panelists articulate their understanding of the virtues so as to be able to answer any questions the class might come up with. (*See additional notes on conducting 'In the Spotlight' activities in the 'Student Activity Tool Kit', page 393 of this resource.*)

EMBRACE THE VISION

We live by the Spirit; we walk by the Spirit

Learning Outcomes
That the young people would:
- recognize the different types of grace;
- understand the concept of our being temples of the Holy Spirit;
- understand the Church's role and authority in providing moral guidance.

Faith-formation Outcomes
That the young people would also:
- become aware of and respond to God's grace in their lives;
- deepen their devotion to Mary, Mother of God and our Mother.

Overview
Section three, 'Embrace the Vision', explores the role and the effects of grace and the Holy Spirit in our lives. We remind the young people that we receive the gift of sanctifying grace at Baptism and we explain the difference between the sacramental graces and actual graces, all of which help us to live out our Christian vocation. We also recall that through the graces of our Baptism we become temples of the Holy Spirit and we receive the seven Gifts of the Holy Spirit which dispose and strengthen us to respond knowingly and freely to God's will. We outline the Church's role in providing us with moral guidance and we explain that the Holy Spirit also blesses the Church with graces to guide her in her teaching. Finally, we advocate turning to Mary, Mother of God and our Mother, as the primary model for living as disciples of her Son.

Supplementary Activities for 'Embrace the Vision'

Teacher Tip: Invite the young people to listen to a song in honor of Mary; for example, 'Hail Mary, Gentle Woman' by Carey Landry.

PowerPoint Activity
Invite the young people to work in groups to research and prepare a set of slides that explain or illustrate the concept of grace and the different types of grace. The young people could present their work to the class.

Worksheet 4: 'Fruits of the Holy Spirit' (*page 380 of this resource*) offers the young people the opportunity to explore how the gift of the Holy Spirit is bearing fruit in their lives.

Teacher Tip: Invite the students to listen to a song in honor of the Holy Spirit; for example 'Everyone Moved by the Spirit' by Carey Landry or 'Spirit' by Sal Solo.

Creative Activity
Invite the young people to write their own prayers to the Holy Spirit asking for the graces, guidance and courage to live and walk by the Spirit.

THINK IT THROUGH

The 'way' of Christian prayer

Learning Outcomes
That the young people would:
- understand the central role of prayer in the Christian life;
- recognize and understand the different expressions of Christian prayer.

Faith-formation Outcomes
That the young people would also:
- try out different types of prayer;
- pray the Lord's Prayer with renewed attention to the meaning of the words.

Overview
Section four, 'Think It Through', examines the practice of Christian prayer and explains why prayer and the Christian life are inseparable. The young people learn how flexible prayer is and how it can help

CHAPTER 12: SUSTAINING THE MORAL LIFE AS DISCIPLES OF JESUS | NOTES AND GUIDELINES | 373 them overcome the obstacles and challenges they encounter in life. We look at the three expressions of Christian prayer, namely, vocal prayer, meditation and contemplation, and the role of prayer in the life of a disciple of Christ. We conclude the section by examining Jesus' own prayer, the Lord's Prayer.

Supplementary Activities for 'Think It Through'

Worksheet 5: 'Prayer Resource' (*page 382 of this resource*) invites the young people to compose their own prayers on specific issues relating to school and home.

Worksheet 6: 'The Lord's Prayer' (*page 383 of this resource*) offers the young people the opportunity to reflect on and write a short commentary about each phrase of the Lord's Prayer.

Teacher Tip: Invite the young people to find and listen to some musical versions of the Lord's Prayer.

Creative Activity
Invite the young people to choose their favorite phrase from the Lord's Prayer, for example 'Give us this day our daily bread', and to create a collage or a video to illustrate what would be happening in the world if these words were to become a reality.

JUDGE AND ACT

Learning Outcomes
That the young people would:
⊙ review the teachings of the Church that they have learned about in this chapter;
⊙ know the story of the Marian devotion to Nuestra Señora de la Caridad del Cobre (Our Lady of Charity).

Faith-formation Outcomes
That the young people would also:
⊙ reflect on the insights they gained through their study of virtue and prayer;
⊙ be inspired by the Cuban people's devotion to Our Lady of Charity.

Overview
In Section five, 'Judge and Act', the young people review the teachings of the Church that they have

studied in this chapter. They also hear the story of Nuestra Señora de la Caridad del Cobre (Our Lady of Charity), a symbol of faith, hope and love for Cuban people.

Supplementary Activities for 'Judge and Act'

Worksheet 7: 'Mary: Model of Discipleship' (*page 385 of this resource*) invites the young people to reflect on and identify five ways in which young people today could learn about discipleship from the life of Mary, the Mother of Jesus.

Worksheet 8: 'Praying to Mary' (*page 386 of this resource*) invites the young people to compose five short prayers to Mary that relate to issues young people might face in their lives.

Additional Prayer Suggestion

Scripture Reflection
(*See instructions for the use of doodling in prayer in the 'Student Activity Tool Kit', page 394 of this resource.*)

Use the following psalm verse to engage the young people in prayer:

> **When you send forth your spirit . . . you renew the face of the ground.**
>
> **PSALM 104:30**

CHAPTER 12 | WORKSHEET 1

NAME:

Images of Hope

When we find it challenging to come to grips with a difficult concept, it helps to use imagery. This worksheet takes an Emily Dickinson poem as a starting point from which to explore the Christian virtue of hope.

READ AND REFLECT
Read and reflect on this poem about hope by Emily Dickinson.

> 'Hope' is the thing with feathers—
> That perches in the soul—
> And sings the tune without the words—
> And never stops—at all—
>
> And sweetest—in the Gale—is heard—
> And sore must be the storm—
> That could abash the little Bird
> That kept so many warm—
>
> I've heard it in the chillest land—
> And on the strangest Sea—
> Yet, never, in Extremity,
> It asked a crumb—of Me.

CLASS DISCUSSION
⊙ How is a bird a good image for hope?
⊙ What point is Dickinson making about hope when she suggests that it is particularly sweet in a storm?
⊙ How is it appropriate to link hope with warmth as she does in line 8?
⊙ What aspect of hope is Dickinson referring to in the last two lines?
⊙ What other images for hope would you suggest, and why?

PAIR AND SHARE
⊙ Read the poem again with a partner. This time, as you read it, think of 'hope' as the Theological Virtue 'through which a person both desires and expects the fulfilment of God's promises of things to come' (*United States Catholic Catechism for Adults*, 515).
⊙ Share with your partner how this 'Christian' hope can be 'sweet' in the face of the 'storms' that challenge your faith, how it provides 'warmth' and 'never stops' as you strive to live as a disciple of Jesus.

JOURNAL EXERCISE
Describe the role hope plays in your faith. What, in particular, do you desire or hope for in relation to your faith? What sustains you in that hope?

CHAPTER 12: SUSTAINING THE MORAL LIFE AS DISCIPLES OF JESUS | WORKSHEET 1 | 375

CHAPTER 12 | WORKSHEET 2

NAME:

Quotations About Love

Love of God and love of others is at the heart of the Christian faith. This worksheet presents a range of quotations about love, especially love of God, and invites your responses.

READ, RESPOND AND SHARE
◉ Read each of the quotations and write a short response, describing what resonates with you in the statement, what you agree or disagree with, or adding an additional insight that comes to mind.
◉ When you have completed the activity, share your responses with a partner.

'The proof of love is in the works. Where love exists, it works great things. But when it ceases to act, it ceases to exist.'
—Pope Gregory the Great

_____

_____

_____

'Charity may be a very short word, but with its tremendous meaning of pure love, it sums up man's entire relation to God and to his neighbor.'
—St. Aelred of Rievaulx

_____

_____

_____

'I have decided to stick with love. Hate is too great a burden to bear.'
—Martin Luther King Jnr.

_____

_____

376 | CREDO | LIVING AND LOVING AS DISCIPLES OF CHRIST

CHAPTER 12 | WORKSHEET 2 (CONTD.)

'Spread love everywhere you go: first of all in your own house. Give love to your children, to your wife or husband, to a next-door neighbor. . . . Let no one ever come to you without leaving better and happier. Be the living expression of God's kindness; kindness in your face, kindness in your eyes, kindness in your smile, kindness in your warm greeting.'

—Blessed Mother Teresa of Calcutta

_____

_____

'What does love look like? It has the hands to help others. It has the feet to hasten to the poor and needy. It has eyes to see misery and want. It has the ears to hear the sighs and sorrows of men. That is what love looks like.'

—St. Augustine of Hippo

_____

_____

'You learn to speak by speaking, to study by studying, to run by running, to work by working, and just so, you learn to love by loving. All those who think to learn in any other way deceive themselves.'

—St. Francis de Sales

_____

_____

'God loves each of us as if there were only one of us.'

—St. Augustine

_____

_____

_____

CHAPTER 12: SUSTAINING THE MORAL LIFE AS DISCIPLES OF JESUS | WORKSHEET 2 (CONTD.)

CHAPTER 12 | WORKSHEET 3

NAME:

Living the Cardinal Virtues

The Cardinal Virtues are the foundation for living a moral and virtuous life. This worksheet invites you to reflect on and identify how you might incorporate these virtues into your daily life as a disciple of Jesus.

REFLECT AND RESPOND

⊙ Reread the information on the four Cardinal Virtues of prudence, justice, fortitude and temperance (self-control) in your theology text before answering the questions below.

Identify some ways in which you could show a commitment to the virtue of **prudence** by the way you live your life. Mention areas where you would most need to practice this virtue.

_____

_____

_____

_____

Identify some ways in which you could show a commitment to the virtue of **justice** by the way you live your life. Mention areas where you would most need to practice this virtue.

_____

_____

_____

_____

378 | CREDO | LIVING AND LOVING AS DISCIPLES OF CHRIST

CHAPTER 12 | WORKSHEET 3 (CONTD.)

Identify some ways in which you could show a commitment to the virtue of **fortitude** by the way you live your life. Mention areas where you would most need to practice this virtue.

_____

_____

_____

_____

Identify some ways in which you could show a commitment to the virtue of **temperance (self-control)** by the way you live your life. Mention areas where you would most need to practice this virtue.

_____

_____

_____

_____

How could your living the four Cardinal Virtues contribute to creating a better world for you and others?

_____

_____

_____

_____

CHAPTER 12: SUSTAINING THE MORAL LIFE AS DISCIPLES OF JESUS | WORKSHEET 3 (CONTD.) | 379

CHAPTER 12 | WORKSHEET 4

NAME:

Fruits of the Holy Spirit

This worksheet offers you the opportunity to explore how the gift of the Holy Spirit is bearing fruit in your life.

REFLECT AND RESPOND

⊙ You received the sevenfold gift of the Holy Spirit in Baptism. The gift of the Holy Spirit enables you to live in such a way that your life bears fruit in the world. The Fruits of the Holy Spirit are charity (love), joy, peace, patience, kindness, goodness, generosity, gentleness, faithfulness, modesty, self-control and chastity.

⊙ On the lines provided, identify a time when each 'fruit' of the Holy Spirit was evident in your life. If you cannot identify a time when a particular fruit of the Holy Spirit was evident in your life, suggest what you need to do to change that.

Charity (Love): _____

_____

Joy: _____

_____

Peace: _____

_____

Patience: _____

_____

Kindness: _____

_____

Goodness: _____

_____

380 | CREDO | LIVING AND LOVING AS DISCIPLES OF CHRIST

CHAPTER 12 | WORKSHEET 4 (CONTD.)

Generosity: _____

_____

Gentleness: _____

_____

Faithfulness: _____

_____

Modesty: _____

_____

Self-Control: _____

_____

Chastity: _____

_____

CHAPTER 12: SUSTAINING THE MORAL LIFE AS DISCIPLES OF JESUS | WORKSHEET 4 (CONTD.) | 381

CHAPTER 12 | WORKSHEET 5

NAME:

Prayer Resource

Along with love and grace, prayer is an essential element in our life of faith. This worksheet invites you to compose your own prayers on specific issues relating to school and home.

REFLECT AND COMPOSE

Take some time to reflect before composing one short prayer for each of the situations listed below.

A birth in the family:

A death in the family:

A good result in a school exam:

A poor result in a school exam:

A conflict at home between a young person and parent(s):

382 | CREDO | LIVING AND LOVING AS DISCIPLES OF CHRIST

CHAPTER 12 | WORKSHEET 6

NAME:

The Lord's Prayer

The Lord's Prayer, which Jesus himself gave us, is the best known Christian prayer of all. But there can be a danger in repeating it frequently without paying due attention to the meaning of the words. This worksheet offers you the opportunity to reflect on and write a short commentary about each phrase of the Lord's Prayer.

REFLECT AND RESPOND

Write a brief commentary on each phrase of the Lord's Prayer. Describe any thoughts that come into your mind as you contemplate what the phrases mean.

Our Father

Who art in heaven

Hallowed be thy name

Thy kingdom come

Thy will be done on earth as it is in heaven

CHAPTER 12: SUSTAINING THE MORAL LIFE AS DISCIPLES OF JESUS | WORKSHEET 6 | 383

CHAPTER 12 | WORKSHEET 6 (CONTD.)

Give us this day our daily bread

And forgive us our trespasses

As we forgive those who trespass against us

And lead us not into temptation

But deliver us from evil

384 | CREDO | LIVING AND LOVING AS DISCIPLES OF CHRIST

CHAPTER 12 | WORKSHEET 7

NAME:

Mary: Model of Discipleship

This worksheet invites you to reflect on and identify five ways in which young people today could learn about discipleship from the life of Mary, the Mother of Jesus.

REVIEW AND RESPOND

- Recall what you know about Mary and how she modeled true discipleship throughout her life—from the moment she accepted God's invitation to be the Mother of Jesus, through all the trials and challenges along with the blessings that accompanied this role. Think especially of how she modeled the Fruits of the Holy Spirit in her life.
- It might help you to reread chapter 1 and 2 of Luke's account of the Gospel, and chapter 19 of the Gospel according to John.
- Now suggest five things that young people today could learn from the example and witness of Mary for their own lives as disciples of Christ.

1.

2.

3.

4.

5.

CHAPTER 12: SUSTAINING THE MORAL LIFE AS DISCIPLES OF JESUS | WORKSHEET 7 | 385

CHAPTER 12 | WORKSHEET 8

NAME:

Praying to Mary

We can pray to Mary for her help and guidance or to ask her to intercede for us with her Son. This worksheet invites you to compose five short prayers to Mary.

REFLECT AND PRAY

Compose five short prayers to Mary that relate to issues young people might face in their lives.

A prayer to Mary about the day-to-day challenges students encounter in school:

A prayer to Mary about pressures on young people as a result of advertising:

A prayer to Mary about needing guidance to discern one's vocation in life:

A prayer to Mary about challenges young people face in witnessing to their faith:

A prayer to Mary about the ups and downs of one's relationships:

---

386 | CREDO | LIVING AND LOVING AS DISCIPLES OF CHRIST

CHAPTER 12 | CHAPTER REVIEW

NAME:

Review of Chapter 12

I. **True/False. Mark the true statements 'T' and the false statements 'F'. In the case of each false statement, cross out and rewrite the incorrect words to make the statement true.**

_____1.   Jesus abolished the Old Law, which centered on the Ten Commandments, and he established the New Law.

_____2.   The model for our love is God's love for us.

_____3.   The term 'grace' comes from the Latin word *gratia*, which means 'generous'.

_____4.   In Confirmation we receive the fullness of the gift of the Holy Spirit.

_____5.   The Gifts of the Holy Spirit dispose and strengthen us to respond knowingly and freely to God's holy will in the circumstances of our daily lives.

_____6.   Catholics believe that we do and can strive to live a life of virtue alone.

_____7.   St. John is the greatest saint of the Church and the model disciple of the Lord.

_____8.   Prayer and the Christian life are inseparable.

_____9.   When the disciples asked Jesus to teach them to pray, Jesus taught them the Hail Mary.

CHAPTER 12: SUSTAINING THE MORAL LIFE AS DISCIPLES OF JESUS | CHAPTER REVIEW | 387

CHAPTER 12 | CHAPTER REVIEW (CONTD.)

_____10. The statue of our Lady of Charity depicts Mary carrying the Christ child in her left arm and with a gold cross in her right hand.

II. Fill in the blanks. Write the letter that corresponds to the correct term in the word bank in the blank space to complete each sentence. There are more terms in the word bank than you will need.

A. believers	**E.** Indefectibility	**I.** Paschal Mystery
B. Christians	**F.** Infallibility	**J.** Hawaii
C. Cuba	**G.** Faith	**K.** Theological
D. love	**H.** merit	**L.** virtue

1. Faith, hope and love are the three _____ Virtues.

2. _____ is 'submission' to God.

3. The *Catechism* uses the term '_____' to identify 'the reward which God promises and gives to those who love him and by his grace perform good works'.

4. The _____ is the Death, Resurrection and Ascension of the Incarnate Son of God.

5. The Greek word *arete*, which is translated '_____', means 'moral excellence'.

6. Mary is the Mother of all _____.

7. _____ means that the Church does not and cannot depart from proclaiming the authentic Gospel without error in spite of the defects of her members.

8. _____ is a gift that flows from the grace of the whole body of the faithful not to err in matters of faith and morals.

9. Marian devotion to Our Lady of Charity is part of the history of the island of _____.

10. 1 Corinthians 13:13 tells us that 'faith, hope, and love abide . . . and the greatest of these is _____'.

388 | CREDO | LIVING AND LOVING AS DISCIPLES OF CHRIST

CHAPTER 12 | CHAPTER REVIEW (CONTD.)

III. Write a brief answer. Explain the teaching of the Catholic Church on 1 or 2.
    1. Sacramental graces
    2. The three expressions of prayer in the Christian tradition

IV. How would you respond? A friend says that the Cardinal Virtues are outdated and old-fashioned ideas that have no relevance in the modern world.

CHAPTER 12 | CHAPTER REVIEW (CONTD.)

V. Make a 'disciple decision'.

1. What is the most important wisdom for life that you discovered in this chapter?

_____

_____

_____

_____

_____

_____

_____

2. Name several ways you can put this wisdom into practice. Choose one of the ways you identify and describe how you will make that wisdom part of your life right now.

_____

_____

_____

_____

_____

_____

_____

_____

_____

390 | CREDO | LIVING AND LOVING AS DISCIPLES OF CHRIST

Student Activity Tool Kit

There is a wide range of activities for students offered throughout the *Credo* series. This 'tool kit' contains suggestions and instructions for getting the optimum benefit from these activities, as well suggesting additional activities and approaches that might be employed.

TOOLS FOR EFFECTIVE LEARNING
- Talk It Over (p. 391)
- Shared Reading Technique (p. 391)
- Jigsaw Reading (p. 391)
- Peer Teaching (p. 392)
- Graphic Organizers (p. 392)
- Mind Maps (p. 392)
- In the Spotlight (p. 393)
- Journal Exercises (p. 393)
- Faith Words Quiz (p. 393)
- Blogs/Blogging (p. 393)
- Vox Pops (p. 393)
- Walking Debates (p. 393)
- Words of Wisdom Collection (p. 394)

TOOLS FOR EFFECTIVE PRAYER
- Doodling as a prayer technique (p. 394)
- Meditations—A guide to facilitate successful meditations (p. 394)
- Sample formats for introducing and concluding guided meditations (p. 395)

Tools for Effective Learning

TALK IT OVER
The 'Talk it over' activities that appear throughout the text may be approached in a variety of ways. The young people may discuss the topic in pairs, in small groups or as a single class group. Before they do so, they should take a few moments just to think about the question(s) to be discussed. Following their discussion they may compare their mental or written notes and identify the answers they think are best, most convincing or most unique. The teacher may then invite them to share their conclusions with others. The teacher may do this by going around each pair or group or by taking answers as they are called out (or as hands are raised). The teacher or a designated helper may record students' responses on the board or overhead.

SHARED READING TECHNIQUE
This technique is useful when students have to read and comprehend a long or difficult text. It is especially useful for reading a long Bible passage.

Step 1: Each student is assigned a reading partner; one will be reader A and the other reader B.

Step 2: Both students silently read the first section; for example, a selection of Bible verses or a paragraph.

Step 3: Student A is initially the summarizer and student B is the accuracy-checker. The summarizer explains in his or her own words the content of the first section. The accuracy-checker listens carefully and offers help or prompts if anything is left out.

Step 4: The students move on to the next section, switch roles and repeat the process until they have completed the text.

Step 5: At the end they summarize the key points.

JIGSAW READING
Step 1: Divide a text into different sections, say five paragraphs.

Step 2: Students split up into groups, each group getting one paragraph to read.

Step 3: In their group the students read the relevant text, discuss the key points and prepare to teach the others in the class what they have learned.

Step 4: Students move around so that one student from each group joins a new group.

Step 5: In the new group they share and teach what they learned in the first group.

This continues until all the information has been shared.

STUDENT ACTIVITY TOOL KIT | 391

PEER TEACHING

Peer teaching is a fun activity, as young people enjoy taking on the role of 'teacher'. It prompts them to think about their own understanding of a topic and how they can enhance their peers' understanding. It also encourages them to take more responsibility for their learning. In addition, it develops their skills in communication and teamwork.

Step 1: Organize the class into mixed-ability groups of three or four students. Divide the section of the course or chapter into different areas, and give each group an area to teach. It is important to give clear guidelines at the start; for example, concerning roles within the group, timing of the exercise, giving and taking peer feedback and so on.

Step 2: Give students time in class to brainstorm on how they will teach the area. The teacher may allocate roles within the group or the group members may do this. The roles assigned might involve collecting information, creating a visual display of the information, or teaching the topic to the whole class. If there are four in a group, one role could be that of question-taker; this student anticipates possible questions from the class and prepares answers to them with the team.

Step 3: Students then research their topic for homework and come up with ideas to teach the topic

Step 4: Give the students time in class to put together their ten-minute teaching session. In addition, they will need time to decide on questions to ask the other groups on their areas.

Step 5: Give each team time to teach their section and five minutes for questions from the class.

Step 6: At the end of the process, the class evaluate each team's performance. If sections were left out or not covered sufficiently, if notes were unclear or if information was not accurate, they should inform the team of this. They also share what helped them remember the material.

Note: Peer teaching can also be done in small groups of three or four, where each group member reads or revises a different section and they teach the other people *within* that group.

GRAPHIC ORGANIZERS

Graphic organizers help students in recording, organizing, summarizing and integrating information. They can take many forms, from Venn diagrams to mind-maps. They may be used for note-making,

for revision, for brainstorming a topic and so on. A number of graphic-organizer templates are provided on pages 397–400 of this resource, which may be photocopied and used for a variety of topics.

MIND MAPS

A mind map is a diagram used to represent words and images linked to and arranged around a key theme or idea. Mind maps can be used to generate, visualize, structure and classify ideas, and as an aid in study, organization, problem-solving, decision-making and writing. Mind maps may also aid recall of existing memories. The process of mind-mapping can be divided into three steps:

Step 1: *Getting Started*
Take a sheet of plain paper and some colored pens. Turn the page so it is in landscape position. In the center of the page draw an image that represents the topic you are working on, and then label the image. Always start in the middle of the page, as this gives you space to spread your ideas in all directions, without being limited by the boundaries found in linear note-making.

Step 2: *Expanding Your Thinking*
The next step entails creating thick colorful branches radiating out from the central image. These branches will represent your main stream of thoughts. There is no limit to the number of main branches, but five or six might be adequate. On each branch, clearly state in bold colorful capitals your main thoughts using a single key word. Use your imagination.

It is important to use colors as they will add energy to your mind map and enhance your creative thinking. To get your thoughts flowing, you may need to ask yourself a few questions. The two main things that make mind-mapping so effective are imagination and association. The brain's thinking processes are naturally image-filled, so in order to incorporate this natural process into the activity it is important to include images and pictures on your mind map. Not only will images save you time in comparison to note-taking, but they are also easier to remember.

Step 3: *Ideas, Thoughts and Associations*
You can use 'association' to expand your mind map to the final stage. Look at the key words on the main branches—these key words should spark off further ideas. Draw smaller branches stemming from the key words to accommodate the associations you make. The number of sub-branches is limitless; it is dependent upon the number of ideas you can think of. The sub-branch may then trigger more thoughts and ideas associated with the key word of that

branch, leading to the development of the next level of sub-branches. Continue this process until all your thoughts and ideas are on your mind map.

IN THE SPOTLIGHT

Throughout this text, students will learn about many famous people. The 'In the Spotlight' activity will help to bring their stories to life. This activity should be used after the class is familiar with the person's story. One student takes on the role of the person being studied. The class must think of questions to ask the person relating to the topic being explored, and the student 'in the spotlight' answers the questions from the famous person's perspective. A number of people can be 'in the spotlight' at the same time to form a panel of experts; for example, the Evangelists Matthew, Mark, Luke and John could lead a discussion on the content of the four Gospels.

Step 1: Begin by asking each student to write a question that they would like to ask the famous person.

Step 2: Select a student or panel of students to be the person(s) 'in the spotlight'. They should sit or stand at the top of the class and answer the questions in character.

JOURNAL EXERCISES

Suggestions for Journal exercises are given throughout the students' text. These allow students to write answers to questions that they might consider too personal to answer in class. They can be particularly valuable because they give students time to pause, reflect and then record their ideas and feelings on a topic. Journal writing can also be a form of prayer. If the Journal activity takes place during class time, you could light a candle (if local fire regulations permit) and/or play some soft music to create a prayerful atmosphere.

FAITH WORDS QUIZ

Faith words are highlighted throughout the text to enable students develop their religious vocabulary. A good way of reviewing the text at the end of the semester is to have a quiz based on these words.

Step 1: Organize the students into teams. Each team divides up the chapters to be reviewed between them. They each take flash cards and write the faith words from the assigned chapters on one side and an explanation on the other side. They may include diagrams or pictures—anything that will help their teammates understand and remember the definitions.

Step 2: Each student takes a turn at explaining the faith words to the rest of their team members.

Step 3: The teacher can lead an end-of-semester quiz based on the faith words, with prizes for the best team!

BLOGS/BLOGGING

'Blogging' is another form of journaling. The term 'blog' is a shortened form of 'weblog'. A blog is a type of website, similar to an online journal. It is usually maintained by the writer and can provide commentary or news on a particular subject or it can function as a more personal diary. Entries are commonly displayed in reverse-chronological order; that is, the last entry is listed first. The word 'blog' can also be used as a verb, meaning 'to maintain or add content to a blog'. Most blogs are set up in such a way as to allow readers to add comments. There are numerous internet sites that provide instructions for setting up and maintaining blogs.

VOX POPS

Vox populi is a Latin phrase that literally means 'voice of the people'. It is a term often used in broadcasting for interviews with members of the general public. Students may use this technique to put a question to other young people in the school or to people in a parish or local club; for example 'Do you believe in God? Why?/Why not?' They could use a video recorder or mobile phone to record the responses and then watch or review them in class.

WALKING DEBATES

A 'walking debate' can be a useful and exciting strategy for helping young people to engage with decision-making, morality and justice issues.

Step 1: Begin by clearing the tables and chairs out of the way to create space in the classroom.

Step 2: Place a sign bearing the word 'Right' on one wall, a sign with the word 'Wrong' on the opposite wall, and a third sign in the middle of the room saying 'Not sure'.

Step 3: According as you read out a list of statements relating to moral decisions, the students move around and position themselves beside whichever sign corresponds with their choice of answer.

Step 4: After each statement, one student standing at each position must say why they have chosen their position. Students can be offered the option of changing their position as they listen to one another.

STUDENT ACTIVITY TOOL KIT | 393

In directing the discussion, you may also invite the young people to consider what factors influence their discernment of what is right and wrong.

WORDS OF WISDOM COLLECTION

There are quotations from Scripture or inspirational people highlighted throughout the *Credo* series. Students may create a personal collection of their favorite words of wisdom in their journal, which they may add to throughout the year. You might like to organize a class project to create a collection of inspirational quotations that could be presented as a class gift at the end of the year.

Tools for Effective Prayer

DOODLING AS A PRAYER TECHNIQUE

The doodle is a ubiquitous feature of teenage culture. Many people doodle without even being aware of what exactly they are doing. For example, students in class will often begin to make shapes on a page while the teacher is talking, which they then decorate and embellish. Generally there is no end in mind, but the very act of doodling focuses the student's attention. Doodling can be used in an imaginative way by the teacher to provide a focus for contemplation. Many high school Theology teachers and other teachers of Religious Education have begun to employ the act of doodling as a technique used in prayer, which young people are very happy to engage in.

Doodling has long been a means for fostering deep reflection, invoking the use of the gift of one's inner imagination as a source of reflection. Recent research clearly indicates that there are a wide variety of 'learning styles' or 'intelligences' by which people learn best and express themselves best. Doodling, in one sense, is a means of expression that particularly suits people whose preferred 'learning style' or 'intelligence' is more visual than verbal. While the use of words is the most common form of learning and expression, for many the use of words is not the most effective and comfortable way of discovering truth and expressing themselves. Employing art and architecture as an expression of faith attests to the power of the 'visual' in passing on one's personal faith in Christ as well as the faith of the Church. The use of doodling in the *Credo* series recognizes the power of simple drawing (or doodling) to be a basic form of reflection on and artistic expression of the faith life for many young people.

In each chapter of the teacher's resource we provide a suggestion for the use of doodling during a prayerful reflection on Scripture.

Preparation:
Each student will need:
⊙ Gel pens, markers or crayons
⊙ A black marker, pen or sharp pencil
⊙ A plain sheet of paper

Note: No erasers are required, as every mark made is part of the entire prayer! The end product will serve as a visual reminder of time spent in prayer.

General Guidelines:
Step 1: Begin by lighting a candle (if the fire regulations of your school permit) to symbolize the presence of God. Say the prayer suggested for the lesson, repeating it slowly a number of times.

Step 2: Play a recording of some soft background music and encourage the young people to become relaxed and calm.

Step 3: Ask the students to write on their page the words of the prayer that they have just heard.

Step 4: Slowly, with their minds focused on the words, they begin to doodle around the words, adding design and color as they like.

Step 5: When they are finished, repeat together the words of the prayer.

Invite the students to take their artwork with them as a reminder of their prayer time.

MEDITATIONS—A GUIDE TO FACILITATE SUCCESSFUL MEDITATIONS

There are opportunities and suggestions for meditative prayer throughout the *Credo* series. The following points are worth noting:

Preparation: It is strongly recommended that you read through each meditation before doing it in class. When you are familiar with it, the piece will flow better, allowing for suitable emphases and pauses as necessary.

Atmosphere: A lighted candle (if local fire regulations permit) and soft background music will help create a relaxed, prayerful atmosphere. You might also like to use incense or some other aroma. It is also worth putting a 'Do Not Disturb' notice on the door.

Remind the young people that this a special time for them to get in touch with themselves and to connect with the presence of God. They should therefore be attentive and avoid becoming distracted or distracting other students.

394 | CREDO | LIVING AND LOVING AS DISCIPLES OF CHRIST

Pace: Pace is crucial—a good meditation should be slow, with plenty of appropriate pauses.

Posture: The best posture is the one that helps you pray. However, for the purposes of a facilitated meditation at school, the preferred option is for students to sit erect in a chair, with their back straight, both feet flat on the floor and hands on lap or on the desktop.

Breathing: Encourage the young people to breathe smoothly, deeply and slowly. Such a pattern, once achieved, inevitably leads to more effective and deeper meditation.

Awareness: Awareness, an essential element of meditation, can best be achieved by learning to listen: to one's own body, thoughts and feelings. Begin by encouraging the young people to listen to the sounds outside the room, then the ones inside the room, then the very slight sounds in their own body (small movements of breath, stomach, heart). By focusing initially on outside sounds, these will eventually cease to be a distraction and can be simply 'let go'.

Centerpiece/Focal point: It is often helpful to have a centerpiece for the young people to focus on, such as a candle, icon or image, or indeed any object or image from nature.

Mantra: Another useful technique is the use of the mantra. Mantras are sacred words or phrases which, when repeated either out loud or in the mind, help to bring the pray-er into a deeper sense of self, or into a higher state of consciousness, or more closely into a sense of the presence of God. A suitable mantra might be a short scriptural phrase such as 'My Lord and My God'. It is often beneficial to say the mantra on the inward or outward breaths or on both.

Sacred Scripture: The Bible is used as a source for many of the meditations in the *Credo* series. A number of mediations are based on Bible stories. Students are often encouraged to place themselves imaginatively in the Bible story. Another form of scriptural prayer that is explored is *lectio divina*, which focuses on four basic movements in praying the Scriptures; namely, *lectio* (reading), *meditatio* (meditation), *oratio* (prayer) and *contemplatio* (contemplation), and sometimes a fifth, *actio* (action).

Personal meditation: The young people should be encouraged to attempt meditation on their own too; for example, in their bedroom or in a little-used room in their home, or even in a secluded place outdoors.

Sample Formats for Introducing and Concluding Guided Meditations

All the meditations in the *Credo* series can be introduced and concluded in a similar pattern. You should adapt the following to suit your own situation and circumstances.

SAMPLE INTRODUCTION
Leader
Times of silence are precious. Our aim during this meditation is to enter into silence—the silence of our own hearts. In order to become still in our innermost heart we must first become still in our body.

And so, we begin by relaxing our bodies. . . . Just close your eyes gently. . . . Sit straight in the chair or desk, leaning comfortably against the back, with both feet flat on the floor. . . . Rest your hands gently on your knees or hold them together loosely. . . .

Bring your attention to your neck and shoulders. . . . Notice any tension you experience there, and just imagine that tension flowing gently down your arms and out of your body through your fingers. . . .

Become aware of your back against the seat. . . . and then, further down, feel your weight pressing against the seat. . . . You are becoming more and more relaxed. . . .

Become aware of your breathing. . . . Don't breathe any more heavily or deeply than you normally do. . . . Notice the colder air at the bottom of your nostrils as you breathe in . . . . and the warmer air as you breathe out. . . . You are now breathing gently and easily. . . . The breath you are breathing now is the breath of life; the breath that God breathed into your body when you were born. . . . Give thanks for this breath, this gift of life. . . .

Now we are going to relax the mind. . . . Images and thoughts and feelings will come into your mind—just let them come and go gently. . . . Don't focus on any thought or image in particular. Just let them come and go of their own accord. . . . Allow all tension or stress to evaporate. . . . You are becoming more and more relaxed. . . .

STUDENT ACTIVITY TOOL KIT | 395

SAMPLE ENDING

The meditator is totally relaxed and at a deeper level of consciousness, so he or she has to be brought back gently to an awareness of the room and the surroundings.

Leader

Return your attention now to your breath. . . . Notice how peacefully you are breathing. . . . Become aware of your body and your posture as you sit in your seat. . . . Notice how calm and relaxed and peaceful it is. . . .

Begin now to stretch your arms and your legs. . . . Open your eyes gently and become aware of the room and the people around you. . . .

GRAPHIC ORGANIZER TEMPLATE

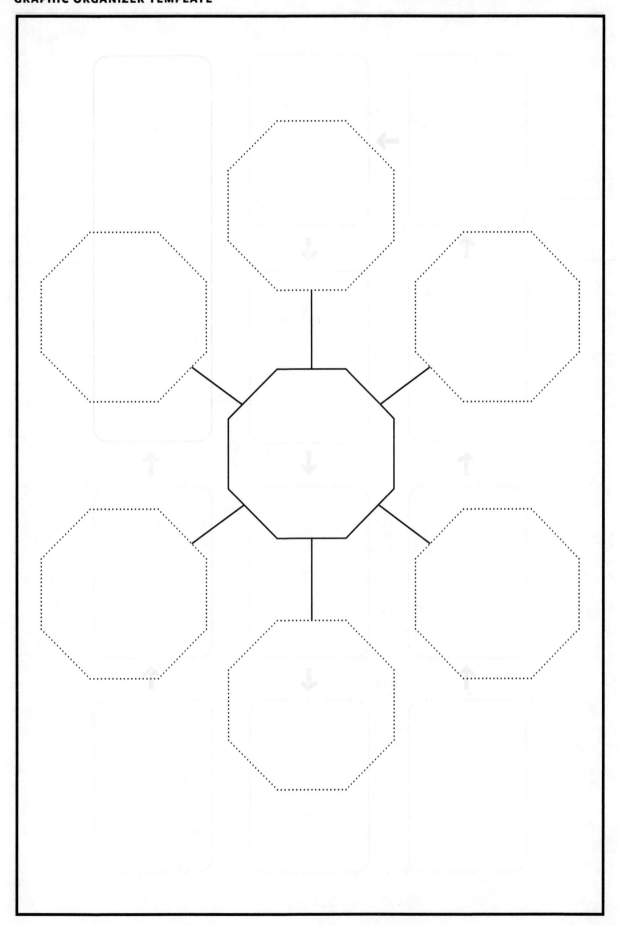

STUDENT ACTIVITY TOOL KIT | 397

GRAPHIC ORGANIZER TEMPLATE

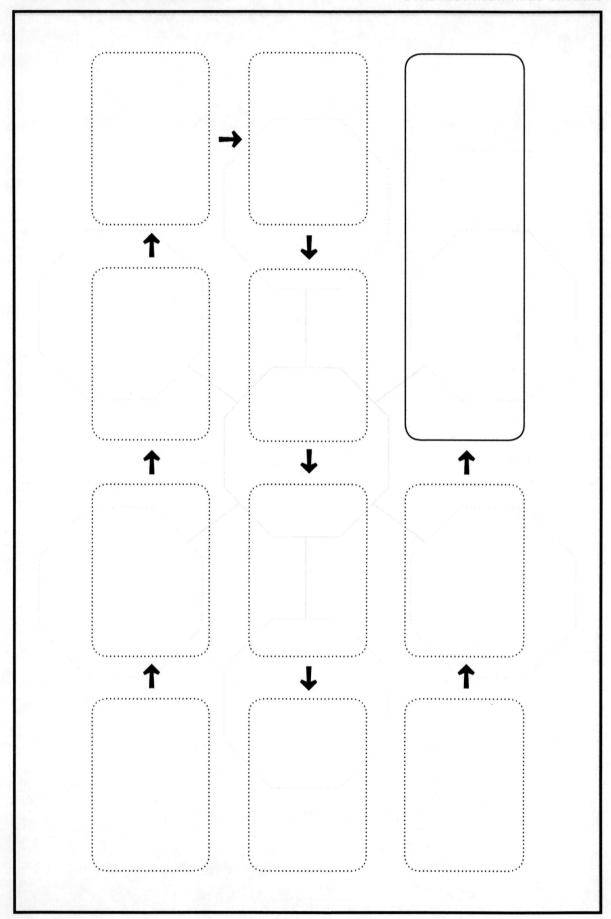

398 | CREDO | LIVING AND LOVING AS DISCIPLES OF CHRIST

GRAPHIC ORGANIZER TEMPLATE

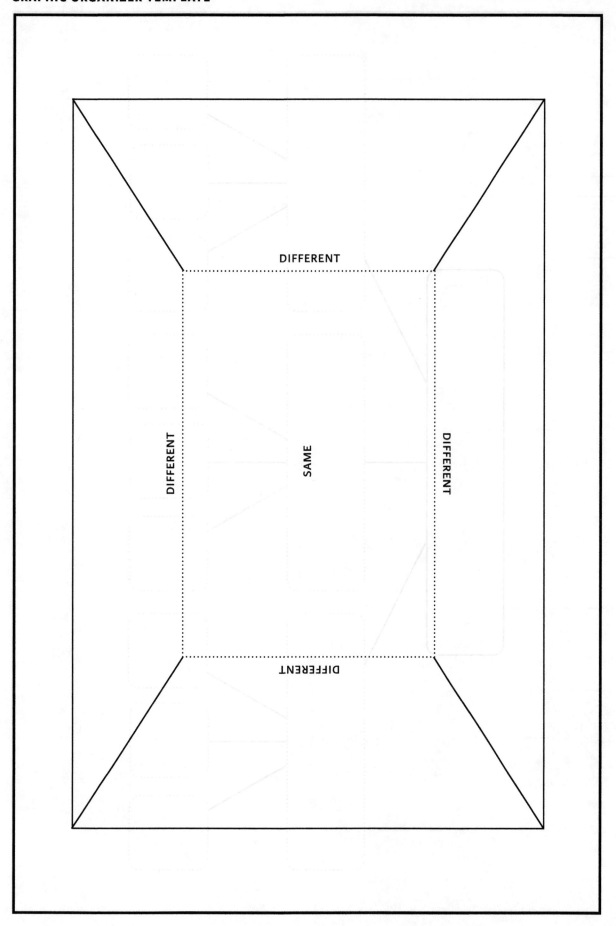

STUDENT ACTIVITY TOOL KIT | 399

GRAPHIC ORGANIZER TEMPLATE

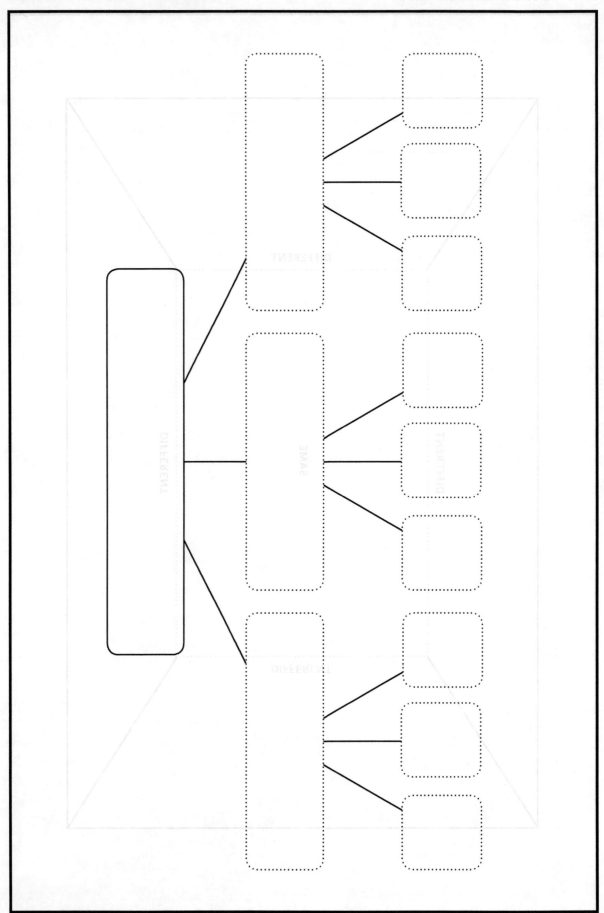

400 | CREDO | LIVING AND LOVING AS DISCIPLES OF CHRIST

Answer Key to Chapter Reviews

Chapter 1: God Desires What Is Best for Us

I. **1.** T; **2.** T; **3.** F (~~fear~~ **love**); **4.** F (~~only with those who never sin~~ **with all people**); **5.** F (~~only specific people, such as priests~~ **everyone**); **6.** T; **7.** F (~~but without~~ **and with**); **8.** F (~~Only evil people face~~ **everyone faces**); **9.** F (~~Because of Adam and Eve's sinfulness, God eventually turned his back on humanity~~ **God never turned his back on humanity**); **10.** F (~~abolished~~ **fulfilled**).

II. **1.** I; **2.** G; **3.** B; **4.** F; **5.** J; **6.** A; **7.** H; **8.** D; **9.** L; **10.** C.

III. **1. Appropriate responses** will recall the story of the original, or the first, temptation, and how the serpent—a biblical symbol for the Devil, or Satan, and evil—tempted Eve to believe the lie that God did not really have her and Adam's 'good' at heart. Eve, in turn, convinced Adam. They knowingly and freely gave into temptation. The Church names that choice Original Sin.

2. Appropriate responses will reflect the understanding that God has gifted all human beings with the capacity to reason and to recognize the voice of God urging us toward what is good. God has also given us free will. Unlike any other creature, we reflect the image of God and have the capacity to choose freely what is good and avoid what is evil, as explained in section three, 'Embrace the Vision', of this chapter.

IV. **Appropriate responses** will reflect an understanding of these concepts: 1) Desire for God is written in the human heart; 2) We are created to share in the eternal love and happiness of God; 3) There is always a longing in our hearts that only God can satisfy; 4) Catholic faith teaches that we achieve true happiness by living as a disciple of Jesus Christ. These concepts are explained in section one, 'Attend and Reflect', of this chapter.

V. **Accept all appropriate responses.**

Chapter 2: Jesus' Response; Our Response

I. **1.** T; **2.** F (~~all four accounts of the Gospel~~ **the Synoptic Gospels of Matthew and Luke**); **3.** F (~~seashore~~ **side of a mountain**); **4.** T; **5.** F (~~song poetry . . . only in the Book of Psalms~~ **in several books of the Old Testament**); **6.** T; **7.** T; **8.** F (~~oneself~~ **others**); **9.** F (~~'Come follow me'~~ **'Peace be with you'**); **10.** F (~~on a small farm in Poland~~ **in the convent**).

II. **1.** F; **2.** B; **3.** H; **4.** D; **5.** C; **6.** L; **7.** J; **8.** K; **9.** I; **10.** A.

III. **1. Appropriate responses** will reflect the understanding that true and lasting happiness lies with God and that Jesus' teachings in the Beatitudes show us the way to live so as to achieve that happiness. The Beatitudes are fundamental attitudes and actions that provide the focus for our attitude toward the world and how God creates us to act in the world, as explained in section one, 'Attend and Reflect', of this chapter.

2. Appropriate responses will reflect the understanding that (1) a beatitude is a form of Hebrew poetry found in several books of the Old Testament that uses rhyming ideas rather than rhyming words to facilitate memorization; (2) it is unlikely that Jesus delivered this 'sermon' word for word, in one time and one place, as it appears in Matthew's Gospel account; rather, Matthew, under the inspiration of the Holy Spirit, wove together a summary of Jesus' most important teachings and placed them at the beginning of his Gospel account; (3) these teachings, which were first passed on by oral tradition, were eventually written during the third stage of the formation of the Gospel and were recognized by the Church as authentic and included in the canon of Scripture, as explained in section two, 'Hear the Story', of this chapter.

IV. **Appropriate responses** will reflect an understanding of these concepts: (1) The

ANSWER KEY TO CHAPTER REVIEWS | 401

Beatitudes are a summary of Christian virtue; they proclaim Jesus' attitude to life in the world; (2) The Beatitudes offer a vision for living in this life that will lead to eternal happiness in the next; they reveal the ultimate goal of human activity, which is eternal happiness; (3) The Beatitudes teach us the final end to which God calls us: the Kingdom, the vision of God, participation in the very life and love of God, our identity as the beloved, adopted daughters and sons of God, and eternal life and rest in God. These concepts are explained in section one, 'Attend and Reflect', and section two, 'Embrace the Vision', of this chapter.

V. **Accept all appropriate responses.**

Chapter 3: God's Law for a Good Life

I. **1.** F; **2.** I; **3.** B; **4.** D; **5.** C; **6.** L; **7.** G; **8.** J; **9.** A; **10.** H.

II. **1.** T; **2.** F (~~revealed to those who were educated~~ **innate in everyone**); **3.** T; **4.** F (~~whom we like best~~ **most in need**); **5.** T; **6.** T; **7.** F (~~cannot~~ **can**); **8.** F (~~always~~ **not always**); **9.** T; **10.** F (~~invade Scotland~~ **divorce Catherine of Aragón and marry Anne Boleyn**).

III. **1. Appropriate responses** will reflect an understanding of the natural law that God has implanted within each one of us that directs us toward what is good and helps us to avoid what is evil. All people possess this natural law within; through reason we can come to know what is right and just, as explained in section one, 'Attend and Reflect', of this chapter.

2. Appropriate responses will reflect the understanding that an erroneous judgment can happen when a conscience makes a judgment that is contrary to natural or revealed law while intending to make a good one. An erroneous judgment can result from ignorance—not knowing clearly what is bad or good in a particular situation. The *Catechism* names these possible sources of erroneous judgment: ignorance of Christ and the Gospel; following bad example given by others; allowing our passions and desires to take over and enslave us; rejection of the Church's authority and teaching; lack of compassion for others, as explained in section four, 'Think It Through', of this chapter.

IV. **Appropriate responses** will reflect an understanding of these concepts: (1) God has implanted the natural law in the heart of all people; it is universal in its precepts and its authority extends to all people; (2) the natural law expresses the dignity of the human person and determines the basis for the human person's fundamental rights and duties; (3) the natural law is unchangeable and permanent throughout history; (4) the natural law is the foundation on which moral rules and civil law are built; (5) the natural law provides universal principles of justice that are immutable and eternal, as explained in section one, 'Attend and Reflect', and section three, 'Embrace the Vision', of this chapter.

V. **Accept all appropriate responses.**

Chapter 4: The Reality of Sin

I. **1.** F; **2.** C; **3.** L; **4.** A; **5.** G; **6.** B; **7.** I; **8.** D; **9.** J; **10.** K.

II. **1.** F (~~remain silent in the face of~~ **stand up against**); **2.** T; **3.** F (~~turned~~ **did not turn**); **4.** F (~~hate and reject the sinner~~ **love and welcome the sinner**); **5.** F (~~to make good decisions~~ **not to fulfill their responsibilities to those in lawful authority**); **6.** T; **7.** F (~~omission~~ **commission**); **8.** F (~~commission~~ **omission**); **9.** T; **10.** F (~~American~~ **French**).

III. **1. Appropriate responses** will reflect the understanding that mortal sin is a total turning of one's back on God, which seriously ruptures one's life-giving relationship with God, with people and with creation. Venial sin is a less serious offense. Venial sins do not sever our friendship with God and do not deny a person the gift of sanctifying grace. These terms are explained in section four, 'Think It Through', of this chapter.

2. Appropriate responses will reflect an understanding of 'social sin' as sin that infects the structures and systems in a society and undermines the dignity of the human person. Social sin may be seen in the exploitation of people, in unjust laws and oppression, and in all forms of slavery and discrimination. We all contribute to social sin by our personal sins and sinful attitudes. Our faith calls us to recognize and to challenge social sin in our society and culture, as explained in section four, 'Think It Through', of this chapter.

IV. **Appropriate responses** will describe the person's argument as 'moral relativism' and will mention that the Church is opposed to such a view of morality. The Church teaches that when actions are contrary to moral law, to the teachings of the Gospel and of the Church, we are to name them as such. Moral actions must always be measured by truth. There are some actions that are just plain evil and contrary to the moral law by nature. The nature of such acts is not changed by the circumstances surrounding the act or by the intention or purpose of the person committing the act. In other words, the end never justifies the means. Moral relativism is explained in section two, 'Hear the Story', of this chapter.

V. **Accept all appropriate responses.**

Chapter 5: The Liberating Power of the Ten Commandments

I. 1. F (Holy Grail **Tablets of the Covenant**); 2. F (ourselves **God**); 3. T; 4. F (Hanukah **Passover**); 5. F (turned around and went back **began to complain against Moses and Aaron**); 6. T; 7. T; 8. F (in keeping with **a departure from**); 9. T; 10. F (The Romans **Pharaoh's daughter**).

II. 1. I; 2. G; 3. J; 4. E; 5. A; 6. F; 7. L; 8. D; 9. B; 10. H.

III. **1. Appropriate responses** will reflect an understanding of idolatry as the divinization of a creature in place of God, or the substitution of some one (or thing) for God. Examples of idolatry would include the worship of money, power or pleasure, or making idols of, for example, the latest fashion or high-end car, or college scholarship or money-making career, or excellence in sport, drama or music, or a diet or exercise routine, as discussed in section three, 'Embrace the Vision', of this chapter.

2. Appropriate responses will reflect an understanding of the natural law that God has engraved on the heart of all human persons, which enables us to tell good from evil, right from wrong, truth from falsehood. The Decalogue contains a privileged expression of the natural law. When we explore the meaning of any one of the Ten Commandments, we recognize from the natural law within us that they make eminent good sense, as explained in section one, 'Attend and Reflect', of this chapter.

IV. **Appropriate responses** will reflect an understanding of the Ten Commandments within the context of the Covenant and God's liberating love. The first of the Commandments affirms that God loved his people first. God revealed the Commandments purely out of love and for our own good. The negative commands of the Fifth through the Tenth Commandments not only point to the evil behavior that enslaves people; they also point to those fundamental deeds that undermine the original plan of goodness—of justice and holiness—that God always wills for humanity. Living the Commandments is our response to

God's love for humanity, as explained in section two, 'Hear the Story', of this chapter.

V. **Accept all appropriate responses.**

Chapter 6: Love the Lord Your God: The Second and Third Commandments

I. 1. G; 2. C; 3. H; 4. I, F; 5. B; 6. D; 7. L; 8. J; 9. K; 10. M.

II. 1. F (God is salvation **beloved**); 2. T; 3. F (You Have Wealth Here **I AM WHO I AM**); 4. T; 5. F (his name **the name of God — 'in the name of the Father and of the Son and of the Holy Spirit'**); 6. F (contrary to both **not contrary to**); 7. T; 8. F (priests **everyone**); 9. T; 10. F (Mindfulness **Spiritual**).

III. **1. Appropriate responses** will reflect the understanding that the First Precept of the Catholic Church requires the faithful to celebrate the Eucharist on Sundays and on Holy Days of Obligation. The First Precept also requires that Catholics rest from work on these days. The Catholic Church has made it all the more possible for us to fulfill these obligations by allowing us to fulfill the Sunday Obligation on Saturday evening and the Holy Days Obligation on the evening prior to the Holy Day, as explained in section four, 'Think It Through', of this chapter.

2. Appropriate responses will reflect the understanding that the Second Commandment prescribes respect for the Lord's name. Responses might mention that the ancient Israelites had a profound reverence for the name of God and that Jesus encouraged his disciples to show the same reverence for the holiness of the name of God by the way he taught them to address God in prayer. Christians have the same honor and respect for the name of Jesus as they have for the name of God. This concept, along with an explanation of those acts that show lack of reverence for the divine name, is explained in section two, 'Hear the Story', of this chapter.

IV. **Appropriate responses** will reflect the understanding that meeting together with one's parish or local Church community for the celebration of the Eucharist is central to the life of a Catholic. Prayer at home cannot be the same as prayer at church, because at Mass we are fed from the Table of the Word of God and the Table of the Eucharist. This principle is underpinned in the first precept of the Church, which is explained in section four, 'Think It Through', of this chapter.

V. **Accept all appropriate responses.**

Chapter 7: Honor Your Father and Your Mother: The Fourth Commandment

I. 1. F ('. . . good **not good**. . . .; I will make him a helper as his partner'); 2. T; 3. F (obliged **never obliged**... even if it **that**); 4. T; 5. T; 6. T; 7. F (Even ... still **obliged not**); 8. T; 9. F (in all circumstances **only when certain conditions exist**); 10. F (America **Africa**).

II. 1. F; 2. G; 3. K; 4. H; 5. J; 6. E; 7. L; 8. B; 9. D; 10. A.

III. 1. **Appropriate responses** will reflect the understanding that Christians fulfill the responsibility to contribute to the good of society by obeying all just laws. We can also speak out and offer constructive criticism of the State when a law is unjust, as outlined in the 'Embrace the Vision' and 'Think It Through' sections of this chapter.

2. **Appropriate responses** will reflect the understanding that just as each human being is created in the image and likeness of God, the family is created in the image of God the Trinity. The Catholic Church teaches: 'The Christian family is a communion of persons, a sign and image of the communion of the Father and the Son in the Holy Spirit' (CCC, no. 2205), as taught in section one, 'Attend and Reflect', of this chapter.

IV. **Appropriate responses** will reflect an understanding of the concepts of filial respect, gratitude, just obedience and assistance, but will also include an awareness of the fact that a child is never obliged to obey a parent, or any person in authority, who asks them to do something that is contrary to God's law, to the Gospel, to the teachings of the Church or to civil law. A child has the right and the freedom to say 'No', as explained in section two, 'Hear the Story', of this chapter.

V. **Accept all appropriate responses.**

Chapter 8: Living the 'Way' of Life and Truth: The Fifth and Eighth Commandments

I. 1. T; 2. T; 3. F (mortal **venial**); 4. T; 5. F (Detraction **Rash judgment**); 6. F (permits **forbids** . . . certain **all**); 7. T; 8. F (Intentional **Voluntary**); 9. T; 10. T.

II. 1. G; 2. D; 3. C; 4. L; 5. K; 6. J; 7. A; 8. F; 9. H; 10. B.

III. 1. **Appropriate responses** will reflect the teaching of the Catholic Church that human life begins with the fusion of a sperm cell and an egg, and, thus, 'the embryo must be defended in its integrity, cared for and healed like every other human being'. Producing and using stem cells from embryos for research is, therefore, contrary to the moral law, as explained in section three, 'Embrace the Vision', of this chapter.

2. **Appropriate responses** will reflect the understanding that, although the Catholic Church allowed the death penalty for capital crimes in the past, and even promoted it for people considered to be heretics, this teaching has evolved to a current position which essentially opposes the death penalty in all but the rarest of circumstances. The Catholic Church now teaches and upholds the State's right to protect its citizens by sentencing those who commit heinous crimes to life in prison, as explained in section four, 'Think It Through', of this chapter.

IV. **Appropriate responses** will reflect the Catholic Church's teaching that when a terminally ill person is facing imminent death, the normal care due to the person must be continued. Any act or the omission of treatment that is done in order to directly end a person's life, even if it is done with the intention of eliminating suffering, is murder. The dying should be given attention and care to help them live their last moments in dignity and peace, as explained in section three, 'Embrace the Vision', of this chapter.

V. **Accept all appropriate responses.**

Chapter 9: The Gift of Human Sexuality: The Sixth and Ninth Commandments

I. 1. T; 2. F (Spirit **Body**); 3. T; 4. T; 5. F (Love **Lust**); 6. F (is the same as **differs from**); 7. T; 8. T; 9. F (does not support **supports**); 10. F (St. Francis of Assisi **St. Thérèse of Lisieux**).

II. 1. B; 2. F; 3. K; 4. C; 5. G; 6. A; 7. L; 8. E; 9. H; 10. D.

III. 1. **Appropriate responses** will mention that the following elements must be present at the time spouses enter a marriage: free and freely entered, unity, indissolubility, fidelity and fecundity, as explained in section four, 'Think It Through', of this chapter.

2. **Appropriate responses** will reflect the understanding that the Catholic Church does not recognize that a civil divorce ends a marriage because the State cannot dissolve what divine law reveals to be indissoluble. However, the *Catechism of the Catholic Church* also teaches that if 'civil

divorce remains the only possible way of ensuring certain legal rights, the care of children, or the protection of inheritance, it can be tolerated and does not constitute a moral offense'. Also, in situations of spousal or child abuse within a family, spouses may separate and discontinue living with each other, but the marriage still exists and the separated spouses are still bound to fidelity to their marriage promises even if they receive a civil divorce, as explained in section four, 'Think It Through', of this chapter.

IV. **Appropriate responses** will reflect the understanding that pornography is contrary to the moral order because it objectifies and strips men and women, youth and children, of their dignity and reduces the person to his or her body parts. This abuse of human sexuality is destructive of both the dignity of persons and the common good of society. Anyone who produces, buys or consumes pornographic materials violates human dignity and seduces others to sin. Pornography is a business and a social sin that is protected legally, but erroneously, in the United States, by the right to freedom of speech. The Catholic Church constantly calls on civil authorities to prevent the production and distribution of pornographic materials, as explained in section three, 'Embrace the Vision', of this chapter.

V. **Accept all appropriate responses.**

Chapter 10: Building a Just and Compassionate Society: The Seventh and Tenth Commandments

I. **1.** T; **2.** F (no a); **3.** T; **4.** F (most all); **5.** F (those who deserve it one another); **6.** F (Legal justice **Social justice**); **7.** F (avarice **envy**); **8.** F (sloth **gluttony**); **9.** T; **10.** F (Argentina **Lima**).

II. **1.** K; **2.** J; **3.** I; **4.** H; **5.** F; **6.** G; **7.** B; **8.** A; **9.** D; **10.** C.

III. **1. Appropriate responses** will reflect the understanding that retributive justice focuses on the punishment of offenders and claims that it is implementing the Mosaic Law of an eye for an eye, a tooth for a tooth. Restorative justice, on the other hand, focuses on the dignity of the human person. While it does not ignore evil acts of injustice and other crimes, it aims at the rehabilitation of the offender and reparation to victims, as explained in section three, 'Embrace the Vision', of this chapter.

2. Appropriate responses will include the

understanding that the moral principle of solidarity enjoins us to unite ourselves with others, to look upon each other as another self, and to share compassionately in each other's joys and sufferings. This involves a love for all peoples that transcends national, racial, ethnic, economic, and ideological differences. It respects the needs of others and the common good in an interdependent world, as explained in section three, 'Embrace the Vision', of this chapter.

IV. **Appropriate responses** will reflect the understanding that privilege and responsibility go hand in hand. In the Seventh Commandment, God directs us to know and live by his divine plan for all creation. The goods of creation are 'destined for the common good'. The Catholic Church names this revealed truth 'the universal destination of goods'. For anyone to possess an excess of goods and to hold them irresponsibly while others go without is an offense against the generosity of God and against one's neighbor, as explained in section one, 'Attend and Reflect', of this chapter.

V. **Accept all appropriate responses.**

Chapter 11: Living New Life in Christ Jesus

I. **1.** T; **2.** T; **3.** F (is is not); **4.** F (rich **poor**); **5.** F (Home **Body**); **6.** F (hierarchy **lay ecclesial ministers**); **7.** T; **8.** T; **9.** F (virginity until marriage **perpetual virginity**); **10.** F (tax collector **fisherman**).

II. **1.** J; **2.** F; **3.** G; **4.** E; **5.** C; **6.** B; **7.** K; **8.** D; **9.** A; **10.** H.

III. **1. Appropriate responses** will reflect the understanding that the baptized have these three essential responsibilities which flow from their Baptism: (i) to be active and faithful members of the Church according to their state of life; (ii) to proclaim the Gospel; and (iii) to serve their neighbors—*all* people, including those who are not members of the Church and non-believers, as explained in section three, 'Embrace the Vision', of this chapter.

2. Appropriate responses will reflect an understanding of the evangelical counsels as vows taken by men or women who enter religious life; there are three vows: poverty, chastity and obedience. By professing and living the evangelical counsel of poverty, members of the consecrated life commit themselves to be 'poor in spirit' *and* 'poor in possessions'. Through the evangelical counsel of chastity, a religious *consecrates* himself or herself totally to God. The vow of 'obedience' includes obedience to God, to the Church and to the

ANSWER KEY TO CHAPTER REVIEWS | 405

authority of the religious community, as explained in section four, 'Think It Through', of this chapter.

IV. **Appropriate responses** will reflect the understanding that laypeople have an important role in the Church. For example, Christian parents share in the mission of Christ through educating and forming their children in the faith of the Church. Laypeople serve as catechists and teachers in schools and parishes and as teachers of theology in colleges and universities. Laypeople also take part in the celebration of the Sacraments, especially in the Eucharist, where they take on various roles, including bringing the Real Presence of the Body and Blood of Christ to the sick and homebound. Laypeople also take part in the governance work of the Church, and they can serve as lay ecclesial ministers or as members of third orders or of confraternities, as explained in section three, 'Embrace the Vision', of this chapter.

V. **Accept all appropriate responses.**

Chapter 12: *Sustaining the Moral Life as Disciples of Jesus*

I. **1.** F (abolished **fulfilled**); **2.** T; **3.** F (generous **free**); **4.** T; **5.** T; **6.** F (do and can **do not and cannot**); **7.** F. (St. John **The Blessed Virgin**); **8.** T; **9.** F (Hail Mary **Our Father**); **10.** T.

II. **1.** K; **2.** G; **3.** H; **4.** I; **5.** L; **6.** B; **7.** E; **8.** F; **9.** C; **10.** D.

III. **1. Appropriate responses** will reflect the understanding that sacramental graces are the gifts of the Holy Spirit received in the Sacraments to help us live out our Christian vocation. In Confirmation we receive the fullness of the gift of the Holy Spirit, first received in Baptism. In the Sacraments of Healing—Penance and Reconciliation, and Anointing of the Sick—God offers us many graces so that we may be healed in body and spirit when we are weakened by sin or illness. In the Sacraments of Holy Orders and Marriage God offers special graces to the faithful whom he calls to serve his Church. In the Eucharist we receive the Body of Christ to strengthen us for our journey of faith, as explained in section three, 'Embrace the Vision', of this chapter.

2. Appropriate responses will reflect the understanding that the Christian tradition speaks of three expressions of prayer, or ways of praying. These are vocal prayer, meditation and contemplation. Vocal prayer is a prayer of words, using a prayer formula, such as the Our Father, or using our own words. The prayer of meditation is a deeper kind of talking with God that is more focused on figuring out how to respond to his words. Meditation brings a person into a deep sense of personal encounter and union with God. In the prayer of contemplation, which is a deep inner prayer, the Father strengthens our inner being with power through the Spirit so that Christ may dwell in our hearts, as explained in section four, 'Think It Through', of this chapter.

IV. **Appropriate responses** will reflect the understanding that the Cardinal Virtues are important for young people today. Prudence provides guidance for our conscience in making moral choices, which all people are faced with on a daily basis. Justice is the constant and firm recognition of what is rightfully due to God and others. Fortitude (courage) is firmness of spirit, especially in times of difficulty. Temperance is also known as moderation or self-control. Temperance does not ask us to denounce all physical goods and pleasures as evil, but guides us in enjoying these created gifts as signs of God's love, as explained in section two, 'Hear the Story', of this chapter.

V. **Accept all appropriate responses.**

406 | CREDO | LIVING AND LOVING AS DISCIPLES OF CHRIST

Acknowledgments

Scripture quotations taken from *New Revised Standard Version Bible: Catholic Edition*, copyright © 1989, 1993, Division of Christian Education of the National Council of Churches of Christ in the U.S.A; all rights reserved.

Excerpts from the English translation of the *Catechism of the Catholic Church* for use in the United States, second edition, copyright © 1997, United States Catholic Conference, Inc., Libreria Editrice Vaticana; all rights reserved.

Excerpts from *United States Catholic Catechism for Adults*, copyright © 2006, United States Conference of Catholic Bishops, Washington D.C.; all rights reserved.

Excerpts from documents of Vatican II from A. Flannery (ed.), *Vatican Council II: Constitutions, Decrees, Declarations* (New York/Dublin: Costello Publishing/Dominican Publications, 1996).

Excerpt, p. 19, from homily of Pope Francis, June 2013, from: *www.catholicherald.co.uk/news/2013/06/07/let-yourself-be-loved-by-god-pope-francis-urges-faithful/*

Reflection, p. 21, from *Praying with Julian of Norwich*, Gloria Durka (St. Mary's Press, 1989).

Verse, p. 31, from 'The Cure at Troy' by Seamus Heaney (Faber & Faber, 1990).

Excerpt, p. 36, from Victor E. Frankl's, *Man's Search For Meaning* (Hodder and Stoughton, 1964), copyright by Victor E. Frankl.

Excerpts, pp. 46 and 47, from Donal Murray, *Keeping Open the Door of Faith: The Legacy of the Second Vatican Council* (Dublin, Ireland: Veritas, 2012).

Excerpt, p. 47, from Eamonn Bredin, *Disturbing the Peace: the Way of Disciples* (Dublin, Ireland: Columba Press, 1985).

Reflection, p. 49, from *Tears of Silence*, Jean Vanier (Darton, Longman & Todd Ltd., 1973).

Excerpt, p. 63, from Megan McKenna, *Harm Not the Earth* (Dublin, Ireland: Veritas, 2007).

Excerpts, pp. 77, from Vincent MacNamara, *The Truth in Love* (Dublin, Ireland: Gill and Macmillan, 1988).

Reflection, p. 79, reprinted with permission from Little Books of the Diocese of Saginaw, Michigan.

Prayer reflection, pp. 83–4, adapted from *Border Lands: The Best of David Adam* (London, SPCK Publishing, 1991).

Quotation, p. 91, by Cardinal John Henry Newman from *The Argument from Conscience to the Existence of God according to J.H. Newman*, by Adrian J. Boekraad and Henry Tristram (Louvain: Editions Nauwelaerts, 1961).

Seven Principles of Catholic Social teaching, p. 94, used with permission of USCCB.

Reflection, p. 103, from Peter McVerry, SJ, *Jesus Social Revolutionary?* (Dublin, Ireland: Veritas, 2008).

'A Prayer', p. 109, and excerpt, p. 114, from *Ruth Patterson: Journeying Towards Reconciliation* (Dublin, Ireland: Veritas, 2003).

Excerpt, pp. 112–13, from Elie Wiesel, *Night* (Bantam Books, 1982).

Poem 'The Sin of Omission', pp. 126–7, by Margaret Sangster (New York: Henry Holt and Company Inc.).

Story 'Down to Earth', p. 128, from *www.neveh.org/price/pricestories1.html*

Excerpts, pp. 130–31, from an article in *The Huffington Post: www.huffingtonpost.com/jim-keady/when-will-nike-just-do-it_b_308448.html*

Excerpt, p. 141, from Pope Francis, quoted in *The Catholic Herald*, 12 June 2013: *www.catholicherald.co.uk/news/2013/06/12/pope-francis-ten-commandments-are-a-signpost-to-freedom/*

Poem, p. 148, by Elaine Campion, copyright © Elaine Campion, 2014.

Excerpt, p. 165, from John O'Donohue, *Benedictus: A Book of Blessings* (Bantam Press, 2007).

Poem 'Magnificat', p. 168, from *The God Who Fell From Heaven* (Allen, Texas: Argus Communications, 1979).

Poem 'Names Never Hurt', p. 182, by Michelle Harper Davies, from: *www.helium.com/items/879504-poetry-bullies*

Excerpts, pp. 200, 202 and 264, from Pope John Paul II, *Familiaris Consortio*, no. 17, copyright 1981, used with permission of Libreria Editrice Vaticana.

Excerpts, p. 201, from Vincent MacNamara, *The Call to be Human: Making Sense of Morality* (Dublin, Ireland: Veritas, 2010).

Reflection, p. 203, from 'Preamble' to the 'Charter of Rights of the Family', October 22, 1983; copyright Libreria Editrice Vaticana.

Excerpt, p. 210, from *The Prophet* by Kahlil Gibran (1883–1931).

Excerpts, pp. 213–14, from address of Pope Francis, May 4, 2013, from *www.vatican.va/holy_father/ francesco/speeches/2013/may/documents/papa-francesco_20130504_santo-rosario_en.html*; used with permission of Libreria Editrice Vaticana.

Excerpts, pp. 215–16, from Fergal Keane's 'Letter to Daniel' (1996), from: *www.pbs.org/wgbh/pages/ frontline/shows/rwanda/todaniel/*

Chart, p. 219, from *Educating the 'Good' Citizen: Political Choices and Pedagogical Goals* by Joel Westheimer (University of Ottawa) and Joseph Kahne (Mills College); from: *www.mills.edu/academics/faculty/educ/jkahne/ps_ educating_the_good_citizen.pdf*

Reflection, p. 229, by Kahlil Gibran (1883–1931).

Excerpt, pp. 231–2, from Pope John Paul II, from 'Television and family: guidelines for good viewing', from *www.vatican.va/holy*; used with permission of Libreria Editrice Vaticana.

'Catching the Sprit', p. 245, by Judy Ball, from: *www. americancatholic.org/Newsletters/MM/ap1100.asp*

Excerpts, pp. 249–50, from Pope John Paul II's 'Letter to Artists', April 4, 1999; used with permission of Libreria Editrice Vaticana.

Excerpt, p. 253, from Message to Graduates, May 11, 2011, from Bishop Kevin C. Rhoades, Bishop of Fort Wayne-South Bend.

Excerpt, p. 254, from United States Conference of Catholic Bishops, 'To Live Each Day with Dignity: A Statement on Physician-Assisted Suicide', June 16, 2011; used with permission of USCCB.

Excerpt, p. 254, 'Protecting Life in the Last Days', June 24, 2011, from Bishop James V. Johnston, Bishop of Springfield-Cape Girardeau,

Quotations, pp. 255–6, from Leo XIII, *Rerum Novarum*, 1891; Pius XI, *Quadragesimo Anno*, 1931; John Paul II, *Evangelium Vitae*, 1995; and Benedict XVI, *Caritas in Veritate*, 2009; used with permission of Libreria Editrice Vaticana.

Excerpt, p. 264, from Fr. Ronald Rolheiser, from: *www. ronrolheiser.com/columnarchive/?id=697*

Excerpts, pp. 265 and 268, from John O'Donohue, *Anam Cara* (Bantam Press, 1997).

Prayer 'For Marriage', p. 289, from *Benedictus: A Book of Blessings* (Bantam Press, 2007).

Excerpt, pp. 290–91, from *Mere Christianity* by C.S. Lewis, copyright @ C.S. Lewis Pte Ltd. 1942, 1943, 1944, 1952; extract reprinted by permission.

Synopsis of story of Ruth, p. 292, from World Council of Churches at: *http://archived.oikoumene.org/uploads/ tx_wecdiscussion/23_THE_STORY_OF_RUTH.pdf*

Quotation by David Cotter, p. 298, from Megan McKenna, *Harm Not the Earth* (Dublin, Ireland: Veritas, 2007).

Quotation, p. 300, from Cardinal Bergoglio (now Pope Francis) at 2007 Gathering of Latin American Bishops (SOURCE: *National Catholic Reporter*) from: *http:// ignatiansolidarity.net/blog/2013/03/13/pope-francis-i-a-voice-for-social-justice/*

Key themes from Catholic social teaching, p. 301, from: *www.usccb.org/beliefs-and-teachings/what-we-believe/catholic-social-teaching/seven-themes-of-catholic-social-teaching.cfm*; used with permission of USCCB.

Reflection, p. 302, from *Values and Visions: A Handbook for spiritual development and global awareness*, Sally Burns and Georgeanne Lamont (Hodder and Stoughton, 1995).

Timeline Activity, pp. 305–6, from: *http://old.usccb. org/campus/teaching-timeline-activity.shtml*; used with permission of USCCB.

Rabbinic tale, p. 309, from *Values and Visions: A Handbook for spiritual development and global awareness*, Sally Burns and Georgeanne Lamont (Hodder and Stoughton, 1995).

Excerpts, p. 311, from speech given by the United Nations Secretary General Ban Ki-moon, from: *http:// www.un.org/apps/news/infocus/sgspeeches/statments_ full.asp?statID=1774#.UWPYo6K8CHh*

Story, p. 313, from: *www.bgnews.com/forum/embrace- ubuntu-way-of-life-work-with-others/article_b04b75c0- 166a-11e2-ae89-0019bb2963f4.htm*

Prayers from Education for Justice: 'Prayer for Social Justice' by Pope Pius XII, p. 319, from: *https:// educationforjustice.org/resources/prayer-social-justice*; 'Justice and Peace Prayer', p. 320, by Jane Deren, from: *https://educationforjustice.org/resources/justice- and-peace-prayer*; 'For Those in Poverty', p. 320, by Education for Justice, from: *https://educationforjustice.org/most-popular*; 'Justice Prayer', p. 320, by Mother Teresa, from: *https:// educationforjustice.org/resources/justice-prayer*; 'Prayer to Make Poverty History', p. 321, by Cardinal O'Brien, from: *https://educationforjustice.org/node/1452.*

Retelling of 'Stone Soup', pp. 322–24, by Marcia Brown, Atheneum Books, (c) 1975 by Marcia Brown, from: */www.michaelppowers.com/prosperity/ stonesoup.html*

Excerpt, pp. 329–30, from Dr. Aidan Donaldson, *Encountering God on the Margins* (Dublin, Ireland: Veritas, 2010).

Quotations, p. 336, from St. Francis of Assisi, from: *www.mycatholicsource.com/mcs/qt/saint_francis_ reflections_teachings.htm#St. Francis of Assisi on Poverty*

Quotation, p. 362, from Pope Francis, World Youth Day, Rio de Janeiro, 2013; used with permission of Libreria Editrice Vaticana.

Quotation, p. 363, from Pope John Paul II, World Youth Day, Toronto, 2002; used with permission of Libreria Editrice Vaticana.

Excerpts, p. 369, from Pope Francis, *Evangelii Gaudium*, 2013; used with permission of Libreria Editrice Vaticana.

Notes

Notes

Notes

Notes

Notes

Notes

Notes